For Phyllis

All' mein' Gedanken, die ich hab',
die sind bei dir . . .

CONTENTS

Introduction   7

PART ONE:
PAST AND PRESENT

1. Historical Perspectives   15
2. Politics in a New Key   35
3. Hitler and the New Generation   61

PART TWO:
CHANGE AND CONTINUITY

4. Religion   83
5. Money   104
6. Germans and Jews   126
7. Women   147
8. Professors and Students   170
9. Romantics   190
10. Literature and Society   213
11. Soldiers   237
12. Berlin: Athens on the Spree and City of Crisis   261

PART THREE:
PRESENT AND FUTURE

13. Democracy and Nationalism   289

APPENDIX

14. 'The Awful German Language'   310
    Bibliography   333
    Index   343

Introduction

The first time I saw Germany was in 1935, when I went there at the end of my junior year in college to do research for the senior thesis that I was expected to submit in the spring of the following year. The subject that I had chosen for this piece of work was "The Rise and Fall of the Weimar Republic," for that ill-fated experiment in democracy had ended in failure two years earlier, and it was, in my view, high time that someone wrote the definitive account of its collapse. There was no doubt in my mind that a few months in Germany would enable me to uncover all the materials necessary to supply this felt want.

My naive expectations were in fact to be disappointed, for, although the essay was completed and accepted, my examiners showed no indication of believing that it was the last word on the subject. On the other hand, my time in Germany had brought its own rewards. It had given me an opportunity to see a good part of Germany and Austria—Munich most of all, where I attended courses in the university, the western lands from Cologne to Freiburg in Breisgau, Vienna, still in a state of shock after the February fighting and the abortive Nazi *Putsch* of the previous year, Nuremberg and the walled towns of Mittelfranken, and the cities of Saxony and Prussia. I had seen Albrecht Dürer's "Four Apostles" in Munich's Old Pinakothek, become an admirer of the work of Cranach the Elder after a day in the Kaiser Friedrich Museum in Berlin, and wondered at the treasures of the Green Vault in Dresden. I had heard my first *Marriage of Figaro* in that same city, the whole of *The Ring of the Nibelungen*, with Frida Leider and Wilhelm Rode, in Munich, and *The Magic Flute* and *Der Freischütz* in the *Staatsoper* on Unter den Linden in Berlin. I had, despite my plodding German, puzzled out the plot of *Götz von Berlichingen* and Heinrich von Kleist's *The Broken Jug*, had been caught up in the rapt silence of the crowded Fountain Courtyard in the Munich Residenz as Elly Ney played Schubert, and, in Salzburg, had been overwhelmed by Max Reinhardt's production of *Faust: Part One*.

These masterpieces of high German culture made a deep and lasting impression on me, but no more so than the many examples that I encountered of abuse of culture and, indeed, of inhumanity and barbarism. Munich, where I spent most of the early summer, was a beautiful city of broad boulevards and leaping fountains, but its charms were not enhanced by banners on storefronts that read "He who buys at a Jewish concern is a traitor to his people!" or by the neatly lettered signs in the English Garden that said "Jews are not wanted here." It was all too apparent that the university, once a symbol of German eminence in the works of the mind, had fallen on evil days. A course on Richard Wagner that I had looked forward to with enthusiasm turned out to be an exercise in nationalism and Nazi propaganda, in which much more was said about Hegel and Hitler than about the composer and in which the argument seemed to be that Hegel had invented the State and Wagner had dreamed up things for it to do, but that their work had been meaningless until Adolf Hitler had given the substance of power to their visions.

Nor was this the worst. One day I walked through the *Lichtsaal* (where seven years later Hans and Sophie Scholl were to shower their fellow students with anti-Nazi flysheets dropped from the upper floors, an action for which they were subsequently sentenced to death) and went to the *Aula* or Great Hall to listen to a lecture on National Socialist racial policy by Julius Streicher, the Gauleiter of Franconia. For three and a half hours, this gross bully, bulging in his brown uniform, poured forth floods of filth that I would not have thought possible in public oratory, let alone from a university lectern, and offered "scientific" evidence of the predatory nature of the Jews, at one point arguing insistently that, if one was attentive while visiting zoos, one would note that the blond-haired German children always played happily in the sandboxes while the swarthy Jewish children sat expectantly before the cages of the beasts of prey, seeking vicarious satisfaction of their blood-tainted lusts. The audience in the *Aula* was attentive, and many took notes.

Despite its offensiveness, the cruelty of Streicher's speech was somewhat attenuated by its generalized approach and the fact that there were no victims present. But one day, traveling from Jena to Dresden, I sat in a railroad compartment with two other passengers, a quiet, rather depressed looking man, who I noticed was wearing the ribbon that indicated that he was a veteran of the First World War, and a red-faced, stocky man with an air of self-confidence and a commanding voice. Seeing that I was a foreigner, the latter undertook to instruct me in the excellences of the regime and the wisdom of its policies, particularly that of anti-Semitism. He made much of the supposed role of the Jews in bringing the collapse of Germany in 1918; he insisted that the inflation of 1923 had been a plot of Jewish speculators; and he maintained that, under the Republic, the Jews had conspired to corrupt youth and undermine morality by means of their control of press, theater, and cinema—all of this accompanied by sly, sidelong glances at the other passenger. When the train slowed and stopped at Neumarck, the latter gathered his bags and departed with a polite farewell. As the door closed behind him, I saw that my interlocutor was beside himself with triumph. "He was one!" he cackled. "Did you see? He was a Jew! I knew it all the time!"

Now and then, in a restaurant or a *Kneipe* one might fall into conversation with a sympathetic person who suggested indirectly that he disapproved of the anti-Jewish policy. But even these people were apt to slide away into exculpation of one kind or another, commenting irrelevantly that, after all, Hitler had solved the problem of unemployment, or that his foreign policy had restored Germany's self-esteem, or that he didn't know about the anti-Jewish excesses, which were the work of his subordinates. It was unwise to argue back, for that was likely to lead to references to lynching in the United States or to the lack of real civilization on the other side of the Atlantic. Xenophobia was never far beneath the surface and sometimes broke forth in ugly forms, as an American friend and I discovered in an inn in the village of Eschenlohe, fifteen kilometers from Garmisch, when menacing looks from a band of muscular hikers in brown shirts and audible sneers about foreigners persuaded us that it was expedient to go to bed early, and again, in a pub in Jena, when we were talking quietly in our own tongue and were interrupted by a drunken shout from a nearby table, "Speak German!"

There was no evidence in the summer of 1935 of any significant popular opposition to Hitler and his policies. The Leader's successful defiance of the Versailles Powers in March, when he repudiated the arms clauses of the Treaty and began a headlong program of rearmament, and his success in June in concluding a naval pact with Great Britain on his own terms had left the majority of the German people in a state of patriotic euphoria that was reflected in the newspapers, in the mood of theater audiences watching the newsreels, and in casual conversation. In those days in Munich, near the point where the Residenzstrasse empties into the Odeonsplatz, there was a plaque on the side of the Feldherrnhalle to commemorate the death of the twelve Nazi "martyrs" who had fallen there in November 1923, when Hitler's Beer Hall *Putsch* had been put down. On either side of this memorial stood an armed sentry, and pedestrians were expected, when they passed, to raise their arms in the so-called *Hitler Gruss*. They always did so, and I was surprised to discover, the first time I walked up the Residenzstrasse, that, when buses went up the street, everybody aboard did the same—drivers, conductors, and passengers together, all of the arms sweeping up in dedicated unison, giving the impression that the vehicle was lifting itself off the pavement. The effect was startling and, the first time, hilariously funny, but that feeling didn't last, and I began to regard the buses as depressing symbols of eager obedience to authority, comic but ominous illustrations of the phrase *"Führer, befiehl! Wir folgen!"* ("Führer! Command and we will follow you!")

I said something of this to the American consul in Munich, a nice man named Charles Hathaway, adding that I found it strange that a people once famous for its irrepressible individualism in religion and philosophy should have made obedience to political authority so supreme a virtue. "Oh my yes," Hathaway replied. "I live in a little village south of Munich, and the people there are hard-working and friendly and not interested in politics in general, and they and I like and respect each other. But if someone in uniform came to them and said, 'March!,' they would march. And if he said, 'Go and cut off Hathaway's head! He is a bad man!,' they would reply, 'We didn't know that!' But they would cut my head off all the same."

The Third Reich, which was just beginning to flex its muscles in 1935, went on to celebrate its flashy but insubstantial triumphs and then vanished, the victim of the arrogance and the hubris of its founder, and a new Germany has emerged, slowly and painfully, but with gathering self-confidence, from the ruins that Hitler left. Given the totality of his work of destruction and the rigors and duration of the process of new birth, is there any real connection between today's Germany and the one that I visited in 1935 or, for that matter, all the other Germanies that lie in the past—those of William II and Bismarck and Frederick II and Luther?

This is a question that has been debated ever since 1945, not only by Germans, but by their neighbors, and it is not surprising that it has been the latter who have been the most insistent in holding that the tie with the past is both real and strong. The French, in particular, have been adamant in their conviction that "the Germans never change" and in their intermittent suspicion that a reversion to the bad old past—a surrender, as one journalist expressed it, to their familiar demons—is not only possible but likely. This annoys the Germans, and in 1977, in response to a rash of stories in the French press about signs of imminent re-Nazification, Countess Marion Dönhoff wrote with some asperity in the influential Hamburg weekly *Die Zeit* that such views were absurd, that too much had changed in Germany and the world to permit a return to the mental attitudes and behavior of the thirties, and that the lines of continuity had been broken, including the continuity of those values that had in the past been the main support of authority in Germany.

The pages that follow will make clear both my agreement with Countess Dönhoff's major premise and my reservations concerning her minor one, that is, her view of continuity. Chapters 2 and 13 below argue that the year 1945 represented a caesura in German history that was sharper and more conclusive than any previous break in modern times, infinitely more decisive than, to take one example, the so-called revolution of 1918. In the aftermath of the Second World War and the tensions of the Cold War, two German States were born with political and economic systems that were radically different from those of the past, and their development upon these new foundations has been so marked that chances of a reversion to the past, on either side of the Wall, are all but negligible.

This does not mean, however, that there are no continuities or that students of contemporary Germany can disregard the past. Just as the habits of obedience that troubled me in 1935 were, as I have tried to point out in Chapter 1, the products less of that indefinable quality that we call national character than of a particular kind—indeed, a unique kind—of historical experience, so do the attitudes and thinking of today's Germans continue to be affected, to a greater or lesser degree, by history and tradition. There is no way, natural or contrived, of divorcing a people completely from its past. This is what Willy H. Schlieker, whose success in building an industrial and shipping empire from virtually nothing made him the most spectacular of the *Wunderkinder* of the 1950s, was implying when he said ironically, "You Americans made one big mistake in your efforts to democratize us Germans, and that is why it never worked properly. . . . In the beginning, you neglected to de-Kaiserize us."

The influence of historical memory and cultural tradition in contemporary German life is difficult to measure with any hope of accuracy, and so is the degree to which the German people can be said to have assimilated their recent past and come to terms with the atrocities committed in their name by the Nazis. But it is the duty of the historian to deal with the contesting claims of change and continuity, trying to remember, as he does so, not to allow his professional predilection for the past to tempt him to undervalue the former or to permit the future-oriented bias of his own generation to blind him to the importance of the latter. This kind of balancing act I have attempted in the second part of this book. Its chapters are intended to suggest the way in which contemporary German attitudes show the effect of old but stubborn assumptions and prejudices: a religious heritage that has always been ambivalent in its simultaneous tendency toward establishmentarianism and revolt; a respect for hard work and the financial rewards that it brings that is combined with the uneasy knowledge, based on traumatic historical experience, that such rewards are apt to be impermanent; a veneration of learning and literature that has traditionally been offset by a disinclination to allow them full freedom of expression; a resistance to change and nonconformity and to those who represent it, whether they are rebellious students or advocates of women's rights; and—associated with this—an inconsistent attitude toward modernity which, through most of the modern period, has expressed itself in the eager adoption of technical and economic innovation and a simultaneous reprobation of its social and moral effects, this latter feeling often assuming romantic, racist, and regressive forms.

It is not the intention here to make predictions about Germany's future or even to make judgments about current tendencies in German thought. As far as the latter is concerned, no people is harder to generalize about than the Germans, perhaps because they have not always been as obedient to the laws of logic as other peoples. Indeed, the only two general statements about them that ever struck me as being sensible may almost be considered as warnings against generalization. The first was Tacitus's famous definition of the Germans as a *propriam et sinceram et tantum sui gentem*, a "distinct, unmixed race, like none but themselves." The second was by Thomas Mann, who once wrote, "The Germans are the really problematical people. . . . Whoever should strive to transform Germany . . . in the sense of the West would be trying to rob her of her best and weightiest quality, of her problematical endowment, which is the essence of her nationality."

PART ONE

Past
and
Present

1

Historical Perspectives

"The Germans," Goethe once said, "make everything difficult, both for themselves and for everyone else." Perhaps that is why there has always been a German problem and why foreigners have periodically confessed their inability to understand German behavior, to say nothing of German philosophy and the German language. In 1860, commenting on the policies of the German states, *The Times* of London said fretfully, "The vagaries of German policy are such that we cannot pretend to follow them. It is useless to look for profundity where, in all likelihood, there is only pedantry, or for a tangible object in what may be only a desire to carry out some dreamy historical notion. Were the ways of the Germans like our ways—were they governed by practical statesmen instead of by martinets and sophists—we should fancy they had some far-seen end in view. . . . But, knowing what they are, we only see in their conduct another instance of that weakness and perversity which has brought on them so many misfortunes."

Sixty years later, somewhat more delicately, Logan Pearsall Smith wrote in that charming but sadly neglected book *Trivia*: "The 'Known World' I called the map, which I amused myself making for the children's schoolroom. It included France, England, Italy, Greece, and all the old shores of the Mediterranean; but the rest I marked 'Unknown'; sketching into the East the doubtful realms of Ninus and Semiramis; changing back Germany into the Hercynian Forest; and drawing pictures of the supposed inhabitants of these unexploited regions. . . ."

These passages, particularly the first, remind us of Henry Higgins's outraged expostulation concerning women: "Why can't they be like us?" The fact is that the Germans aren't like anyone but the Germans and, in view of their history, can hardly expect to be. While England and France were powerful national entities before the end of the fifteenth century, it was not until the seventh decade of the nineteenth that Bismarck's diplomacy and the efficiency of the Prussian army brought the fragmented German lands together and established a centralized realm with a single government. In the two centuries that preceded that event, much of what we now call Germany was, for reasons that will become clear, relatively untouched by the great movements of Euro-

15

pean history. Not unnaturally, its inhabitants acquired the habits of mind and the attitudes toward life and politics that were best suited to their situation, and many of the characteristics that we regard as "typically German" originated in this period. These did not disappear when Germany became a united nation in 1871; indeed, the nature of German politics in the century that followed continued to be profoundly influenced by them, and some of the failures of understanding between Germany and the West are explicable in their light.

I

It is paradoxical that the Germans, chronically torn and divided, in Friedrich Hölderlin's phrase, throughout most of the modern period, seemed during the middle ages, and particularly between the tenth and twelfth centuries, to be politically more mature, and closer to establishing effective political institutions, than their neighbors. It was the German tribes who inherited and cherished the tradition of the Roman Empire and the legacy of Charlemagne, and, when the Carolingian Empire collapsed under the pressure of new barbarian invasions, the Germans were the only element of stability in northern and central Europe. It was they who drove the Norsemen back into the sea, repulsed the Slavic incursions in the east, and, by forming a strong union with the Papacy, established peace in the European center. After the coronation of Otto I as Emperor in 962, it was possible to speak of a German hegemony over Europe, and, in the course of the next century, there were indications that the first truly national State in Europe was emerging in the German lands. Records dating from the tenth century speak of a *regnum teutonicorum* as an accomplished fact, which suggests that a recognizable national identity or self-consciousness also existed. This feeling was doubtless encouraged by the marked revival of commerce and the beginnings of urban civilization, which came earlier to the German states than it did elsewhere, and also by the persistent efforts of the German king-emperors to break down provincial barriers and consolidate their own domains.

This promising development did not continue. The very increase of economic prosperity added to the strength and pretensions of local princes, who were in any case restive under the domination of Imperial power. More serious was the revival of the Papacy from its earlier weakness. In the tenth century, the Papacy and the German kings were closely allied; in the eleventh the popes found that, in order to preserve their own position against the ambitions of the German kings, it was useful to find allies among their unhappy vassals. This policy was effective. The well-known struggle between Pope Gregory VII and Emperor Henry IV ended with an Imperial capitulation at Canossa, a result that would have been impossible if the princes had not been on Gregory's side; and, although Canossa was by no means a definitive papal victory, its results in Germany were significant. It marked the beginning of a fateful tendency in German history, the dualism between central authority and princely power, which, in the end, destroyed the former and fastened upon the realm the particularism that was to affect all aspects of German life in the modern period.

The eventual victory of this process was hastened in the twelfth century, when the Hohenstaufen emperors became fascinated with the possibility of conquering Italy and became in result involved in new conflicts with the Papacy, which now began systematically to follow an anti-Imperial balance of power policy. As this struggle developed, the German emperors were themselves compelled to bargain with their vassals and to grant concessions in return for support. These donations, which gave the princes the right to maintain courts of their own, to build castles and raise levies of arms, to collect taxes and mint money, and to control the towns lying within their territories, cut the ground out from under the feet of the German monarchy. By the thirteenth century, the process known as the territorialization of Germany was well advanced—the fragmentation of the German lands into a bewildering congeries of independent units, governed under separate rulers and recognizing only the vaguest connection with the Imperial authority; and by the fourteenth, when the Golden Bull gave legal recognition to the rights and sovereignty of the most important princes, the German crown was a nullity and German unity a mere façade.

As if to emphasize this development, Germany's European position changed for the worse. In the days of the Saxon and Hohenstaufen emperors, the German Empire had been the greatest power in Europe, and none of its neighbors had dared to threaten its borders. Now new pressures were felt on every side, and Germany became in a true sense what it was often called later on, *das Land der Mitte*, the country in the middle. By the fifteenth century, border territories that had long been considered German had broken their ties or were absorbed by stronger neighbors. Prussia, won by the Teutonic Knights, was lost to the Poles; Bohemia asserted its independence; the Netherlands and Switzerland drifted away; and in the west the emerging power of France began to encroach upon the Rhenish lands. In a Europe that was rapidly changing, it was apparent that the fortunes of a disunited state in the middle would be neither enviable nor comfortable. As the German historian Hermann Oncken wrote later, "Taken all in all, the Reich seemed to become smaller, the neighbors to come nearer, the boundaries to be no longer fluid but rigid, and an encirclement . . . was becoming more apparent on all sides."

Had there been leaders with any sense of German national interest, this condition of vulnerability might have been exploited to galvanize new forces of cohesion and growth, and the German states might have begun to follow the road that England and France had already taken. This did not happen, largely because the Imperial title now passed to the possession of the Habsburg dynasty. The new rulers were often able and energetic men, but family interest disinclined them to use their talents for Germany's advantage. By a policy of judicious marriages, they had accumulated far-flung territorial possessions from the lower Rhine and the Scheldt to the eastern Alps and from Spain to the lands along the Danube. To them, Germany was of secondary importance, convenient as a connecting link between their dispersed holdings and as a battlefield, or alternatively a field for annexations and compensations, in their growing rivalry with the royal power of France. A Maximilian I and a Charles V might talk about the necessity of a thoroughgoing reform of the old Imperial structure, but nothing was ever accomplished. This was because their hearts weren't in it, because the consolidation of the power of the German princes had already gone too far, and finally because of the complications caused, in the sixteenth century, by the Protestant Reformation.

Upon the German mind and, indeed, upon the German language, this great revolution of the spirit had profound effects that will concern us later in this volume. For the moment, we need note only its most fateful consequence, namely, that it destroyed the one shadowy semblance of unity in Germany and inaugurated a long period of religious conflict that culminated in the terrible war that erupted in 1618 and raged across central Europe for thirty years.

If the Thirty Years War began as a conflict between confessions, religious zeal soon proved in many cases to be a mere disguise for political opportunism, and the war was transformed into a gigantic duel between Austria and Spain on the one hand and France, Sweden and the maritime powers on the other, with Germany the arena in which their struggle for mastery was played out. When one remembers it, it is not for the exploits of its great captains, although their names, to be sure, have come down to us. But Peter von Mansfeld, Albrecht von Wallenstein, Gustavus Adolphus, Johann von Tilly, Ambrosio di Spinola and Bernard of Saxe-Weimar distinguished themselves neither by strategical genius nor operational élan; they are recalled rather as commanders who had little control over the brutal *Soldateska* whom they brought into Germany, as men, indeed, who stood helplessly by as the war they pursued broke through the purposes for which it was ostensibly being fought and—as Karl von Clausewitz in his military writings said was the inherent tendency of war—assumed its absolute and most unconditional form.

Consider what happened to the flourishing town of Magdeburg in the thirteenth year of the war. As the armies of the Habsburg Emperor Ferdinand II, having extirpated Protestantism in Bohemia, pressed their campaigns to the north, the Protestant forces received welcome new support from the young King of Sweden, Gustavus Adolphus, who in July 1630 landed at Usedom in Pomerania with sixteen troops of Swedish horse and a strong detachment of artillery and ninety companies of foot, mostly mercenary Scots and Germans, and marched southward. In order to deny him possession of Magdeburg, the key fortress on the Elbe, and also to supply his own troops, worn out in bloody but fruitless attacks upon Gustavus's lines of communications, the Imperial commander Tilly invested the town and took its outer fortifications in April 1631. Although he was known as the monk in armor because of the blameless rectitude of his personal life, Tilly was no religious fanatic and wanted no needless expenditure of life. He therefore called upon the inhabitants to remember their allegiance to the Emperor and to open the gates, promising to respect their liberties and property. The town magistrates, who knew that their stores of powder were all but exhausted and that the remaining defenses of the town, hastily built of loose earth, could not long withstand assault, were inclined to yield. But whenever they sought to do so they were overborne by the eloquence of the pastor of the Ulrichskirche, a dedicated Lutheran named Gilbert de Spaignart, who declared that it would be infamous in the eyes of the Lord to surrender to the papists, and by the promises of the commander of the town's defenses, the Hessian soldier Dietrich von Falkenberg, that the Swedish King was on his way to Magdeburg and would raise the siege.

This delay was suicidal. Tilly's troop leaders, especially the impetuous Gottfried Heinrich Graf von Pappenheim, apprehensive lest they find themselves caught between the town walls and a Swedish army, pressed their commander to let them storm Magdeburg, and the growing insubordination of their troops, bored with the rigors of camp life and greedy for the creature comforts of the town, added urgency to their arguments. With heavy heart, Tilly gave the order to attack. Between six and seven o'clock on the morning of May 19, the Pappenheimers burst through the northern walls before the startled garrison could bring effective fire to bear upon them, and the outer streets of the town were filled with *Landsknechte* bent on liquor, plunder and rape. It was soon apparent that there was nothing that the officers could to do restrain the blood lust and mania for destruction that seized their troops. Tilly himself, riding through scenes of unimaginable carnage with a baby that he had found crying in the arms of its dead mother, told the prior of a local monastery to try to direct women and children to take refuge in the cathedral. This certainly saved some lives, although their number was dwarfed by the fatalities. During the assault, Pappenheim had set fire to one of the town gates, and sparks from this, carried by a strong wind, set fires that raged through the wooden structures of the town, killing natives and invaders alike and reducing Magdeburg to a sea of smoldering cinders. Of the town's 30,000 inhabitants, only 5000 survived, and many of those were carried off by Tilly's retreating army as concubines and servants.

Magdeburg was not the only town to fall victim to the ravages of the war. Before the conflict was over, Berlin had lost half of its population and Chemnitz eighty percent. When the Spanish troops came to Munich, they brought the plague with them, and within weeks 10,000 people died. The poet Andreas Gryphius voiced the despair of townspeople in every part of Germany that was visited by the war, when he wrote:

Wir sind doch nunmehr ganz, ja mehr denn ganz verheeret!
Der frechen Völker Schar, die rasende Posaun,
Das vorn Blut fette Schwert, die donnernde Karthaun
Hat aller Schweiss and Fleiss and Vorrat aufgezehret.

Die Türme stehn in Glut, die Kirch ist umgekehret,
Das Rathaus liegt im Graus, die Starken sind zerhaun,
Die Jungfraun sind geschänd't, und wo wir hin nur schaun,
Ist Feuer, Pest und Tod, der Herz und Geist durchfähret.

[We are now wholly, yea! more than wholly devastated.
The band of presumptuous nations, the raving trumpets,
The sword oily with blood, the thundering cannon-royal
Have consumed the fruits of all our sweat and travail.

The towers stand in flames, the church is overturned,
The town hall lies in ruins, the stalwart are hacked to bits,
The maidens are deflowered, and everywhere we look
Fire, plague and death oppress the heart and soul.]

The suffering of the rural population was equally great. In the fifteenth chapter of the second book of Hans-Jakob Grimmelshausen's contemporary picaresque novel *Simplicius Simplicissimus*, the author describes the adventures of his hero as a member of a troop of foraging Croats, who "swept through the villages, stole and took what they wanted, mocked and ruined the peasants and violated their maids and wives and daughters and, if the poor peasants didn't like that and dared to be brave and to rap one or the other forager across the knuckles because of these deeds, then one cut them down, if one could catch them, or at least sent their houses up to heaven in smoke." All along the trail of the war, from Swabia and the Palatinate in the south, through Thuringia and Magdeburg and Brandenburg, to Mecklenburg and Pomerania in the north, peasant communities suffered this kind of treatment, not once but repeatedly in the course of the war, and were sometimes reduced to cannibalism in their desperate attempts to survive. By 1641 the population of Württemberg had been reduced from 400,000 to 48,000, and the Palatinate had lost four fifths of its inhabitants. Bohemia, which had a population of 3 million in 1618, had only 780,000 at the end of the war, and of its 35,000 villages, only 5000 still existed. Swedish troops alone destroyed 18,000 villages in the last eighteen years of the war, along with 1500 towns and 200 castles.

Although there were areas that remained relatively unaffected by the war—Upper and Lower Saxony, Holstein, Oldenburg, Hamburg and Prussia—Germany as a whole suffered a population loss of about 35%, declining from 21 million people to about 13½ million, and this and the destruction of property that accompanied it turned it for an appreciable time into an impoverished and handicapped country. This condition was not improved by the settlement that ended the war, for the Great Powers who concluded the Peace of Westphalia in 1648 compounded the difficulties of recovery by depriving Germany of access to the sea. After Westphalia, the mouth of every great German river was under foreign control. From Memel to the mouth of the Vistula, the Poles held the coast of the Baltic; the Oder and the surrounding coast were in Sweden's hands, as were the Weser and the left bank of the Elbe. Holstein and the right bank of the Elbe were controlled by the Danes, and the mouth of the Rhine was Dutch. There had been a time when Germany was the land of the Hansa, the league of cities that sought their fortunes on the open sea; it had now become a landlocked nation, at the very moment when other European nations were winning colonial empires. The effect of this on Germany's towns, already crucially weakened by the war, is not difficult to imagine. They now became mere shadows of themselves, sad reminders of a happier past.

The peacemakers of 1648 also imposed upon Germany a political settlement that confirmed and legitimized the atomization of Germany by recognizing over 300 German states as sovereign entities. This was the reason that the French successors of Richelieu, determined to humble the Habsburg power, regarded Westphalia as "one of the finest jewels in the French crown" and argued that any attempt to interfere with "German liberties," by which they meant the rights of the petty states, would constitute a breach of international law. German disunity and powerlessness thus became part of the natural European order, acquiesced to by all Great Powers, including the larger German states. At the Congress of Vienna in 1815, the Prussian delegate Wilhelm von Humboldt justified this by taking the line that the divisions of Germany were conducive to international peace, adding, "Its whole existence, therefore, is based upon a preservation of balance through an inherent force of gravity. This would be entirely counteracted if there were introduced into the ranks of European states, besides the larger German states considered as single units, a new collective state. . . . No one could then prevent Germany, as Germany, from becoming an aggressive state, which no good German can wish."

As late as 1866, the French were still using this argument. On the very eve of Prussia's war with Austria, which was the first long step toward German unification, the statesman and historian Adolphe Thiers, like his predecessors at Westphalia and Vienna, defended the "German liberties" in a speech in the French Chamber of Deputies. "I beg the Germans to reflect," he said, "that the highest principle of European politics is that Germany shall be composed of independent states connected only by a slender federative thread. That was the principle proclaimed by all Europe at the Congress of Westphalia." A union of Germany, he added, would simply subvert the European balance of power.

II

Upon the inhabitants of the German lands, the social and psychological effects of the Thirty Years War and the imposed settlement were protracted. With respect to the former, the war greatly strengthened the privileged position of the aristocracy at the expense of the educated and prosperous burgher class and the peasantry. The decline of the towns and the consequent decrease in the demand for food caused so sharp a fall in grain prices that small landowners were often forced to sacrifice their independence in order to maintain themselves. Particularly in the East Elbian lands, in Mecklenburg and Pomerania and Prussia, the local nobility was able to take advantage of this situation to increase their own holdings and to impose new obligations upon local peasants in the form of rents and services and restrictions upon movement. Their princes, who required the military and administrative services of the nobility, either tolerated these practices or—as was true in Prussia under Frederick William I (1714–1740)—encouraged them and made them the basis of a social contract with the aristocracy at the expense of the other classes.

In general, the power of the princes was enhanced by the war and the settlement, and it was a sign of the times that princely residences, like Würzburg and Karlsruhe and Mannheim, now replaced in prominence and splendor the old commercial centers like Nuremberg and Augsburg and Lübeck. At these princely courts, the nobility held a virtual monopoly of the principal ministerial positions, but in the upper reaches of the civil service, in the fiscal administration, for example, there were opportunities for educated members of the bourgeoisie, who now found such careers more attractive than the commercial life that they might have followed a century earlier. In all German states, the ruling class was now composed of the landed aristocracy, the military service nobility and the higher officialdom, which was largely non-noble, and this elite was to continue to occupy the seats of power, despite the transition in the nineteenth century to constitutional forms of government, until the First World War. This sociopolitical hierarchy was in turn served by a host of lesser officials—police, customs officials, tax collectors, teachers, even clergymen—who also derived their authority from the prince.

It is not too much to talk of a progressive bureaucratization of Germany in the seventeenth and eighteenth centuries and a concomitant growth among the inhabitants of the German states of habits of deference toward authority that seemed excessive to foreign observers. These last may have had ancient roots—it was a medieval pope who called Germany the *terra obedientiae*—but there is little doubt that they were encouraged by the traumatic effects of the war. The daily presence of death, the constant *Angst* of which Gryphius speaks in his poems, made the survivors willing to submit to any authority that seemed strong enough to prevent a recurrence of those terrors. They accepted the swollen pretensions of their princes uncritically and with an atavistic fear of the likely consequences of any dissolution of existing social relationships; and in time this acceptance came to appear normal and acquired the weight of tradition. To some extent, this was true because, in a land untouched by the secularization of the West, it found powerful support in a prevalent religious ethic, imparted, as we shall see, by

State-dominated and State-supporting churches, and was also unchallenged by any alternative view of the relationship between ruler and subject. That unsparing critic of the foibles and weaknesses of his countrymen, the Württemberg publisher Karl Friedrich Moser, wrote in 1758, "Every nation has its principal motive. In Germany, it is obedience; in England, freedom; in Holland, trade; in France, the honor of the King."

As far as the Germans were concerned, the motive retained its force long after external circumstances had ceased to be a potent argument for authoritarian rule. Even in the nineteenth century, when both the horrors of the Thirty Years War and the more recent exactions of Napoleon Bonaparte were comfortably remote, agitation for an expansion of popular rights of participation in government was countered by insistence that social order depended upon undeviating obedience to existing authorities. This argument was a constant ingredient of textbooks in elementary schools, but it was not restricted to such official materials and was pervasive. The family magazine *Daheim,* for instance, preached loyalty to throne and altar with undiminished fervor until the end of the century, and both the literature of the educated classes and the popular reading of the masses were permeated by the same authoritarian zeal. Thus, Victor von Falk's novel of the Berlin underworld, *The Executioner of Berlin,* which was published serially in short installments and sold hundreds of thousands of copies, was filled, despite its sensational tone, with small sermons on obedience. ("I carry out what the judges have decided and my Emperor has approved. Surely it is no disgrace to execute the commands of such men.")

Acceptance of the authority of the prince assumed a willingness to obey the commands of his agents, no matter how petty their position or arrogant their manner. The willingness of Germans to tolerate the most offensive behavior from anyone wearing a uniform or official insignia was something that always surprised Western visitors. The satirist of the Weimar period Kurt Tucholsky once explained it as the result of a conviction that bureaucracy, with all its faults, was ordained. "What little reason the German possesses divides the country horizontally into two layers: above, the bureaus; below, the subjects. And believes at the same time that the bureaus have fallen from the moon, along with the bureaucrats and everything which, with its official stamps and sarcastic tone and boring incompetence, oppresses the poor innocent citizenry."

The life of the average German in the eighteenth and early nineteenth centuries was provincial in the extreme. There were, of course, some exceptions. The citizens of Berlin and Munich, capitals of states with international pretensions, were not untouched by influences from the outside world, and natives of the great harbor-city Hamburg could be described as holding cosmopolitan views. But this could not be said of those who lived in the villages of Lower Bavaria or the sandy reaches of East Elbia and the Baltic littoral, and it was certainly not true of the inhabitants of what might be called the German heartland. This was the part of Germany that the nineteenth century ethnographer W. H. Riehl called "middle or differentiated Germany," which stretched from Westphalia to the Danube and from the Rhine to Upper Saxony. This, Riehl said, was the "motley encyclopaedia of our society," filled with middle-sized communities set in rolling country that contrasted with the open landscape and the larger towns of Prussia to the north and Bavaria and Austria in the south. Until 1806, when Napoleon finally abolished the Holy Roman Empire, these communities represented its real substance, and their individuality was protected by this fact and by the provisions of the Treaty of Westphalia which made the Empire part of the European balance and forbade territorial change or amalgamation within it.

The characteristic features of these "home towns," as they have been called in a brilliant modern study, were institutional eccentricity and close social integrity. It was here that local custom and tradition and guild privileges survived until the middle of the nineteenth century, and here that modern law and administration, modern learning, skills and industry, modern population movements and growth were most vigorously opposed. Because they were small—generally ranging from a thousand to ten thousand inhabitants—these communities had neither the kind of government by patriciate that divided the citizenry of older and larger towns nor large bodies of noncitizens or partial citizens or transients. Their dwellers compensated for their separation from the general tendencies and interests of the larger society by their strong local pride and community sense and their pronounced *Geselligkeit* or sociability, which was reflected in their pleasure in family and community feasts and frolics, in the celebration of anniversaries and namedays, and in activities of the innumerable organizations to which they belonged—church societies, choirs and instrumental groups, skat and skittles clubs, and the like. (In the small town that William Sheridan Allen studied for his book about the rise of National Socialism, he discovered that in 1930 there were 161 clubs, an average of one for every sixty persons.)

Because of their relative isolation, moreover, the towns of the heartland were a principal source of that remarkable diversity of German life which Goethe praised as the positive side of particularism. Until very recent times, a person traveling through Germany could count on encountering ever new varieties of speech and dress, of food and drink, of song and story, and not least of all of humor. In his *Little Geography of German Wit,* Herbert Schoeffler pointed out that just as the northern cities had their distinctive styles—Hamburgers being given to realistic melancholy and black humor, denizens of Cologne delighting in the zany non-sequiturs of their local gods Tünnes and Schäl, and Berliners being masters of the witty rejoinder and the *jeu d'esprit*—so was this true of the world of Gmünd, Aalen, Bopfingen, Biberach, Leutkirch, Reutlingen and the other Imperial cities and hometowns, and that there was as wide a difference between the humor of the Swabians and the

Saxons* as there was between the astronomical system of Kepler, who with typical Swabian love of order made the planets follow leftward elliptical courses, in order to avoid collisions, and that of Gottfried Leibniz, whose Saxon dislike of quarreling led him to postulate a *Gemütlichkeit* of the spheres.

Even with respect to humor, however, the heartland tended to be parochial and defensive. In the early nineteenth century, a pastor who probably lived in the differentiated Germany of which we have been speaking, wrote about Berliners and northerners in general: "They have only wit, which wounds, rather than humor, which conciliates. And here they make us aware of the elements of a foreign nationality by which they are characterized. The Viennese have humor, and to the German *Gemüt* that atones for a thousand sins. And in this word, this expression *Gemüt*, the whole antithesis that divides Germany into two parts comes to a head. *Gemüt* means the south, truly German, tender, intimate, full, warm; *Jemüt* [as a true Berliner would pronounce the word] means the north, sharp, industrial, blasé, superficial, and mixed with foreign, Jewish and French elements."

These words are significant as indicating the author's preoccupation with the question of what was truly German, and this too was characteristic of the heartland. In no other part of Germany was the adjective "German" so heavily used; indeed, it often appeared that the unadorned noun represented something of lesser value than that connoted by "German" wine, "German" song, a "German" maiden, the "German" forest (*O du mein deutscher Wald!*), "German" industry, "German" valor, "German" loyalty, and "German" gaiety (which Nietzsche arbitrarily associated with the names Luther, Beethoven and Wagner, defining it as the sweetness of spirit that comes from having overcome adversity and adding that it could not be understood by other peoples). This emphasis upon uniqueness may have been a reflection of a yearning for a lost identity, as has often been suggested. In his essay "What is German" (1865), Richard Wagner said something of the sort when he wrote: "After the complete destruction of the German essence (*Wesen*), after the almost complete extinction of the German nation as a result of the indescribable devastations of the Thirty Years War, it was this most intimately homely world [the area between the Rhine and the Alps, the truly German lands of Swabia, Saxony, Franconia and Bavaria] from which the German spirit was reborn. German poetry, German music, German philosophy are today highly respected by all peoples of the world; but in his longing for 'German glory' the German can usually

---

*Saxon humor is supposed to incline toward the philosophical, as in Wilhelm Pinder's story of the Saxon who died and went to heaven's gates, where Peter told him to go up to the second floor and knock on the door of Room 247 and he would be admitted. He did this, but nothing happened, so he put his shoulder to the door and with much effort got it open, "and there stood Lord Jesus in all His glory, and He said, 'Yes. It always sticks a little.' "

dream of nothing else but something similar to the restoration of the Roman Empire."

But, if this was so, the emphasis upon Germanness was also an indication of a search for assurance in a rapidly changing world, and an attempt to accomplish this by differentiating local traditions and local values from external ones. This defensiveness is understandable. As the years passed, the world of these small communities—so admirably portrayed in Goethe's idyll *Hermann und Dorothea,* with its emphasis upon private values and its indifference even to such a world-shaking phenomenon as the French Revolution, in the canvases of the Biedermeier painter Moritz von Schwind, and in Albert Lortzing's light operas *Der Wildschütz* and *Der Waffenschmied*—was threatened by the forces of bureaucratic centralization and nascent capitalism and industrialism. In the end, these developments overwhelmed and destroyed the political environment that had nourished the hometown culture.

Even after this had happened, however, and the differentiated communities had been submerged in the Empire of Bismarck and William II, their psychology survived in the form of regional resentments, philistinism, and bigotry. Their most perceptive analyst, the American historian Mack Walker, has written that "belief in the primacy of communal membership, mistrust of floating individuals, and righteous hostility toward the outside were the hometown legacy to the Germany of the later nineteenth century and at least the first half of the twentieth century." To that legacy we shall have occasion to return later in this book.

III

If one remembers the degree to which the traumatized Germany of 1648 was cut off from the outside world and the kind of political and cultural attitudes that this condition encouraged in the greater part of the German population in the subsequent period, one can understand the relative failure in Germany of that great intellectual movement of the eighteenth century known as the Enlightenment.

This had its origins in Great Britain with the epochal discoveries of Isaac Newton and the determination of his followers to base a science of society and a moral philosophy upon Newtonian conceptions of natural law. It spread rapidly to the continent and in France found an inspired spokesman in the person of Voltaire. Its reception in Germany was not so impressive, and there were German states that were untouched by its influence. Even so, the German contribution was not negligible, and the leading German spokesmen for the *Aufklärung,* as it is called in Germany, were so eloquent that they were accorded a degree of international attention that no German thinkers since Luther's time had been able to command.

In the most general terms, the Enlightenment was a movement of people who desired to improve the human condition and believed that this could be done most expeditiously by the rigorous application of the rule of reason to all of the ideas that dominated men's minds and all of the institutions that determined the conditions in which they lived. These *philosophes,* as they were sometimes called, had many differences among themselves when they were confronted with specific issues. But they were generally agreed that the correlatives of rationality were secularism, humanity, cosmopolitanism and freedom—freedom from arbitrary power, freedom of speech, freedom to make the most of one's talents, freedom of moral choice. And they were further united in their absolute commitment to criticism, their fearlessness in facing new ideas, and their willingness to be modern, in the sense of breaking away from the burden of past superstitions and orthodoxies. This, in general, was the credo of people like Montesquieu and Voltaire, David Hume and Denis Diderot, Thomas Jefferson and Jean-Jacques Rousseau, Jeremy Bentham and the Marquis de Condorcet.

Chief among the German *Aufklärer* was the King of Prussia, Frederick II (1740–1786), whose rationalization of the Prussian government—("A well-conducted government," he said in his Testament of 1752, "ought to have a system as coherent as a system of philosophy")—was so exemplary an application of the principles of the Enlightenment that it aroused much admiration abroad. Frederick was the enlightened despot *par excellence,* and his inaugural decree granting equality of rights to all religious creeds in his realm and his encouragement of the formulation of rules of war as a means of introducing a measure of restraint to the century's intermittent bloodletting are examples of many actions that might be cited to demonstrate that the King's dedication to the principles of the *Aufklärung* was not a mere matter of theory but was meant to be expressed in institutional and legal forms.

This could not but impress the rest of Germany, and in his memoirs Goethe writes of how his native city, Frankfurt on the Main, where no love was ordinarily lost on the Prussians, was nevertheless *fritzisch* in his youth. Even so, when German intellectuals at the end of the eighteenth century talked of living in a Frederician age, they were sometimes referring not to the monarch in Sans Souci, but to his namesake, the Berlin bookseller Friedrich Nicolai. It has been said of Nicolai that there would have been no German Enlightenment without him and that it was he who transformed Berlin from a provincial *Residenzstadt* (official residence of a monarch) into the spiritual and cultural capital of the still divided Germany.

This is only slightly exaggerated. Certainly Nicolai's literary journal, the *Allgemeine deutsche Bibliothek,* which he founded with Moses Mendelssohn and Gotthold Ephraim Lessing and directed single-handedly for almost forty years, was the indispensable means of keeping the German reading public informed, not only about what was being written in their own fragmented land, but about cultural and intellectual developments in other countries as well. The importance of the journal as a critical forum is shown by the fact that it published reviews of 80,000 books during Nicolai's editorship. The tone of these notices was never bland and often contentious, for Nicolai was the embodiment of the Enlightenment's faith in the critical method. "Criticism," he once wrote, "is the only helpmate we have which, while disclosing our inadequacies, can at the same time awaken us to the desire for greater improvement."

Nicolai was nothing if not energetic. In addition to his editorial duties, he was the proprietor of Berlin's biggest bookstore, which he made a meeting place for intellectuals who shared his own progressive views and in the running of which he stoutly refused to compromise his philosophical principles for the sake of commercial profit. He once said, "I am not so enamoured of material advantage as to want to purchase it at the price of injury to the whole world. I love the enlightenment of the human race." The same motivation inspired his novel *Sebaldus Nothanker,* a sadly neglected masterpiece that was inspired by Oliver Goldsmith's *The Vicar of Wakefield* and told of the trials of a country parson in the most benighted parts of eighteenth century Germany. Compared with other contemporary novels, *Sebaldus Nothanker* was remarkable for the richness and detail of its social descriptions and the bluntness of its criticism of injustice and inefficiency. Its vast popularity (Goethe was annoyed by its surpassing *Wilhelm Meisters Lehrjahre* in this respect) is to be explained by its urgent plea for the emancipation of the bourgeoisie from the restrictions placed upon it by the conservatism of the feudal-absolutist State (Nicolai exempted Prussia from this category) and by the obscurantism of the orthodox Lutheran clergy.

It was, however, in Nicolai's friend Lessing that the German Enlightenment found its noblest expression. A critical intelligence of the first order—his writings on the drama helped to break the domination of French convention and to open the way to the development of a national theater, and his famous critique of Johann Winckelmann's aesthetic theory in his essay "Laokoon" exerted decisive influence upon the classical revival in Germany—Lessing used his gifts to strike out at all forms of prejudice and all barriers to the full development of the human potential. The most charming of his dramas, the lively comedy *Minna von Barnhelm,* is at once a plea for the reconciliation of the old enemies Prussia and Saxony and a lesson in the folly of allowing irrational conceptions of honor to frustrate natural emotions; the tragedy *Emilia Galotti* is a corrosive revelation of the privilege and corruption of the minor German courts; and his early play *The Jews* and the more famous *Nathan the Wise* are bold attacks upon the prevailing prejudice against the Jewish minority, the latter, in which the protagonist answers the Sultan Saladin's insistent question "What is the true religion?" making a plea for toleration that is as moving today as it must have been when it was written.

Like other spokesmen for the Enlightenment, Lessing believed that untrammeled reason was the key to progress; and in his essay "The Education of the Human Race," he wrote confidently, "No, it will come, it will surely come, the time of the completion, when the individual, the more convinced his reason becomes of an ever better future, will have no need to borrow motivational grounds for his behavior from that future, but will do the good because it is the good and not because arbitrary rewards are attached to it."

Lessing's numerous disciples tried in their own ways to realize this dream of human progress, some of them concentrating on the struggle for political rights, like Georg Forster, the logic of whose convictions led him to the advocacy of political democracy, the establishment of a short-lived republic in Mainz in 1793, and death in Paris during the Terror, others by seeking to combat those forces inside Germany that they felt were inimical to intellectual freedom and progress. Notable among the latter was the Göttingen mathematician and astronomer Georg Christoph Lichtenberg, whose *Aphorisms* are among the great achievements of the German spirit in the eighteenth century. Like Lessing, Lichtenberg was a formidable critic who directed his shafts against charlatans, mystagogues and purveyors of false science, like the physiognomist Johann Lavater. He was also an inveterate opponent of provincial patriotism, that *"Teutschheit"* which was really a disguised form of xenophobia, and his brilliant sallies against this recurrent German disease were to win the praise of people like Heinrich Heine, Leo Tolstoi, Karl Kraus and Albert Einstein, all of them spiritual heirs of the Enlightenment.

In 1784, the philosopher Immanuel Kant, in an essay called "An Answer to the Question: What Is the Enlightenment?" wrote, "If someone asks, are we living in an enlightened age, the answer would be No. But even so, we are living in an age of enlightenment." The statement was less paradoxical than it seemed. What Kant meant was that whereas, wherever one looked, one could find evidence of man's inhumanity to man, of social inequity, of outworn and ineffective institutions, of prejudice and entrenched reaction, it was also true that dedicated and energetic people were doing their best to correct these things. "A few who think for themselves," Kant wrote, "will always be found, even among the installed guardians of the multitude, who, after they have themselves thrown off the yoke of nonage, will spread about them the spirit of a rational estimation of the proper value and of the vocation of every man to think for himself." And from that impulse would come general enlightenment and social and political progress.

In the latter half of the eighteenth century, Germany had no dearth of such preceptors, but unfortunately their influence was neither pervasive nor protracted. For one thing, religious faith, which, as we shall see later in this book, was deeply rooted in the German people and embodied in a learned and active clergy, was strong enough to blunt, in the German *Aufklärung,* the ideas of social contract and popular sovereignty that were salient features of the Enlightenment in the West. At the same time, the death of Frederick II and the coming of the French Revolution marked a decisive change in the intellectual atmosphere, and one that was not conducive to the implementation of advanced ideas of any kind. Indeed, the apostles of the Enlightenment—the *Nikolai-iten,* as they were called in Berlin—were now attacked as subversives, opponents of monarchy, sympathizers with the radical forces in Paris. Nicolai was deprived of control over his literary journal, and his friends found it expedient to trim their sails to the winds of fashionable doctrine. The German *Aufklärung* shriveled under a cloud of defamation and petty persecution and died without leaving the kind of legacy that the Enlightenment in Great Britian, France and America made to future generations.

IV

One of the ideas of the Enlightenment that had been congenial to the educated middle class of the larger states had been that of cosmopolitanism, the view that the cultivated person was a member of a society that transcended national boundaries. Lessing had said that patriotism was not a quality that he coveted, since it "would teach me to forget that I must be a citizen of the world," and the leaders of what is now called the classical age of German literature agreed, Friedrich Schiller once saying, "I write as a citizen of the world who serves no prince. At an early age, I lost my fatherland to trade it for the whole world." But this, like other ideas of the Enlightenment, faded quickly at the century's end and was replaced by a philosophy of nationalism that was much closer to the prejudices of the citizens of the German heartland than to the ideals of the *philosophes*. The agents of this change were Herder and Napoleon.

To call Johann Gottfried von Herder a nationalist is to run the risk of distorting his views. The student of Kant and J. G. Hamann, he had little interest in politics and had a deep and abiding detestation of all forms of centralization, coercion, regulation and imperialism, which he associated with the entity that he contemptuously called the State. The State was a cold monster, intent on the acquisition of power. It robbed men of themselves; it turned them into machines of obedience; it distorted and vitiated their noblest impulses.

But if Herder hated the State, he believed in the nation, and in two works that influenced his own and subsequent generations—*Another Philosophy of History* (1774) and *Reflections on the Philosophy of the History of Mankind* (1776–1803)—he argued eloquently for the idea of belonging, and recognizing that one belonged, to a nation. This he defined as the community that was made up of kinship and history and social solidarity and cultural affinity and was shaped over time by climate and geography, by education, by relations with its neighbors and by other factors, and was held together most of all by language, which expressed the collective experience of the group. "Has a nation anything more precious?" Herder asked. "From a study of native literature we have learned to know ages and peoples more deeply than along the sad and frustrating path of political and military history. In the latter we seldom see more than the manner in which a people was ruled, how it let itself be slaughtered; in the former we learn how it thought, what it wished and craved for, how it took its pleasures, how it was led by its teachers or its inclinations."

The British historian of ideas Sir Isaiah Berlin has pointed out that in
Herder's view to be a member of a group or nation was to think and act
in a certain way, in the light of particular goals, values, pictures of the
world. To think and act in this way was to belong, to be part of the
whole, to be attuned to its spirit. The ways in which Germans spoke and
moved, and ate and drank, and made love and laws would be different
than those patterns of behavior and feeling in other peoples. And there
was a quality common to all those patterns, a common ingredient, a
Germanness, a *Volksgeist* that could not be abstracted and defined but
represented the individuality of the nation.

Not its superiority, however. Herder was a pluralist who believed in
the equality of all cultures under the eye of God. He flatly rejected
Enlightenment notions about an ideal man and an ideal society. No
person to him was like any other person, and no nation like any other
nation. All were part of Humanity, the infinitely rich panorama of life
to which every individual and every nation made its characteristic contribution.

The young intellectuals of the years before the outbreak of the French
Revolution—the so-called Storm and Stress generation—claimed
Herder for their own, moved by his passionate defense of individuality
and his insistence that literature should express the variety and passion
of life. It is doubtful whether they were aware of the inner contradictions and the ambiguous political implications of his doctrine of cultural
nationalism. With the advantage of hindsight, it is possible to argue that
the doctrine of belonging was an unfortunate bequest to a middle class
that had no share in the political decisions of their governments, since it
could be used as a rationalization of their present condition and an
excuse for not doing anything about it. This was the explanation of the
lethargy that lay over German political life in the years when democratic revolutions were shaking the American colonies, Geneva, the
Austrian Netherlands, England and Ireland, Poland, Hungary and
France. Closing their eyes firmly to reality, the middle class took refuge
in their Germanness, persuading themselves that, since they were im-
bued by the undying group spirit, they were already in a state of
grace.

Was it not inevitable, moreover, that Herder's theories would be misused and turned into a justification, not only for the kind of State power
that he detested but also for the kind of xenophobia that he deplored?
And was not Herder himself partly responsible for this? It was all very
well for him to say that he was not interested in politics and patriotism,
and that cultures were incommensurable and had equal rights to exist.
Why then did he feel called upon to say with such insistence that "the
savage who loves himself, his wife and child . . . and works for the
good of his tribe as for his own . . . is in my view more genuine than
that human ghost, the . . . citizen of the world, who, burning with love
for all his fellow ghosts, loves a chimera. The savage in his hut has room
for any stranger; . . . the saturated heart of the idle cosmopolitan is a
home for no one"? And what is to be made of his not infrequent summons to Germans to be German and to protect their values from foreign

corruption. Statements like "Awake, German nation! Do not let them ravish your palladium!" and "Germans, speak German! Spew out the Seine's ugly slime!" show how difficult it was to keep politics out of cultural nationalism, to prevent claims that nations were individual and unique from degenerating into the claim that some nations were superior, and one's own most of all. It was Herder's tragedy that the essential humanity of his philosophy was to be perverted into narrow political nationalism by patriotic tub-thumpers, and that his views on the individuality of the nation were to be transformed by philosophers like J. G. Fichte and Georg Friedrich Hegel into an idealization of the State as a kind of super-Personality to which the individual citizen owed complete allegiance, which, indeed, alone validated his existence.

The catalyst in effecting this transformation was Napoleon Bonaparte, whose conquest of Germany and reduction of Bavaria, Austria and Prussia to the position of satellites brought home to all Germans the extent of their powerlessness. It was not surprising that, in contemplating this, some Germans should have idealized the power that they did not possess and sought to give armor to the *Volksgeist* that Herder had told them was the essence of Germanity. In this spirit, Fichte, in his *Addresses to the German Nation* in 1807–1808, postulated a State that was a necessity for the individual citizen, who realized himself in serving it; and the young Hegel went a step further in arguing that the State, as the embodiment of collective life, could not be controlled by the individuals who composed and served it, but went its own way and fulfilled its destiny by means of the power that was its essence. In the clash of State wills that was the substance of politics, there was no moral restraint upon the State's activities. "There can," Hegel wrote, "be no talk of means. Gangrenous limbs cannot be healed with lavender water; gentle counter-measures are not suitable in a situation in which poison and assassination have become the customary weapons; and the near putrefaction of life can be remedied only by the most violent means."

This cult of State power did not find universal acceptance. In the struggle against Napoleon, a second school of thought emerged, which was represented by the Prussian reformers Karl vom und zum Stein, Karl August von Hardenberg, Gerhard von Scharnhorst, August von Gneisenau and Wilhelm von Humboldt in the years 1807–1813, who maintained that the strongest government was the one that could mobilize the energies of its subjects by giving them rights to match their responsibilities. The idea of a constitutional government, responsive to an educated and self-reliant citizenry whose rights were clearly defined and protected, became the program of nineteenth century liberalism. Its progress was always, however, handicapped by the political backwardness of the majority of the German people, their exaggerated respect for constituted authority, their ingrained habits of obedience, and their suspicion that constitutional government was somehow un-German. It was further hampered, after the educated middle class became its chief proponents and the struggle for German unity had begun in earnest, by the bourgeoisie's inherited lack of confidence, its secret admiration of power, and its willingness, in the breach, to give it preference over freedom.

These deficiencies were painfully apparent in the crucial constitutional struggles of the nineteenth century, and this helps to explain why both the revolutions of 1848 and the attempt of the Prussian parliament in the sixties to restrict the military prerogatives of the Crown ended, after initial triumphs by the liberals, with definitive victories by the forces of absolutism and reaction. As a result, the Empire created in 1871 by Bismarck's diplomacy and Prussian military power, despite its institutional similarities to the Western constitutional regimes, was, and remained, an authoritarian State that recognized neither the theory nor the practice of popular sovereignty and self-government; and that meant that Germany entered the twentieth century without the kind of tradition that might have enabled it to meet the hard problems that were awaiting it.

This was a problem that worried many thoughtful Germans, and after the First World War—a conflict that was due, in large part, to the absence in Germany of effective constitutional restraints upon the arbitrary use of power—the philosopher and theologian Ernst Troeltsch sought to come to terms with it. In a lecture before the Hochschule für Politik entitled "The Ideas of Natural Law and Humanity in World History," he addressed himself to what he called "the theoretical and permanent problem of the difference between the German system of ideas—in politics, history and ethics—and that of Western Europe and America." The basis of Western political thinking, he argued, was the view of all men forming a single society, which Dante had called *humana civilitas,* and being governed by a common law, *jus naturale;* but this had never in modern times been congenial to the German mind. In England and America, the idea of Natural Law had inspired the demand for personal liberty and for the right of the people to control the leaders they had themselves chosen; in France, it had become a theory of direct self-government, equality, and full participation in the control of the State. Such ideas had never taken root in Germany, largely because of the failure of the Enlightenment, and the mainstream of German philosophical thought had subsequently rejected "the universal egalitarian ethic, . . . the whole of the mathematico-mechanical spirit of science of Western Europe, [and] a conception of Natural Law that sought to blend utility with morality. . . ."

Instead of these Western ideas, the Germans had emphasized the inner development of the individual and of the German nation as a unique cultural expression. Their downright obsession with this made them indifferent to the Western view that human beings and nations should seek, "on the basis of equality and by a mere process of incessant climbing, to increase the range of reason, well-being, liberty, and purposive organization, until they attain the goal of the unity of mankind." At the same time, their inward-directedness had induced them to leave the practical realities of existence and the decisions affecting the life and well-being of ordinary people in the control of the State and its agents.

Troeltsch's essay was written in 1922, only four years after the military defeat of Germany had led to the collapse of the Empire and the establishment of a Republic in its place, but at a time when it was already becoming clear that the democratic experiment was doomed to failure because of an insufficiency of democrats. For the problem that he analyzed so incisively, he had no solution, beyond suggesting that his fellow countrymen might profit from more self-criticism and from a new conception of history that rose above "the being of the particular nation . . . to a view of the being of that nation as connected with the being and development of the whole world." But he admitted that for anything like that to be effective, generations of time would be needed. Meanwhile, German political thinking continued to be impregnated by the feeling, half mystical and half metaphysical, that interpreted the idea of individuality, which in the West had connotations of personal liberty and popular sovereignty, "as meaning the particular embodiment from time to time assumed by the Divine Spirit, whether in individual persons or in the super-personal organizations of community life."

It may be that the twenty years that followed Troeltsch's lecture—years in which Adolf Hitler and the Nazi State became the ultimate incarnation of that kind of thinking—were a more effective cure than that proposed by Troeltsch himself. However that may be, the founding of the German Federal Republic in 1949 at least opened the way for a new attempt to discover whether the democratic instinct was stronger than the traditions and habits of thought that had prevented its growth and consolidation in the past. If this should turn out to be true, the gulf between Germany and the West of which Troeltsch wrote would be diminished and the problems of mutual communication and understanding eased.

2

Politics in a New Key

One of the questions most frequently asked in political discussions after 1945 was "Is Bonn Weimar?" It was natural that it should have been phrased this way, for the fragility of the new West German Republic was very apparent in its first years, and the memory of the drastic results of the last failure of German democracy was still vivid. Even so, the question was inappropriate. The Weimar Republic had failed for a number of complicated reasons and because of the operation of economic and foreign-political forces that were not always amenable to control by the Germans themselves, but not the least important of the causes of its collapse was the fact that its inception had in no way marked an effective break with history and political tradition. What was called the revolution of 1918 was not a revolution in any real sense, and the Republic of 1919 was an improvised regime in which too many important positions remained in the hands of people whose primary allegiance was to the past and its institutions and values.

No such continuity was possible in 1945. The ravages of the war had reduced Germany to the condition described by Willy Brandt in his memoirs, a chaos of "craters, caves, mountains of rubble, debris-covered fields, ruins that hardly allowed one to imagine that they had once been houses, cables and water pipes projecting from the ground like the mangled bowels of antediluvian monsters, no fuel, no light, every little garden a graveyard and, above all this, like an immoveable cloud, the stink of putrefaction. In this no man's land lived human beings. Their life was a daily struggle for a handful of potatoes, a loaf of bread, a few lumps of coal, some cigarettes." This was *Stunde Null*, Hour Zero, a time in which life was reduced, as it never had been in 1918, to the barest essentials.

It was not a time that was conducive to nostalgia, but rather one in which the Occupying Powers encouraged the Germans to reflect upon the consequences of their past political behavior, while they themselves pursued a policy of denazification, disarmament, dismantling and democratization that was designed to prevent a reversion to old ways. The occupation period, which lasted for four years, was a hiatus in German political life in which the finishing touches were put to Hitler's destruction of Germany's past; and, before it was over and the Germans had

35

been authorized to resume organized political activity on the local and zonal level, old structures and elites had been demolished so completely that there was no possibility of building a new system upon them.

Not that there was any inclination to try to do so among the men who now assumed responsible roles in German politics. In the Soviet zone, the founders of the Socialist Unity Party (SED) set out to establish a Communist regime that would mark a complete break with the past. In the west, when the Social Democratic Party (SPD) resumed its work after twelve years of silence and when the Free Democratic Party (FDP) and the Christian Democratic Union and its Bavarian ally the Christian Social Union (CDU-CSU) began their activities, their leaders were men who had witnessed Hitler's success in undermining the Weimar democracy and were determined to build a new Republic on a firmer basis than the old.

In both cases, their success was greater than historically minded observers had, in the first years, believed possible.

I

The decision to establish a separate republican State in the western part of Germany was the consequence of the breakdown of interallied collaboration in the first postwar years, but the successful establishment of the Federal Republic and its acceptance by the West German population were due primarily to the efforts of five German politicians of the prewar generation: the Socialists Kurt Schumacher and Ernst Reuter, the liberal Theodor Heuss, who was to be the Republic's first President, Ludwig Erhard, the author of what came to be called West Germany's "economic miracle," and Konrad Adenauer, who was to serve as Federal Chancellor for the first fourteen years of the Bundesrepublik's existence.

It can be fairly said of Kurt Schumacher that, at a time when the political instincts of the German people were still stultified by the effects of the war and when Communism seemed likely to be the beneficiary of prevailing apathy, he was the first man of stature to opt for democracy and to organize a mass party on that basis and the first politician to appeal to those of the younger generation who wanted vigorous leadership that was unencumbered by association with the Nazi past. He was himself a symbol of what Hitler had done to his country. During the twelve years of the Third Reich, he had sat almost uninterruptedly in concentration camps, as punishment for the biting anti-Nazi speeches that he had made as a member of the Reichstag in the years 1930–1933, and, when he was released, he was a dying man, for a serious circulatory disease had gone unattended during his imprisonment. A breakdown in 1948 forced the amputation of his right arm, and the four years of life that were left to him were rarely free of suffering. But his ailments merely strengthened the resolve that he had made during the years in the camps, to refound the Social Democratic Party and lead it to the position of responsibility that he believed it alone among the German parties deserved by virtue of its unblemished record of opposition to Hitler.

Schumacher's great achievement after 1945 was to prevent the effective incursion of Communism into the Western occupation zones. He hated the German Communist Party for its collaboration with the Nazis in the Berlin transport strike of 1932; he believed that it had shared responsibility for Hitler's accession to power and had lamed resistance to National Socialism in the years 1939–1941; and he denied the democratic character of the reorganized KPD and condemned it for its dependence upon the Soviet Union, which made it, in his eyes, a "foreign party." When it became evident in 1945 that the Social Democratic Party organization that had been set up in the Soviet zone was moving, under the leadership of a left-wing Socialist named Otto Grotewohl, toward fusion with the Communist Party, Schumacher forestalled the possibility of the spread of this movement to Western Germany by establishing a Social Democratic Party in the British zone, proclaiming the thesis of a Socialist renovation of Germany by democratic means, and, in May 1946, called a party conference in Hannover, which was attended by delegates from the other Western zones and which took a firm stand against fusion. Moreover, when Grotewohl's joint party, which now called itself the Socialist Unity Party, sought to extend its authority over the whole of Berlin, Schumacher flew to that city and pleaded with Socialist groups to resist the SED's claims. As a result, a group of younger leaders demanded a plebiscite on the issue, and, when it was held, 80% of the voters in the non-Soviet sectors of the city supported Schumacher's views, and a Berlin delegation subsequently appeared at the national party deliberations in Hannover.

It was Schumacher's view that the party that emerged from that conference should not be a mere copy of the old party of August Bebel and Philipp Scheidemann and Otto Braun. That party had been too often the victim of its own shibboleths, caught in rigid theoretical positions that alienated voters because they seemed either impractical or unpatriotic. Schumacher insisted that the new party be pragmatic and realistic, following a consistent program of political democracy, based on parliamentarianism and unrestricted recognition of civil rights, economic democracy, based upon progressive taxation, planned economy, and socialization of industry and finance, and a foreign and military policy that was free from the party's prewar doctrinaire positions and was truly national. His views on these points, and his insistence that the party give up the oppositional stance that it had maintained during most of the Weimar years and be prepared and eager to assume responsibility for governing the country, were persuasive, at least to his younger disciples, like Fritz Erler and Willy Brandt. (Some of the older ones were harder to move, and Horst Ehmke, who later attained ministerial rank under Brandt, tells of being asked after the party's defeat in the elections of 1953 why he looked so sad. "Because we lost," he replied. "*Na, Junge,* cheer up!" replied one of the old stalwarts. "Things could be worse. We might have won!") His philosophy was to find its ultimate expression in the Godesberg platform of 1959, where the remnants of the party's old Marxist ideology were discarded as inappropriate for a democratic party that was open to all citizens regardless of class affiliation, as well as in the independent foreign policy followed by his successors Willy Brandt and Helmut Schmidt.

Schumacher was an abrasive man, with a caustic tongue that made enemies easily. He alienated all of the occupying authorities—the Russians for obvious reasons, the English and the French because he was "too arrogant" and "too German," the Americans because he was "too socialistic." The violence of his attacks upon the policies of the conquerors and his peremptory demands for greater independence aroused so much indignation in London and Washington that there was some danger they would impede the return of political sovereignty to the Germans. It was the great service of Schumacher's colleague Ernst Reuter that he tempered Western alarm by dramatizing the struggle against Communism in his own person and removing the lingering American suspicion that socialism and communism were virtually indistinguishable.

Reuter managed this by the defiant position that he struck in June 1948, when the Soviet authorities cut off access from the West to Berlin in an effort to exact concessions for themselves in Western Germany or, if that failed, to take over the whole city. It is sometimes forgotten that, when the Soviet action began, there was considerable doubt in the West that it could be countered effectively. It was Reuter, the *de facto* if not the legal Ruling Mayor of Berlin (the Soviets had vetoed his election to that post), who insisted, in meetings with Western officials, that the Berliners would resist as best they could whether the Western Allies supported them or not, but that, if help were forthcoming, he was sure that the blockade could be defeated. His attitude won the unstinted admiration of General Lucius D. Clay, the U.S. Commandant in Berlin, and it influenced the decision to launch the airlift that eventually persuaded the Soviets to abandon their experiment. During the months of the blockade, Reuter worked tirelessly to maintain the spirits of the beleaguered population, and his speeches were widely circulated and were not without effect in the West. "With all the means at our disposal," he shouted to an audience of 80,000 Berliners early in the struggle, "we shall fight those who want to turn us into slaves and helots of a party. We have lived under such a slavery in the days of Adolf Hitler. We want no return to such times." And then, invoking uncomfortable memories,

> There are always people who, in a critical hour, start talking of the necessity of putting up with realities. We Germans have had our experience in this regard. . . . They wanted always to "avoid the worst" and in the end Germany was in ruins. We had not only lost our freedom, but we were also thrown back for a generation, condemned to a beggar's existence. Today, it's the same all over again. Today also,

> Germany can only live if she learns to fight for her freedom
> and her right.
>   In this crisis, we not only ask you to have confidence in us;
> rather we appeal to you to have confidence in yourselves.

This, and the response it elicited, revealed something new in German politics, and the Western authorities, still suspiciously watching for the recurrence of antidemocratic behavior, could not but be impressed by it. They had already decided, at a meeting in London in June 1948, to ask the West Germans to set up a government for the whole of the area covered by the three Western occupation zones. Reuter's example of militant democracy during the blockade was an earnest that that venture had a good chance of succeeding.

The task of creating a new state is never an easy one, and previous German experience in drafting democratic constitutions, in 1848 and in 1919, was not encouraging. The Council of Parliamentary Delegates from the various states that came together in September 1948 to begin the task of drafting a basic law for a government for Western Germany had the good fortune to do so at a time when the economic chaos of the last years was beginning to lift, thanks, as we shall see in a later chapter, to a currency reform promulgated in the Western zones in June. Even so, they could hardly have succeeded had it not been for the good sense and the collaborative spirit of the leaders of the three political parties that had organized themselves in the last three years and, in particular, the mediatorial efforts of the founder and leader of the Free Democratic Party, Theodor Heuss.

Like Schumacher, Heuss had been a member of the last Reichstag of the Weimar years and, as one of the few surviving delegates from the German Democratic Party, he had—when Joseph Goebbels shouted, "What are you doing here? You have no following anymore!"—answered simply, "I represent my own opinion here." A sometime professor and a writer of distinction on philosophical and political subjects, Heuss was always the scholar in politics, a man of known probity and independent judgment who could be counted upon to resist trendiness and question conventional wisdom. His role in the Parliamentary Council was to warn his colleagues, on the one hand, against writing into the Basic Law stipulations that might compromise the future reunification of Germany—their work must necessarily be considered provisional—and, on the other, against the kind of timidity in the delegation of power that would prevent their creation from governing effectively. In his opening speech, he warned his colleagues that their memory of how the Nazis had abused power should not lead them to deprive the new government of authority and that their eagerness to break with the past should not prevent them from adopting older institutional forms that had proved their usefulness. The Weimar Republic had failed, he argued, not because of its constitution but because it was established in an atmosphere poisoned by the stab-in-the-back theory, by ideas of monarchical restoration, and by political Romanticism. Since those forces had now been destroyed, one need not insist unecessarily upon an originality that might be self-defeating.

In this spirit, Heuss successfully opposed the view, expressed in the so-called Herrenchiemsee draft of a constitution, that the new West German Republic should be a Federation of German States (*Bund deutscher Länder*), arguing that anything that promised to be as loosely structured as that term implied would appear to the younger generation, not as a new political beginning, but rather as an evasion of political responsibility. Similarly, he warned against the idea, also implicit in the Herrenchiemsee draft, that the rights of the individual must always be given priority over those of the central government. A representative of the tradition of that South West German liberalism that had historically resisted the pretensions of the absolute State, Heuss nevertheless insisted that anti-Hegelianism could be carried too far: the State must be recognized as the symbol of national dignity and communal feeling, and it could not be left without power.

> Every State, even the democratic State, rests upon the power
> to command and the claim to obedience. The essence of the
> democratic State lies in the fact that it possesses a mandate
> to rule that has a limit and hence is revocable.

Heuss was by no means the dominant figure in the meetings of the Parliamentary Council and, at the crucial moment in its fortunes, in March 1949, when the three Occupying Powers became concerned lest the federal government be given too much power at the expense of the states, it was the violent and determined attitude of Kurt Schumacher that prevented capitulation to their point of view. But it can be said that, during the constitutional deliberations, Heuss's was always a voice of reason and common sense, and his influence was perceptible in the final result, the establishment of a federal State (*Bundesstaat*) that retained such features of the Weimar Republic as parliamentary government based on popular sovereignty, a multiple-party system, a bicameral legislature with a *Bundestag* to represent the popular will and a Federal Council to represent the states, a supreme constitutional court to watch over the rights of individual citizens, and a presidential office. The salient differences from the Weimar constitution were to be found in the absence of any provision for proportional representation, which had had the effect of multiplying splinter groups and complicating the task of forming parliamentary majorities, or for popular initiative, which had had disruptive effects in the 1920s, and a decided reduction in the powers of the Federal President, particularly the elimination of his right to suspend the constitution in time of emergency.

The Basic Law was completed at the begining of May 1949 and, after ratification by the various regional governments, was promulgated on May 23, with a preamble which declared that its purpose was "to give a new order to political life for a transitional period" (that is, until a constitution for the whole of Germany became possible) by creating a "democratic and social federal State." It is worth noting that the law was not submitted to the people for their approval; the continuing insecurity of the times seemed to make this inexpedient. Lewis J. Edinger, the foremost student of the politics of the West German Republic, has written that it was generally understood by the drafters of the Basic Law and was implicit in the governmental structure that they established (and their deliberate reduction of the role of direct democracy) that "strong governmental leadership would need to ensure the smooth operation of the new system and to create political orientations that would give the regime legitimacy among the mass of the population."

The new Republic was fortunate in this respect, not least of all because of Heuss's efforts. As the Federal Republic's first President, a position that he held for ten years, he was a representative figure, standing above the political strife of the parties and the specific issues of the day. But, as he said when he assumed office, he did not intend to interpret neutrality as meaning to have no views of his own. He made the most of the symbolic and integrative powers of the presidency, but he also used it to do what Walter Bagehot once said was the principal function of the constitutional monarch in Great Britain—"to encourage and to warn," to address himself to the broader issues of human existence and, in his blunt Swabian way, to remind his countrymen of their virtues and their weaknesses. He knew the weaknesses well, and his speeches were filled with quiet warnings—statements like "the sense of self-irony is too undeveloped in our people" and "the Germans find it very hard to remain sober when they get close again to the sweet delights of hubris" and similar admonitions—but he was also confident that they could be inspired to rise to the challenges of the new age. "External power has been gambled away," he said when he became President. "Moral power must be won." Through his own example and by the speeches he made at home and abroad, during his trips to Israel and England, for example, he sought to create the image of a Germany that was serious about changing its image in the world, and his not inconsiderable success in this endeavor helped restore German self-pride and assurance and, by extension, to strengthen the foundations of the new Republic.

These services were undeniably important, even if overshadowed by those of his colleagues, Erhard and Adenauer.

II

The first elections after the acceptance of the Basic Law were held in August 1949, and it had been generally expected that the Social Democratic Party, under the forceful leadership of Kurt Schumacher, would win a majority. But when the votes were counted, it was the CDU-CSU of Konrad Adenauer that came out ahead, with 31% to 29.2% for the SPD and 11.9% for the FDP.

There can be little doubt that bread and butter issues determined this surprising result. The violence of Schumacher's attacks upon the Mar-

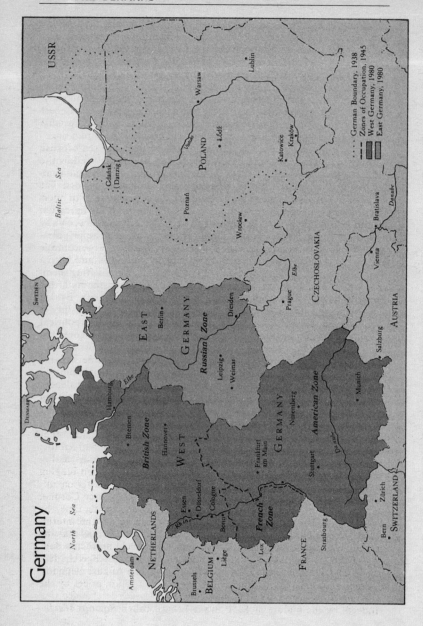

Germany

German Boundary, 1938
Zones of Occupation, 1945
West Germany, 1980
East Germany, 1980

shall Plan for European recovery as nothing but thinly disguised American imperialism, his demand for the nationalization of heavy industry, and his insistence that West Germany opt for a planned economy seem to have alarmed large numbers of voters, and the CDU exploited this feeling. Adenauer shrewdly based his campaign on tangible goals rather than abstract principles, focusing upon issues that concerned most Germans in 1949—food, housing and employment—and presenting evidence to show that something would be done about them. His best weapon in the work of persuasion was the man who was to be his most valuable associate for the next fourteen years, Ludwig Erhard.

An economist of some distinction, whose career had suffered because of his refusal to join the Nazi Party, Erhard had been discovered by the U.S. military command after 1945 and made minister of economics in Bavaria. In 1948, when the Western occupation authorities decided that currency reform was needed to end the galloping inflation in their zones, he had helped to work out the details of that elaborate operation but had insisted that it would be inadequate in itself to put the economy on a sound basis. What was needed, he argued, was the complete abolition of rationing and of the whole network of price and wage controls that the Occupying Powers had inherited from the Nazis and left in force, presumably because they feared the consequences of lifting them. Nor would he take no for an answer. Despite the grave doubts of his superiors, he used his authority as economic director of the joint British and American zones to promulgate an emergency law which, on July 7, 1948, suspended existing controls. For its author this step had political as well as economic implications. When he announced his law over the radio, he said: "Only when every German can freely choose what work he will do and can freely decide what goods he will consume will our people be able to play an active role in the political life of their country." Only by freeing themselves from their accustomed economic dependence upon government would they become free to exercise political responsibility.

For most Germans, this was less than persuasive, for the first result of the lifting of controls was an increase in the cost of food and other consumer goods, while simultaneously the currency reform had led to a rise in unemployment. Despite strong pressure to reverse himself, Erhard went further in the direction he had chosen. Once again braving the disapproval of the Occupying Powers, he reduced tariffs on imported goods, in order to put a brake on inflation and to force German manufacturers to become more competitive. At the same time, he organized a crash program to provide cheap clothing for the interim period. Even as early as the summer of 1949, there were signs that the economy was on the mend, for the currency reform had brought a doubling of the gross national product within twelve months. This made a positive contribution to the CDU-CSU victory in the August elections. By Christmas, Erhard was confidently predicting a fall in prices by the spring, and this proved to be no idle boast.

Indeed, by the middle of 1950, what Erhard called *Soziale Markt-*

wirtschaft, or "socially responsive free market economy," had survived
the testing period and was beginning to register solid successes, and it
now received additional encouragement when the outbreak of the Korean War in June created a flood of orders for machinery, tools and
heavy industrial equipment, which West Germany, with the largest pool
of cheap skilled labor in Europe, was prepared to supply. Thus began
the *Wirtschaftswunder*, or economic miracle. In the next seven years,
all aspects of the economy showed improvement, with national income
rising by 112% and wages and salaries, after taxes, by 119%, while
prices were kept in balance by an income tax schedule that bore heavily
upon all classes of society but was alleviated by tax incentives, available
to all citizens, that fueled the productive capacity of the nation. The free
market economy brought prosperity and full employment to the German people while providing them also with an elaborate social security
program that included health insurance, free medical care, unemployment benefits, and old age pensions, and in addition it proclaimed the
principle that management and labor should not consider themselves to
be antagonists but should work together as social partners, an idea that
was given some substance by the introduction of the principle of co-
determination (*Mitbestimmungsrecht*) in the direction and policymak-
ing of the coal and steel industry.

Erhard's economic policies, which transformed Western Germany
into the third-ranking economic power in the world, freed the Federal
Republic, during its formative years, from the kind of financial and
social problems that had contributed to the failure of its predecessor.
That was a great boon, although not in itself conclusive. Whether the
Bundesrepublik was to survive was less an economic question than a
psychological one. The traumatic effects of the Nazi years and the
shock of the military defeat and its aftermath had seriously shaken the
confidence of the German people in all forms of political organization
and activity, while at the same time affecting them with a latent yearning for direction and leadership. This disoriented mood was potentially
dangerous to the growth of democratic government, and it was perhaps
Konrad Adenauer's greatest achievement that he was able, by sheer
force of personality, to neutralize and transform it. He was the first
German statesman who was able to overcome the unconscious tendency
of his countrymen to believe that leaders could only be taken seriously
when they wore uniforms. His political style, which was stern, earnest,
and patriarchal, convinced them that the authority for which they
longed could be found in a democratic government under his leadership,
and they never seriously wavered in that faith until his retirement.

But Adenauer was no mere father figure, instilling confidence in a
shaken people by means of the appearance of wisdom that sometimes
comes with age. He was, to be sure, old—his political career had begun
in 1907; he had been Lord Mayor of Cologne from 1917 to 1933; and he
was seventy-three years old when he became Federal Chancellor in
1949—but his energies were unimpaired. In 1917, when he became
Lord Mayor of Cologne, he had spoken words that may be taken as

descriptive of the mood with which he took up the far more difficult tasks that confronted him thirty-two years later. "There is nothing better than life can offer," he said, "than to allow a person to expend himself fully with all the strength of his mind and soul and to devote his entire being to creative activity." Throughout his long career, this creative drive was directed and balanced by the juristic rationalism in which he was trained as a young man, and by his religious faith, and these together deepened his sense of duty and gave him a self-assurance that no German statesman since Bismarck had possessed in the same measure. It would be difficult to define the moral component of Adenauer's statecraft, but its role was certainly more important in motivating him than considerations of personal power or prestige.

The historian Golo Mann once described Adenauer, using words that he found in Plato, as a cunning idealist, and this is apt, for, although his long life in politics had left him with an awareness of the frailties of human beings that bordered on cynicism (he once said that it was a pity that God had limited human percipience but placed no bounds on human stupidity) and endowed him with all the tricks of persuasion, dissimulation and obstinacy that are useful in exploiting and manipulating them, he employed these gifts for objectives that were neither selfish nor narrowly nationalistic. When he became Chancellor, he decided to leave economic and domestic problems largely in the hands of Erhard and his other ministers and to devote himself to the task of restoring the self-confidence of his people by winning back for them their full sovereignty, while at the same time directing their aspirations to goals nobler than those that had led them to forfeit it. No more than Theodor Heuss did he desire to see a restoration of national hubris. "When you fall from the heights as we Germans have done," he said on one occasion, "you realize that it is necessary to break with what has been. We cannot live fruitfully with false illusions." The day of the Greater German Reich was over. Germany's future lay in collaboration with other democracies in an integrated Western European union.

If this was idealism, it was not bereft of a strong component of realism. Adenauer was aware that a policy that was oriented clearly to the West would expose him to the criticism that he was needlessly jeopardizing the possibility of reunification and was sacrificing the 17 million Germans who lived in the Soviet zone. There is no doubt that Adenauer's foreign-political preferences were influenced, then and later, by his strong anticommunism, but, even so, he was persuaded that, in the first place, there was no sign that the Soviets were going to be accommodating in the matter of reunification and, second, that to raise the issue in the atmosphere created by the recently terminated blockade of Berlin would annoy the Western Powers and make them unwilling to relax the controls they still maintained over the German people.

The most onerous of these was the dismantling policy, which threatened to impede the recovery of Germany's industrial production. In November 1949, at Petersberg on the Rhine, after protracted negotiations in which the Occupying Powers became for the first time aware, to their cost, of the German Chancellor's skill as a negotiator (the French High Commissioner sighed wearily after one session, "It is a very hard task, making presents to the Germans!"), Adenauer won an agreement that dismantling would be terminated in important sectors of the economy in return for German adherence to the Ruhr Statute, which had been announced by the Occupying Powers in December 1948 and had set up an international authority for that important industrial area. This was a concession that Adenauer did not regard as onerous, compared with the economic benefits accruing from the end of dismantling, and in any case he believed, as he said in a speech in Bern a few months later, that the Ruhr Statute might be "a promising starting point for general and comprehensive cooperation among the nations of Europe." In this, he was not far wrong, for the Statute was soon superseded by the Coal and Steel Community, and that was followed in turn by such international institutions as Euratom, the Common Market, and the short-lived European Defense Community.

Given the corrosive nationalism that had in the past distorted the German spirit, Adenauer's dedication to the idea of Europe was impressive and even startling. Certainly there was nothing in the literature of German statecraft to compare with his description of his hopes concerning the Coal and Steel Community, or *Montanunion*, as the Germans called it. "I was convinced," he wrote, "that the *Montanunion* in its results would change, not only the economic relations of our continent, but the whole manner of thinking and the political feeling of Europeans. I was convinced that they would lead the Europeans out of the confines of their national State existence into the broad reaches of the European area, which would give the life of the individual a greater and richer meaning. The youth of all European peoples longed for this, to gain experience and to learn and to work in other countries. . . . People whose feelings were still in our time determined by suspicion, the desire for advantage, and resentment would become neighbors and friends."

In the years from 1949 to 1954, Adenauer held before the German people the vision of a new European order that would be founded on the twin pillars of the Coal and Steel Community and the European Defense Community and upheld by the goodwill of ordinary citizens in all countries. That this vision captured the imagination of Germans was attested by the magnitude of the Chancellor's victory in the elections of 1953, and there is little doubt that his devotion to it helped convince the Western Powers of his reliability and thus speeded up the return of full sovereignty. It is, of course, true that his private assurances (private because he had not seen fit to communicate them to the Bundestag) that the Federal Republic would be prepared to raise a contingent army for an international force affected their thinking in this regard, for the outbreak of the Korean War in June 1950 had caused them to change their views concerning the advantages of German demilitarization. Thus, when the European Defense Community, which would have placed careful restraints on any West German force and deprived it of independent command above the divisional level, finally shattered on the reefs of the French parliament in August 1954, the British and the Americans did not hesitate to bring the French back into line and persuade them to agree to the admission of the Federal Republic into the North Atlantic Treaty Organization with full sovereign rights, including that of raising an armed force of 500,000 officers and men.

Adenauer described the month of the EDC's defeat as "the terrible month" and, in a conversation that was overheard by a news reporter, lamented that the French had forced a national army upon Germany, adding, "When I am no longer on hand, I don't know what will become of Germany, unless we still manage to create Europe in time." The turn of events had, in fact, created difficulties for him. While bringing full national independence rather more quickly than he had expected, it had disenchanted the believers in the European idea, outraged antimilitarists, and given new ammunition to those who had argued from the beginning that his pro-Western policy would postpone reunification indefinitely. It was the last group of critics who were the most outspoken during the Bundestag debate on the ratification of the treaties admitting the Bundesrepublik to NATO, and, although Adenauer showed a mastery of parliamentary tactics in carrying the house and public opinion with him, he was injudicious in his repeated insistence that a policy of strength, based upon German rearmament and adhesion to the Western Alliance, would force the Soviet government, in due course, to permit reunification.

The best that can be said for this argument is that the British and particularly the Americans believed in it even more fervently than the Chancellor. But at the Geneva Summit Conference of 1955, the Russians showed not the slightest indication of interest in the German question and, in September of that year, when Adenauer went to Moscow, hoping to persuade them to change their minds, he was unsuccessful. His diplomatic adviser, Herbert Blankenhorn, wrote in his diary: "In our principal objective, the reunification of our country, we made no progress. There was no talk of free elections. We had the impression that the Soviet point of view has significantly hardened, and that the Russians will not—certainly for a long time—let the East zone out of their sphere of influence." The behavior of the Soviet negotiators, especially Nikita Khrushchev, was not always courteous and, in order to secure a promise that 10,000 German prisoners of war, still held in Russia, would be released, Adenauer had to agree to the diplomatic recognition of the Soviet Union by the Bundesrepublik—that is, the establishment of diplomatic relations between the two countries—a concession that was bound to alarm the Western Powers and could be interpreted as a first step toward the recognition of the German Democratic Republic.

This trip augured ill for the next phase of the Chancellor's foreign policy. What was left of the policy of strength evaporated during the Suez and Hungarian crises of 1956; in the subsequent period, the effect of Khrushchev's Berlin ultimatum caused Adenauer to have intermittent fears of a deal between the Superpowers at Bonn's expense; and, after the building of the Berlin Wall in August 1961, the hope of German reunification appeared to become impossibly remote. Nor were these disappointments offset by progress in the West. Adenauer's faith in West European unity had not wavered, and he had never ceased to work for what he considered to be the key to such union, namely, a genuine rapprochement between Western Germany and France. In 1949, when he became Federal Chancellor, he had declared that "the Franco-German antagonism, which has dominated European politics for hundreds of years and given occasion for so many wars and so much destruction and bloodshed, must finally be unconditionally removed from the world"; and in July 1962, when he traveled to Paris to sign the Franco-German Treaty of Friendship, he must have felt that the great work was crowned. But within the year Charles de Gaulle had vetoed Great Britain's entrance into the Common Market, and critics of Adenauer's policy could now argue that, having placed the Western community above reunification, he was now sacrificing that community to his friendship for France.

This was overstated, and, in any case, de Gaulle's obstructionism was eventually overcome. When one remembered the state of Germany in 1949, when Adenauer took office, the failures seemed less impressive than the achievements. By his diplomacy and his advocacy of international collaboration, he had brought a disoriented and universally detested nation back into the international community as an equal. In the words of former U.S. High Commissioner John J. McCloy, he had "met the great imperative of his moment in German history—the restoration of national self-respect without the revival of intransigence."

At the same time, his long tenure of office had provided the West Germans with a sense of continuity and stability and the necessary time to become used to democratic institutions and to learn how to make them work. Paradoxically, this manifested itself, in Adenauer's last years, in mounting objection to his own political style, to his unsubstantiated attacks upon political opponents, his resistance to constitutional forms of consultation, and his insensitivity to the dubious past of some of his associates; and the massive criticism of his high-handed methods in the so-called *Spiegel* case of 1962, when he authorized patently unconstitutional procedure in an attempt to give substance to charges of breach of state security by a journal that had been critical of him, seemed to indicate that the Germans were no longer as tolerant as they once had been of government interference with basic liberties.

It was reassuring that, during the Adenauer era, none of the weakness that had driven the Weimar Republic to its death had recurred. Thanks to the continuing economic prosperity and the successful integration of the refugees and expellees from Eastern Germany (a process that was facilitated by the Equalization of Burdens Law, which, by means of a levy on property that had survived the war, provided the homeless with the means for a new start), conditions favorable for the formation of extremist parties did not exist. The neo-Nazi Sozialistische Reichspartei and the Communist Party were outlawed, in 1952 and 1956 respectively, on constitutional grounds, and other parties of protest, whose activities fell within the limits of the law, soon perished for want of followers, as the most successful of them, the National Democratic Party (NPD), was to do in 1970. By 1961, only three parties regularly polled more than the 5% minimum share of the vote that was necessary for representation in the Bundestag or the state legislatures, the CDU-CSU, the SPD and the FDP; and, while they differed on individual issues, they had a similar commitment to the preservation of the existing political system. This similarity was underlined in 1959, when the SPD, tired of continuing defeat in national elections, decided at its party conference in Godesberg to broaden its electoral base by jettisoning the Marxist dogmas, the doctrinaire antimilitarism, and the advocacy of nationalization of industry that had been its stock in trade in the past. It adopted a policy paper that stated: "The consumer's freedom of choice and the worker's freedom to choose his job are fundamentals of a socialistic economic policy, while free enterprise and free competition are important features of it"; and, at the same time, it assured potential voters that Christian convictions were not incompatible with Social Democratic principles. To the displeasure, and later often vocal opposition, of its left wing, the SPD had in fact become a *Staatenpartei*, a system-supporting party, like the others, and like them it addressed its appeals henceforth to all sections of the population, rather than regarding itself as representative only of the working class. After Godesberg, the possibility of interparty collaboration on the state and federal level was greatly enhanced; and, even after the long Socialist domination of national politics began in the seventies, the CDU majority in the Federal Council made it possible for political scientists to talk of a "secret coalition" that maintained stability in the country.

The Federal Republic benefited from the absence of two further antidemocratic forces. The old Junker-nationalist consortium that had played such a malevolent role in the last years of the Weimar Republic had disappeared as a result of Hitler's policies and the division of the country, and the army, while restored under Adenauer, had, as we shall see, lost all political influence. As Peter Katzenstein has written, the elimination of these forces enhanced the political importance of a centralized business and an equally centralized labor community, which operated, however, in collaboration with, rather than in opposition to, the party system, which thus provided an arena not only for democratic participation but for collaboration between the various elites as well.

As for the State, that mysterious entity that had traditionally served to condone domestic absolutism and foreign adventurism, it had been demythologized and depersonalized and was regarded by most West Germans, as Lewis Edinger had written, not so much as an expression of the *Volkswille* but as a "giant impersonal corporation with its managers (government), supervisory board of directors (parliament) and administrative staff (civil service)." The tie between the individual and this kind of State was pragmatic rather than romantic. In the contractual relationship provided by the Basic Law, the individual citizen had learned to expect tangible returns for the power he vested in his governors.

At the end of the Adenauer era, therefore, the foundations of the Republic seem to have been well and truly laid. If there was a disturbing note, it was the growing emphasis upon conformity that characterized the domestic system and the rigidity and lack of movement in the Republic's foreign policy.

III

The origins of the German Democratic Republic go back to April 1946 when the Social Unity Party (SED) was established in the Soviet zone and declared its mission to be the promotion of a "united, peace-loving, antifascist, democratic German Republic." Its success in this endeavor was prevented by Kurt Schumacher's work in founding an independent Social Democratic Party in the west, and in 1948–1949, when the Cold War began, the SED transformed itself from a radical-democratic mass party to a cadre party of the Stalinist type and became the organizing force in the DDR when it was formally established in October 1949. Under its leadership, the Soviet example was followed in every aspect of economic policy, as became clear in the Five Year Plan proclaimed at the SED's third party conference in 1950. At the same time, the party approved a policy of "intensified internal class struggle" and, by the vigorous destruction of traditional forms of property in banking, industry and agriculture—a policy begun by the Soviet occupying authorities as early as 1945–1946—and the abolition of the professional civil service and the trade unions, began the systematic conversion of the country into a Communist, one-party State, a process that involved the use of ideologically inspired mass terror against whole social groups and sects.

The key figure in the execution of these policies was Walter Ulbricht. A man who had neither the eloquence of Schumacher and Reuter nor the presence and wit of Konrad Adenauer, Ulbricht nevertheless possessed exactly the kind of talent needed for the circumstances in which he made his way. The quality of charisma and the talents of a People's Tribune were not qualifications that assured success in a satellite State dominated by Stalin's Russia. For survival, one had to be an organization man, and Ulbricht had always been the *Apparatschik* par excellence.

The son of a tailor who had been a lifelong SPD member, Ulbricht grew up as a Socialist of the left and always retained the old-fashioned pre-World War One orthodoxy in which he was trained. He was described by comrades of the early days as reticent, friendless, with few ideas or conspicuous talents; yet he was a believer and a hard worker and, when he became a Communist in 1919, these qualities stood him in good stead. He never became involved in the ideological debates that racked the German Communist Party in the 1920s; his Marxism was too simple for doctrinal refinements, and he was, in any case, interested more in concrete tasks than in theorizing. In 1923, he had already been called to the central party organization in Berlin; in 1924, he went to Moscow and served in the Comintern for four years; in 1928, he was a member of the KPD delegation to the Reichstag; and from 1929 to 1933, he was leader of the party in Berlin.

Ulbricht's biographer has written that Adolf Hitler and Joseph Stalin collaborated in advancing Ulbricht's career after 1933, for the concentration camps of the former and the purges of the latter eliminated many people who might have been his rivals. He not only survived but helped condemn many of his former comrades as "agents of Fascism." He was adroit in following every shift in the Moscow party line (he had been one of the most fervent supporters of the Nazi-Soviet Pact in 1939 and one of the most skillful in rationalizing it later on), and this flexibility and loyalty commended him to the Soviet occupation authorities after 1945. Nominally, Wilhelm Pieck and Otto Grotewohl were his superiors, but he possessed the real power. He was the liaison man with the Soviet military command; he was the planner of the agricultural reform and the supervisor of the first Two Year Plan. He helped transform the SED into a Bolshevist party of a new type and became its Secretary General in 1950 and its first Secretary in 1953; and, when Pieck died in 1960, he became the head of the Council of State as well.

Ulbricht's long years in office—he dominated the affairs of his country from 1949 to 1971, longer than any German statesman since Bismarck—provided the DDR with the kind of political continuity that Adenauer's shorter tenure gave the Federal Republic, without, however, the quick prosperity or the internal stability that were notable in Western Germany. The revolutionary changes in the nature of property-holding—particularly the expropriation without compensation of all farms exceeding 100 hectares in extent and the division of these properties, which had formerly belonged to the Junker class, among small peasants and agricultural laborers—caused a disruption of normal production that lasted for years and was exacerbated by the dogmatism of party bureaucrats who neither understood, nor made any concessions to, the imperatives of the sowing and harvest seasons. In contrast to the situation in Western Germany, the economy was deprived of economic stimuli like the Marshall Plan and was burdened by a heavy reparations load that the Soviets exacted without regard to its effects upon recovery, while the nationalization of industry was so complete that all normal inducements to efficiency and productive zeal were stifled. The government's attempt to correct this by raising production norms and work loads had little success beyond goading a working class that was already exasperated by the unavailability of consumers goods and the continued rationing of staples into open revolt. On June 17, 1953, construction workers in East Berlin downed tools and called for a general strike which rapidly spread to other industrial centers like Halle, Magdeburg and Leipzig. When what had started as a protest against working and living conditions threatened to change to a massive demand for the

restoration of unions and free elections, the government became a-
larmed and appealed for Soviet intervention, and the rising was put
down with considerable bloodshed and with an aftermath of heavy
punishment for hundreds of participants.

For twelve years after the founding of the Democratic Republic, an
additional burden upon the economy was the constant brain-drain represented by the flight of intellectuals, scientists and doctors, technicians
and engineers to the West. The causes of this were obvious enough. The
never-ending heresy-hunting and the horrendous penalties meted out
for supposed crimes against the State, particularly during the long
tenure of "Red Hilde" Benjamin as minister of justice, the unrelieved
thought control, and the tedious nagging by party watchdogs made life
in the DDR intolerable for spirited and talented people; and even many
who were ideologically committed to the Communist cause, like the
historian and literary critic Alfred Kantorowicz and the philosopher
Ernst Bloch, were moved to leave the country by Ulbricht's periodic
striking out at people he considered dangerous opponents, like Wolfgang Harich, professor of Marxist philosophy, who was sentenced to ten
years at hard labor in 1957 for demanding intellectual liberty and a
more flexible form of Socialism. Escape was easy enough—one needed
only to go to Berlin, make one's way to the Western sectors of the city,
and apply for assistance in flying to the West—and the numbers avail-
ing themselves of it assumed embarrassing and economically ruinous
proportions. Between 1949 and early 1961, the exodus averaged
230,000 a year. Seventy-four percent of these refugees were under for-
ty-five, and 50% under twenty-five, and they included many specialists
whose skills were badly needed in the DDR and some whose loss could
hardly be hidden, as when the entire law faculty of the University of
Leipzig defected within a year. In August 1961, despite increased vigilance on the part of the police, the number of escapees reached 2000 a
day.

It says something for Ulbricht that, through all of these difficulties,
he retained the confidence of the Soviet Union and, indeed, like Adenauer, succeeded in steadily increasing the freedom of his country from
close Soviet supervision. His firmness in dealing with the rising of June
17 and in eliminating doubters and dissenters in the months that followed its suppression seems to have convinced the Soviets that their
satellite was in good hands. In 1955, the Soviet Union recognized the
sovereignty of the DDR in all questions of domestic and foreign policy,
and from that time until his retirement in 1971 Ulbricht was recognized
by Stalin's successors as the most reliable of their allies, and his advice
was carefully listened to when crises affected any of the Soviet Union's
Warsaw Pact partners, as happened in 1968 in Poland and Czechoslovakia.

This was not the case, however, in 1961, when Ulbricht seems to have
believed that the problem of flight from the DDR must be solved by a
renewed and final blockade of Berlin, so that, as he said in a press
interview in June, no one would fly in or out of that city without his

permission. The prescription was apparently too drastic for the Soviets, and at a meeting of the Warsaw Pact representatives on August 11 Ulbricht was authorized (the irrepressible Khrushchev later said he had "ordered" him) only to cut off the traffic between the Eastern and Western sectors of the city. As a result, on August 13, 1961, the East German police began to string barbed wire and erect roadblocks along the inner boundary of the eight districts of the Soviet sector of Berlin, and in the days that followed, when no effective Western retaliation materialized, to replace this temporary barrier with a cement wall that cut the entire city in two and was guarded along its length by means of watchtowers and armed sentries with orders to shoot anyone attempting to scale it.

The construction of the Wall ended the rapid seeping away of the DDR's vital energies and gradually brought a new measure of stability and economic progress. The sense of despair that affected many people in the first months after the closing of the Berlin escape hatch was in time replaced by a spirit of accommodation and a readiness to make the most of the existing situation. The government responded to this mood by the promulgation, at the Sixth Party Congress in January 1963, of a "New Economic System," which was characterized by more reasonable production goals, a less frantic insistence upon record-breaking, a greater emphasis upon achievement and managerial skills, and a professed willingness to protect plant managers from excessive bureaucratic interference. The desire to raise the standard of living united party and working class, and progress toward that goal was not unimpressive. Even before the events of August 1961, there had been some signs of economic improvement, particularly in agriculture, where the growth of cooperatives (more than 10,000 in 1959) and the law of June 1959 on "voluntary collectivization" gave more security, if less independence, to small farmers, provided greater opportunity for rationalization, technical improvements, and scientific farming, and did away with rationing. This progress continued during the sixties, while industrial production showed marked growth, and the development of foreign trade steady and considerable increase in its tonnage. There was even some improvement in the supply of consumer goods, and articles that had once seemed unattainable luxuries came within the reach of workers and employees. Ownership of television sets increased from 42% to 74.5% between 1963 and 1967, of refrigerators from 15.7% to 43.7%, of washing machines from 18.1% to 44.3%, although in 1967 fewer than 10% of ordinary citizens were owners of automobiles.

The changing of the guard in the DDR came in 1971, when Ulbricht, on grounds of ill health, surrendered his post as Party Secretary to Erich Honecker, who, four years later, took over the chairmanship of the Council of State as well. Although he had devoted his whole life to Communism, the new leader was reputed to be less likely than his predecessor to take the strict Soviet line on all questions, and there were those who expected a liberalization of governmental controls over areas of life that in the West would have been considered private. As we shall have occasion to see, in some things, like religion, this proved to be true, although for special reasons; in others, like the arts, the contrary was the case.

The distinguishing characteristic of Honecker's policies in his first years was the emphasis placed upon strengthening the tie between the ordinary citizen and the existing State form. At the Eighth Party Conference in 1971, a new social policy was launched, which, in the next two years, took the form of a program of increased benefits for old people and invalids, social insurance for the sick, rental allowances for the disabled, loans to facilitate marriage, vacation leave with pay for working mothers, and other social welfare measures. At the same time, most of the remaining private concerns and firms that had continued to operate under partial government control were fully nationalized, on the grounds that this would make for more efficient management and hence an increased range of social benefits, including higher wages.

Simultaneously, party agitators and propagandists began an intensified campaign to create a *sozialistisches Staatsbewusstsein*, a sense of identification with the Socialist State, working primarily through schools, youth organizations, rural collectives, army indoctrination centers, factory councils and the like. This was doubtless motivated in the first place by the onset of détente and the increased contacts that it brought, for the first time since the building of the Wall, between DDR citizens and Western visitors. It is significant that, although détente proved economically desirable for the DDR, since it brought hard currency into the country, Honecker continued to play down common ties with West Germany, even going so far in 1974 as to drop the national German emphasis that was prominent in the 1968 State constitution and to announce that the legitimacy of the DDR lay in the fact that it was a "Socialist State of Workers and Farmers." An additional motive for the new ideological campaign was the desire to counter a growing restiveness among young people, who gave increasing signs of being discontented with an overbureaucratized country that had little to offer them in the way of spiritual satisfaction and denied them access to the places and things that they saw every day, beamed from the West, upon their television screens. The consciousness program was an attempt to counter the most serious of the problems caused by the improvement of economic conditions, that of rising expectations, particularly among the young.

IV

In 1960, the novelist Hans Werner Richter, returning to Western Germany from a trip to the DDR, wrote that he was shocked by the contrast between the vitality that he found in Eastern Germany and the prevailing indifference that he sensed in his own country: "There in the dictatorship, a lively political interest, and here in the democracy a lazy lack of political feeling." At about the same time, the Berlin theologian Helmuth Gollwitzer carried the same point further, writing that the line

between the two Germanies was "a division between Western materialism and Eastern idealism."

These observations were less impressive as accurate perceptions of
reality in the German Democratic Republic than as reflections of a
political and moral malaise that seemed to grip the Federal Republic at
the end of the Adenauer era. The old man's last years in office were
marked by a decline in his personal prestige, caused in part by his failure to react strongly to the building of the Berlin Wall but more perhaps
by his stubborn refusal, from 1959 on, to heed the wishes of those of his
party who felt it was time for him to step down in favor of a younger and
more vigorous leader. As Adenauer held on, new ideas and initiatives
were postponed; an air of tentativeness settled over Bonn; and the authority of the government began to suffer. This was not wholly corrected
when the Chancellor finally handed his office over to Ludwig Erhard,
for the father of the *Wirtschaftswunder*, although an undeniably vigorous man, lacked his predecessor's charisma and his political sense. He
was soon involved in intraparty feuds, while simultaneously being attacked by the left for a lack of attention to basic social reforms. In the
elections of 1965 he did well enough to hold on to a majority in the
Bundestag, with the support of the liberals, but a temporary recession
the following year and differences on tax policy led the FDP to withdraw its members from the cabinet, and this led to Erhard's resignation.

The feeling of people like Richter and Gollwitzer that political energy
and idealism were in short supply in the Bundesrepublik seemed to be
confirmed by two events of the mid-1960s. The first was the emergence
of the National Democratic Party, which was accused of being neo-
Nazi in leadership and philosophy (a plausible charge, since twelve of
its eighteen-member directorate had been active Nazis) and which
showed greater strength in regional elections than previous parties of
this stripe. The second was the decision of the Social Democratic Party,
in late 1966, to enter a coalition government with the CDU-CSU and to
accept as Chancellor the minister president of Baden-Württemberg,
Kurt-Georg Kiesinger, who had entered the National Socialist Party in
1933 and remained a member until 1945. This led the novelist Günter
Grass, a hard-working member of the SPD, to write a vigorous protest
to Willy Brandt, the leader of the party, and to address a public letter to
the new Chancellor, in which he asked: "How are young people in our
country to find arguments against the party that died two decades ago
but is being resurrected as the NPD if you burden the Chancellorship
with the still very considerable weight of your past?"

Grass's concern about the feelings of the younger generation was not
misplaced, and it was at this time, as we shall see later, that the movement of protest in the universities, which originated in large part as a
reaction to antidemocratic and conformist tendencies in society, grew
in strength and violence. But his objections did not deter the Socialists
from entering the coalition, and it may be that, in doing so, they saved
themselves from the discouragement and disunity that destroyed the

energies of their sister parties in France and Italy. Their participation in the governing coalition gave them an opportunity for positive action, and Willy Brandt as foreign minister and Karl Schiller as minister of economics in particular made the most of this and displayed new initiatives that were not always to the taste of their coalition partners. The effect on the electorate was favorable, and, aided by the lifting of the recession, the SPD gained so many seats in the parliamentary elections of October 1969 that they were able to form a coalition with the FDP and take over the reins of government. Willy Brandt became the Republic's first Socialist Chancellor.

Born in Lübeck, the son of a sales clerk, Brandt became a member of the Socialist Youth Movement as a schoolboy and in 1931 joined the Socialist Workers Party, a splinter group between the SPD and the KPD. His mentor was Julius Leber, the Socialist leader who was later murdered by the Nazis, and it was for Leber's *Lübecker Volksboten* that he wrote his first political essays. In 1933, he emigrated to Norway and began to study history, while working simultaneously as a journalist, an occupation that took him to Spain during the civil war. Stripped of German citizenship by the Nazis in 1938, he became a Norwegian citizen, but two years later, when the Nazis occupied Norway, fled to Sweden, where he remained until the war's end. After his return to Germany in 1945, he was drawn back into Socialist politics by Kurt Schumacher, became a close associate of Ernst Reuter in Berlin, and took over the management of the party's Berlin secretariat in 1948. From 1951 on, he was a member of the Berlin House of Representatives, becoming its president in 1955 at the age of forty-one. A politician of authority and great popular appeal, he won international recognition as Ruling Mayor of Berlin during the crisis years from 1958 to 1961, and he became his party's candidate for the Chancellorship for the first time in the elections of 1961, which he lost after a campaign that was marked by a scandalous amount of personal vilification by his opponents, the most prominent member of the CSU, Franz-Josef Strauss, not hesitating to say: "We have a right to ask Herr Brandt: What were you doing abroad for twelve years? We know what we were doing in Germany!" After losing a second time to Erhard in 1965, he resolved not to try again, but this decision was vitiated by events, and his domination of the Great Coalition brought him to the Republic's leading office three years later.

Although he was known for his uncompromising opposition to concessions to the Communists, Brandt became convinced, after the building of the Wall, that a policy of mere confrontation was useless and that a search must be made for *ad hoc* arrangements that would ease relations with the governments of Eastern Europe and particularly with the DDR. The lessening of Cold War tensions after the settlement of the Cuban missile crisis in 1962 had created a more favorable atmosphere for such explorations, and Erhard's foreign minister, Gerhard Schröder, had taken advantage of this to send trade missions to Poland, Rumania, Hungary and Bulgaria and to offer to conclude agreements for the renunciation of force in the case of disputes. Neither the Erhard government nor the Great Coalition made conspicuous progress along these lines, but despite the Soviet intervention in Czechoslovakia in 1968 Brandt remained determined to push what his colleague Egon Bahr called *Wandel durch Annäherung* (change through rapprochement).

The dramatic symbol of this determination was Brandt's trip to Erfurt in East Germany in March 1970, four months after he became Chancellor. In his first policy statement, in October 1969, he had announced that he intended to seek conversations with both the Soviet and the Polish governments, and almost immediately Bahr was despatched to Moscow to sound out Andrei Gromyko on the possibility of a normalization of relations, while Georg Duckwitz, State Secretary in the Foreign Office in Bonn, began similar talks with the Poles. The approach to the DDR Brandt reserved for himself, doubtless because of the intensity of his feelings concerning the necessity of restoring contact between Germans who had been brutally separated by the results of the Cold War. On January 22, 1970, he wrote to the chairman of the Council of Ministers in the DDR, Willi Stoph, and suggested a personal meeting to discuss "practical questions . . . that could alleviate the life of people in divided Germany," and after some diplomatic sparring, in which Stoph sought to make the talks conditional upon preliminary concessions by the Bundesrepublik, he received a favorable reply, possibly because of Soviet pressure on East Berlin. On March 19, a day that seemed to many European observers to mark a decisive change in the direction of central European politics, Brandt arrived in Erfurt.

The ensuing talks, as Brandt makes clear in his memoirs, were difficult and inconclusive, for Stoph varied between accusations against the Federal Republic for having caused the division of Germany and insistence that attempts to close the breach were impossible and that the Bundesrepublik would be best advised simply to accord diplomatic recognition to the German Democratic Republic. Brandt did not yield to these tactics. One should remember, he pointed out, that

> German policy after 1945 was . . . in the last analysis a function of the politics of the powers who conquered and occupied Germany. The power confrontation between East and West had since then overshadowed the German situation and divided Europe. We cannot simply undo this division. But we can endeavor to alleviate the results of this division and to contribute energetically to a process that begins to fill up the trenches that separate us in Germany.

Moreover, he added, this was the best contribution that Germans could make to general détente in Europe.

Brandt did not expect to register a great success in Erfurt, or at the follow-up meeting in Kassel in West Germany, which was, as it turned out, marred by public demonstrations by rightist groups protesting Stoph's presence and leftist groups demanding immediate recognition of the DDR. His goal had simply been to take the initiative in a way that, if it accomplished nothing else, would neutralize negative East German influence in Moscow while the Bahr-Gromyko talks were proceeding, while at the same time letting Eastern European governments see that there were areas of policy in which the Federal Republic was able and willing to conclude bilateral agreements. Without in any way loosening his ties with the West, Brandt was making it known that the Bundesrepublik was prepared to follow an independent line in the interest of general appeasement.

This had positive results. In August 1970, the Moscow talks ended successfully with the signature of a Soviet-West German treaty that provided for the pacific resolution of all disputes between the signatories and recognized the existing frontiers between the two Germanies and between Germany and Poland, while not excluding the possibility of German reunification "in free self-determination." Four months later, a similar treaty normalized relations between the Federal Republic and Poland, stipulating the recognition by the former of the inviolability of Poland's frontiers, including the Oder-Neisse line, which the Western governments had long insisted was a merely provisional border.

The momentum created by these agreements facilitated progress on the German question. In August 1971, a Four Power agreement on Berlin clarified and guaranteed Western rights in Berlin and recognized West Berlin's ties with the Federal Republic, and in December this was amplified by detailed intra-German agreements for its implementation. Finally, the outlines of Brandt's *Ostpolitik* found their completion in the Basic Treaty between the Federal and Democratic republics in December 1972, in which each agreed to respect the other's territorial integrity and to renounce the use of force in settling disputes, which promised collaboration on practical and humane questions, and which made contact between Germans on opposite sides of the Wall somewhat easier.

For his work in promoting these agreements, Brandt received the Nobel Prize in 1971. The reception in Germany was less friendly, the CDU-CSU mounting a massive campaign against the ratification of the treaties, and some FDP members of the Bundestag abandoning the Chancellor when the crucial battles were fought. On April 27, 1972, Brandt successfully defeated the first formal vote of no-confidence in the Bundestag's history and, five months later, he risked his office and the success of his policy by provoking and deliberately losing a second confidence vote, in order to be able to call for new elections, in which he was subsequently vindicated and returned to office with a forty-five-vote majority for the SPD-FDP coalition.

These tactics assured the ratification of the treaties but did not ease Brandt's continued tenure in office. His Chancellorship coincided with the worst phase of the student revolt and with the beginning of the energy crisis; his preoccupation with foreign affairs led him to neglect his earlier vow to be "the Chancellor of domestic reform," although his administration brought about notable changes in worker-management relations and pension programs; and he was not as attentive as he might have been to the administrative efficiency of his own party organization. It was the last of these failings that brought him down, for in May 1974 it was revealed that one of the prominent officials in the Chancellor's office, Gunter Guillaume, was an East German spy, and Brandt immediately assumed full responsibility for this and submitted his resignation to the President of the Republic.

The manner of his going was not unimpressive, David Binder, in the *New York Times*, pointing out that it was hardly possible to imagine any of Brandt's predecessors acting in the same way. All things considered, he continued, historians might come to conclude that Brandt's most durable achievement lay not in foreign, but in domestic, policy, "in institutionalizing the practice of democracy in a nation with limited democratic experience. For the Brandt Chancellorship was rich in successful tests of the 1949 Bonn Constitution, breathing fresh life and spirit into that remarkable document," while "in his governing style he brought about domestic reform through his insistence on teamwork and consensus in his cabinet, [and] his inspiration toward greater citizen participation in politics, culminating in the turnout of 90% of the eligible voters in 1972."

The smoothness with which the crisis was surmounted gave some support to these views. Without delay and with no evidence of doubt or dissent, the SDP-FDP coalition united behind the team that was to remain in power for the next eight years, Helmut Schmidt (SPD) as Chancellor and Hans-Dietrich Genscher (FDP) as foreign minister. The new Chancellor had served under Brandt as defense minister and later as finance minister and had the reputation of being a tough pragmatist with an aggressive style. A Paris newspaper, betraying the fixed French view that the Germans are happiest with authoritarian leaders, wrote, "Helmut Schmidt's inclinations are always controlled by his sense of realities. Germany can afford this. Despite the D-Mark revaluations and despite the energy crisis, it has great prosperity, consistent industrial dynamics, and considerable monetary reserves. Only the Iron Chancellor was missing. Now he has arrived." The truth was, one of Schmidt's former associates wrote, he was authoritarian only in his willingness to make decisions and his ability to make them promptly. But the decisions were always preceded by lengthy discussions; there was always a feedback process between the upper and lower ranks; and nothing was settled on a purely hierarchical basis. He was a strong leader who nevertheless believed in participatory democracy and encouraged and inspired it.

It was clear that the new government would be called upon to deal with serious problems, both in foreign policy, where the implementation of the Eastern Treaties did not promise to be easy, and on the home front, where tax reform and new codetermination proposals posed difficulties and urban terrorism had, as we shall see, assumed frightening proportions. But there was little disposition to doubt the stability of the Republic, and on May 23, the twenty-fifth anniversary of the Basic

Law, it is likely that more people than not agreed with two statements among the many made to celebrate that occasion. The first was the speech of the Federal President Gustav Heinemann, Heuss's second successor, in which he said:

> No constitution can soothe all the world's wounds. There is no known answer about the purpose of life, and one is not likely to become known to us. What the Basic Law can do, has done, is to offer us a democracy, a State with equal justice for all, a socially conscious State. It is incontrovertible, despite all that still has to be improved, that the Federal Republic of Germany in its twenty-five years of history has achieved a status that could be described this way: We have joined those States that have been able to provide a high degree of civil liberties, economic well-being and social security.

The second was a comment on the Saar Radio: "Democracies require tradition. For this, twenty-five years are too few. But enough time has elapsed to be able to say that the Germans of the Federal Republic of Germany can be content with their constitution."

3

Hitler and the New Generation

He died by his own hand on an April day in 1945, shortly after three o'clock in the afternoon, and his body was carried into a courtyard swept intermittently by Soviet machine-gun fire and incinerated, the remains being gathered after some hours in a sheet and stamped into a shell crater. A definitive enough death, one might have thought, but not so definitive as to prevent his shade from having a remarkable facility for troubling the lives of those who survived him and of their children. In contemporary Germany, it is difficult to look at a map or to listen to Wagner's music or to discuss the curricula of the lower schools or to think about the past without his memory touching the mind, and periodically numbers of Germans become concerned that a process of rehabilitation is under way to restore him to honor, while equal numbers become exercised lest the schools allow the memory of his brutalities to sink into oblivion. "He has played a trick on us," Horst Krüger has written in his book *The Shattered House: A Youth in Germany.* "This Hitler, I think he'll remain with us until the end of our lives."

I

Early on the morning of March 15, 1939, after the elderly President of rump Czechoslovakia had yielded to the threat of imminent bombardment of his capital city and had placed the fate of his country in Germany's hands, Hitler burst into the office of his secretaries and invited them to kiss him. "*Kinder!*" he cried. "This is the greatest moment of my life! I shall go down in history as the greatest German!"

That ambition was not to be realized. After the easy conquest of Czechoslovakia, there was no turning back for Hitler. His foot was already on the course that was to lead, through scenes of unimaginable carnage and barbarity, to the physical destruction and moral shame of his country. Nor can it be doubted that he willed the ultimate holocaust. Did he not choose the road of war with a sublime indifference to the limits of Germany's resources and the superior potential of its enemies? Did he not shut his eyes to the possibility of a peaceful settlement of his claims on Poland in 1939 and boast, "After all, I did not raise the army

61

in order *not* to use it?" Did he not, through impatience over the stalemate in his struggle with Great Britain, rush into war with the Soviet Union, and did he not, after his first setback on the eastern front, willfully and as if bent upon self-destruction, widen the circle of his enemies by declaring war upon the United States? Did he not, a month later, order the "Final Solution" of the Jewish question, as if to compensate for the military victory he knew he could no longer win, later boasting of his responsibility for this horror, when he said publicly on November 8, 1942:

> You will remember the meeting of the Reichstag when I declared: If the Jews imagine that they can cause an international world war to wipe out the European race, the result will not be the destruction of the European race but the destruction of the Jews in Europe. People always laughed at my prophecy. But of those who laughed then, countless numbers are doing no more laughing now, and perhaps in a little time those who still laugh won't do it any more.

And finally, when the cruel end was near, did he not take the easy way out, not neglecting to place the blame for the debacle upon the German people before escaping its consequences by suicide? "If the war is lost," he had said spitefully, "the people will be lost also. It is not necessary to worry about what the German people will need for elementary survival. On the contrary, it is best for us to destroy even those things. For the people has proved itself to be the weaker, and the future belongs exclusively to the stronger people of the East. Those who will survive this struggle will in any case be inferiors, for the good are already dead."

Golo Mann had called Hitler "the unpleasant subject," and one can see what he means. The monster of destruction, the mass-murderer, stands athwart German history. But so does the uncomfortable fact that there was a time when many Germans were indeed willing to regard him as the greatest German, when painters portrayed him in shining armor, like a new Parsifal come to heal Germany's wounds, when poets described him as the embodiment of the elemental, the inevitable, the ever-expanding and comprehending grasp of historical transformation, when historians saw him as a Hegelian Hero, a world-historical individual who sensed what was inherent in his age, who knew best how to realize it, and who rallied others to his standard because they believed that he was right, when university professors had declared him to be infinitely wise and Christian clergymen infinitely good, and when the great majority of the German people, regardless of class and status and occupation, accorded him veneration and unquestioning obedience. How was one to account for the capitulation of a country generally considered to be among the most civilized in Europe to a man who was contemptuous of all of the values of civilization? And how was this to be explained to posterity, to new generations of Germans who would be born and would grow up in a Germany and a world that had been shaped and burdened by Hitler's crimes and who would ask how these things had come to pass and why their parents and grandparents had accepted Hitler as a leader?

At the outset, it was left to the historians to undertake this delicate task, and they went about the job almost reluctantly. The dean of German historians at the end of the war was Friedrich Meinecke, a scholar who had spent his life studying the complicated relationship between German nationalism on the one hand and the cosmopolitan influence that had originated in the Enlightenment on the other, and who had argued, in one of his most impressive books, that the humanist tradition, far from being crushed by the dominant position won by Prussia in the nineteenth century, had found its logical culmination in the unification of Germany under Bismarck's leadership. The policy that Germany had pursued during the First World War—and what Meinecke once called "the boundless demands of the Pan German-militaristic-conservative combine"—had created some doubt in his mind about the validity of his own argument, and the rise of Hitler and the support given to his policies by the German people deeply depressed him. In a letter to a friend at the end of the war, he wrote: "It always seems to me now that Schiller's Demetrius is a symbol of our fate: pure and noble when he began, but in the end a criminal. Puzzling—but in any case very tragic. I can't get it out of my head."

In his last book, *The German Catastrophe*, Meinecke tried to solve the puzzle but, in his tangled and illogical argument, less a historical analysis than an attempt to come to terms with himself, he came dangerously close to committing what has been called the cardinal German sin of taking refuge in destiny. "Must we not always be shocked," he asked, "at the precipitous fall from the heights of the Goethe era to the swamp of the Hitler period? Passionately, we Germans ask ourselves how this was possible within the selfsame nation. We are reminded of [Franz] Grillparzer's mid-nineteenth century words, which are both a diagnosis and a prognosis: 'Humanity-Nationality-Bestiality.' "

But these words, Meinecke continued, still did not provide an adequate answer to the question; nor did the idiosyncrasies of German development or the unique events that had determined its history. It might be true that the German temperament had always had "a stormy inclination to rise up suddenly from the limitations of the reality that surrounded it," and that this desire for emancipation had too often led to a glorification of strong leaders and an idealization of power. And it might be, he added sadly, that Bismarck's creation of the Reich had not been an unambiguously good thing, that it had encouraged the organized cult of power in the form of militarism and had followed a course that deviated from Western liberal ideas. But none of this could explain what Germany had condoned under the leadership of "the unholy man," the "demonic personality," whose outstanding characteristic, Meinecke quoted the social historian Otto Hintze as having said, was that he did not "belong to our race at all. There [was] something wholly foreign about him, something like an otherwise extinct primitive race that is completely immoral in nature."

Why then did the country of Luther and Goethe submit to him? Meinecke could only answer that it had been the result of the play of chance. "In view of the monstrous success of Hitler's rise to power, may one not venture to question whether after all it resulted from general causes? Did not chance, fatally for Germany, weave its thread into the pattern? And precisely at the decisive points during Hitler's rise to power in the State in the years from 1930 to 1933?" It was impossible to avoid the question, Meinecke concluded helplessly. One was caught between having "with gloomy fatality to explain the misfortune that Hitler brought upon Germany as an inescapable destiny" and accepting the possibility that "the demon chance [came] to the aid of the daring gambler and monstrous swindler Hitler in his rise to power and in his final call to the office of Chancellor."

There was rather too much *Dämonie* and *Schicksal* in this tortured account to make it plausible to Meinecke's fellow historians. The key to the Hitler problem, they argued, was Hitler himself, a real rather than a diabolical appearance, and it was necessary for historians to learn as much about him as they possibly could. Unfortunately, some of those who applied themselves most rigorously to that task were almost immediately accused in the letter columns of newspapers of having fallen in love with their subject and of seeking to restore his reputation. This was the experience of Werner Maser, who dedicated his energies to exhaustive investigations of Hitler's family history and early years and to such controverted questions as who his father had been and whether he had Jewish blood in his veins, and this was what happened also to the distinguished medievalist Percy Schramm. During the last stages of the war, Schramm had had the job of keeping the war diary of the OKW, the Supreme Command of the Wehrmacht; he had been present at the so-called Führer Conferences at Hitler's military headquarters and had had other opportunities to observe Hitler in various settings. He was appalled by the one-dimensional and stereotyped portraits of Hitler as "the house-painter" and "the carpet-chewer" and "the drummer" that were the stock-in-trade of the newspaper press. Hitler, he insisted, was a much more complicated person than was commonly realized, and it was precisely that fact that made him so menacing. To elaborate his point, Schramm in 1964 took the occasion of the publication of a new edition of Henry Picker's book *Hitlers Tischgespräche (Hitler's Table Talk)*, the record of conversations that Hitler had with his associates in the years 1941 and 1942, to contribute a long introduction. In this, he described the Führer's private life, his relations with his most intimate subordinates, the sort of things he liked to talk about, his taste in music, art, books and food, his gift of mimicry, his delight in jokes (provided they were not indelicate), his personal charm and his gifts of ingratiation, especially with women, his loyalty to his old comrades, and other aspects of his personality.

Schramm's introduction was serialized in the weekly news magazine *Der Spiegel*, and almost immediately the editors were deluged with letters from readers who felt that the professor was presenting a "Biedermeier Hitler" and providing "advertising for Fascists, even if indirectly." One reader wrote ironically, "The fact that Hitler loved dogs and children is not new and cannot move anyone any longer. But that he secretly raised the wages of ballet girls three hundred percent in order to save them from the threat of a life of prostitution brings tears to the eyes of the most hard-bitten among us." The historian Golo Mann took a more serious view. "All of the things that Percy Schramm describes may be true," he wrote. "But doesn't the professor understand that a complete picture is a matter of how the details are ordered? Doesn't he understand that a man should be judged by his deeds and not by his love of children and animals?"

The hullabaloo over Schramm's essay was an indication of the sensitivity of the Hitler theme and the pervasiveness of the feeling that even the Führer's reconstructed image might have the power to seduce the German people from their newfound, but perhaps still shallow, democratic convictions. (Even as late as 1979, when the Supreme Constitutional Court in Karlsruhe freed a bookseller from charges of anticonstitutional behavior, after he placed two copies of *Mein Kampf* on sale, the literary critic Fritz J. Raddatz protested against the judgment, writing, "The scars are still too fresh, the bacillus too lively, the danger of infection too acute.") But the historians were not put off by this, nor did they reject the Schramm approach as trivial. Among those who busied themselves with the Hitler problem—and few major historians neglected it completely—the major tendency was to seek the explanation for Hitler's rise to power and his success in winning and retaining the support and confidence of the German people in the interplay of personality and circumstance and, more particularly, in the victory of political genius and organizational skill over a demoralized democracy.

The materials to support this view were assembled for the first time by the Berlin historian Karl Dietrich Bracher in 1957 in an enormously detailed study called *The Destruction of the Weimar Democracy* that was to anticipate the conclusions of most of what was written about the Hitler problem in the next twenty years. Bracher analyzed the structural, legal and psychological defects of the Weimar Republic, its horrendous economic problems and its subordinate position in the international community, both of which eroded its basis of popular support, the irresponsibility of its political parties, and the general failure of leadership that was notable from its early years. This system, he made clear, could not but be vulnerable to the fatal combination of Adolf Hitler's will and energy and the nature of his party, which was more a religion of hope than an ordinary political organization, a steadily growing horde of true believers whose bond of effective unity was their faith in their Führer.

In Bracher's book—and in its sequel, *The National Socialist Seizure of Power*, written in collaboration with Wolfgang Sauer and Gerhard Schulz in 1960—Hitler's personal tastes and social gifts received small attention. The emphasis was rather upon his political qualities, and particularly his ability to ingratiate himself with the resentful and deprived elements of the nation and to retain their allegiance in times of discouragement, his superb sense of timing, his almost uncanny ability to take advantage of the mistakes made by political antagonists, and the speed and ruthlessness with which he expanded the relatively limited power that was placed in his hands in January 1933, so that, within a year, he was master of the nation.

The sixties and seventies saw a steady stream of biographies and special studies of Hitler and the Third Reich, the best of which showed the influence of Bracher's pioneer studies, as of the brilliant biography of the Englishman Alan Bullock, *Hitler: A Study in Tyranny* (1957), which was widely read in Germany, and the work of his fellow countryman H. R. Trevor Roper, particularly his essay "The Mind of Adolf Hitler." The first notable German biographies were those of Helmut Heiber (1960) and Hans Bernd Gisevius (1963), the first remarkable chiefly for the brevity with which it recounted the known facts of Hitler's life and career, the second because it was written by a man who had been an active member of the resistance movement and had, indeed, in 1938, when Neville Chamberlain's decision to go to Berchtesgaden had lamed the resolution of those General Staff officers who had been planning a coup against Hitler, pleaded with General Erwin von Witzleben to take action despite the British collapse. Despite some lack of balance between its parts, the Gisevius book contributed to the search for a convincing explanation of why Germans accepted Hitler as a leader by describing in convincing detail his undoubted intellectual gifts, his diplomatic skill and tactical virtuosity, and by giving striking examples, from Gisevius's own experience, of the Führer's ability to make elite groups as amenable to his persuasive powers as the untutored masses.

Since 1973, the standard German biography has been the brilliant work of Joachim C. Fest, *Hitler: A Biography*, a book based on exhaustive and meticulous research and covering every phase of his career with masterful authority. Fest's account is filled with challenging hypotheses, not the least striking of which is his view that by his very nature Hitler was bent upon self-destruction and that, after 1939, he abandoned the world of rational politics and devoted himself to that end. But how did he reach the position of eminence that enabled him to pull the world down with him? Fest suggests three answers. In the first place, he exploited what Fest calls *die grosse Angst* (the Great Fear) that affected the German bourgeoisie in the last decades of the nineteenth century and particularly in the wake of the First World War—a panic that was rooted in part in apprehension over the rising tide of Communist revolution, but whose deeper cause was a fear of modernity. The technical-economic process of modernization came later to Germany than to other countries but was then much faster and more radical in its realization, and as a result it aroused more irrational fears and more violent movements of reaction. The relentless advance of industrialism and urbanism eroded all inherited cultural and moral values and seemed to threaten the individual with a society of scientific management and assembly lines; and fear and disgust over this prospect allied themselves with a romantic longing for the lost past. The Great Fear was a compound of cultural pessimism, social resentment and racial antipathy (for the Jews were widely believed to be the prospective beneficiaries of the process of change and decay); and the foundation of Hitler's power over the German people was his ability, from the moment when he began to make speeches in the beer halls of Munich in 1919, to articulate and mobilize these feelings of anxiety and give them direction and thrust. "None of the followers whom he began, after a shaky beginning, to attract," Fest writes, "was able to express the basic psychological, social, and ideological motives of the movement as he was. He was never only their leader, he was always their voice." He was at once the embodiment of the "backward-looking utopianism" of millions of his countrymen and the promise that it would be achieved by means of a satisfyingly violent vengeance upon all those who had brought Germany to this critical pass.

The key to Hitler's political rise was, in the second place—as most of Hitler's biographers had recognized—his superb oratorical gifts. It was perhaps difficult for Fest's contemporaries to understand the compulsive force of his speeches when they listened to old recordings of his performances on the podium, and the bathos of the sentiments expressed and the incomparable vulgarity of the style made it even harder. The secret lay in the magic bond that was established, as soon as the first sentences had been uttered, between the speaker and the individual auditor. Hitler spoke to every one's secret grievance and hidden desire as well as to the collective mood. Fest says, "Without this correspondence between the individual- and the social-pathological situation, Hitler's acquisition of such a magically demanding power over their spirit is unthinkable. What the nation was momentarily experiencing— the succession of disenchantment, collapse, and loss of status, and the search for objects of guilt and hatred—he had long ago experienced himself. Since then he had all the explanations and excuses at hand and knew all the formulas and culprits, and that gave his own formulations of understanding an exemplary character, so that the people, as if electrified, recognized themselves in him."

Finally, to an unpolitical people who distrusted politics and whose antipathy seemed to have been justified by the venal and ineffectual party trafficking of the Weimar period, Hitler offered salvation by means of art and myth. He had always regarded himself as an artist rather than a politician, and Thomas Mann once wrote an essay called "Brother Hitler" in which he argued that he was not mistaken in doing so. In 1923, Houston Stewart Chamberlain, the philosopher of racism, said that Hitler was "the opposite of a politician," adding that "the ideal politics is to have none; but this nonpolitics must be boldly recognized and forced upon the world." Hitler appears to have taken these words to heart, replacing the usual pedestrian goals of the working politician with a grandiose conception of German destiny and aestheticizing the rituals of politics in such a way as to dramatize it. The Weimar politicians had had no psychological sense. In contrast, Fest writes:

Hitler was the first—by means of firm screening effects,
theatrical scenery, ecstasy and the tumult of adoration—to
give back to public occasions their intimate character. Their
striking symbol was the dome of lights: walls of magic and
light against the dark, threatening outside world. And if the
Germans might not share Hitler's hunger for space, his anti-
Semitism, the vulgar and brutal traits that were a part of
him, the fact that he had once more given to politics the great
note of destiny and had mixed it with an element of dread
brought him applause and adherents.

One more notable book should be mentioned in this brief catalogue,
trivial in scope in comparison with the Fest biography, but admirable in
its insight and its focus on practical matters often forgotten, and that is
Sebastian Haffner's brief essay in book form, *Comments on Hitler*
(1978). Speaking directly to the question of the German submission to
Hitler, and with particular reference to the years 1938–1939, Haffner
writes:

Today, the question "How could we have?" comes easily to
the tongues of the elderly, and the question "How could you
have?" to those of the young. But then, it required a quite
extraordinary sharpness of vision and incisiveness to see in
Hitler's achievements and successes the hidden roots of the
future catastrophe, and a wholly extraordinary strength of
character to abstract oneself from the effect of those achievements and successes. Hitler's barking and ravening
speeches, which, listened to again today, arouse disgust or an
impulse to laugh, at that time had often a foundation in fact
that silenced the listener's rebuttal, and it was the factual
foundation, not the barking and the ravening, that counted.

Haffner cited a speech of April 28, 1939, in which Hitler had boasted
that he had overcome the chaos in Germany, restored order, increased
production in all branches of industry, eliminated unemployment, united the German people politically and morally, "destroyed, page by
page, that treaty which, in its 448 articles, included the most shameful
oppression ever exacted of peoples and human beings," restored to the
Reich the provinces lost in 1919, returned to their fatherland millions of
unhappy Germans who had been placed under foreign rule, restored the
thousand-year-old unity of the German living space, all without shed-
ding blood or inflicting the scourge of war upon his own or other
peoples, and all by his own efforts, although, twenty-one years earlier,
he had been an unknown worker and soldier. This outburst, Haffner
commented, was "nauseating self-adulation," couched in a "laughable
style. But, *zum Teufel!*, it's all perfectly true—or almost all! . . .
Could people reject Hitler without also giving up everything that he had
accomplished, and were not all of his unpleasant characteristics, and his

evil deeds as well, mere blemishes compared with his accomplishments?"

Few people who spent any time in Germany in the 1930s can deny the thrust of this question. Provided they were not Jews or Communists (a dreadful proviso that they preferred not to think about), most Germans profited materially and psychologically from the first six years of Hitler's rule, and they were quick to point this out when criticism of any kind was leveled against the Leader. Moreover, as Haffner also noted, when that criticism was particularly acute, there was an instinctive tendency to argue that the Führer did not know about the matter in question and would not have tolerated it if he had. The devotion that Hitler won from the Germans by the positive achievements of the years before the war was remarkably resistant to reason and reality. The Führer's hold over the German people was, of course, reinforced, once the war had begun, by patriotism on the one hand and the efficient brutality of his system and his monopoly of force on the other; but the continuing loyalty of many Germans was a personal one, a willingness to believe, in the face of all the facts, that the man who had done so much for them in his first years could do no wrong and would somehow emerge, victorious and immaculate, to confound his enemies and detractors.

Not all of those who wrote about the German experience during the Third Reich were willing to accord to Hitler the respect that one finds in the works of Bracher, Gisevius, Fest and Haffner. It is worth noting that no biographies of Hitler have been written in the German Democratic Republic, and this fact is, of course, a reflection of the ideological insistence of Marxist historiography upon the primacy of economic forces over accidents of personality. In this spirit, those writers in the West who preach what is called *Faschismustheorie* argue that Hitler had no essential importance but was merely a creature of the forces of late capitalism that were intent upon preserving their mastery over their disintegrating world at any cost and chose an instrument who was a sufficiently proficient practitioner of force and terror to accomplish this. What this amounts to, of course, is that Hitler was the tool of the bankers and the industrialists, an argument that happens not to be true, for recent research has shown that Hitler was much less dependent upon financial support from big business in the days before he came to power than was once supposed, and there is not a scintilla of evidence that he ever deferred to the wishes of the interests that are supposed to have controlled him.

"Fascism-theory" nevertheless enjoys great popularity among left-wing university students, who are apt to be vehement in expounding it. Some years ago, when I undertook with a young colleague to give a *Hauptseminar* in the Friedrich-Meinecke Institut of the Free University of Berlin on the subject of Adolf Hitler, the group's first session was a stormy one, one group of students expressing outrage that we should be considering a "biographical" approach to a serious subject and demanding that the seminar be restructured. We refused to accept this suggestion, and the seminar went about its business, but there were other acrimonious moments, for example, when we asked the students to read the preface to Fest's biography, which is a disquisition on historical greatness and an inquiry concerning the extent to which Hitler fitted the great Swiss historian Jakob Burckhardt's definition of that term, and again when one of the group leaders suggested that Hitler was the only political genius to emerge during the Weimar years. Finally, when we announced that the seminar would visit the Reichstag building to see the Erwin Leiser film *Mein Kampf*, a work that places considerable visual emphasis upon Hitler's oratorical skills and propaganda techniques, the rebellious section of the group agreed only on condition that we also go to the Arsenal Theater to see the Soviet film by Ivan Ropp called *"Der gewöhnliche Faschismus"* ("Ordinary Fascism"), which exemplified the Marxist interpretation by pairing Hitler with Mussolini and making them both faintly ridiculous persons in the grip of forces they could not withstand.

In a review article in which he rejected the Fascist theory out of hand but expressed strong reservations about Sebastian Haffner's more pragmatic approach to the Hitler problem, the late Jean Améry, who had been a member of the Belgian resistance and later a prisoner in Auschwitz, wrote that the most important thing to remember about Hitler was that "the German people were *ripe* for him, in which respect a gruesome-prophetic George poem . . . echoes as tragic background music." This was a reference to Stefan George's "The New Reich," a typical expression of the political Romanticism of the 1920s, about which more will be said in a later chapter. George wrote:

> Der sprengt die ketten, fegt auf trümmerstätten
> Die ordnung, geisselt die verlaufenen heim
> Ins ewige recht wo grosses wiederum gross ist
> Herr wiederum herr. Zucht wiederum zucht. Er heftet
> Das wahre sinnbild an das völkische banner.
> Er führt durch sturm und grausige signale
> Des frührots seinen treuen schar zum werk
> Des wachen tags und pflanzt das Neue Reich

> [He breaks the chains, sweeps order on the dump heaps,
> Scourges the dispersed and scattered back home
> To the eternal right where great is once more great,
> Master once more master, discipline once more discipline.
> He fastens
> The true symbol upon the people's banner
> And leads through the storm and dreadful signs
> Of the early dawn his loyal troop to the task
> Of the wakeful day and plants the New Reich.]

The suggestion that Adolf Hitler was in the last analysis a projection of latent forces in the German soul, a culminating expression of German Romanticism, has found its most brilliant exponent in Hans Jürgen

Syberberg, who has elaborated it in his film trilogy consisting of *Requiem for a Virgin King,* which deals with Richard Wagner's patron, King Ludwig II of Bavaria, and his attempts to escape from reality by means of art, *Karl May,* which focuses upon the last mystical phase of the great master of escapism, and *Hitler,* a seven-hour reflection upon Germany's final flight into destruction. In the last of these films, in which, incidentally, Hitler usually appears as a marionette, the Proteus-like narrator, speaking to him, says: "You believed you were the motor, and it was you yourself who was moved, mirror of our desire and of our dreams of the power of the community. There was no other choice. The course of history and the multiple experiments of German democracy proved it." And then, turning to the audience, "Everything led to him. He was the only solution—no accident, no error, no violation. Between him and us, from step to step everything was logical. The goddess of history, providence had spoken, and was right, terribly right. He was Germany and Germany was he in the twentieth century."

It is surely worth noting that none of these German writers, however much they may have differed concerning Hitler's role and the reasons for his ascendancy over the German people, sought to palliate his crimes. One must look abroad for experiments of that nature. In a provocative and lively book called *The Origins of the Second World War* (1962), the British historian A. J. P. Taylor, in one of his not unusual willful moods, advanced the thesis that Hitler was really no different from any of the other national leaders in the 1930s, that he had no clear idea where he was going, the ideas of *Mein Kampf* having long been forgotten when he took power and the objectives announced in his meeting with his military commanders on November 5, 1937, never meant seriously, and that he was rather surprised in the end to find out where he had gotten to. This odd view was probably the result of Mr. Taylor's frequently expressed irritation with historians who claimed to know what Hitler was thinking, but it placed him in the same position as those hapless leaders of the democracies in 1933 who refused to take any of Hitler's earlier utterances to heart and believed that he would play according to their rules. Mr. Taylor's critics pointed out that it was surely not without significance that Hitler's foreign policy and his program of conquests resembled in faithful detail those laid out in his speeches in the twenties and in *Mein Kampf* and his second book in 1928.

Mr. Taylor was, of course, not trying to rehabilitate Hitler; he was really intent on proving the stupidity of *all* of the statesmen of the thirties. But there were other writers who were more determined to attack the general view of Hitler's crimes against civilization. In 1964, it was announced that an American writer named David L. Hoggan had been made the recipient, by German societies financed by groups with conservative political views, of awards bearing the names of Germany's most famous historian, Leopold von Ranke, and one of its most courageous humanists, Ulrich von Hutten. The awards were made in recognition of a very long book that was published in Germany in 1961 under the title *Der erzwungene Krieg*. In this work, Hoggan had argued that the responsibility for bringing war upon the world in 1939 was not Adolf Hitler's but rather that of the foreign ministers of Great Britain and Poland, Lord Halifax and Colonel Józef Beck. Hence his title, which might properly be translated as "The War Forced on Germany."

Since both Hoggan's thesis and the curious ways he used documents in his attempts to support it had been subjected to devastating criticism in the leading historical journals of the United States and Germany, the news of the awards touched off a row of major proportions. The *Berliner Tagesspiegel* deplored "these spectacular honors for a historical distortion," both as an attempt to launch a new historical legend and as an affront to the memory of Ranke and Hutten, who had fought steadfastly for freedom and truth. The Association of German Writers and the executive board of the German Trade Union Council echoed these sentiments, and in the Bundestag the minister of the interior described the awards as "crude impertinence" on the part of right-radical groups and promised an investigation. Finally, the government of Baden-Württemberg refused to permit the presentation of the Hutten Prize to take place in Heidelberg Castle as planned, and the Bavarian Bureau of State Palaces, Gardens and Lakes ruled that the Munich Residence could not be used for a reception in the author's honor. Nothing much more was heard of Mr. Hoggan's book after that.

A more formidable champion of the dead Führer was the Englishman David Irving, who in 1976 published a book entitled *Hitler's War*, which he described as an attempt to scrub "years of grime and discoloration from the façade of a silent and forbidding monument" and to reveal the true Hitler underneath. Irving claimed that the record had been distorted by professional historians (he was inordinately proud of not having been trained professionally) who didn't know how to read the evidence and merely repeated each other's prejudices; and certainly the Hitler who emerged from his version of the past was a far different one than was to be found in earlier works—less brutal and ruthless, more human, and deserving of sympathy, since he was always being let down by others. This result was achieved, however, not by the presentation of new evidence but rather by means of the technique employed by the author. In his introduction, Irving wrote that his book "view[ed] the situation as far as possible through Hitler's eyes, from behind his desk," and this method had the effect of bringing the scene at Hitler's wartime headquarters to the reader with a dramatic immediacy rarely achieved in earlier accounts of the war. But this also meant that, when judgments were made, they were Hitler's own judgments and that they were uncontested. Thus, Mr. Irving, who did not hesitate to use formulations like "Hitler was cheated of the ultimate winter victory," accepted the Führer's attribution of all military setbacks to the incompetence or disloyalty of the General Staff and the commanding generals, without making any appraisal of Hitler's own deficiencies as a commander, which included, among other things, an irresponsible profligacy with respect to material and human resources. In a reconstruction of Hitler's thinking in October 1941, Irving described him as agonizing over German losses in the field ("What would be left of Germany and the flower of her manhood?"), but forebore to mention that this was the same man who, when told somewhat later on about the high casualties among junior officers on the Russian front, said, "But that's what the young people are there for!"

Irving's generosity toward Hitler assumed its most excessive form in his treatment of the Final Solution. Claiming that the personal role of the Führer in this matter had never been examined and that conclusions had been drawn about it without justification, he argued that there was no proof of Hitler's having ordered the liquidation of the Jews, whereas, on the contrary, there was "incontrovertible evidence" that he forbade it. In Irving's view, the Führer had wanted the Jews out of Europe and had ordered that they should all be swept into territories in the east, but the SS authorities and the *Gauleiter* and regional commanders and commissars in Poland and other areas had "proved wholly unequal to the problems caused by this mass uprooting in midwar." They simply "liquidated the deportees as their trains arrived," a procedure that Hitler knew nothing about until October 1943, if not later.

In the English edition of his book, Irving complained bitterly that his German publishers, without consulting him, suppressed or revised these views on the grounds that they were "an affront to established historical opinion" in their country. This, if somewhat high-handed, was understandable, for Irving's "incontrovertible evidence" of Hitler's guiltlessness was of the flimsiest kind. Disregarding the commonsense view that, given the enormity of the Final Solution and the potential results of its revelation, it was not surprising that written evidence of Hitler's ordering the action did not exist, and brushing aside as inconsequential the repeated instances of Hitler's speaking publicly or privately of his intention of exterminating the Jews—his statement to the Czech foreign minister in January 1939 ("We are going to destroy the Jews! . . . The day of reckoning has come!"), and speeches and statements on January 30, 1941, January 30, February 24, September 30, and November 8, 1942—Irving based his argument on a single notation in Heinrich Himmler's telephone log, dated November 30, 1941, and reading *"Keine Liquidierung"* ("No liquidation"). It was difficult to prove anything from this. Scholars were quick to point out that there existed a somewhat less laconic statement of Himmler's of May 1944 that intimated that he did have superior orders to commit the enormities that virtually eliminated the Jews of Europe; and, by analyzing the other scribbles on the same telephone sheet, the historian of the Holocaust, Lucy Dawidowicz, showed that the notation that Irving made so much of referred not to Jews in general but to a single individual whom Hitler wanted removed from a convoy passing through Berlin.

Irving was undaunted by the critical reception of his work and, in July 1978, he did not hesitate to appear at a gathering of historians and political scientists who met in Aschaffenburg to discuss the theme "Hitler Today—Problems and Aspects of Hitler Research," where he cheerfully attacked German scholarship for laziness and lack of critical sensitivity. One of the onlookers wrote later that to listen to the British writer shouting, "Do you want to know the whole truth?" was to be reminded of Joseph Goebbels' speeches in the Sportpalast and that Irving seemed to be sustained by a sense of mission derived from the fact that, according to his own account, he had learned from Hitler's personal ear, nose and throat doctor that the Führer had hoped that one day an English historian would write a fair biography of him.

If the Aschaffenburg conference, which included leading writers on the Hitler problem from all over Germany, was in accord when it came to rejecting Irving's views (and to closing its ears to Werner Maser's attempt to prove that Hitler had a son in France), it could agree on very little else. Variations of all the hypotheses that have been mentioned above found expression in a discussion that at times became stormy, but in the end it was clear only that the debate would have to go on, without foreseeable end. In his account of the meeting in the newspaper *Die Zeit,* Karl-Heinz Janssen wrote: "There we sit after more than thirty years—the Empire in ruins, the East German homeland lost, Berlin divided, Prussia abolished, the old society with all its values destroyed, the new still without contours, the world filled with the rattling of weapons, hearts filled with secret fears, of atomic catastrophe, of inflation and unemployment, of terrorists—and, despite all that, ever again Hitler, Hitler, Hitler—one can't stand it!"

II

To what extent did this unending discussion affect the popular consciousness and, more particularly, how was it reflected in the curricula of elementary and secondary schools? From the very beginning of the Federal Republic, the schools were periodically accused of not doing enough to protect society against the danger of a revival of undemocratic behavior by teaching their pupils the truth about Hitler and the crimes of his regime.

During the 1950s, that criticism was, to a large extent, justified, although for some special reasons. At that time, the older teachers were relics of the last Hitler years and were, one way or another, too involved in the question of guilt to teach about the Nazi past with objectivity. In a great many schools all over Germany, historical instruction dwelt on the remote past or came as far as Bismarck and then stopped abruptly and in some confusion. To do justice to teachers and boards of education, it should be remembered that materials were not available to make adequate coverage of the modern period possible. Books and curricula that had been used in the 1940s were not suitable for instruction in the schools of a democratic State, and it took considerable time before new textbooks could be written and new faculties could begin experimenting with films, tapes and documentary sources of various kinds.

This situation was corrected more expeditiously than might have been expected, partly as a result of a temporary revival of right-radicalism at the end of the fifties and a rash of incidents that involved the smearing of swastikas on public buildings and vandalism against synagogues, mostly by small groups of juveniles. This galvanized the regional governments into action, and in 1962 the ministers of education of the ten federal states issued uniform directives about how the history of the Third Reich was to be taught in the schools and accepted a teaching plan that included stipulated curricular units on National Socialism as a political and administrative system, anti-Semitism and the Holocaust, Hitler's foreign policy, and his responsibility for the war. The basic document declared that the Third Reich "must be observed in the context of German history so that the seductive appeal of a synthesis of nationalism and Socialism can be comprehended, a synthesis that was then revealed to be devoid of all human and social content, based on a premise of biological nationalism."

Simultaneously, the necessary materials began to be available, not only because of the research of university historians, but because of the efforts of school supervisors and teachers to prepare texts that were not burdened down by the paraphernalia of academic scholarship but would answer the questions and speak directly to the concerns of young readers. A notable example was Werner Klose's *Hitler: A Report for Young Citizens* (1961), which began by citing a tribute to Hitler, written by an unknown poet for a ceremony of the *Reichsarbeitsdienst* (Reich Labor Service) in 1935 and which described the Führer and the flag.

Nun schwenkt er sie im Wind, schwenkt sie mit Macht,
Und lässt sein Rufen hallen durch die Nacht.
Da horchen all die alten Kämpfer auf,
Die deutsche Jugend rottet sich zu Hauf.

Er schwenkt die Fahne, schwenkt sie hin und her,
Er ruft die deutschen Männer ins Gewehr.
Er schwenkt die Fahne hoch, schwenkt sie mit Macht
Und lässt die Trommeln wirbeln in der Nacht.

[He waves it in the wind, waves it with might,
And lets his summons echo through the night.
Then all the Old Fighters prick up their ears,
And German youth assembles in a troop.

He waves the banner, waves it to and fro.
He calls German men to arms.
He waves the banner, waves it with might,
And lets the drums roll in the night.]

"We don't know," Klose wrote, "what became of that young man, who serenaded his Führer in this way in 1935. But we know that the Führer shot a bullet through his head at 3:30 in the afternoon on April 30, 1945, when his banner was in shreds and his drum broken in the desert of ruins that he had made out of Germany. How that came about deserves to be told to German youth, of whom one would like to hope that they will reflect before they again assemble 'in a troop' around someone who waves a flag." In his account, which was written in economical but often eloquent prose and illustrated with telling cartoons, Klose spared his readers none of the horrors of the Hitler period, and in his chapter on the attentat of July 20, 1944, he did not hesitate to ask, "If it had not been for the heroism of the women and men of the resistance, what right would our people have to look those of other nations in the eye?"

Even more successful than Klose's book was Hanna Vogt's *Schuld oder Verhängnis?* (published in the United States as *The Burden of Guilt*). For six years a town councillor in Göttingen and later official reporter for the Hessen State Center for Political Education, Frau Vogt set out to write a book that would deal with the questions that she had heard young people ask in innumerable discussions that she had attended and with the rationalizations and half-truths that one heard in private conversations and in the speeches of the less responsible brand of politician—such questions as: did Hitler really come to power because of an iniquitous peace treaty? were the Western Powers as much at fault as Germany for the coming of war in 1939? was there a moral duty to resist Hitler? how should non-Jews have reacted when the persecutions began? how could Germany shape an honorable future? Published in 1961, her book was an immediate success, 400,000 copies being sold in the first two years. The minister of education in Hessen made it prescribed reading in all final classes in the *Volksschulen,* and it was put on the approved lists of ten other ministers of education and of the Senate of West Berlin.

All in all, there was every reason to believe by the middle of the sixties that the materials being used by the schools for instruction about the history of the Third Reich were meeting the objectives set by the federal ministers in 1962. In an independent report of progress made, Grace Richards Conant, an expert on German education and wife of U.S. High Commissioner and Ambassador to West Germany James Bryant Conant, wrote that, in a country that had been notorious for the extreme nationalism of its historical scholarship, it was reassuring to note that publishers of schoolbooks had fallen into the habit of submitting manuscripts to the International Schoolbook Institute in Braunschweig for analysis and correction of bias and error, while state governments had demonstrated their willingness to withdraw books from use when they failed to meet the standards of that organization. After examining ten of the most widely adopted history texts, Mrs. Conant found them free of the kind of distortion that had marred German schoolbooks in the interwar period and noted that, without exception, they contained drastic judgments of German national policy after 1933 and provided detailed accounts of the brutalities practiced by the Nazi government against fellow Germans before 1939 and of the horrors of the Final Solution pursued during the war years.

This improvement in the reading materials used in the schools did not, of course, provide any assurance that the students themselves were acquiring the kind of knowledge that would protect them against the blandishments of a new Leader or against an exciting new combination of nationalism and Socialism; and opinions about the results, as opposed to the methods, of historical instruction were apt to vary widely. In 1965, David Schoenbaum, an American journalist living in Germany, spent six weeks sitting in on a study group of twenty young men, aged nineteen and twenty, who were about to graduate from a secondary school in North Rhine Westphalia and subsequently wrote a report on this experience for *The New York Times Magazine*. Schoenbaum participated in discussions of the relationship between Hitler's movement and the churches, the treatment of the Jews (concerning which the class read quotations from the Nuremberg Laws, the transcript of the Wannsee conference of January 1942, the diary of Rudolf Hoess, the commandant of Auschwitz, and the diary of the poet and novelist Jochen Klepper, who committed suicide with his Jewish wife and his daughter in 1942), the problem of resistance, the nature of Nazi foreign policy, the prosecution of the war, and the question of the nature of the responsibility that citizens of the Bundesrepublik bore for the crimes committed by Hitler's government. Schoenbaum was impressed by the knowledge of the students and the serious nature of their responses to the problems put to them.

Eleven years later, however, on the initiative of an educationist in Kiel named Dieter Bossmann, 102 teachers of 110 schools in various parts of Germany asked students in 121 classes of different grades to write essays on the theme "What I Have Heard about Hitler." Bossmann spent seven months reading and making excerpts from the 3042 essays sent to him and, at the end of his labors, said that the result was "an unlimited catastrophe." Many of the respondents admitted knowing nothing about the subject; some boasted of shutting their ears when Hitler was mentioned, because politics didn't interest them; and a very large number confessed to merely fragmentary knowledge, a good deal of which proved to be alarmingly incorrect. There were students who believed that Hitler had been born in 1819, that he was an Italian, that he had fought in the Thirty Years War, that he had made the first moon landing, that his accession to power in 1933 was the result of an electoral victory over Bismarck, that he had placed all of his opponents, whom he called Nazis, in the gas chambers, that he drank a lot of whiskey and sang a lot of songs, and that he was a Communist. There were others who wrote that he had done a lot of good for Germany and that while he was in power there were no hippies or rockers or terrorists. There were those who recalled nothing except details, generally exaggerated, about his sexual preferences and practices, and others who mentioned his racial and euthanasia programs but seemed to feel that these were compensated for by his success in alleviating unemployment. There were students who believed that the conspirators of July 20 included Rommel, Goering and Speer, as well as Hindenburg, Rosa Luxemburg and

Karl Liebknecht, and there were others who asserted that Hitler had survived the war to become an associate of Konrad Adenauer and a member of the CDU with friends in the Bundestag.

Heralded by an article in *Der Spiegel,* excerpts from the essays appeared in book form at the end of 1977 and caused reactions of shock and outrage. These might not have been so violent had Mr. Bossmann's revelations not coincided with what was being called a "Hitler wave" in the Bundesrepublik. In 1976, Jean Améry had warned that "the time of rehabilitation" was dawning.

> In England one will discover that Oswald Mosley [founder of the British Union of Fascists] was not such a fool after all. In France a bemused public opinion will weigh [Marshal] Pétain and [Pierre] Laval on scales brought by false weights to a pseudo-historical balance. And in Germany? After all the measures of classification and qualification have been taken, Hitler will not be denied his place in the hall of honor. . . . We are already being told that historical objectivity lies beyond good and evil, which means that evil will be relegated without discrimination to the files, and good will vanish from the day's agenda.

To some people, 1977 seemed to promise the fulfillment of that prediction. Suddenly, the illustrated magazines were filled with articles about the Führer, or his paladins, or the triumphs of his propaganda. There were new Hitler records in the music shops and the announcement of a forthcoming rock opera called *Hitler Superstar.* The Führer's automobile license plates and items of his raingear sold for fabulous prices in auctions in Munich. All over the country, the film *Hitler: A Career,* based on Fest's biography, was showing to packed houses, and Hitler's face stared from placards advertising it on every city street. The French newspaper *Le Monde* announced that a poll by the Leo Burnett Company and IRES of Düsseldorf had disclosed that 41% of the persons interrogated felt that, while Hitler had "committed numerous errors," one should not neglect "the positive aspects of his action"; and both the Italian and the French press were up in arms about what was called the "Kappler scandal"—the daring exploit of a German woman faith-healer who had effected the escape to Germany of the seventy-year-old Herbert Kappler, a former colonel in the SS who had been condemned to life imprisonment by an Italian court in 1948 for the massacre of 335 hostages in the Fosse Ardeatine near Rome during the war. What infuriated the foreign press was the refusal of the Bonn government to accede to Italy's demand that Kappler be extradited. Disregarding provisions of the West German Basic Law that made this impossible, they declared that the attitude of the Bonn authorities was an additional sign of the revival of Nazism or something very like it in Germany.

Coming on top of all this, the news that there was considerable confusion in the minds of German schoolchildren about the realities of the

Third Reich seemed, even to so sensible a journal as *The Economist* of London, to be an ominous circumstance. In fact, there was no substantial basis for alarm. The so-called "Hitler wave" subsided as quickly as it had arisen and was a thing of the past even before the Fest film had completed its run in the major cinema houses. Simultaneously, people began to have second thoughts about Mr. Bossmann's disclosures. New tests of fifteen- to eighteen-year-olds in various schools revealed not only that they had more command of the history of the Nazi period than his excerpts had seemed to show, but that they were capable of making shrewd judgments about the reasons for Hitler's rise to power, popular reactions to his policies and the possibility of a repetition of the Hitler phenomenon. Educational theorists pointed out, at the same time, that it was well known that students in the middle grades, who had formed a considerable percentage of Mr. Bossmann's respondents, were characterized by a disinclination to learn about subjects that did not concern them directly, that their interest was difficult to awaken, and that their attention span was extremely short. This was true not only for German children. Had the historical knowledge of young English students or Americans been tested by asking them to write essays about Winston Churchill or Franklin Delano Roosevelt, there was no doubt that the same kind and the same number of howlers and inanities would have shown up in the results.

This hardly excused the kind of confusion that had led some students to believe that Hitler had been a Communist or a member of the CDU and had led one of them to write that big industry had created the NSDAP out of fear of Communism and that Hitler was the figurehead of the Fascism that resulted, which would have come even if he had never existed. But, as Werner Klose wrote, one did not have to look very far in order to find an explanation of those errors. It was characteristic of the society in which the students lived that their elders used political labels with no discrimination. The term Communist had long been used by politicians and churchmen to describe anything that offended them, and of late the misuse of the terms Fascist, Nazi, and "Faschistoid" had been no less profligate. "Who," Klose asked, "will complain about the lamentable historical knowledge of fourteen-year-old students, when in many university institutes not only sectarian students but even their teachers are convinced, and say so more or less openly, that the victims of the terrorists were, at the very least, 'Faschistoid' because they served the Bundesrepublik in this function or that? When our 'System' (a Hitler term for parliamentary democracy!) is twisted by demagogues into this unhistorical concept of hate, *Faschismus,* the historical reality of National Socialism simply becomes incomprehensible for part of our young people."

These arguments helped to place Bossmann's experiment in perspective, and the reaction to the American *Holocaust* TV-film in February 1979, which will be discussed below and which was particularly positive among young people, served to reassure many of those who had been deeply troubled by it. But not everyone was comforted by this, and before long the ghost of Hitler was troubling the consciences of Germans again. The source of concern this time was the growing militancy of right-extremist groups. Such organizations had long existed on the fringes of the law and had been tolerated because they were of trifling size and were composed for the most part of aging veterans of the Movement. But in 1978 and 1979, a network of new, professedly neo-Nazi groups appeared, which were loosely associated in an *Aktionsfront nationaler Sozialisten* headed by a former Bundeswehr lieutenant named Michael Kuhnen and were composed for the most part of males under thirty. These groups began a series of actions, using tactics similar to those of the left-wing terrorists. It was alleged that Kuhnen had planned armed attacks on garrisons and exercise places in Hamburg and Bergen-Hohne that succeeded in seizing arms and munitions, as well as robberies of banks and business firms that netted him 150,000 DM, and it was said that his organizations were planning an operation to free Hitler's deputy Rudolf Hess from his detention in Spandau and to mount an assault upon the Berlin Wall.

There was little danger that these still minuscule groups would be able to carry out these ambitious plans, let alone—as Kuhnen boasted was his intention—to "reawaken Germany," "refound the NSDAP," and "restore the Reich to its old strength," for by the latter part of 1979 they were under as close police supervision as the left-wing terrorists. Even so, it was disheartening to hear the old slogans being shouted in public again, and even more so to speculate about how many people there might be who harbored thoughts like Kuhnen's in secret. A Munich institute commissioned by the Chancellor's Office in 1979 to investigate popular susceptibility to right-radical slogans found that the problem was more serious than had been supposed and that the saying "Germany was better off under Hitler" was no longer uncommon. It was clear, one and a half generations after his death in the bunker, that Hitler was like the little man upon the stair in the old song. He wasn't there, but he wouldn't go away.

PART TWO

Change
and
Continuity

4

Religion

Considering the number of times that Germany's intellectuals have declared that God is dead, its newspapers devote a surprising amount of space to news about religion. This cannot be described as the result of editorial whim or confessional zeal, although there are, to be sure, more important journals of confessional persuasion in Germany than there are in the United States. It is rather a reflection of the fact that despite the secularizing tendencies that have affected all Western countries in the industrial age, religion has remained a vital force in Germany. This is shown not only by the fact that 95% of the population of the German Federal Republic acknowledge themselves to be, at least formally, members of one of the Christian denominations, but also by the activity of religious leaders and professing Christians in the politics of both the Federal Republic and the German Democratic Republic. Most of all, perhaps, it is illustrated by the liveliness, if not acrimony, of disputes within the two principal confessions concerning church reform and the appropriate role of Christianity in contemporary society.

These activities and internal debates are not, of course, new. Indeed, they reflect convictions and differences that have, in some cases, existed among confessing Christians since the beginning of the modern era and have been exacerbated by memories of the behavior of the Protestant and Roman Catholic establishments during the Nazi years.

I

To illustrate this, we must start by going back to the Reformation, a point in time that is perhaps less remote to the Germans than it is to us, since they are still surrounded by its memorials. This great revolution that destroyed the unity of the German Church was the result of a coincidence of general tendencies and individual initiative. During the last years of the fifteenth century, there had been a growing conviction, even among the most dedicated believers, that the Church of Rome was in bad need of reform, and this feeling was strengthened by an incipient German nationalism, nurtured by Ulrich von Hutten and other humanists, who found the subordination of the German Church to Rome demeaning. This was not the last time that German Catholicism was to

83

be moved by these feelings, which are, indeed, not negligible in strength today. In the sixteenth century, they assumed compelling force when Martin Luther became their embodiment.

In a famous passage in his *History of Religion and Philosophy in Germany*, Heinrich Heine wrote that Luther was "not merely the greatest but also the most German man in our history, so that in his character all the virtues and failings of the German were united in the most magnificent way." He was at the same time mystic and practical man of affairs, "the tongue as well as the sword of his age, . . . a cold scholastic word-cobbler and an inspired, God-drunk prophet who, when he had worked himself almost to death over his laborious and dogmatic distinctions, in the evening reached for his flute and, gazing at the stars, melted in melody and reverence."

The contradictions that Heine noted marked both Luther's temperament and his personal style, which varied between the moving eloquence of his songs and the coarse invective of his attacks upon his enemies; and they were most notable in his religious reform. His enunciation of the doctrine of justification by faith alone, with its implicit rejection of the necessity of any intermediary between the individual believer and his God, his belief in a priesthood of all believers drawing the principles of their faith from Scripture, and the marvelous force of the pamphlets that he wrote to propagate these ideas amounted to an unprecedented declaration of intellectual liberty. On the other hand, his uncompromising support of secular authority against those whom his words encouraged to demand social and political change not only appeared to limit that freedom to the inner realm of the spirit but placed a conservative stamp upon the Protestant movement from the moment of its birth.

This was, perhaps, inevitable. Luther was himself a conservative, who believed that the existing political and social order, with all its inequalities and injustices, was an expression of the will of God, Who had also created government by secular authorities for the enforcement of law and order. The secular world was not a Christian order; most men were unregenerate sinners and had to be controlled by worldly wisdom or by force. But it was a necessary one, since, without an imposed order, chaos would result, and the existence and spread of Christianity would become impossible. Therefore, the individual Christian, who lived in a community of mercy and love, also had to fulfill his duty in the world of violence and sin. Bound by his conscience to an ethics of love, he also owed allegiance of the secular order, whose preservation was ordained by God; and, if he were called upon to serve it, as a soldier or officeholder, he must do his duty and regard his service as a form of worshiping his Maker.

Luther's attitude toward the disorders inspired by his teaching was, therefore, not surprising. In 1522, when there was a rising of the lesser knights led by Franz von Sickingen, the Wittenberg Reformer disassociated himself from it and regarded its eventual suppression as a judgment of God; and, two years later, when the great rebellion of the peasants began, he not only took an unequivocal stand against it but wrote a notorious pamphlet in which he bade the princes to "fight confidently and use the sword in good conscience as long as there is a fiber of resistance. For the advantage is that the peasants have a bad conscience, fighting for an unrighteous cause, and every peasant who is killed for it loses body and soul to the devil for all eternity. . . . These are peculiar times, so peculiar that a prince who sheds blood earns heaven much more than many a man who prays."

Not all of those who had been moved by Luther's defiance of the authority of the Roman Church felt this way. Thomas Münzer, who fought on the side of the peasants at the battle of Frankenhausen and was captured and executed after that debacle, was—despite his later canonization by Friedrich Engels as a precursor of Communism—an ardent Christian who had originally followed Luther but had become convinced that it was not enough to believe that religion was an inward, spiritual experience. He believed that when the individual, through a process of trial and suffering, had received the Holy Spirit, he was converted into an instrument for the extermination of evil in the world and must join with other converts in an unremitting struggle to complete the course of human history by ushering in the Kingdom of God. When the peasants' revolt began, Münzer saw in it the beginning of this process of transformation. He had already, a year earlier, founded a secret military organization called the League of the Elect among the miners of Mansfeld and, when the disorders began, he mobilized it with the words: "Do not despair, be not hesitant, and stop truckling to the godless villains! Begin to fight the battle for the Lord! Now is the time! Everywhere in Germany, France and the neighboring foreign lands there is a great awakening! The Lord wants to start the game, and for the godless the time is up!"

Within a decade of Luther's challenge to the Roman Church, therefore, his Protestant faith was opposed by a theology of social and political action, based—in the words of Münzer's biographer—on the belief that "words of faith had to become deeds; the individual's rebirth through the advent of the Holy Spirit in the soul must be translated into . . . action revealing God's will for the world." With Luther's encouragement, that theology was ruthlessly suppressed by the princes; but it was not the last time that it would inspire men who, like Münzer, had a deep compassion for the sufferings of the vulnerable sections of society, to challenge the assumptions of their religious leaders.

In the sixteenth century, however, Luther's view prevailed, and in the subsequent period orthodox Lutheranism became an increasingly uncritical supporter of secular authority, carrying this to a point, indeed, where it lost the autonomous position that the Roman Church had been able to maintain by means of the confessional and the power of excommunication. In the sixteenth and seventeenth centuries, in the areas where Protestantism spread, the territorial princes seized the judicial rights and the properties that had belonged to the Roman Church and, since the new Lutheran congregations could not support them-

selves by their own means, became their patrons. In time, patronage was
interpreted to mean the right to examine the financial and physical
needs of the congregations and to intervene in doctrinal questions, like
forms of worship and school curricula and appointments; and, when the
territorial prince was ultimately recognized as the highest bishop or
summus episcopus of the body of congregations,which happened inSax-
ony, the Guelf duchies, Mecklenburg, Hesse-Darmstadt, and Württemberg, the transformation of the Lutheran Churches into official
churches was complete. Luther himself had condoned this development.
The physical aspects of church organization had never been of burning
concern to him, and even in doctrinal matters he had, after his conflict
with Münzer and some experience with other sectaries, come to fear
unlimited subjectivism in Biblical interpretation and to place increasing
emphasis upon dogma and theological leadership. Supervision by secular authority was, in his eyes, merely an additional safeguard.

In most of the areas where Lutheranism prevailed, it tended to encourage a passive obedience to authority on all levels from the local
landholder to the prince. In the state of Brandenburg-Prussia, however,
an important difference is to be noted. Here, while the bulk of the population remained Lutheran, the ruling Hohenzollern dynasty was converted in 1613 to Calvinism. The doctrinal and organizational differences between the two forms of Protestantism are less important here
than the fact that Calvinism brought into the country, from the Netherlands and the France of Henri IV, ideas of *raison d'état*, of science of
government, and of State growth that most of the lesser Lutheran
princes were incapable of comprehending, but which the Hohenzollerns,
ambitious to make their State an independent power in Europe, found
congenial. The Calvinist court preachers of the Hohenzollern family,
located not only in Berlin but in twenty other towns throughout the
realm, were the nucleus of a growing body of officials who, from their
positions in church consistories, in the Joachimsthalschen Gymnasium,
the most important Calvinist school in the country, and in the civil service, spread the idea of active obedience and service to the State and
were agents of State centralization and power. Upon Prussian Lutheranism, these influences were not lost, and in 1817, when the Reformed
(Calvinist) and Lutheran churches were merged, organized Protestantism in Prussia had become the dedicated supporter of the centralized
absolute power.

The growth of powerful official churches was bound to arouse, among
some concerned Christians, feelings analogous to the opposition to the
Roman Church in the sixteenth century. Even in Luther's time, there
was a pronounced growth of individual sects and conventicles that
sought spiritual solace in mystical experience and chiliastic visions and
regarded the church that was founded in Luther's name as nothing
more than a bureaucratized orthodoxy served by "priests of Baal" who
made idols out of ritual and dogma. More significant, because better
organized, was the Pietist movement, which had its inspiration in the
work of Philipp Jakob Spener (1635–1705). A man whose Christian

conscience was matched by his pastoral energy, Spener set out to promote a program of active Christianization of daily life outside the regular church organization. In 1666, he organized a Bible college (*collegia pietatis*) in Frankfurt which held daily meetings for Bible reading, special prayer and the cultivation of individual piety and was open to people of all classes.

These activities, and Spener's additional teaching that Christian life would manifest itself in work of social amelioration, aroused wide attention, and similar groups were formed in other parts of Germany, often in the homes of the nobility and the upper burgher class. In the University of Leipzig there was a particularly active group under the leadership of August Wilhelm Francke (1663–1727), which placed so much emphasis upon Christian works and upon the reform and rebirth of church, university and society that the orthodox Lutheran leadership became alarmed and communicated its concern to the various governments. One can understand this reaction. The heart of Pietism was the moral renovation of the individual, achieved by passing through the anguish of contrition into the overwhelming realization of the assurance of God's grace. This experience was the result of introspection and prayer and was completely personal and unique to the believer. He had no need of theologians to point the way for him, nor could he derive any benefit from religious hierarchies dominated by the various German states. Help could be provided only by searchers for grace like himself, and the true Christian life could be lived only in small communities of awakened Christians. This ideal seemed, in short, to challenge the very existence of the establishment; and before long aroused authority was seeking to prevent the spread of the new movement. Anti-Pietist laws were passed in Saxony (1690), Brunswick and Lüneburg (1692), Brandenburg (1700), Hesse-Kassel (1703), Bremen (1705), Nuremberg (1707), and in other Lutheran centers.

Even so, Pietism found a refuge in larger towns like Frankfurt and Hamburg and, despite some initial resistance, in Brandenburg-Prussia. Francke and his associate, the jurist Thomasius, joined the faculty of the new university of Halle, founded by the government of Brandenburg in 1694, and Francke immediately began a program of social activity remarkable for his time, forming a school for the poor in 1695 and Germany's first organization for the education of orphans, the famous *Waisenhaus*, in 1698, and establishing a publishing house for the production of cheap Bibles and religious literature for distribution through the country.

Francke's activities received official patronage (and this may be regarded as the beginning of the taming of Pietism) when Frederick William I assumed the throne of Prussia in 1713. A remarkable social reformer in his own right, Frederick William is reported to have said, "If I build and improve the land and make no Christians, then everything I do is worthless." It was Pietist social activism as well as zeal for the Reformation that led this forthright ruler to destroy the Catholic Marienkirche in Brandenburg in order to use its stones for a military orphanage in Potsdam, and the King's admiration of Francke led him to use his writings for the religious instruction of his troops, so that they might fight more staunchly for God's purpose as defined by their sovereign. Frederick William also sensed and approved the pedagogical originality of Francke's experiments in education, which soon included noble and bourgeois children of both sexes, as well as orphans and children of the poor, and which were planned so as to adjust the nature of the education to the gifts of the individual student and to develop his talents as far as possible. Francke was especially interested in preparing gifted young people of whatever class for government service and, in this, was actively encouraged by his monarch. Indeed, one of the most striking results of Pietism was the strong and lasting effect that it had in the Prussian bureaucracy and the officer corps of the army and the social classes from which they were principally recruited.

On the other hand, although it started as a movement of protest against the bureaucratization of religion and official Church indifference to social ills, Pietism never aimed at anything like a total reform of Church or State. In the areas in which they were strongest—in Saxony, in the East Elbian districts of Prussia, and in Württemberg, where the movement had a genuinely popular basis—the Pietists became known in the eighteenth century as the *Stillen im Lande*, the quiet ones, a name that summed up both the inwardness of their concerns and their relative indifference to politics. The mutual antagonism that had marked their relations with the leaders of the Lutheran Church soon diminished, and it was significant that most Pietist groups—even the Brethren's Community in Herrnhut, a refuge for exiles from Bohemia that was founded by Count Nicholas Ludwig von Zinzendorf and was open to Christians of any confession—remained within the Lutheran Church and in time, as we shall see, were co-opted by its establishment.

Meanwhile, what may be called mainstream Lutheranism had overcome the fierce doctrinal wrangling that had characterized its history in the sixteenth and seventeenth centuries and become increasingly influenced by a rationalism that stemmed originally from the attempts of Leibniz and Christian Wolff to reconcile religion and philosophy in the form of a positive religion that accepted belief in God and in the immortality of the soul as "natural" and placed its emphasis upon the moral freedom of the individual. This development and the influence of Wolff's philosophy of religion upon intellectuals in general help explain why the Enlightenment had such limited results in Germany. In contrast to the situation in France and England, there were no atheists or republicans among the German *Aufklärer*, who, having no doctrinal obscurantism to complain of, were not driven to religious alienation and who were less interested in political goals than they were in the perfectibility of the individual and of humanity. Pietism also had something to do with this, for the work of people like Francke demonstrated that there was no incompatibility between piety and enlightened social policy; and so did the deeply felt religious instinct that was the result of the cultural influence exercised ever since Luther's day in the most remote parts of Protestant Germany by a dedicated and well-educated clergy.

The distinguished analyst of French and German culture Robert Minder has written persuasively of the impact of the vicarage (the *Pfarrhaus*) on German literature, and the German novel from Jean Paul to Wilhelm Raabe and Theodor Fontane affords rich testimony to this. But the moral and spiritual influence of the *Pfarrhaus* on the emerging middle class was no less profound and, during the Enlightenment, it served to modify their objectives and expectations and make them less intent on secular goals than the bourgeoisie in the west.

The coming of the French Revolution and Napoleon's conquest of, and eventual expulsion from, Germany had a quickening effect upon religious faith in general, which continued after the peace settlement of 1815 and was sustained by the exaggerated fear of renewed revolution that affected the German upper classes. In these circumstances, Pietism, which had begun to wane in the last years of the eighteenth century, not only revived but was transformed into a conservative force within the Lutheran Church. During the war of liberation, many high-ranking officials in the Prussian civil service and the officer corps of the army had become members of Pietist circles, perhaps because an emotional God-directed religion seemed the best ideological armor against French rationalism and secularism, and in the subsequent period— indeed, until the end of the 1840s—such devotional groups continued to be a normal aspect of the life of the nobility of the East Elbian lands. It is worth noting in passing that the greatest German statesman of the second half of the nineteenth century, Otto von Bismarck, was brought into such a circle in the home of his friends the von Thaddens of Trieglaff, and that he experienced a religious conversion that had permanent effects upon his personality and statecraft. Students of Bismarck's policy have too often tended to regard statements of his like "I am God's soldier, and where He sends me there I must go," or "I believe I am obeying God when I serve my King," or "It is precisely my living evangelical and Christian faith that lays upon me the duty, in behalf of the land where I was born and for whose service God created me, to guard that office against all sides" as hypocrisy or rationalization. This is far from being true, and to think that it is, is to fail to appreciate the source of the assurance with which Bismarck conducted foreign policy and to misunderstand the ethos of the Prussian nobility, which, in our own time, was so important a factor in their participation in the conspiracy against Hitler's life.

The general fear of revolution and rationalism that prevailed after 1815 persuaded high officials at the Prussian court, some of whom came from these East Elbian circles, that religious fervor was the best guarantee against political agitation by the masses and that the way to propagate it was to ensure that henceforth truly religious—that is, Pietist— candidates for the clergy be given preference in scholarship awards and appointments. This policy was instituted during the reign of Frederick William III and carried to an extreme by his successor, Frederick William IV, who had romantic notions of founding a Christianized Prussia that would be a bulwark against progressive political tendencies. The leading positions in the Ministry of Cults and the hierarchy of the

Christian Evangelical Church were filled with neo-Pietists who proceeded to conduct a campaign of harassment against clergymen of too pronounced rationalist views—like the so-called Young Hegelians and those preachers who, under the influence of D. F. Strauss's *Life of Jesus* (1835), had doubts about the authenticity of the Bible account—and against opponents of the liturgical reform that had accompanied the union of the Lutheran and Reformed churches, like the remarkable Berlin preacher Friedrich Schleiermacher.

Not for the last time in German history, such a blatant intrusion of politics into the religious sphere, accompanied as it was by an attempt to exclude nonconformists from the body of the faithful and to make the Church an instrument of political reaction, awakened a storm of protest among the public. In June 1841, the pastor Leberecht Uhlich called the first of a series of meetings to protest against doctrinal directives issued by the Protestant leadership, and from these meetings grew the movement known as the Friends of Light (*Lichtfreunde*) which, by 1845, was bringing thousands of people together from every part of the country, including many women, a fact that impressed and angered government officials because it was so unprecedented. In these assemblies, protests were raised against the rigidity of the government's Church policy, and there were demands for a more representative Church constitution, with greater lay participation in governance, and other reforms that would bring the Church into accordance with progressive tendencies.

The movement did not last or achieve great results, and it is memorable chiefly as an early illustration of the way in which, in time of political instability (Germany was moving toward the revolutions of 1848), religion could serve as a focus for antigovernment agitation. One of Metternich's agents said with alarm in 1845, "Religion is now the axis around which the world, and with it political affairs, revolves." As it turned out, he was wrong. When the revolution came, the militant pastors of the *Lichtfreunde* did not play a prominent role. Their oppositional stance was restricted to the sphere of religion, and when political reality broke in they retreated. In the years that followed the debacle of 1848, the majority of Protestant pastors—not only in the Evangelical Church in Prussia but in the Lutheran churches in Saxony, Hannover and Württemberg and the Reformed congregations in other states— outdid themselves in preaching reprobation of revolution and unconditional loyalty to the existing authorities. This was a stance that was consistent with the prevailing conservatism of German Protestantism since Luther's time. Whether it was appropriate for the new industrialized Germany that was gathering its strength and was to emerge in the Reich of 1871 was questionable.

II

The fortunes of German Catholicism since the Reformation had taken a different and more difficult course. By the middle of the sixteenth century, four fifths of Germany was Protestant, and it seemed not unlikely that the remaining pockets of Catholic resistance, like the bishop-rics of Cologne and Würzburg, and Augsburg and the rest of Bavaria would be unable to withstand the onward push of the triumphant Lu-theran reform. This was prevented by a dramatic recovery by the shak-en Church of Rome, which was instituted by the Council of Trent (1545–1563). This effected a clarification and redefinition of Catholic doctrine and began a systematic removal of the kind of abuses that had precipitated Luther's revolt. The subsequent recovery of the Catholic position in Germany was effected under the political leadership of Em-peror Ferdinand II and princes like the Elector Maximilian I of Bavaria and, although it was accompanied by the dreadful bloodshed that reached its height in the Thirty Years War, it was so successful that, after the Treaty of Westphalia, Mainz, Cologne and Trier and their adjacent territories, Würzburg, Constanz, Bamberg and Münster, Bad-en, Bavaria, Austria and numerous petty states in the north and along the Rhine were Catholic territories.

The cultural reconquest of these lands was as important as the polit-ical. For this, the Society of Jesus, founded in 1540, was chiefly respon-sible, for its members led the way in correcting the deplorable lack of education that had been characteristic of the lower Catholic clergy. This was a task that required years of devoted labor, in which new seminaries and schools were founded and the Jesuits sought to establish themselves in the theological faculties of universities like Würzburg, Bamberg and Fulda. Although they often had to put up with the oppo-sition of local prelates or of prince-bishops who were resistant to the decrees of the Council of Trent, the Jesuits not only effected a sensible improvement of the curricula of Catholic educational institutions and made them vital centers in promoting the Counter-Reformation, but they demonstrated their belief in practical Christianity by missionary activity in the countryside, the establishment of hospitals for the sick and homes for the indigent, and experiments in basic education for the poor.

Not the least important of the cultural achievements of the Jesuits was their bringing of the baroque style of architecture into Germany. This seventeenth-century import from Italy, which profoundly affected Austrian church building and found its first impressive embodiment in Germany in the Theatinerkirche in Munich, not only gave visible form to the religious zeal of the Counter-Reformation but helped to commu-nicate it to the masses. In the richness and extravagance of its orna-mentation, which was in sharp contrast to the stark simplicity of Prot-estant church architecture, it illustrated the conviction of Ignatius Loyola, the founder of the Jesuit order, that the most effective way of making converts to the Roman Catholic Church, or of winning back those who had left it, was to appeal not to their reason but to their senses, by overpowering them with impressions that would dazzle and move them, sweep them up into the heart of the drama of redemption, and give them a glimpse of the beauty and magnificence of God's throne and the joy that awaited the faithful. The new churches that were founded in the seventeenth and eighteenth centuries by the Jesuits and other orders used baroque internal decoration for didactic purposes, and the style gradually spread through Bavaria and other Catholic areas, finding magnificent expression, for example, in both the religious and secular architecture of the ecclesiastical principalities of Bamberg and Würzburg.

Even more impressive were its humbler manifestations. Particularly after its early heaviness and Italianate bombast had been lightened by the influence of the French rococo style—a change that can be seen in the churches decorated by the brothers Cosmas Damian and Hans Georg Asam in Munich, St. Johann Nepomuk and the charming Annenkloster, and in the Jesuit Church of the Guardian Angel in Eichstätt—the baroque had great popular resonance. Local masons, woodcarvers, stucco-workers and fresco-painters brought their adaptations to country cloisters and village churches, sometimes with astonishing results, as in the case of the unique pilgrimage church called the *Wies*, near Steingaden. In much the same way as the sacred music of Johann Sebastian Bach affected the German Protestant, so did the baroque style seem to appeal to the ordinary Catholic believer, and for the same reasons: it made the invisible palpable and carried the individual into the heart of the divine drama.

Throughout the eighteenth and nineteenth centuries, German Catholics were never entirely free from preoccupation with the fact that they constituted a religious minority in the country and that, because of their tie with the Papacy, they were viewed with distrust by many of their Protestant countrymen. Concern about their minority status increased as a result of political developments. As long as the Holy Roman Empire existed, Catholicism was more than adequately represented in the political affairs of Germany as a whole; but the coming of Napoleon put an end to that, for he abolished the Empire and secularized the ecclesiastical states that had been the basis of the German Catholic Church's temporal power, conferring much of the lands and population of these states upon non-Catholic princes. Napoleon's ultimate defeat did not repair this damage; and, indeed, the political fortunes of Catholicism were to suffer more formidable blows as the new century advanced. Once the national unification movement gathered strength, it became clear that its liberal standard-bearers were intent on excluding Austria, the strongest of the German Catholic states, from the union to which they aspired; and, if the revolution of 1848 had not failed, they would have done so. Eighteen years later, as a result of its victory at Königgrätz, the Prussian army did what the liberals had failed to do. Confronted with the prospect of a Prussian-dominated Germany without Austria, a German Catholic wrote sadly to his brother, "*Lieber Georg, die Welt stinkt.*" To protect their interests against the prospective Protestant majority, Catholic leaders and laymen founded the Center Party, which was to play an important and, at critical moments a crucial, role in German politics until 1933. In the first years of its existence, however, this confessional party seemed to inflame even further the suspicions that German Protestants harbored against Catholicism; and in the 1870s the Chancellor of the new Empire, Otto von Bismarck, exploited those feelings in his attempt to smash the new party in the famous campaign that liberals called the *Kulturkampf*, or "struggle for civilization."

The *Kulturkampf* was justified on the assumption that the German Catholic Church was a mere instrument in the hands of a foreign power, the Papacy, which had, liberals felt, demonstrated its opposition to all modern ideas by the promulgation of the Syllabus of Errors in 1864 and had revealed ambitions with serious political implications in the declaration of the doctrine of papal infallibility in matters of faith and doctrine in 1870. This was, however, an assumption that had little support in history. Ever since the seventeenth century, relations between the German Catholic leadership and Rome had been less than cordial, the papal establishment finding German churchmen too ready to make arrangements of convenience with their Protestant colleagues, the German Church finding Rome too complacent when abuses of absenteeism and nepotism occurred in the sees of the princely German bishops. During the Enlightenment, Catholic reformers were markedly antipapal in their views; Bishop Sailer of Landeshut openly championed ecumenism; and the auxiliary bishop of Trier, Febronius, talked of the necessity of founding a national Catholic Church. This last idea, which predated the Reformation, was to surface repeatedly in the years that followed and was particularly strong among young priests during the turbulent events of the 1840s.

The extreme conservatism of Pope Pius IX, whose pontificate lasted from 1846 until 1878, increased the tension between Rome and the German Catholics, and it was German bishops who most staunchly opposed the doctrine of papal infallibility. Their spokesman was Josef Ignaz von Döllinger (1799-1890), a man who combined great scholarly gifts with political penetration and courage, and a consistent champion of the concept, first expressed by him in 1848, of a church that would be neither "the instrument of a police state" (as it had become in Austria, and as the Evangelical Church was becoming in Prussia) nor "the tool of bureaucratic administration." Döllinger became convinced that the growing absolutism of Pius IX and the increasing doctrinal rigidity of the Curia threatened the independence of the German Church; and, in 1865, after the issuance of the Syllabus of Errors, he wrote, "Ultramontanism is no fiction any longer, no ghost, but a real and aggressively advancing power" that must be opposed. When the Vatican made plans to call a Council in 1869, he foresaw that it would be used to issue new dogma that would be hard to justify historically and impossible for progressive minds to accept; and he used his pen to combat this danger. Ordered to conform to the decree of papal infallibility, he refused to do so on grounds of conscience and was excommunicated, an action that profoundly stirred the German Church and led numerous members of the clergy to join Döllinger in spiritual exile.

This division would have done more damage to the Catholic Church if

Bismarck's *Kulturkampf* had not followed so closely upon it. That ill-advised campaign, with its concomitant expulsion of the Jesuits and dissolution of their seminaries, its imposition, in Prussia, of official requirements for ordination, and its transfer of disciplinary authority over the Church to government agencies, backfired in a spectacular way. Not only did it bring German Catholics together in an impressive solidarity that was reflected in the doubling of the popular vote of the party that Bismarck had wanted to destroy, but it effected a marked diminution of anti-Catholic feeling in the nation as a whole. One Protestant theologian wrote, "The State cannot conduct a war against a large part of its own population without causing, on all sides, profound injury to the moral consciousness." Bismarck himself was shrewd enough to see that he had blundered, and at the end of the seventies dismantled the anti-Catholic campaign.

III

Throughout the history of the Second German Empire, both confessions had to face the challenge of modern science on the one hand and industrialism and urbanization on the other, and in both respects German Catholicism showed itself better prepared. The enlightened policies of the Church of Rome during the pontificate of Leo XIII (1878–1903) and the new fervor induced at home by the *Kulturkampf* helped the Catholic Church meet the assaults of biblical criticism and Darwinism with more equanimity and resilience than the Protestant theological establishment could muster. Indeed, the leading Protestant theologians of the age—Julius Wellhausen, Albrecht Ritschl and Adolf von Harnack—showed such a readiness to abandon the mystical and intuitive elements of the Christian tradition and to sacrifice doctrinal positions that the ability of the Protestant Church to compete with the new secular religions of the age—nationalism, Socialism, and the like—was gravely compromised.

The threat to religious faith that was posed by the prevailing materialism of the age and, as far as the lower classes were concerned, by the deracination caused by industrialization, both confessions sought to combat by ameliorative social work. In this field, the Catholics had a long tradition, dating from the pioneer missionary work of the Jesuits in the sixteenth century. During the Enlightenment, Bishop J. M. Sailer of Landshut had shown intense interest in pastoral work, and his student Franz von Baader, professor of philosophy in Munich, had been one of the first to discern that the growth of the propertyless class would confront the Church with urgent problems. In the 1840s Catholic thinkers were among the first to call for State factory legislation, and Adolf Kolping, a lay member of the Church, founded Catholic journeymen's associations to give free vocational training to working men. In the 1870s, these early experiments were given new vigor by Wilhelm Emmanuel von Ketteler, the bishop of Mainz, who sought to combat the demoralization of increasing industrialization by establishing cooperative societies, recreational organizations, and Christian trade unions. Ketteler's brand of Social Catholicism became a prominent part of the program of the Center Party, and his trade union movement remained active until it was abolished by the Nazis in 1933.

In the ranks of the Evangelical Church, there were social reformers as dedicated as Ketteler: J. H. Wichern, the founder of the Inner Mission, and Adolf Stoecker and Friedrich Naumann, who were concerned by the growth of irreligion among the proletariat, were anxious to promote Church programs of social welfare. But these reformers found less support in the Church hierarchy than their Catholic colleagues did; and, as the government's concern over the growth of Social Democracy grew, so did the Church leadership's opposition to Christian social programs. In 1895, the Supreme Church Council sternly reprobated what it called "attempts to turn the Evangelical Church into an active agent in the political and social disputes of the day." This, it added, could only "divert the Church from the goal set for it by its Maker: namely, the creation of blessedness for the soul."

Stubborn reformers continued to argue, as Friedrich Naumann did in the pages of his journal *Die Hilfe*, that both Church and society were menaced by the growing gulf between the classes that the slum conditions caused by industrialization and urbanization and the indifference of the upper classes to the miseries of the poor were creating. But the Protestant leaders seemed to feel that any attempt by their church to correct these things might be regarded as implied criticism of the government and would make them appear as disloyal as the Catholics, whose Center Party did not hesitate to oppose the government on a wide range of issues from finance to armaments and colonial policy. As in Luther's day, the Protestant Church put its faith in princes and enjoined upon its members the doctrine that it was their duty to believe in God and remain true to the demands of their calling and leave politics to their rulers. In 1887, when the Center joined with the Progressive and Socialist parties to vote down a government military appropriations bill, the most respected Evangelical theologian of his day, Albrecht Ritschl, denounced the action as the result of an unholy alliance of Aquinian and Jesuitical principles of natural law and an assault upon the rights of the State, which had received its legitimacy from history. Despite the social insensitivity of the Imperial government and the dangerous irresponsibility of its foreign and military policy, the Protestant churches gave it unflinching support until its collapse in military defeat in 1918.

The coming of the Weimar Republic in 1919 did not diminish the ingrained conservatism of German Protestantism. The clergy, long used to regarding the princes as their titular leaders, found it difficult to accept a regime in which the Socialist and Catholic parties played such a dominant role, and either held to a stubborn monarchism (the Synod of the Prussian Evangelical Church sent an address of thanks to the exiled William II in 1920 for his services to the nation) or gave their support to nationalist, and implicitly antirepublican, movements. The majority of middle class and lower middle class Protestants, critical of the Republic's economic policies and fearful of a Communist revolution, were not disposed to object, even when some of their religious leaders began to interest themselves in the growing National Socialist movement.

The experience of the Catholics was not much different. Although the Church gained in independence as a result of the revolution of 1918, being freed from the disabilities it had formerly suffered from in Protestant states, and, although Catholic trade unionists and the small peasants of southwest Germany were supporters of the Republic, the Catholic industrialists of the Rhineland and Silesia were ambivalent in their attitude from the beginning, and some of the bishops, like Cardinal Faulhaber of Munich, were vocal in their opposition to the new order. The Catholic Center Party, which had been part of the original Weimar Coalition, grew steadily more opportunistic after 1924 and found alliances with the right more congenial than its old partnership with the Social Democrats. In the crucial years from 1930 to 1933, it was conservative Centrists like Monsignor Ludwig Kaas and Franz von Papen who steered the course toward Adolf Hitler and, on March 23, 1933, it was the vote of the Center Party's Reichstag delegation that assured the passage of the Enabling Act that vested dictatorial power in the Nazi leader.

It did not take long before both confessions had reason to regret their feckless political behavior. The Concordat of July 1933 between Hitler and the Vatican, which Kaas, Faulhaber and Cardinal Bertram of Breslau hoped would assure the continued independence in a Nazi State of Catholic schools and other organizations, was won at the price of a denial to the clergy of the right of political activity and was followed by the forced dissolution of the Center Party. Nor did Hitler abide by the terms of the Concordat that he signed. Conflicts between Nazi officials and Catholic school administrators were continual after 1933; State surveillance over the content of Catholic sermons and literature became steadily more oppressive; and arrests of priests who, in the Nazi view, had misused the liberties that the Concordat assured mounted in number in the late thirties.

In the case of Protestantism, the Nazi threat was even more direct, amounting to a blatant attempt to unify the Protestant Churches under a *Reichsbischof* chosen by the Führer in a new Germanic religion that would be purged of the Jewish features of the traditional faith and from which pastors with Jewish racial background or oppositional views would be banned. Momentarily successful in unseating the old leadership of the Protestant Churches in all parts of Germany except Hannover, Bavaria and Württemberg, this German Christian movement soon encountered opposition from a group of concerned pastors led by Martin Niemöller of Berlin-Dahlem, who courageously told Hitler: "You have said that I should leave the care of the German people to you. I am bound to declare that neither you nor any power in the world is in a position to take from us Christians and the Church the responsibility God has laid upon us for his people." This resistance grew significantly when Karl Barth, a Swiss Reformed theologian who had taught at German universities since 1921, and Hans Asmussen, a Lutheran pastor of Altona, called an assembly at Barmen-Gemarke in May 1934 that was attended by 140 representatives of nineteen Lutheran, United, and Reformed state churches. This body issued an appeal to congregations and individual Christians to "try the spirits whether they are of God," denounced the German Christian movement in explicit terms, and announced that "Jesus Christ . . . is the one Word of God, whom we are to hear, whom we are to trust and obey in life and death." The Confessing Church, which emerged from this meeting and subsequent ones, claimed to be the only legitimate German Evangelical Church and—despite constant persecution that led to Barth's expulsion from his chair of theology and the harassment and arrest of hundreds of pastors, especially after the formal repudiation of the German Christian movement from the pulpits in March 1935—it forced Hitler virtually to abandon his attempt to form a Nazified Christian Church.

This victory, and the opposition of the Catholic Church to the government's euthanasia program, which forced its curtailment, and the success of both confessions in preventing their youth movements from being supplanted by the *Hitlerjugend* did not alter the fact that the churches, in Karl Barth's words, remained for a long time "silent on the action against the Jews, on the treatment of political opponents, on the suppression of the freedom of the press in the new Germany, and on so much else against which the Old Testament prophets would certainly have spoken out." It was only slowly and by degrees that they carried their resistance outside of the purely religious sphere. Within the Protestant Church, where the Lutheran doctrine of the "two Kingdoms" had made for a traditional subservience to the State in political matters, the transition was difficult; and in the Catholic Church the argument that the important thing was to maintain the "internal cohesion" of the Church (a legacy from the *Kulturkampf*) was used to discourage political activism.

Even so, a new doctrine of resistance won growing acceptance as the horrors of Nazi persecution and inhumanity became increasingly clear. Even before the dreadful pogroms of November 1938, individual preachers had stopped listening to the warnings of their more cautious brethren and had started to move from a general and parochial form of opposition to a more direct one. Some of them used their pulpits for direct attacks upon the regime and suffered for it with long prison sentences or death—like Martin Niemöller, who was imprisoned in the Sachsenhausen concentration camp from 1938 to 1945, Paul Schneider, who died in Buchenwald, and the provost of the Berlin Hedwigskirche, Bernhard Lichtenberg, who received a two-year sentence in prison for offering public prayers for the Jews, was not released at the end of that time, and died in transit to Dachau. Others, like Dietrich Bonhöffer, who also paid for his activities with his life, embarked on the road of conspiracy, seeking contact with groups of like-minded persons who wished to oppose the government's policies in a more effective way or to overthrow it entirely. In the active resistance to Hitler, it cannot be said that dedicated churchmen and churchwomen of both confessions did not play a worthy part. Even so, when the Third Reich came to its terrible end, there were many Christians who felt guilty because of what they had not done and who silently echoed the words of the ten leaders of the Confessing Church who said, in the Stuttgart Declaration of October 1945, "We accuse ourselves that we did not witness more courageously, pray more faithfully, believe more joyously, love more ardently."

IV

It was the hope of many Protestants after 1945 that, with all of the old ties to the State broken, their church might make a clean break with its past and begin an era of evangelical freedom, in which the congregations were independent, making their own decisions through their own boards of elders or synods, running their own financial affairs, existing without bishops and elaborate bureaucracies. This was Martin Niemöller's desire, when he called after 1945 for a church, not of pastors, as in the past, but of "brotherly organization and brotherly life." And this represented the feelings of many young Catholics also, who dreamed of a church organization that would be closer to that of apostolic times than that of the prewar period.

These desires were not realized. The advantages of a close link with the State seemed too palpable to be rejected: such a connection would provide the financial support needed for rebuilding and would also— since the Occupying Powers would certainly not permit the growth of another authoritarian regime—give the churches more power than earlier to exert a healthy influence on government policy. To assure such influence, both confessions collaborated in the formation of the Christian Democratic Union, which became the majority party in the politics of the Bonn Republic from 1949 to 1968.

While the Catholic and Protestant churches were restored to their old form, there was no return to past habits of deference to authority. Both confessions lived under a heavy burden of guilt for errors of omission or commission during the Nazi period, errors that they were not allowed to forget, since works like Carl Amery's The Capitulation (1963), Rolf Hochhuth's drama The Deputy (1963), and Heinrich Böll's novel The Clown (1964) dwelt on the past obliquities of organized Christianity. They were both aware that, while 95% of their fellow citizens paid the federal church tax, which was obligatory for all but those who were willing to declare themselves to be unbelievers, regular church attendance was practiced by only 50% of the Catholic population and 20% of the Protestant, and that, if they were to improve those figures, particularly among the young, they must avoid any appearance of conformity and political and social conservatism. They were further aware that the very fact that they received tax support made such avoidance a delicate matter, since on issues of social controversy they ran the risk of public criticism if their views seemed too progressive. It was not surprising that many clergymen in both confessions felt that it would be easier for their church to play its proper role in society if the church tax were abolished.

Even so, the Evangelical Church in Germany, as it was now called, showed a commendable independence of spirit. It could claim a good deal of credit in the 1960s for opposing the prevalent line of government foreign policy and calling for a political accommodation with Poland at a time when that question was still taboo, thus influencing the shift to *Ostpolitik* and détente. It was stubborn in its insistence that the political division between the two Germanies not be a barrier to cooperation with Protestant churches in the German Democratic Republic, and through such cooperation it strove to discourage tension between the two governments and to find a basis for at least ad hoc arrangements that would bring advantage to the people of the DDR.

In domestic politics, the Evangelical pastorate took independent positions on questions on which public passions ran high. Thus, Helmuth Gollwitzer, who had been Niemöller's successor in the Dahlem Church in 1937 and was later a prisoner of war in Russia, stood on the side of the student left during the university disorders of the 1960s and fought strenuously against excessive government reprisals; and similarly his spiritual successors in the seventies and eighties pleaded for justice for terrorists or took their places in the columns marching in protest against the nuclear waste plant at Gorleben. The fact that their behavior infuriated many of their fellow citizens could not be regarded as a bad thing by anyone with a historical memory, although there was no doubt that, at the congregation level, it was bound to cause cleavages that would not be easy to close. In the climate of the sixties and seventies, the old dispute between Luther and Münzer about the limits of Christian engagement became alive once more.

Nor was the Catholic Church untouched by this dispute. In June 1980, when the *Katholikentag der Jugend* brought 80,000 West Germans to Berlin, 70% of them under thirty, it was noted in the press that a large number of these seemed less interested in devotional questions than in nuclear energy, the constitutional rights of radicals, opposition to military service, youthful unemployment, equality for homosexuals, and other issues that, in the local congregations, were the source of friction between young people and their priests and older co-religionists. In this respect, Hermann Steinkamp, professor of pastoral sociology in Münster, commented that the problem of youth and the Church was too often one of "We (the Church of the older communicants)'re OK; you (the young)'re not—or at least not yet—OK."

Both confessions, moreover, had to deal with doctrinal questions of some delicacy. As in the nineteenth century, theologians were anxious to reduce discrepancies between received doctrine and the results of modern scholarship and science, in the hope of making the truths of Christianity more understandable and acceptable, and at times the Protestant hierarchy felt called upon to reprobate the ways in which they did so. In 1980, after extensive hearings, a board of the Evangelical Church withdrew the right of holding Church office from Pastor Paul Schulz of Hamburg because his interpretation of Christian doctrine was in marked variance, on important points, with the traditions of the Evangelical Church. This decision was not surprising, because Dr. Schulz had declared that "the principle of love" was "the origin, the motivation and the goal of all being" and, in explicating this view, had cast doubt on the active role of God, had declared that Jesus was to be regarded purely as a model of the principle of love in action, had denied the idea of immortality of the soul, had defined the Evangelical Church as a purely social organization and denied the presence of Christ within it, had attributed to the confession of the Church, to which he had pledged himself at the time of his ordination, a merely historical significance, and had, in addition to all this, been frivolous and insolent when questioned during his hearing about these contentions. But in the current atmosphere of permissiveness, which is as pronounced in Western Germany as it is in the United States, an act of discipline always attracts inordinate, if not always intelligent, attention, and the Schulz case led to some criticism of the Protestant churches as being unresponsive to modern needs and realities.

More complicated, and of more potential damage to his Church, was the case of the Catholic theologian Hans Küng, who in December 1979 was deprived by papal action of his rights as a Catholic teacher and theologian on the grounds that his writing departed from "the full truth of the Catholic faith."

A member of the Catholic theological faculty of the Protestant university of Tübingen, Küng was a thorn in the side of the Vatican as early as the 1960s when his first books, which dealt historically with the evolving structure of the Church, were denounced in Rome. The basic cause of this disapproval was Küng's belief that the development of a centralized Church had succeeded in dividing Christendom, a view that he expressed after his dismissal in the words: "The predominant Roman juristicism, centralism and triumphalism in doctrine, morals and Church discipline, particularly after the eleventh century but widespread even earlier, is neither justified by old Catholic tradition nor by the Gospel and was subject to criticism at the Second Vatican Council. Yes, it was the chief cause of the split with the Eastern Church and with the reforming churches."

The Vatican's displeasure grew in 1970 when Küng published his book *Infallible?*, which threatened to reopen the Döllinger dispute by analyzing the origin and the meaning of the doctrine of papal infallibility. Although the Curia had abolished the old Index of forbidden books in 1965, the Congregation of Faith (which had in the same year replaced the old Holy Office) placed Küng's book on what amounted to a secret index; and he was ordered not to circulate it further or to have it translated before he had appeared before a colloquium in Rome. Küng refused to appear unless the charges against his book and the names of the officials who would press them were made known and unless he had the right of choosing his own defender, and the matter was dropped, after strenuous representations by the Tübingen theological faculty and the energetic intervention in Rome of the chairman of the German Bishops Conference, Cardinal Döpfner of Munich.

Subsequently, the publication of Küng's widely read *To Be a Christian* brought him into conflict with Döpfner's successor, Cardinal Höffner of Cologne, principally on matters of Christology and Mariology; and, in 1977, without a formal hearing, the Bishops Conference decided that Küng did not provide his readers with "the whole Christ" or present "his deed of salvation in its wholeness." Two years later, this curious formulation became the basis of Küng's condemnation by Rome, despite an earnest attempt by Bishop Moser of Rottenberg to convince the Congregation of Faith that Küng had no intention of causing a new dispute over infallibility, that on the question of Christology his view was congruent with that of the councils of the ancient Church, which he was attempting to interpret for modern readers, and that there was no precedent for the Congregation's making complicated questions of Christology and Mariology the subject of an inquiry.

The dismissal of Küng from his sacred offices caused a welling up of protests in Germany, particularly since, unlike Pastor Schulz in Hamburg, he had been condemned unheard. It was recalled that in 1963, in an unprecedented criticism of the Holy Office at the Second Vatican Council, Cardinal Frings of Cologne had made the stern demand that henceforth "in this Office no one will any longer be the subject of complaint and condemnation, unless he and his local bishop are heard in advance, unless he knows the charges that have been brought against him, and unless he has been given the opportunity to answer what has been written and said against him." Küng had not been given those rights, a fact that cast a shadow of reaction over the Mother Church while fanning the always latent German opposition to papal authority. The effect of the decision upon the mass of Catholic believers in Germany would be difficult to estimate, but the violence of the immediate reaction indicated that it was not inconsiderable.

For those churchmen who had worked long and hopefully for the principle of ecumenism, the Küng case could not help being discouraging. Roman Catholic interest in a rapprochement between the confessions had in any case appeared to slacken in recent years—there were fewer joint services, and Catholic partners in mixed marriages were often excluded from their local churches—and the dismissal of the leading German Catholic advocate of ecumenical theology seemed to indicate that the hierarchy intended to adopt an increasingly parochial position. This impression received some support in October 1980, when it was announced that Pope John Paul II would visit Germany.

This caused great excitement in the country, as well it might, since no head of the Roman Church had visited Germany in almost 200 years; but the effect of the visit was marred by the maladroitness of the Pope's hosts, the Roman Catholic Bishops Conference. They first neglected to include in the Pope's schedule a special audience for the presidium of the Evangelical Church, an omission that was corrected belatedly and not very graciously, and then made the mistake of approving and distributing a *Little German Church History* that included an essay by a Freiburg theologian upon Martin Luther, which argued that he had divided the Church out of presumption, emotional instability and mistaken theological assumptions, and which intimated that his marriage was sacreligious, lewd and, because it took place during the bloodshed of the Peasants War, callously immoral. This exercise in Counter-Reformation rhetoric was disavowed, after protests from churchmen and laity in both confessions, but it was an unfortunate prelude to the visit of a pope who was already becoming known for the conservatism of his views on doctrinal matters and who, indeed, during his visit to Germany in November, gave no indication that he was very interested in exploring new possibilities of confessional reunion.

The Küng case and the row over the papal visit did at least show that religion was still a vital force in the secularized society of the West. It was no less so in the DDR, where over 8 million Evangelical Christians and about 1 million Roman Catholics lived under an avowedly atheistic regime. During the long period when Walter Ulbricht was Secretary of the SED, every effort was made to break the independence and undermine the faith of these congregations, and official pressure and individual harassment at the local level, often extending to the exclusion of young people who were churchgoers from privileges open to other citizens, and even from the *Abitur* (school-leaving examination) and the right to university study, were not without effect. In 1969, the Eastern congregations dissolved their tie with the Evangelical Church in the Federal Republic and formed their own federation; the number of churchgoers sank to about half; and a party-oriented Pastors' League began to serve as an SED propaganda front.

The nonconformists, however, were numerous, and they were stubborn enough to withstand and eventually to wear down this persecution; and particularly in the seventies, when disenchantment with the regime became pronounced among young people, the resisting congregations began to be attractive to them. This was not lost on the regime, and shortly after Erich Honecker succeeded Ulbricht, the Evangelical Church was informed that henceforth the inner sovereignty of the *Kirchenbund* would be recognized and that "the further development of normal relations between State and Church" would make possible the regulation of other outstanding problems. Shortly thereafter the Pastors' League was dissolved, and the government's State Secretary for Church Questions entered into direct contact with the *Kirchenbund*; in 1976, the SED incorporated into its program a formal guarantee of freedom of religion and belief; and in March 1978 Honecker, in the first meeting of the heads of State and Church in thirty years, met with the Eastern bishops and discussed common problems with them, assuring them that henceforth confessing Christians would enjoy the same respect and rights as other citizens.

The motivation of the government was clear enough. The Church's notable work with the retarded and physically incapacitated had indicated that it was capable of performing important social functions. Its attractiveness to a disillusioned younger generation was an even stronger argument for the kind of relationship between Church and State that would place the latter in a position to defuse a potentially dangerous situation. Finally, it was hoped that the new relationship would improve the DDR's image abroad.

The leaders of the Evangelical Church were realistic enough to see the value that the relationship had for the regime and to use it for religious ends. They were able to persuade the government to end its ban on church-building, to allow the Church greater use of radio facilities, and to grant technical assistance for annual conferences—all concessions of importance to an organization that had in the past found it difficult to maintain contact between its congregations. Nor did it hesitate to make its opinion known on more political matters. Even in the Ulbricht years, it was able to persuade the government that conscientious objectors to military service should not be put in prison but rather assigned to productive work in construction or other State services; and in the wake of the unprecedented meeting with Honecker, Evangelical pastors did not hesitate to raise their voices in a common declaration from the pulpit to protest against the government's declared intention of introducing military training into school curricula for students aged fifteen and sixteen and to announce that they would give whatever support they could to any parents whose consciences led them to oppose this policy.

This *Kanzelerklärung* was not effective in deterring the government; indeed, it was made only after private remonstrances had been rejected. But the Church's action showed confidence and a determination not to refrain from criticism out of fear of jeopardizing the new relationship with the government. Given the political circumstances, this can be taken as one more indication of the vitality of religion in contemporary Germany.

5

Money

In Goethe's *Faust II*, that remarkable work that the German literary critic Hans Mayer has called an "electrocardiogram of the German character," Mephistopheles, bent upon showing the protagonist all the pleasures of this world in the hope of finding one that will please him so intensely that he will give his soul in return for its prolongation, takes him to the court of the Emperor. Their visit comes at a time of financial embarrassment for the ruler; his treasury is empty, his victualers are threatening to cut off supplies, and his mercenary troops are restive because their pay is in arrears. Always eager to demonstrate his fertility in expedients, Mephistopheles tells the Emperor that he is rich beyond his knowledge, for the earth belongs to him, and it is filled with hidden treasures and deposits that can serve as the collateral for an issue of paper money. The Emperor is hard to persuade, but his Treasurer is more responsive and, after some sleight of hand, he and the Steward are able to report to the bewildered monarch:

> Remember, Sire, yourself it was last night
> That signed the note. You stood as mighty Pan,
> The Chancellor came and spoke in words that ran,
> "A lofty festal joy do for thyself attain:
> Thy people's weal—a few strokes of the pen!"
> These did you make, then thousand-fold last night
> Conjurors multiplied what you did write;
> And that straightway the good might come to all,
> We stamped at once the series, large and small,
> Tens, twenties, thirties, hundreds, all are there.
> You cannot think how glad the people were.
> Behold your city, once half-dead, decaying,
> Now full of life and joy, and swarming, playing!
>
> . . . .
>
> Like lightning notes were scattered on the run.
> The changers' shops are wide to everyone,
> And there all notes are honored, high and low,
> With gold and silver—at a discount though.
> From there to butcher, baker, tavern hasting,

One half the world seems thinking but of feasting,
The other in new raiment struts and crows;
The draper cuts the cloth, the tailor sews.
In cellars "Long live the Emperor!" is the toasting;
There platters clatter, there they're baking, roasting.

Reading this, one is tempted to credit the poet with pre-vision, for the manipulation that he described was to take place on a grand scale on more than one occasion in the history of his own country. When it did so, the results were no happier than he hints they eventually were (note the words "at a discount though") in Mephistopheles's experiment in currency flotation, and they left fateful traces in the German psyche. There is good reason, therefore, for us to consider the role of money in Germany's recent history.

I

The lust for gold seems to have been one of the primal instincts of the human race, for the struggle to acquire precious metals is portrayed in its earliest legends as the center of human endeavor, and the most primitive tribes seem, from the records we have of their lives, to have delighted in their possession. For centuries, gold was desired not for use but for show; and just as hoard-building was characteristic of the tribal chiefs of remote antiquity, so was the possession by rulers of the early modern period of treasure chambers filled with gold and silver plate, embossed goblets and richly decorated armor and weaponry, a custom that continued in some countries—one thinks of the marvelous Green Vault in Dresden—until the seventeenth and eighteenth centuries.

Long before that, however, the interest of Europeans had shifted from the piling up of objects made from precious metals to the accumulation of gold and silver in forms that could serve as the equivalent of objects and be used for payment of services or for exchange. In the high middle ages, this was reprobated and described as a sin to which priests and Jews were particularly prone, but it is clear that it was common to all classes. In the early fourteenth century, Dante castigated the nobility and the burgher class of Florence for being "all too intent upon the acquisition of money," and the Blessed Giovanni Domenici, fourteenth century Dominican reformer and popular preacher, said that "the accursed hunger after money" had affected rich and poor, clerisy and laity, noble and commoner and that it led "these infatuated fools to every kind of evil."

The economic historian Werner Sombart once pointed out that for centuries the desire for money had no direct connection with the prevailing economic organization of society, which continued to be based on the principle of production for subsistence rather than profit. Persons who desired to accumulate wealth did so outside of the productive and commercial activity of their time and used the moneys they acquired for other than economic purposes. The usual methods of seeking wealth were force (raids by robber barons like Götz von Berlichingen and the Quitzows or more elaborate military forays against wealthy neighbors), magic (treasure-hunting and alchemy), the invention of projects, or get-rich-quick schemes to extract money from the gullible, gambling, and the lending of money at a profit. The germs of a capitalistic money economy were to be detected in some of these practices, although they were generally too limited in scope and organization and motivated too exclusively by the desire to acquire money that could be spent immediately in ostentatious living and extravagant pleasure to be capitalistic in spirit. The transition to a genuinely capitalist economy came only when there was a coincidence between the desire for money and the entrepreneurial spirit, embodied in a new class of men, whom a French historian has called *les bourgeois conquérants*, who combined vision with a talent for organization, whose projects were practical and backed by a determination to succeed and the kinds of negotiating skill and attention to detail that would assure success, whose personal desires were modest and restrained by their sense of thrift and moderation, and who were, in fact, inspired by a new ethos that was summed up in the response of Germany's first great merchant-banker, Jakob Fugger, to a relative who urged him to give up business in his old age and enjoy the wealth he had accumulated with such effort. Fugger replied that he had no intention of doing so, that he wished to make a profit as long as he could.

In Germany, this transition came later than in other countries, and it was indeed, until very late, intermittent. In the late middle ages, the merchants of the Hansa, a federation of harbor towns, played a leading role in the trade of northern and eastern Europe and had great influence on both its productive trades and its public finance. By the fifteenth century, however, the Hanseatic League was in decline, and the center of German economic activity moved to the south, where the capitalist spirit found an embodiment in the commercial and financial activities of the Welser and Fugger families of Augsburg, who based the organization of their financial systems upon techniques that the great Italian banking houses had elaborated since the thirteenth century. Under Jakob Fugger the Rich (1459–1525), the Fuggers, who had started modestly as merchants of fustian cloth, not only began to concentrate on mining and the trade in ore, but became the principle bankers of Emperor Maximilian I and his successor Charles V, while at the same time supplanting the Italian bankers in the handling of papal finances, acting as the intermediary for most of the moneys that the Holy See received from Germany, Poland and Hungary.

These activities have led a contemporary German dramatist, Dieter Forte, in a play called *Martin Luther and Thomas Münzer, or The Introduction of Bookkeeping* (1971), to portray Jakob Fugger as the most important single figure in the German Reformation, whose manipulations had more to do with determining the course of history than the religious issues. Forte shows Fugger talking with Duke Frederick of Saxony, Luther's protector, about the importance of a new ethic of work.

Do you know that we have over a hundred church holidays a year? Over a hundred, my dear prince. Church masses, pilgrimages, I don't know what. The people eat and drink themselves full and don't give a thought to work. . . . And then these fast days! I'm always having to petition for new exceptions for my workers. A worker should work and not fast! This has finally got to be regulated. Daily work should be sanctified. People should thank God that they can work at all. They can receive their reward in heaven. Then they won't need so much on earth, and we shall finally have cheaper labor costs. So much for your Luther.

This is certainly an exaggeration, and it is to be doubted whether the capitalist spirit was as widely spread in Germany as the far-flung enterprises of the Fuggers might seem to indicate. Most of the publicists of the age from Luther and Erasmus to Hutten and Sebastian Franck were bitterly opposed to *Fuggerei*, and their views were more representative of public attitudes than those of the Augsburg bankers. In any case, these sixteenth century manifestations of the capitalist spirit were shortlived, for the prevailing conditions in Germany for the next two centuries were hardly conducive to the expansion of business activity, and, as we have seen, the Thirty Years War not only cut Germany off from the outside world and destroyed the most thriving commercial centers in the nation but created political conditions within the German states that militated against the rise of a vigorous bourgeois class. It was not until the eighteenth century that industrial and commercial activity began to revive, and even then its development was impeded by the interstate conflict that was almost continuous from 1740 to 1763 and was all but destroyed by the revolutionary and Napoleonic wars that extended from the early 1790s until 1815.

As a result of all this, Germany's economic development was significantly retarded, and there was no broad-based advance until the middle of the nineteenth century. The economic world described in Schiller's poem "The Song of the Bell" was still a precapitalist one of small trades and guilds, and the commercial firm T. O. Schröter in Gustav Freytag's novel *Debit and Credit* was limited in its operation by its narrow financial base. It was only in the 1850s that the first signs of large-scale capitalist enterprise became evident, and only after the German states were united in 1871 that economic development was continuous and expanding.

The role of capital—that is, of money—in this process was crucial. In the evolution of the first major industrial enterprises in the fifties and sixties, banks played a strategically significant role, and after 1871 industrial development, commercial expansion, and banking activity went hand in hand. The first great joint-stock banks were established in the seventies—the Deutsche Bank and the Diskonto Gesellschaft in 1870, the Dresdner Bank in 1872—organizations that appealed to large numbers of shareholders by virtue of the newly recognized principle of limited liability and were thus able to supply credit, in excess of the deposits of gold and silver that were held in reserve, to the large-scale enterprises that needed it for their activities, which involved the gradual absorption, in one form or another, of the business of the nation. It was with respect to this process that Werner Sombart wrote: "The traffic in credit in modern banks [was] at once the regulator and the measure of economic life. In the offices of the great banking houses, decisions were made not only with respect to war and peace, and the friendship or enmity of great empires, but decisions that, in the last analysis, determined both the fate of the small tradesman on the Polish frontier and the continued existence of the mightiest iron foundry."

II

In the new integrated capitalistic society, money possessed a power and a seductive attractiveness that it had not possessed for the masses of society during most of human history. It thus assumed palpably magical qualities.

The most accessible of nineteenth century philosophers and the most congenial to the cultivated German middle class once explained why this should be so. "That people's wishes are principally focused on money," Arthur Schopenhauer wrote, "is often used against them as a reproach. Yet it is natural, indeed unavoidable, to love that which, as an indefatigable Proteus, is ready at any moment to transform itself into the current object of our so changeable and multifarious desires. In point of fact, any other property can satisfy only one desire or one need . . . and such properties are, therefore, only relatively good. Money alone is the absolute property, because it satisfies not merely one need *in concreto*, but need as such *in abstracto*."

More critically, Karl Marx wrote in 1844 that money was more than a mere means of satisfying desires; it was a talisman that had the property of transforming the capabilities of the persons who possessed it, as well as their relations with others. In a natural world, a world of truly human relationships, wrote the future founder of the Communist movement, love could be exchanged only for love and trust bought only by trust; the enjoyment of art would require a capacity to understand it; and influence over others would be the result of force and attractiveness. All interpersonal relationships and all relationships between persons and the external world would be determined by qualities of character and will. But in the world of capitalism, these qualities were no longer necessary and, indeed, became increasingly irrelevant, for their functions could be performed just as well by that magic substance for which all humankind yearned. Money had the property of buying everything and appropriating all objects and qualities. It was omnipotent and could be used to mediate between people and their desires, bringing the latter into the possession of the former and vesting in the former the qualities that, in a natural world, they would have needed to achieve their desires. It was the universal "galvano-chemical power of society."

Money, Marx wrote in this remarkable passage, is the pimp between man's need and the object. "That for which I can pay . . . that am I. The extent of the power of money is the extent of my power. . . . I am ugly, but I can buy for myself the most beautiful of women. Therefore, I am not ugly, for the effect of ugliness—its deterrent power—is nullified by money. I, in my character as an individual, am lame, but money furnishes me with twenty-four feet. Therefore, I am not lame. I am bad, dishonest, unscrupulous, stupid; but money is honored, and therefore so is its possessor. Money is the supreme good, therefore its possessor is good. Money, besides, saves me the trouble of being dishonest; I am therefore presumed to be honest. I am stupid, but money is the real mind of all things and how then should its possessor be stupid? Besides, he can buy talented people for himself, and is not he who has power over the talented more talented than the talented? . . . Does not my money therefore transform all my incapacities into their contrary?"

In this tirade—for that is what it was, the first of many attacks upon a society that, through money, could transform values into commodities—there was a profound political truth. It could perhaps be said that, because Germany was not unified by a successful middle class revolution but by the old feudal classes through the agency of the Prussian army and Bismarck's diplomacy, and because, in addition, the middle class did not receive the political power and responsibility that it attained in England and France, money did not talk quite as loudly as it did in those countries. Even so, the triumphs of German industry in the last quarter of the nineteenth century—the first of those German economic miracles that impressed the Western World—did tend to create gigantic private fortunes, and there is no doubt that the attribution process that Marx described did take place and that possession of great wealth was taken to be equivalent to the possession of every kind of admirable quality. Great industrialists, in particular, were accorded an immoderate degree of admiration and, in some ways, became the culture heroes of their day.

Three cases can be cited to illustrate this, the first that of the so-called Cannon King Alfred Krupp. The descendant of a family that had been prominent in Essen since the sixteenth century, and the son of a father who had frittered away the family reputation and fortune in a premature attempt to produce cast steel in competition with British industry, Alfred Krupp took over the family firm in 1826. After a modest beginning, in which he shored up the family fortunes by making a machine for the mass production of tableware and manufacturing cast steel mills for the rolling of gold, the coming of the railway age offered him opportunities to which he responded with energy and imagination. His smelters turned out the cast steel from which railway equipment was made in firms all over Germany, and the Krupp firm was the first to produce seamless wheels that would not crack under high speeds. In the late forties and fifties, production for the railways was the backbone of the business, and it was supplemented when the firm began to make navigational equipment as well, in the form of axles and screw propellers for river and oceangoing steamships.

The real turning point in Krupp's fortunes, and the beginning of his international reputation, came in 1851, when at the Crystal Palace Exhibition in London the attention of thousands of visitors was captured by a display in which the principal item was a six-pound field gun whose barrel, instead of being made of the usual bronze, was made of cast steel. The exhibit won a gold medal for Krupp, for it was his gun. More important, it brought him customers, and he was soon selling guns to Egypt, Russia, Holland, Great Britain, Switzerland, Spain and Austria. He had more difficulty in his own country, where he had been trying to interest the Ordnance Department of the Prussian army in his gun barrels since 1843. It was not until 1859, as a result of the intervention of Prince William (the later King-Emperor William I) that Krupp received his first Prussian order, for 300 cast steel rifled barrels for field guns. Because the ordnance experts refused to accept Krupp's advice that his tubes would work most effectively with breach mechanisms of his own design and casting, five of the 160 cast steel guns used in the war against Austria in 1866 exploded in the field. After that, the Prussians saw the light and relied upon Krupp's judgment, and he in turn became the armorer of the German Empire.

By 1887, when Alfred Krupp died, he had become the greatest industrialist on the European continent. His firm had a working force of 20,000 men, was delivering a yearly total of 23,000 guns all over the world from Switzerland to China and from Japan to Montenegro, and was turning out daily a total of 1000 shells, 500 steel wheels, axles and springs, and almost 200,000 rails. This impressive productive capacity was to be expanded by his successors, for Alfred Krupp was the founder of a dynasty that survived not only the collapse of the Empire but that of the Third Reich, for which it had provided weaponry with the same zeal that had been the distinguishing characteristic of the Cannon King himself.

If, in a nationalist age, Krupp was considered to be a heroic figure and a pillar of the Empire, Hugo Stinnes, whose career reached its height in the first years of the Weimar Republic, enjoyed popular esteem because he appeared to possess qualities of vision and will that the Republican leaders lacked. Stinnes did not look like a hero. The writer and diplomat Harold Nicolson, who saw him shaking his fist under the noses of the French delegation at the Spa Conference of 1920 on disarmament and reparations, wrote that he had "the appearance of Ahasuerus [the Wandering Jew] dressed as a gamekeeper." But there was no doubt about his energy and ruthlessness as an entrepreneur, and before his death he had built an industrial empire that dwarfed that of Alfred Krupp.

Stinnes started modestly enough in 1893, when he took over a family enterprise that had specialized in the coal trade and domestic shipping, but from the beginning he showed a determination to branch out and a willingness to take risks, and the latter quality in particular had, within ten years, brought him control of the German-Luxemburg Mining Company and the Rhine-Westphalia Electric Company, the leading power supplier in the Ruhr. In the postwar years, taking advantage of the depreciated currency and the hard money made available to him by his foreign holdings, he swiftly built up an industrial complex which at its height included 1535 legally independent concerns with 2888 branches, extending from mines, the coal trade and ocean and domestic shipping to the production of paper and cellulose, steel and energy, printing and publishing, banking and insurance. The ingredients of his success were his eye for the main chance, his early recognition of the possibility of vertical concentration of undertakings and of the significance of diversification, and his unflagging energy; and the secret of his popularity lay in the fact that the success of his enterprises seemed a blow in the face of the Allies who, it was widely believed, were seeking to keep Germany in an impoverished condition. There seemed to be no limit to his genius for accumulating wealth; and when he died the Munich satirical journal *Simplicissimus* showed a picture of St. Peter ringing a bell at heaven's gate to summon the angels and saying: "Stinnes is coming! Wake up, children, or in a fortnight he'll own the whole works!"

A more remarkable case than that of Stinnes, and one that showed the power that money had to transform failure into success and to confute the reason of wise men, was that of Friedrich Flick. Born in 1883, the son of a Rhenish farmer who supplied pit props for mines, Flick grew up with the idea of a career in coal and steel firmly fixed in his mind and methodically went about the job of preparing himself for it in the *Realgymnasium* (secondary school) in Siegen, in a three-year apprenticeship as a bookkeeper in a foundry in Weidenau, and in the University of Cologne, where he took the Diploma in Commerce. This secured him the position of confidential clerk in the Bremer Foundry, a position that he held for five years before being invited to join the directorate of the Minden and Schwarte AG, one of the largest iron works in the Siegerland. The twenty-nine-year-old director took advantage of this improvement in his position to marry, choosing the daughter of a textile manufacturer in Siegen who brought with her a dowry of 30,000 RM. Because he was employed in an industry vital to the war effort, he escaped service in the trenches during the war of 1914–1918, and that conflict brought him opportunities for high profits and the purchase and reorganization of plants less efficient than his own, opportunities that Flick, who possessed a genius for speculation, did not neglect. In 1915, he had moved to the Charlottenhütte GmbH in Niederschilden, a firm with 2000 workers that controlled mines, smelting furnaces and rolling mills. By the end of the war, he had doubled its size.

Like Stinnes, Flick profited from the postwar inflation and invested heavily in new mills and mines; and by 1926 he had merged his various holdings in a trust called Vereinigte Stahlwerke. This was almost forced into bankruptcy during the Great Depression but was saved by the intervention of the Heinrich Brüning government, which bought up shares in Flick's Gelsenkirchen mines at three times their stock exchange price. This experience convinced Flick of the importance of being on good terms with those in political power, no matter who they might be, and in consequence he not only supported the policies of the Nazi regime after 1933 but profited from its Aryanization program by acquiring control of the formerly Jewish firm Hochofenwerke Lübeck AG. This collaboration led to his trial at Nuremberg for war crimes and a sentence of seven years (five of which he served) in prison.

The Nazi defeat also destroyed his industrial empire, for three quarters of his holdings were in East Germany, and these were confiscated by the new Communist regime, and the American occupation authorities in the west seemed determined to force the deconcentration of his other holdings. Determined to rebuild, Flick was nevertheless canny enough to follow the advice of his Wall Street lawyers and, rather than fight deconcentration proceedings, to sell his properties and take the proceeds, which were tax free since the sale was forced, and reinvest them in other enterprises. Just at the time when the new German economic miracle was gathering force and when money was in short supply and interest rates high, Flick sold his coal-mining properties to a French syndicate for $26 million plus 19 million in blocked funds that could be invested only in French companies. He then began secretly to buy up shares in the Daimler-Benz company, acquiring 37.5% of the firm's stock for $20 million and making profits that eventually reached 3000% over par. With his other funds, he purchased shares in steel companies in France and Belgium and acquired the Feldmühle paper works, Dynamit-Nobel, and the Krauss-Maffei tank and military equipment plant, while retaining ownership in four German steel plants and shares in 227 enterprises that had been part of his pre-1945 empire. This was a comeback in the grand style, and, when Flick died in 1972 at the age of eighty-nine, he was described as the richest man in Germany and perhaps in Europe.

In looking at the careers of these three industrial giants, one is hard put to discover any trace of nobility or generosity of spirit. It has been said of Krupp that he never spent a penny on the arts or the sciences or the poor or the community, and this was no less true of Stinnes and Flick. It would be difficult to detect in any one of them true dedication to his country. Krupp gave Prussia no prior claim on his weapons and cheerfully sold his most dangerously efficient ones to powers that might use them against his fellow Germans. Stinnes made a reputation as a patriot by his defiant speeches at Spa about what would happen to the French if they tried to exact reparations by force; but, when the French did precisely that, three years later, by marching into the Ruhr, he not only profited from the ensuing inflation, which he sought to prolong by refusing financial assistance to his hard-pressed government, but also did his best to conclude mutually profitable deals with French concerns. As for Flick, there is no evidence of national concern in any of his undertakings.

These aspects of the careers of the three industrialists were not, of course, generally known, or at least not sufficiently so to diminish the admiration in which thousands of Germans held them. That feeling may be accounted for by the very intensity of their absorption in their work.

Krupp is supposed to have said that work was his prayer, and this was a remark that would have been appropriate in the mouth of Stinnes or Flick. All three could have repeated the litany that booms through the public address system in Heinrich Mann's powerful story *Kobes*, a satire on Stinnes's life: "I have simple thoughts, simple goals. I am nothing special. Politics I don't understand. A busy merchant am I, the symbol of German democracy. No one can fault me. I am Kobes. No gluttony for Kobes. No boozing for Kobes. No dancing for Kobes. No whoring for Kobes. Kobes works twenty hours a day."

This attitude was bound to commend itself to ordinary Germans, who were inclined to the belief, which Luther enunciated but which certainly existed before his time, that God had assigned to every person a calling or *Beruf* and that it was his duty to perform it as well as possible. Whether the obsessiveness and exclusivity with which the Krupps, Stinneses and Flicks applied themselves to the ceaseless pursuit of wealth could be justified by that doctrine, most people did not pause to inquire; their success seemed sufficient answer for any questions and sufficient cause for praising them. In their attitude toward the careers of their wealthiest industrial barons, many Germans were no more critical than Adolf Hitler was in 1930 when he rejected the advice of his radical party comrade and later opponent Otto Strasser that the Nazi social revolution would have to start with the expropriation of the great industrialists. Hitler answered: "Do you think I'd be so crazy as to destroy heavy industry? Those producers worked their way to the top by their own merits and, because of this process of selection, which proves that they are an elite, they have a right to lead."

III

The admiration that the German people had for successful industrialists did not extend in anything like the same measure to pure financiers. Industrialists, after all, dealt—or seemed to the unsophisticated to deal—with tangible objects like steel rails and tons of coal, whereas financiers worked with the primal magic substance itself, money, and hence were regarded as belonging in the same category as sorcerers or *Hexenmeister*. An occasional exception was made. Carl Fürstenberg, the head of the Berliner Handels Gesellschaft in the Bismarck years and during the reign of William II, became an admired and even popular Berlin personality, partly because he steadfastly refused to accept any title or preferment or decoration from the Imperial Court but more, perhaps, because he was a wit after the Berlin fashion, and his *jeux d'esprits* were told and repeated all over town. Much could be forgiven in a man who referred to the deep but disappointing *décolleté* of the finance minister's wife as an "uncovered deficit," who told a man who complained that his beautiful wife was betraying him with two friends that he'd much prefer to have "a 30% share of a good thing than 100% of a bad," who could answer his confidential clerk, who said, "Guess who's just died?", with the words "Today anyone will do," and who, having secured a whole sleeping compartment to himself on a crowded train, and being importuned by an acquaintance who said, "Herr Fürstenberg, your upper berth is free. Let me have it! Money is no object!", answered, "*Na schön*—but let me sleep on it first."

But in general suspicion of financiers was, and had been from earliest times, deep and uncompromising. Even Jakob Fugger had not been free of it. His role in papal finances, and particularly his handling of the indulgences that the Pope had granted to Albrecht of Brandenburg, seemed to many patriotic Germans to be nothing more than a corrupt bargain for profit that by causing large exports of gold from the country constituted a serious strain upon its economic life. And from Fugger's time onward, similar distrust, sometimes rising to deep hatred, was focused on the whole class of court financial advisers and bankers. This was largely true, of course, because, as a result of the long respected Church prohibition of usury, the most efficient and best-established financiers were Jews: Oppenheimer and Wertheimer in Vienna, Liebmann, Gompers, Ephraim, Itzig, Isaak in Berlin, Behrens in Hannover, Lehmann in Halberstadt, Baruch and Oppenheim in Bonn, Seligmann in Munich, Kaulla in Stuttgart, and Rothschild in Frankfurt and Vienna. Germans found it difficult to believe that Jewish bankers could be other than self-serving, and their resentment was not always confined to verbal assaults and social boycott, as the notorious case of Joseph Süss-Oppenheimer showed.

An ambitious young man who had held minor offices at the courts of the Palatinate, Hessen and Electoral Cologne, Süss-Oppenheimer became personal accountant to Prince Karl Alexander of Württemberg in 1732. He must have been extraordinarily diligent in discharging his duties, for when Karl Alexander became Duke of Württemberg a year later, he made him his chief financial adviser and gave him extraordinary powers.

He would have been well advised to use these modestly, for the situation was a delicate one. In a Protestant land, Karl Alexander's Catholicism was not popular, and his penchant for absolutism was not calculated to wear well with subjects who prided themselves on their ancient liberties. But the new financial adviser was not a cautious man, and he not only encouraged the tendencies of his master but supplied him with new ideas. Following mercantilist principles that were of questionable appropriateness in this agricultural land, he introduced State monopolies on salt, leather, wine and tobacco; he founded a bank and a porcelain works in which he had a private interest; and he was reported also to profit from the State lottery and from gambling casinos and coffee houses of ill reputation which, to the indignation of the pious, were allowed to operate without apparent restriction. These things aroused increasing hostility, and the *Finanzrat* (financial adviser), now generally known as Jud Süss, was made responsible for actions that might have been more appropriately placed at the door of his master, who by all accounts was a profligate and demanding man. On the very day that Karl Alexander died, in 1738, Süss-Oppenheimer was arrested, convicted swiftly of high treason in a trial that was filled with irregularities and presided over by judges who were his personal enemies, and hanged.

There were, at least until Nazi times (when the story was made the subject of a viciously anti-Semitic film by Veit Harlan), no other cases like that of Süss-Oppenheimer. But the combination of Jewishness and banking continue to cause unfavorable reactions, and even the powerful Bismarck was unable to protect his chief financial adviser from them. In 1858, when Otto von Bismarck received his appointment as ambassador to St. Petersburg, he asked his friend Baron Mayer Carl Rothschild of the powerful international banking dynasty to recommend a reliable banker in Berlin, specifying, according to legend, that he should be Jewish. Rothschild recommended Gerson Bleichröder, whose father had been the Rothschilds' Berlin agent in the 1830s and who had maintained that connection while becoming a highly successful banker in his own right, with customers in the highest ranks of society.

Bleichröder handled Bismarck's private financial affairs for the rest of his life and, in addition, provided him with information about the economic and fiscal conditions of other countries that Bismarck found invaluable after he assumed control over the foreign affairs of Prussia and, after 1871, of Germany. It is clear from Fritz Stern's splendid study of the relationship of the two men that Bleichröder's influence was a restricted one. The Chancellor made use of his assessments and listened to his advice. But he did not always accept the latter, as was shown in 1887 when he used financial pressures to restrain Russian adventurism in the Balkans, a course that Bleichröder deplored. Even so, although there was not a scintilla of evidence to support them, many of Bismarck's countrymen believed, or pretended to believe, that he was a mere tool in Bleichröder's hands. In 1877, the right-wing publicist Rudolf Meyer wrote that the Chancellor permitted his "*Hausfreund*" Bleichröder, a man who was known to be guilty of "scandalous greed and dirty business practices," to corrupt the upper classes of society and make them "an easy prey for Social Democracy."

Parenthetically, it may be noted that Bleichröder was not the last prominent banker to be accused, on inadequate evidence, of possessing unwarranted political power and manipulating it for his own sinister purposes. During the last years of the Weimar Republic, this reputation attached itself to Jakob Goldschmidt, the witty, highly cultivated and enormously able chairman of the Darmstädter Bank, who was a friend of both Heinrich Brüning, Reich Chancellor from 1930 to 1932, and General Kurt von Schleicher, who helped bring both Brüning and his successor Papen down but was less successful in his efforts to outmaneuver Adolf Hitler. It was easy, on the basis of his associations, to believe that Goldschmidt was the real wire-puller in the complicated politics of the last phase of the Weimar Republic, just as it was easy to believe that Hermann J. Abs, the chief executive of the Deutsche Bank in the 1960s and the member of twenty-six other boards of directors (eighteen of which he chaired), was the *éminence grise* behind the government of Konrad Adenauer, who was known to consult him. And as in the case of Bleichröder, there was no dearth, either on the extreme right or the extreme left, of people eager to accuse Goldschmidt and Abs and others like them of contributing to the corruption of society.

That the source of corruption lay not in the supposed manipulators but in money itself was clear to more consequential thinkers. In 1843, in a review of a study on "the Jewish Question" by Bruno Bauer, Karl Marx wrote: "Let us consider the real Jew: not the *sabbath* Jew, whom Bauer considers, but the *everyday* Jew. . . . What is the profane basis of Judaism? *Practical* need, *self*-interest. What is the worldly cult of the Jew? *Huckstering*. What is his worldly god? *Money*. Very well: in emancipating itself from *huckstering* and *money*, and thus from real and practical Judaism, our age would emancipate itself." This passage has often been cited as an example of Jewish self-hate, but it is clear that Marx's animus was directed less against his own people than against the activity to which history had assigned them and against the permeation of society by the acquisitive instinct. In his later works, the emphasis on the Jews fell away, and Marx focused his criticism upon the social system itself, which in his eyes had been fatally compromised by the universal striving after wealth. "Modern society," he wrote in *Capital*, "which soon after its birth pulled Plutus by the hair of his head from the bowels of the earth, greets gold as its Holy Grail, as the glittering incarnation of its very principle of life." The only road to liberation, to freedom from the inequalities and injustices and brutalities that this false system of values had caused, lay in the destruction of society in its present form, in the abolition of capitalism as a result of a successful proletarian revolution, and in the ushering in of the Socialist millennium.

No less unconditional in his view was Marx's contemporary Richard Wagner. This may seem surprising, for his early operas were faithful representations of the preoccupations and aspirations of the preeminently capitalistic class, the bourgeosie. As the distinguished German literary scholar Hans Mayer has pointed out, *The Flying Dutchman* (1843) was filled with the regressive utopianism and the optimistic revolutionary hope of the German middle class in the years from 1830 to 1848; *Tannhäuser* (1845), despite its legendary setting, was a *Künstlerdrama* with a theme that was recurrent in middle-class literature, the conflict between genius and the practical world of affairs in which it must live; and *Die Meistersinger von Nürnberg* (1868) both recalled the days of a proud and self-reliant burgher class, of which the Nuremberg of Hans Sachs and the master-singers was the symbol, and expressed the current political hopes of the German bourgeoisie on the eve of German unification, aspirations that Wagner had himself expressed in his writings and fought for during the revolution in Saxony in 1848.

But even in *Lohengrin* (1850), there were hints that Wagner was becoming impatient with the failure of the middle class to recognize the legitimate claims of the artist: the tragedy of Lohengrin is that, if he remains true to himself, he cannot expect to find either comprehension or sympathy in bourgeois society; he cannot at one and the same time be a Knight of the Grail, a husband, and a politician, and when he recognizes this he leaves Elsa of Brabant and her world to return to the realm of the spirit. In the years that followed the composition of *Lohengrin*, as the unification of Germany brought growing materialism, Wagner's criticism deepened. As Thomas Mann once wrote, he inclined increasingly to the view that the state of the arts was the best criterion for judging bourgeois values, and what he saw around him was the degradation of art to a mere instrument of enjoyment. He saw earnestness and dedication shouldered aside by frivolity and routine, and he saw unbelievable amounts of money squandered, not to promote the true purpose of art, but to produce cheap effects. When he found that no one was as affected by this spectacle as he was himself, when he encountered a yawning indifference to his complaints, he concluded that the political and social conditions that permitted this sort of thing called for revolutionary transformation.

This was the message of *The Ring of the Nibelungen*, a musical drama based on the sagas of the Volsungs but speaking to Wagner's own age and condemning its social and cultural values. In the composer's view, Alberich's curse in *The Rhine Gold*, after the golden ring that he stole is stolen from him, had fulfilled itself as fully in the real world as it did in the opera.

Wie durch Fluch er mir geriet,	As it came to me with a curse,
verflucht sei dieser Ring!	Let this ring be accursed!
Gab sein Gold	As its gold gave me
mir Macht ohne Mass,	Power without limit,
nun zeug' sein Zauber	Let its spell now
Tod dem, der ihn trägt!	Bring death to its bearer!
Kein Froher soll	Let no happy man
seiner sich freun,	Delight in it,
keinem Glücklichen lache	Let no fortunate soul
sein lichter Glanz!	Enjoy its shining gleam!
Wer ihn besitzt,	Let whoever possesses it
den sehre die Sorge,	Be consumed with care,
und wer ihn nicht hat,	And whoever does not
den nage der Neid!	Be gnawed by envy!
Jeder giere	Let every man lust
nach seinem Gut,	After its delights,
doch keiner geniesse	But let no one find
mit Nutzen sein!	Any profit in it!
Ohne Wucher hüt' ihn sein Herr;	Let its possessor hoard it without pleasure,
doch den Würger zieh' er ihm zu!	But let it bring the murderer upon him!
Dem Tode verfallen,	Doom-stricken,

fessle den Feigen die Furcht:	Let him cringe with fear:
so lang er lebt,	As long as he lives,
sterb er lechzend dahin,	Let him long for death,
des Ringes Herr	The Ring's Lord
als des Ringes Knecht . . .	As the Ring's slave . . .

The Ring of the Nibelungen was a bourgeois parable that found its climax in Siegfried's funeral march in *The Twilight of the Gods*, a lament for lost virtue and misguided valor. Whether anything could be saved from the universal degeneration of values Wagner did not make very clear. The ending of the drama was ambiguous. That the composer had the utopian hope of a world redeemed by art and based on justice and brotherhood and love was, however, apparent, and so was his belief that, in order to make that possible, the ring must return to the Rhine, that is, gold must cease to be a function and revert to its natural form. In this, Wagner reminds us of another poet who was alienated from the world of bourgeois values, Rainer Maria Rilke, who once wrote: "The ore is homesick. And it wants to forsake the coins and the wheels that teach it a petty way of living. And out of the factories and out of the money chests, it will return into the veins of the gaping holes that will clamp shut behind it."

IV

It didn't, of course, do any such thing. Instead, it continued to be the motivator of Germany's economic life and to exercise its usual influence upon its politics, the social attitudes of its people, and the condition of its arts and sciences. Its power, moreover, to affect the thinking of both the simple and the sophisticated remained undiminished and sometimes took dramatic forms, as three incidents from Germany's modern history illustrate.

In 1871, as the price of military defeat, the French government ceded to Germany the provinces of Alsace and Lorraine, with their highly developed textile industry and their rich deposits of iron ore and potash, and in addition agreed to pay a war indemnity of 5 billion francs plus interest. Bismarck hoped that this liability would weigh heavily upon the French for years and would prevent their military recovery, but he was disagreeably surprised when the government in Paris discharged the debt by May 1873, and he was probably even more disconcerted by the results that flowed from this unwelcome punctuality. Of the sums that were received from France, the German Imperial Government retained less than half, paying the rest out to the separate states. But both the federal and the state governments proceeded to spend the windfall, the former on making good the depletion of military equipment as a result of the recent fighting and on an expansion of the forces to meet new needs, the latter on the liquidation of war loans and the payment of pensions, on local building programs, and on the construction of highways and railroads. One way or another, the greater part of the French indemnity ended up, in the form of pension payments, salaries and business contracts, in the pockets of German citizens. Since a government currency reform was simultaneously adding 762 million marks to the amount of free capital in circulation, the result was a significant overheating of the economy.

What followed was the greatest speculative boom that Germany had ever known, triggered by the fateful combination of large amounts of unemployed money and a liberalization of laws governing the establishment of joint-stock companies that greatly expanded the opportunities for investment. Rumors of fortunes being made in railways, in the building trades, and in new industrial undertakings brought floods of people from all walks of life into the offices of company promoters with their life savings in their hands, and for a time their wildest expectations were realized, and they were able to live riotously and spend lavishly in the belief that there was no end to the easy money that was rolling in. But this, all too soon, proved to be fool's gold. In May 1873, as a result of speeches in the Reichstag about unscrupulous operators preying on the small investor, shares in the railroad enterprises of Bethel Strousberg, which had been the principal dynamo in the bull market, fell precipitously, and the boom dissolved, involving dozens of reputable companies and hundreds of marginal ones in the collapse, and wiping out thousands of gullible people who learned the hard lesson that paper profits are evanescent but paper losses real unless covered.

From this debacle, the economy recovered in time, but its psychological effects were more persistent. As in all such setbacks, there were demands for an investigation to determine the culprits, and as in most of such cases public opinion found them without waiting for a systematic inquiry. The crash of 1873 was blamed in the first instance upon the National Liberal Party, which as the strongest party in the *Reichstag* had been responsible for passing the new currency reform and the liberalized banking and corporation laws and which, as one newspaper said ominously, was altogether too conciliatory to the financial community, perhaps because several prominent party leaders had relatives who were bankers. These charges seriously weakened both the reputation of the National Liberal Party and its self-confidence, an ominous development that made it vulnerable to Bismarck's attacks at the end of the decade and led to the definitive defeat of German liberalism and the reorientation of German policy in a conservative antimodern direction.

The more fateful significance of the crash was that it caused the revival of virulent anti-Semitism in Germany. Many of the National Liberal leaders were Jews, and prominent banking houses like Bleichröder and Oppenheimer had participated in the boom and in efforts to contain the bust. It was the former activity that was remembered, particularly by people who had lost money as a result of their own cupidity and heedlessness; and it was these people and the conservative press that spread the persistent notion that the stock market crash of 1873 had been a Jewish manipulation.

An even more dramatic example of the power of manipulated money to leave a poisonous residue in the minds of its victims came in the ruinous inflation of 1923. As in the 1873 case, this gigantic expropriation of the lower middle class had its origins in war, specifically in the financing of Germany's war effort in 1914–1918 by loans rather than by taxes. In August 1914, when the Reichstag not only authorized the Imperial Government to borrow up to 5 billion RM to support the war but also suspended the legal restrictions upon the circulation of notes not covered by gold reserves, it created precisely the situation described in *Faust II*.

> Arrears are paid as they were due,
> And all the army's pledged anew;
> The soldier feels his blood made over.
> Landlords and wenches are in clover.

The printing press became the principal means of meeting the needs of government, army and business for the duration of the war, but the practice quintupled the amount of money in circulation, and by 1918 the Reichsmark had declined to about one half of its prewar parity with gold.

The imposition of a horrendous burden of reparations on the defeated Germany, the fact that the Versailles Treaty deprived it of resources that might have facilitated the payment of these (colonies, merchant marine, rolling stock, mineral deposits), and the disinclination of the Allies to accept payment in labor services or manufactured goods confronted the new Republic with a liability which it did not have the gold reserves to liquidate but which it had to pay off if it were not to lose more territory. Not unnaturally, it did what its predecessors had done and printed more money. Had the reparations figure been renegotiated within a reasonable period, this solution might have worked, but all conferences for that purpose failed, and the German currency began to depreciate at an alarming rate. In 1923, the situation got completely out of hand when, as a result of a trifling default, the French occupied the Ruhr, Germany's only remaining coal and iron complex, and when the German government responded with a program of passive resistance. This was a defiant gesture but an ill-considered one: the striking miners and railway and factory workers and officials in the Ruhr had to be given government support, and the cost of this was staggering. Not having the courage to resort to a capital levy on its wealthier citizens, the government madly multiplied paper money (by the end of 1923, 133 plants with 1783 presses were turning out notes day and night) which lost its value as fast as it was printed.

The story of the German inflation is reasonably well known. When I was a boy in Canada in 1923, I bought a nickel candy bar one day and found under the wrapper a ten thousand RM note, a colorful but worthless "prize." In Germany at that time, workers were being paid twice a day and were rushing off with cigar boxes filled with notes of even larger denominations to try to spend them on food or other necessities before the next dollar quotation arrived and deprived their money of half its value. It was a good time for people with foreign assets, for speculators who operated across international borders, buying cheap in Germany and selling dear in Holland, and for the great tycoons like Stinnes who had the resources to expand by means of loans that could be paid back in depreciated currency. But to thousands in the middle class, it was an upside-down world in which everything that Marx had said about the ability of money to transform values became clear—a world in which profligacy was rewarded and providence punished, in which the brother who had drunk up his share of the family inheritance but had saved the bottles fared better than the one who had put his share in a savings bank where its value disappeared overnight, in which the simplest of objects were now valued in monstrous sums and the cost of things like food and fuel and clothing and doctors' fees and hospital care were astronomical. In these lunatic conditions, the most vulnerable people were those who lived on pensions or other fixed incomes and the aged and the young. But manual workers, whose unions were successful for a time in getting their pay adjusted to the inflation rate, were by 1923 suffering from mounting unemployment and were abandoning their unions by the millions because they were no longer able to protect either their jobs or the rights that labor had won in 1918–1919, while small shopkeepers and independent tradesmen were in no better shape, hopelessly watching their costs for materials and goods soar while their returns dwindled even as they were being counted.

The traumatic effects of this victimization were long felt. That the trade unions were ineffective in 1932–1933 in defending the Republican government from rightist attacks, that associations representing artisans and small traders and unions of white collar workers were active in the National Socialist movement, and that the bulk of the lower middle class looked to Adolf Hitler as a savior was due less to the great depression of the thirties, although that to be sure was not insignificant, than to the memory of the great inflation of 1923. The failure of the first German experiment with republican government was foreordained when the one commodity that more than any other seemed to give people a means of rational assessment of their situation lost its power to do so any longer. For millions of Germans, that unprecedented and bewildering event hopelessly compromised faith in representative government and encouraged the growth of messianism and utopianism. The beneficiary of that transformation of values was Adolf Hitler.

V

By a curious irony, Germany's second attempt to build an effective democracy was inaugurated in circumstances not entirely dissimilar to those of 1923, and it may be argued that it was another manipulation of money that assured its success. This is a hypothesis, however, that does not enjoy universal agreement even in Germany, and where one stands on it depends to a large extent on what one means by success.

Germany ended the Second World War, as it had ended the First, with a large debt, the prospect of a staggering liability for war damages and related claims, and a currency that had deteriorated seriously during the war and was soon to become almost valueless. The agency of accelerated depreciation was the occupation mark, the currency that was issued by the victorious powers for the purpose of paying the salaries of their occupation forces and other services and of serving as legal tender in transactions between their troops and German civilians. This was made equivalent in value to the Reichsmark and was redeemable in British and U.S. currency at a rate of ten to the dollar. This might have been tolerable had it not been for the growth of the black market, on which members of the occupying forces began to sell commodities like tobacco and coffee for vastly inflated prices in RM, which they then redeemed in their own currency at profits ranging to 100 and 150 percent. This led the American military authorities to replace the occupation mark with military script that could be used in military installations but not in dealings with civilians. The cure proved to be worse than the disease, for its result was to make the American cigarette the new medium of exchange. Edwin Hartrich has written: "The cigarette became the yardstick of values, and prices were quoted in packs and *Stangen* (cartons), which also served to further eliminate the inflated and virtually worthless Reichsmark as a viable currency."

As in 1923, there were people who lived happily in these conditions, and others who became their victims. The occupying troops, who had access to the post exchange shops and could, in addition, ask their families to ship them cigarettes and other commodities that were sought after by German civilians, made great profits, as did native speculators. But when the average weekly pay of a semiskilled worker was 80 RM and a one-dollar carton of cigarettes was retailed at 1000 RM or more, it was clear that existence for most Germans would be at the bare subsistence level unless they had family possessions that could be sold on the black market for the cigarettes with which they could buy a few creature comforts from those who were hoarding them for profit. In time, this began to worry the occupation authorities, who did not want to be accused of what they had charged the Nazis with at the Nuremberg trials, the plunder and spoliation of a defeated nation. In 1947 the United States army tried to regularize and control the black market and to see that German citizens received fair value for the goods they bartered there. When this proved less than satisfactory, the Western occupation authorities determined to carry through a basic currency reform.

In June 1948, it was announced that the citizens of the Western zones of occupation would be required to register the amounts of RM that they had in their possession or in bank deposits and that these would be converted into new Deutschmark, at a rate of 1 DM: 10 RM, each German being allowed to exchange 400 RM at the outset and 200 RM two months later. This decree, which wiped out hundreds of billions of RM in securities, war bonds, mortgages, and reserves, seemed draconian and was promptly labeled as such by the Soviet government, which had long since stopped following a joint economic policy with the Western Powers and would have preferred a continuation of the Western inflation as being potentially conducive to Communism. Yet it eliminated the cigarette economy that had debauched the old medium of exchange and introduced a new kind of money which, despite the fact that it had no gold or silver backing, established itself quickly as a hard currency in relation to others.

It did this by that magic power that money has to transform situations by effecting changes in psychological moods. The economist Henry Wallich wrote that the currency reform "transformed the German scene from one day to the next. On June 21, 1948, goods reappeared in the stores, money resumed its normal function, the black and gray markets reverted to a minor role, foraging trips to the country ceased, labor productivity increased, and output took off on its great upward surge. The spirit of the country changed overnight. The gray, hungry, dead-looking figures wandering about the streets in their everlasting search for food came to life as, pocketing their 40 DM, they went out on a first spending spree." The German economy was back in operation, and the *Wirtschaftswunder* would soon astonish Germany's neighbors.

VI

To a not inconsiderable number of Germans, this sudden transition was a misfortune rather than a boon, a gift to the new Federal Republic that compromised it from the moment of its birth in 1949. In an address on the tenth anniversary of the war's end, the Dahlem pastor Helmuth Gollwitzer said, "We should be thankful that the great misery of the postwar period could be overcome so quickly—but is it really good for us that things go so well for us again and so soon? The full stomach should not deceive us about the hollowness of the convictions, the brittleness of the inner foundation of countless persons, the indifference with which many pass over the fate of our own people and the need of others. Our repletion is a greater danger than the hunger of ten years ago." More direct and uncompromising were the words of the Catholic intellectual Carl Amery in 1963:

> Currency reform established overnight the new society, the society of capitalism. And immediately in a very modern form: of mass production and consumption, of marketing and the satisfaction of economic needs. It is pointless to complain of this. The new counters were thrown on the gaming table (sixty units for each; capital goods in addition, under the counter) and the gentlemen were requested: *Faites vos jeux*. They did so. Political consciousness, mastering of the past, the craftsman's virtues: all these lost their importance. . . . Political consciousness? We had indeed just learned how far people had got if they knew the racket. And mastery of the past? My God, we wanted to forget. Forget

the end of the nation, forget our own shady part in that end, forget the ticking of the nuclear clock. That indeed is what we are playing at. . . .

Scarcely anyone knows that it is impossible in this casino to remain decent—at any rate, not as our fathers were "decent." None of them has deliberately renounced the old values; they have simply deposited them in the cloakroom. They think that they can go out at any time and collect their overcoats on presentation of a cloakroom ticket. This of course is an illusion; it is impossible to spend six, eight, ten hours a day behind the counters and still remained the "decent" man of yesterday. The game changes values, it alters characters.

Thus, with the economic recovery came a sense of guilt, a feeling shared by many sensitive people and particularly, as we shall see, by academic youth that it had all been too easy and too quick, that it had shut off the debate on options too soon, that it had foreclosed opportunities for fruitful innovation, and that it had brought not a brave new world but a Restoration, in which all the wrong things had been restored—a restored world of money and materialism and militarism (for the decision to rearm Western Germany followed hard on the currency reform) which would end the way all the other old worlds had ended.

Out of thoughts like this came the pervasive cultural pessimism that affected so many of Western Germany's intellectuals and the recurrent doubts about the viability of German democracy that we find in plays like Bodo Strauss's *Gross und Klein* (1978), with its repeatedly posed question *"Wohin*?" ("What's it all about?") and its implied motto "Instead of war, we have this." To what extent this is shared by ordinary Germans it would be difficult to say. In 1979, Peter Iden of the *Frankfurter Rundschau* expressed the opinion that it was more widely spread than was generally realized and was reflected in catch phrases that implied doubt about the permanence of things. People, he said, were constantly using words like *wahnsinnig* (crazy) and *geheimnisvoll* (mysterious) in connection with quite normal and ordinary things, as if to express surprise over their existence or ability to function. They were always saying *"Alles klar!"* as if desperately resolved to give clarity to a situation that no longer warranted it, or assuring others that such and such a thing would be done *"mit Sicherheit!"* so emphatically as to suggest that they no longer believed in any form of durability.

And yet it is to be doubted whether a better or more viable Germany would have resulted from a continuation of the conditions that preceded the currency reform. Indeed, it is not impossible that the calculations of the Soviet government would have been proven to be accurate and that economic misery would have led to a victory of Communism in both parts of Germany. If that had happened, the cultural pessimists might have had a different view about a lot of things, including money. It is not irrelevant to point in this connection to the quandary of Erich Honecker, who, at the end of the seventies, found himself being compelled, in order to win tolerance for his other policies, to allow the D-mark of the west to circulate as a second currency in the German Democratic Republic, a means of providing for his fellow citizens comforts that he had been unable to give to them. Needless to say, this was an experiment that was viewed with grave displeasure by his Soviet masters, who remembered their Marx and had reason to fear the transformative power of money.

6

Germans and Jews

In Edgar Allan Poe's story "William Wilson," the protagonist has a schoolmate who bears the same name as he and resembles him so closely in age, form and features that they might be brothers. He finds it impossible to accept this likeness. Toward his double, he feels a mixture of "petulant animosity, which was not yet hatred, some esteem, more respect, much fear, with a world of uneasy curiosity"; but "the feeling of vexation . . . grew stronger with every circumstance tending to show resemblance, moral or physical, between my rival and myself." In the end, after he has sought vainly to escape from his schoolmate, who follows him to the university and has a habit of appearing at critical moments in his later life, his irritation hardens into hatred, and he kills him.

Poe's tale is not without relevance to the tragic story of the relationship between the Germans and the Jews. The family resemblance between the two peoples is striking and is evident in their industry, their thrift and frugality, their perseverance, their strong religious sense, the importance they place on the family, and their common respect for the printed word, which has made the Jews the People of the Book and the Germans *das Volk der Dichter und Denker*. They are alike also in the nature of their intellectual pretensions, refusing to restrict themselves to pragmatic and utilitarian goals, but sharing the Faustian ambition to find the secrets of the universe and to solve the riddle of man's relationship to God, the objective equally of German metaphysicians like Kant, Hegel and Schelling and of the Jewish cabbalists.

Their kinship is apparent also in their negative traits, and Jörg von Uthmann has recently pointed to "that feverish activity in business that has made them so unloved in the world . . . , their common belief in the absolute and the obsessiveness with which they push every good thing to the point where it becomes a bad one, [and] that inimitable combination of tactlessness and sensitivity, of arrogance and subservience, of pride in belonging to the Elect and self-contempt" that distinguishes both peoples.

Even if we are impressed by these similarities, however, we must ask ourselves whether there was any necessary connection between them and the *dénouement* of the relationship, which was as dreadful as that in

126

Poe's story. Why did not these resemblances lead to integration rather than to the destruction of the Jews by their fellow citizens? Why was Heinrich Heine's prophecy not fulfilled, that the Germans and the Jews, the two ethical nations, as he called them, would create a new Jerusalem in Germany, "the home of philosophy, the mother soil of prophecy and the citadel of pure spirituality"? Uthmann and others have argued that their affinity in itself prevented this, leading instead to a deadly sibling rivalry. There may be something in this, although it seems, if not an inadequate explanation, at least an incomplete one. Surely the answer to the problem of German anti-Semitism, as to others, must be sought in the belated evolution of Germany to nationhood, and more particularly in the failure of the Enlightenment on the one hand, and, on the other, in Germany's difficulty in adjusting to rapid industrialization and social change.

I

The more remote causes of anti-Semitism were, of course, religious. Even in Roman times, the Jews were viewed with suspicion because their strict monotheism made no concessions to the deification of the emperors and the rites that celebrated this, and in some parts of the Empire their stubbornness on this score led to anti-Jewish riots and pogroms. But it was only with the rise of Christianity that such violent expression of hostility toward the Jews became a regular feature of Western life. To Christians, the Jews were an obdurate people who had refused to recognize Jesus as the promised Messiah, and who not only still persisted in that error but were burdened with the guilt of deicide, which, according to the Gospel of St. Matthew, they had themselves acknowledged, by crying, at the time of Jesus's condemnation, "His blood be on us and on our children!" Jesus himself, according to the Gospel of St. John (8 : 42–45), had declared them to be sinful and unregenerate ("Ye are of your father the devil, and the lusts of your father ye will do"). and his followers found it easy to believe that there was no crime of which the Jews were not capable. In the fourth century, St. John Chrysostom declared vehemently, "I know that a great number of the faithful have a certain respect for the Jews and hold their cere-monies in reverence. This provokes me to eradicate completely such a disastrous opinion. . . . Since they have disowned the Father, crucif-ied the Son, and rejected the Spirit's help, who would not dare to assert that the synagogue is not a home of demons? God is not worshiped there; it is simply a home of idolatry. . . . The Jews live for their bel-lies, they crave for the goods of this world. In shamelessness and greed, they surpass even pigs and goats. . . . The Jews are possessed by dem-ons, they are handed over to impure spirits. . . . Instead of greeting them and addressing them by so much as a word, you should turn away from them as from the pest and a plague of the human race."

The very exclusivity of the Jews, their preference during the middle ages for living in closed communities, made them the object of wild surmise and superstitious fear. No crime was committed, no child disappeared without responsibility being placed at their door. It was widely believed that obscene practices and ritual murder were a normal feature of their religious observances, that they were poisoners of wells and seducers of the young, and that their demonic powers enabled them to call down earthquakes, pestilence and tempests upon their Christian neighbors. Not unnaturally, in time of calamity, they became the victims of mob violence.

In Germany, sporadic outbursts of popular anti-Semitism were common throughout the middle ages and the early modern period. They were often encouraged by the Church, which sometimes made it easier for rioters to identify their victims by forcing Jews to wear distinctive items of dress (yellow patches or horned caps, which was the custom in Bamberg in the fifteenth century), or by Christian merchants who were jealous of the competition of Jewish peddlers, or by people who wished to free themselves from debt to Jewish moneylenders. It was recognized by people with any sense of reality that the Jews generally stimulated economic life and brought prosperity to the localities in which they settled, and in many parts of Germany Jewish traders were placed under the protection of the Emperor or of local rulers. But the rights granted them varied from state to state and were limited in duration and always at the mercy of local conditions and the whims of town councilors.

The coming of the Reformation led, at least temporarily, to an increase of intolerance. Martin Luther seems at first to have believed that the Jews would respond positively to the new dispensation and would renounce their past errors and embrace Christianity.

> For our fools, the popes, bishops, sophists, and monks—the coarse blockheads!—dealt with the Jews as if they were dogs and not human beings. They have done nothing for them but curse them and seize their wealth. I would advise and beg everybody to deal kindly with the Jews and to instruct them in the Scriptures; in such case we could expect them to come over to us.

When, however, the Jews were unresponsive, the Reformer raged against them with a coarseness of language unequaled before the Nazi period. In a long treatise called "Concerning the Jews and Their Lies" (1543), he asked:

> What then shall we Christians do with this damned, rejected race of Jews? . . . Since they live among us and we know about their lying and blasphemy and cursing, we cannot tolerate them. . . . In this way we cannot quench the inextinguishable fire of divine rage . . . or convert the Jews. We must prayerfully and reverentially practice a merciful severity.

This, he continued, would include "setting fire to their synagogues and schools and covering over what will not burn with earth so that no man will ever see a stone or cinder of them again," "breaking and destroying their houses . . . so that they have to live in stalls like gypsies and learn that they are not the lords in our land as they boast and must live in misery and captivity," depriving them of their holy books, silencing their teachers, forbidding them the right to travel or to trade, and seizing their wealth on the grounds that "everything that they possess they have robbed and stolen from us by their usury."

These harsh prescriptions were not put into general practice, although it is doubtless true that, thanks to Luther's personal animus and to the heightened emphasis placed upon the text of the New Testament in Lutheran observance, that church acquired a prejudice against the Jews that was never completely eradicated. On the other hand, the devastation brought upon Germany by the prolonged religious warfare that originated with the Reformation hardly encouraged attacks upon the Jews, for it was they, more than any other element in society, who by means of their international contacts and their access to credit facilitated the economic recovery of Germany after 1648. In the second half of the seventeenth century, many of the territorial princes welcomed Jewish settlement, while making the immigrants pay for the privilege, and the so-called Court Jews (*Hofjuden*), who have been mentioned earlier, played an indispensable role in the financial administration, not only of the minor German courts, but of Austria during the reign of Leopold I and his successors Charles VI and Maria Theresia.

Of all of the German states, Brandenburg-Prussia showed the greatest degree of toleration toward the Jews. When four thousand Jews were expelled from Vienna in 1670, the Great Elector gave permission for fifty families to take up residence in his lands and granted them privileges (the right to acquire houses and to conduct public worship) that were denied to them in other states. To the economic growth of Prussia, this reception of the Jews was as important as the Great Elector's decision to give a home to the French Huguenots after the revocation of the Edict of Nantes. The last years of the seventeenth century and the first half of the eighteenth saw a systematic rationalization of the financial administration of the State and a steady growth of trade and manufacturing that was due in large part to the shrewd management of the *Hofjuden* and *Hoffaktoren;* and Eda Sagarra has written that it is no exaggeration to say that Prussia was enabled to escape defeat in the Seven Years War and to repair the material losses caused by that conflict with celerity only by the heroic efforts of economic advisers like Veitel Ephraim and Daniel Itzig.

These services were recognized not only by the court, which extended the privileges of its Jewish subjects, but by Prussian society as well, which showed an increasing willingness to accept them. This was particularly true in Berlin, where, at least on the cultural level, there was at the end of the eighteenth century a kind of symbiosis between the rich Jewish families and the more enlightened sections of the Prussian aristocracy and the upper middle class.

The way for this was prepared by Moses Mendelssohn, the son of a

Thora copier (*Sefer*) in Dessau, who had come to Berlin in 1743, penniless and unable to speak the German language properly, and who had subsequently become the friend of Lessing and one of the leading figures of the German Enlightenment. Mendelssohn believed that the Jews must liberate themselves from the spiritual ghetto in which they had lived for centuries by ceasing to regard themselves as a separate nation, accepting German culture as their own, freeing their religion from outworn rituals and working for its acceptance as one denomination among others. He sought to break down the social barrier between Jew and Gentile by making his home a meeting place for intellectuals, distinguished foreign visitors, and the Berlin *haute volée*, hoping to promote mutual understanding and to demonstrate that the Jews were not an exotic people but Germans with the same interests as other enlightened members of German society.

Mendelssohn's example was followed by his daughter, Dorothea Mendelssohn Veit, who in the last years of Frederick II's reign had a "reading society" that met twice a week and attracted Berlin writers and scholars without respect to religious difference, and by the wives and daughters of other Jewish merchants and professional men. These included Frau Hofrat Bauer, whose circle included the brothers Wilhelm and Alexander von Humboldt, Henriette Herz, whose beauty and wit brought even the sober-sided Nicolai to her knees and made Schleiermacher declare that she was his "most intimately connected substance" without whom life would not be worth living, and the spirited Rahel Levin (later Varnhagen), where the political observer Friedrich von Gentz and the Swedish ambassador Karl Gustav von Brinckmann commingled with writers like Ludwig Tieck, Adalbert von Chamisso, Clemens von Brentano and Friedrich Schlegel, and where one might find Frederick the Great's gifted nephew, Prince Louis Ferdinand of Prussia, with his mistress Pauline Wiesel and his brother-in-law, the mathematician and composer Prince Radziwill.

The pleasure that Rahel's non-Jewish guests took in her company was a far cry from the popular disposition to regard Jews as less than human. In 1743, when Moses Mendelssohn had trudged through the Berlin gate, the customs officer had noted in his watchbook, "Today there passed six oxen, seven swine, and a Jew"; and the laws of most German states still breathed the spirit of that notation. But in the days when the salons dominated Berlin's social and intellectual life, it was easy to believe that conditions were changing and that the differences that existed between Jews and Germans could be removed, in Berlin and elsewhere, by goodwill and enlightened statecraft. In his widely read treatise *On the Civic Improvement of the Jews* (1781), Christian Wilhelm von Dohm expressed the Enlightenment's faith in the capacity of rational legislation to change the way people thought by calling upon the German governments to take the initiative in this by giving the Jewish community the same rights that they gave to other subgroups in society, by tolerating its special traditions and customs as they did in the case of the aristocracy, the university professoriate, and the various Christian communities, and by encouraging it and all such groupings to cherish the common bond of citizenship, which should make out of them all a harmonious whole.

The optimism that inspired Dohm's treatise seemed to be justified when, in the following year, Emperor Joseph II issued a patent of tolerance for all Jews in his realm. In reality, this provided for only the rudiments of toleration and, like other general declarations of its kind, broke down in local practice. The high hopes of the ideologues of the Enlightenment were, in fact, to be disappointed because they were not shared by the masses of the Christian population, who did not visit salons or read the treatises of the *philosophes*. In Lessing's play *Die Juden*, a mysterious traveler arouses the admiration of a German baron by the elegance of his dress and manners, his courage when the baron and his daughter are in danger, and his wealth, all of which seem to indicate that he is a member of the highest rank of society. When the baron begins to entertain notions of marriage between his daughter and the traveler, the latter says, "I am a Jew." "What difference does that make?" the baron's daughter asks. Her maid tugs at her elbow and whispers, "Psst, Fräulein! Psst! I'll tell you afterwards what difference it makes."

Here was the voice of that part of the population that was untouched by the Enlightenment and retained a prejudice against the Jews that came from the middle ages and was to persist into the nineteenth century, impervious to rational argument and assuming ugly forms in moments of economic privation or national crisis.

II

Even among the cultivated sections of society, the willingness to tolerate the Jews faltered and in many cases died. In the first instance, this was due to the outburst of patriotic feeling that took place during the years of Napoleon's domination of Germany. Anti-French agitation was propagated by societies like the Deutsche Tugendbund and the Christlich-deutsche Tischgesellschaft, which reacted strongly against the progressive and cosmopolitan views of the Enlightenment and preached a doctrine of integral nationalism with a strong admixture of Christianity. In a pamphlet written in 1815, the Jewish publicist Saul Ascher described this new movement as "Germanomania" and wrote bitterly:

> Christianity and Germanness were soon melted into one, an easy task for transcendental idealists and identity philosophers. They reasoned this way. Germany could be saved only by means of oneness and identity of the people in the Idea. Oneness and identity in religion expresses this requirement completely. . . . It ought not to seem strange that, according to the ideas of these enthusiastic idealists . . . the antithesis to their theory lay in the Jews, and this explains the coarse and menacing tone in which, from Fichte at the end of the eighteenth century to his students and admirers today, the Jews and Jewry have been stormed at.

Ascher cited a recent book called *Jewish Pretensions to German Citizenship,* in which the author took sharp issue with Dohm's case for a greater measure of civil rights for Jews and argued that only conversion to Christianity could justify the grant of citizenship, demanding further that restrictions be placed upon new Jewish immigration into Germany and suggesting that there should be a clearer legal definition of the relationship between Germans and Jews, which implied a tightening of restrictions upon non-Christian subjects.

Views like these, and the cruder anti-Semitism of pamphlets like Grattenauer's *Against the Jews,* which jeered at Jews who "to prove their culture . . . publicly eat pork on the *shabbes* . . . and on the promenades learn Kiesewetter's *Logic* by heart," created a climate of opinion that was unpropitious to any real progress toward assimilation. In the countries of the west, the Jews had owed their emancipation to the conquest of power by the wealthy and educated middle class. Such a bourgeois revolution did not take place in Germany, and the Jews had either to be content with the minimal toleration granted to them by the laws of the states in which they lived, which gave them rights that gradually (but not until the 1860s) amounted to legal equality but fell far short of winning for them complete social acceptance, or to seek equality and integration by their own individual merits and achievements.

For many, this latter course proved to be a heartbreaking task. Rahel Varnhagen was to discover that even those who had been proud to be seen at her brilliant evenings were unwilling to accept her as an equal— that is, as a German like them—and that there was nothing she could do to free herself from what she called "the ever continuing and self-renewing misfortune of my false birth. These words, so easily spoken . . . are the bows from which, my whole life through, the most painful and poisonous arrows have been discharged. No art enables me to escape them—no reflection, no exertion, no industry, no submission. . . . When I think I must be a queen or a mother, I discover that I am *nothing.* No daughter, no sister, no lover, no wife, not even a citizen." And again, "How wretched it is always to have to legitimize myself! That is why it is so disgusting to be a Jew." Few Jews were unaware of those wounding darts, whose sting was felt in moments of triumph and defeat alike and interrupted moments of felicity, when one least expected it. "It is like a wonder!" Ludwig Börne once said. "I have experienced it a thousand times, and yet it always remains new. These people reproach me for being a Jew, and those forgive me for it, and still others praise me for it; but they all think of it. They are as if enchanted in the magical Jewish circle, and no one can get out."

For any sensitive person, the dilemma was a cruel one. If they remained true to their tradition and their religion, the Jews were regarded as an alien element in the social body; if they accepted Christianity and sought to prove themselves good Germans, they were often criticized for arrogance and presumption, their very achievements being used against them to prove that they were un-German. The *casus classicus* to illustrate the latter reaction is that of Heinrich Heine.

Born in a ghetto, Heine accepted baptism as "the entrée card into

European culture." He wrote later, "I make no bones about my Jewishness, to which I have not returned because I never left it." But there was as little doubt about his Germanness as there was about his Jewish origins. He devoted his life to a vain effort to create an ideal fatherland by criticizing the faults of the real one, and no one who reads the poems he wrote in exile—

> Denk ich an Deutschland in der Nacht,
> Dann bin ich um den Schlaf gebracht
>
> [Thinking of Germany in the night,
> I am robbed of sleep]

or

> O, Deutschland, meine ferne Liebe . . .
>
> Mir ist, als hört ich fern erklingen
> Nachtwächterhörner, sanft und traut;
> Nachtwächterlieder hör ich singen,
> Dazwischen Nachtigallenlaut.
>
> Dem Dichter war so wohl daheime,
> In Schildas teurem Eichenhain!
> Dort wob ich meine zarten Reime
> Aus Veilchenduft und Mondenschein.
>
> [Germany, distant love of mine . . .
>
> From far away I seem to hear
> Night-watchman bugles, soft and clear.
> Night-watchman songs are sweetly ringing,
> And far-off nightingales are singing.
>
> At home in Schilda's oaken grove,
> How well the poet thrived! I wove
> My tender-hearted verses there
> Of moonlight and of violet air.]—

can question the depth of his love for his country or his right to the title that he claimed for himself, "a German poet."

Yet, although he was the greatest German lyric poet after Goethe and an acknowledged master of prose style, Heine never received, in his own time or later, the honors that are usually given to great writers. Indeed, as early as the 1830s, the fatal verdict of "un-German" had been pronounced against him. In a brilliant analysis of Heine's early critics, Jost Hermand has summed up their complaints. "Because Heine's approach was so subjective, he appeared to his critics to be unrestrained and formless. Because he was so formless, he seemed frivolous and immoral.

Because he was inclined to be immoral, he was regarded as a Socialist of the St. Simonian school. Whoever inclined to such a doctrine was understandably regarded by conservatives as a Francophile. As a Francophile, he immediately fell under the suspicion of wandering around the world in a restless way. Anyone who was rootless could only be a Jew. As a Jew, one was laden with the odium of being not genuine—et cetera ad libitum in infinitum."

The nature of Heine's writing and the circumstances of his life laid him open to these criticisms. He was a satirist among a people that did not take easily to satire and expected literature to be serious and respectful of things that deserved respect. What was one to do with a writer who apparently did not take even the products of his own pen seriously, and who could write, as Heine did in his fourth series of *Travel Sketches (The Baths of Lucca):*

> There is nothing more boring upon this earth than the reading of an Italian travel account, unless it is the writing of it, and the only way the author can make it minimally tolerable is to talk about Italy as little as possible. Although I have fully accepted this procedure, I cannot promise you, dear reader, much entertainment in the next chapters. If you become bored with the wearisome stuff that is in them, comfort yourself by thinking of me, who have to write all this rubbish.

This sort of thing was as irritating to many German readers as Heine's habit of leading them into sentimental moods and then, when their defenses were down, confronting them brutally with reality. Nor did they appreciate his irreverent sallies at respected institutions like universities and churches—his intimation in *Journey in the Harz* that the University of Göttingen was essentially no more important than the local lying-in hospital, or the passage in *The History of Religion and Philosophy in Germany* in which he noted that St. Peter's Church in Rome was built with the moneys gained by selling indulgences and thus was "a monument to fleshly lust like that pyramid built by an Egyptian concubine with the moneys she gained by prostitution," going on to contrast this southern carnality with the sobriety of the north, "where the climate facilitates the practice of the Christian virtues and where, on October 31, 1517, when Luther nailed his theses on the door of the Augustinerkirche, the city canal in Wittenberg was perhaps already frozen, and people could skate on it, which is a very cold pleasure, and no sin."

Finally, they found insufferable Heine's persistent habit of writing about the German people with a good-natured contempt as a race of philistines, as "a great fool that calls itself the German people," of jeering at Germany's impotence in comparison with other nations—

> Russia and France control the land.
> Great Britain rules the sea.

> Ours is the cloudy realm of dreams
> Where there's no rivalry—

and of suggesting that the Germans, like the dancing bear Atta Troll in his political satire of that name, liked to make speeches about freedom but secretly enjoyed being in chains.

Heine's early critics were fond of spicing their attacks upon him with references to his frequently expressed admiration of France, as if to prove him a traitor to his own country. But essentially it was his Jewishness that supplied them with everything that they needed to satisfy themselves that he was not worth consideration as a German artist. Indeed, the virulence of their attacks upon him in the 1830s and 1840s showed how disingenuous were the claims of many Germans that they had no objection to Jews as long as they were willing to be converted to Christianity. With a forthrightness that made no attempt to hide his racial prejudice, Eduard Meyer wrote in 1831, with reference to Heine and his fellow exile in Paris, Ludwig Börne:

> Baptized or not, it's all the same. We don't hate the religion of the Jews but the many hateful characteristics of these Asiatics, among them their so frequent impudence and presumption, their immorality and frivolity, their noisy behavior, and their so frequently base approach to life. . . . They belong to no people, no State, no community; they rove about the world as adventurers, sniffing around . . . and they stay where they find lots of opportunity for speculation. Where things go quietly and in accordance with the law, there they find it uncomfortable.

Even more vituperative was Wolfgang Menzel, a respected literary critic with a university chair, who professed to be shocked by Heine's essay *Voyage from Munich to Genoa* and wrote: "We see in it the Jewish youth with his hands in his trouser pockets, standing impudently in front of pictures of Italian madonnas," and went on to talk of "Jewboys from Paris, dressed in the latest mode but very *blasé*, enervated by dissoluteness, and with a characteristic smell of musk and garlic."

After the founding of the Reich in 1871, the most implacable of the now dead poet's foes was the historian Heinrich von Treitschke, a significant fact because Treitschke was considered by many to be a sort of official spokesman for the new Germany. In his widely read *German History*, which was designed to explain to his countrymen what and who had made them great, Treitschke was careful to deny Heine any share in Germany's rise to nationhood, although he was generous in writing of the contributions of other writers. He could not deny that Heine's poetry had enjoyed wide popularity, and still did, but, he wrote, "Slowly, very slowly, did the understanding gain ground that Heine's witticisms could never be truly congenial to German minds. Of all our lyric poets, he was the only one who never wrote a drinking song; to him, heaven seemed full of almond cakes, purses of gold, and street wenches, for the oriental was incompetent to carouse after the German manner. It was long before people realized that Heine's *esprit* was far from being *Geist* in the German sense." And, more sternly, this time with reference to Heine's great satirical poem *Germany: A Winter's Tale*, he wrote, "This poem, one of the most brilliant and characteristic products of Heine's pen, is an index for the Germans of what severed them from this Jew. The Aryan nations have their Thersites and their Loki, but such a character as Ham, who uncovers his father's nakedness, is known only to Jewish saga."

The intemperance of this attack is perhaps understandable. Heine was the chief of those German-Jewish writers who have been called "disturbers of the peace," and *Germany: A Winter's Tale* was doubtless a thorn in Treitschke's flesh because the reactionary opposition to civil liberty and social progress that Heine had discovered in the Germany of the 1840s and pilloried in his poem was still all too evident in the Bismarckian Reich. That his poem would outrage people like the nationalistic historian, Heine had foreseen, writing in his introduction: "I already hear your beery voices: 'You have violated our colors, you scorner of the fatherland, you friend of the French, to whom you would surrender the free Rhine!' Calm yourselves! I will honor and respect your colors when they deserve it, when they no longer represent a slavish play-acting. Plant the black-red-gold flag on the heights of German thought, make it the standard of a free humanity, and I will give my best heart's blood for it. Calm yourselves! I love the fatherland as much as you do. Because of this love, I spent thirteen years in exile, and because of this love I return to exile perhaps for ever."

Forever is a long time, but one would hesitate to state with any firmness that Heine has yet received from the Germans the acceptance that is his due. After 1945, his name was honored in the German Democratic Republic, partly because of the poet's association with Marx and Engels and partly because of his sympathy for the proletariat of Paris in the 1840s, and *Germany: A Winter's Tale* was used in elementary schools for polemical purposes. It is doubtful that the poet, who fought so hard for freedom, would be happy about being honored by a State that is so far from being free. Meanwhile, in the Federal Republic, a movement to name the university in his native town Düsseldorf after him was twice defeated by the academic Senate and by student plebiscites for obscure reasons, among which latent anti-Semitism was surely not absent.

III

In 1921, in one of many articles that he wrote on anti-Semitism, Kurt Tucholsky, the greatest German satirist after Heine, imagined General Erich Ludendorff arriving at heaven's gate and being asked sternly how he could justify his having caused the deaths of 2 million men during the war. "Dear God," Ludendorff answered, "it was the Jews!"

Tucholsky's fancy was not as exaggerated as it might seem. During the nineteenth century, the Jews were blamed for every calamity that befell their country and when the war came, if they were not made the scapegoats for the defects of Ludendorff's generalship, they were accused of stabbing the army in the back in 1918 and of having helped impose a shameful peace settlement upon the country. Subsequently, every economic setback suffered by the Weimar Republic—the horrendous inflation of 1922–1923, for example—and every feature of its foreign policy that offended German patriots was blamed upon them.

It was, of course, not unnatural, in time of economic troubles, to regard the Jews as the persons responsible. In the predominantly rural economy of the early nineteenth century, they were often the vital element, the peddlers and the dealers in grain and livestock, the moneylenders whose advances carried the peasants over hard winters. They were not usually beloved of their customers, and in hard times had to bear the brunt of popular hatred. The period between the Congress of Vienna and the revolutions of 1848 was marked by frequent anti-Jewish riots, in southern Germany and the Rhineland in 1819, in Hamburg in 1830, and in Baden in 1848. Concerning the last of these, the ethnographer W. H. Riehl wrote, with his usual pro-peasant bias, that it was "the natural enmity of the exclusive peasant class spirit against the alien interloper, it was the pride of the owner of land toward the wandering homeless breed that expressed itself here." That the rural economy depended to a large extent upon the services of the objects of his contempt does not seem to have occurred to him.

The economic transformation of Germany during the second half of the century was dramatic, and the very speed with which the process of industrialization was effected caused painful social dislocation and a deracination that involved considerable personal tragedy. The superior ability of the Jews to adjust to new conditions—the ease with which, in contrast to many small-town Germans, they adapted themselves to urban life—was held against them and reinforced the suspicion that they promoted and profited from social disintegration. Their prominent role in the clothing trades, which took advantage of cheap rural labor, exposed them to accusations of exploitation, and the proliferation of Jewish banks and investment firms in Berlin, Frankfurt and Vienna had even more fateful results. It is not too much to say that anti-Semitism in its modern virulent form had its origins in the stock-market crash of 1873, a debacle precipitated by the overextension of the railroad empire of the Jewish entrepreneur Bethel Strousberg and the manipulations of less reputable Jewish traders who had exploited the reckless greed of small investors. Amid the furious attacks upon Jewish swindlers that followed the crash, the public overlooked the fact that it was a Jewish Reichstag deputy, Eduard Lasker, who had tried repeatedly to warn against the fragility of the speculative boom, and that it was the energetic intervention of Jewish banks like Bleichröder and Company that prevented the damage from being greater than it was. The harm was now done, and the image of the Jewish businessman as Shylock intent on getting his pound of flesh became indelible.

It was in the wake of the crash of 1873 that a new breed of professional anti-Semites appeared in Germany who far exceeded Heine's critics in their use of racial arguments to support their opposition to the

Jews. In the lectures and pamphlets of people like Eugen Dühring and Paul de Lagarde and Wilhelm Marr, the Jews were no longer accused of being un-German because they refused to accept Christianity but were described as being by their very nature an alien element in German society, as being carriers of a disease that contaminated its vital forces and threatened it with degeneracy and death. It is doubtless true that these philosophers of racial theory were unknown to most Germans and that the violence of their fulminations and the pornographic cast of their fantasies repelled many of those who learned of them. But what they had to say, which was often couched in spurious scientific terminology and embellished by random quotations from anthropologists, biologists, psychologists and theologians, was not unimportant, for it impressed the gullible and often confirmed, or helped give form to, suppressed or unconscious prejudice against the Jews.

The spread of this new anti-Semitism was encouraged, moreover, by the frankness with which men of prominence and influence admitted their own reservations about the Jews. Readers of Treitschke's *German History* or the speeches of Court Preacher Adolf Stoecker were not always sophisticated enough to sense the distinction between their religious arguments and the racist exaggerations of the Dührings and the Marrs; the stature of the former figures, therefore, lent credibility to the wildest charges of the latter. Even more important was the support the racists received from Richard Wagner, a man whose influence on the generation before the First World War, through his ideas as much as through his music, would be difficult to overestimate.

Wagner's anti-Semitism probably had its origins in resentment against Jewish financiers and impresarios who failed to support him at the start of his career and against Jewish competitors, like Giacomo Meyerbeer, whose triumphs were at first greater than his own; and this found expression in his essay on "Jewishness in Music" (1850) and in the dozens of references to Jewish sharp practice and exploitation of Christians that clutter the pages of Cosima Wagner's diary. But, in addition to this accumulated spleen against fancied enemies, a strong element of fear affected his thinking. His sometime friend Friedrich Nietzsche was to write in *Beyond Good and Evil* of anti-Semitism being "the instinct of a people whose type is still weak and undetermined, so that it could easily be effaced, easily extinguished by a stronger race." This may have been a reference to Wagner, who combined a hidden admiration for the Jews' success in surviving centuries of oppression with strong doubts about the ability of his own people to retain its individuality in conditions of free competition. He expressed his anxieties in attacks upon the Jews as enemies of German culture.

This obsession was in no wise moderated by the fact that some of the most dedicated propagators of his own musical ideals were Jewish, like the opera director Angelo Neumann, the pianist Josef Rubinstein, and Wagner's favorite conductor Hermann Levi (whom he treated with good-natured contempt and total lack of sensitivity, as is shown by the fact that he seriously considered pressing him to undergo baptism as the condition for being allowed to conduct the première of *Parsifal*). Despite his many Jewish admirers, he prided himself on his services to the anti-Semitic cause. After reading a speech by Stoecker in the late 1870s, Cosima Wagner wrote in her diary, "We laughed over it, because really it appears that Richard's essay about the Jews was the beginning of this battle," and Wagner himself insisted that Wilhelm Marr's *The Victory of Jewry over Germanness*, which went through twelve printings between 1873 and 1879, was merely a reflection of his own views. His anti-Semitism affected his judgment on all other subjects (his constant denigration of Bismarck was based in large part on Bismarck's contempt for Jew-baiters, which led Wagner to accuse him of having "*verjudert*" Germany; and the fact that Bleichröder was allowed to give a dinner for the delegates to the Congress of Berlin in 1878 persuaded him that that gathering was "a shame for Germany"); and it often assumed disgusting forms. After the fire in the Vienna Burgtheater in 1881, in which hundreds of people, including 400 Jews, died, Cosima reported that Wagner had made a "hearty joke," saying that "all the Jews should be burned up at a performance of [Lessing's] *Nathan*."

There is no doubt that Wagner's openly expressed dislike of the Jews, and the opinions of other eminent people like Treitschke and Stoecker, helped to legitimize anti-Semitism, to give it a spurious social and intellectual respectability. This was true also of the treatment of Jews in some of the most widely read novels of the late nineteenth century. It would be difficult to support the claim that writers for the more cultivated part of the reading public, like Wilhelm Raabe, Gustav Freytag and Felix Dahn, were consciously anti-Semitic in their writing; indeed, they were often sympathetic in their portrayal of the material and psychological hardships of German Jews. Nevertheless, for dramatic effect, they resorted in their most popular books to the technique of parallelism, placing in contrast the careers of their Christian protagonist, who was always portrayed as being honorable, idealistic and dedicated to the service of others, and his Jewish counterpart, who was self-centered, cowardly, materialistic, and unscrupulous. This was the method employed in such long-time best-sellers as *Der Hungerpastor, Soll und Haben*, and (handled somewhat differently) *Ein Kampf um Rom*; and it is not unlikely that readers of those books were more deeply impressed by the machinations of the Jewish villains than they were edified by the dull rectitude of the Christian heroes. As for the 20 million Germans who derived their spiritual nourishment from the trashy novels that appeared in weekly installments, they became accustomed to stereotyped portraits of Jews as usurers, well-poisoners, child-murderers and master criminals.

It is, of course, possible to exaggerate the influence and the uniqueness of German anti-Semitism. With respect to the latter, it is probably true that anti-Jewish feeling was as strong before 1914 in France and other countries as it was in Germany. With respect to the former, it is true that none of the manifestations of anti-Semitism mentioned here and none of those that might be cited—the conquest of university fraternities in the 1890s by anti-Jewish prejudice, the Tivoli Program accepted by the Conservative Party in 1892, which expressed opposition to "the widely obtruding and decomposing Jewish influence in our popular life," or the existence of an Anti-Semitic Party with seventeen seats in the Reichstag in 1893—hurt Germany's Jewish subjects in any tangible way. The radical program of Hermann Ahlwardt, a half-demented schoolmaster who had been dismissed for embezzlement before becoming a popular demagogue and who advocated the imposition of the most stringent restrictions upon the Jews, a decree proclaiming them foreigners on German soil, their exclusion from public and cultural activities, and, eventually, the confiscation of their wealth and their deportation, attracted no significant support. The emancipation that had been achieved in 1867 was unaffected by the violent resolutions passed in rightist party conferences, and the statute books remained free of discriminatory legislation.

But this was hardly comforting. Before 1914 anti-Semitism was like a stubborn low-grade infection that did not seriously impair the health of the social body but defied all attempts to cure it. There were people who were deeply alarmed by its persistence and who tried to find means of combating it but had to admit defeat. The historian Theodor Mommsen, who in the late 1870s had been the first to take up arms against the anti-Jewish writings of his colleague Treitschke, said with discouragement a decade later:

> You are mistaken if you believe that anything could be achieved by reason. In years past, I thought so myself and kept protesting against the monstrous infamy that is anti-Semitism. But it is useless, completely useless. . . . It is a horrible epidemic like cholera—one can neither explain nor cure it. One must patiently wait until the poison has consumed itself and lost its virulence.

The sickness that he feared did not show its true malignance before 1914, but it was, nevertheless, slowly poisoning the collective psyche and eroding its powers of moral and intellectual resistance. After 1918, in a radically different emotional atmosphere, infected by national humiliation and economic stringency, the malady was gradually to consume the whole body and to drive it to the madness in which it inflicted ghastly wounds upon its own members.

In a fine study of anti-Semitism in Germany and Austria, Peter Pulzer has pointed out that there was no essential difference between the anti-Semitism of the pre- and postwar periods. Every argument that National Socialist orators used against the Jews had been made before 1914; the only difference was that the Nazis had the strength of their convictions and turned those arguments into a program of action. The concept of the Holocaust was, after all, inherent in Ahlwardt's program in the 1880s. All that was needed was Adolf Hitler's demonic will to transform it into reality.

IV

It was the tragic dilemma of the German Jews that, like William Wilson's *Doppelgänger*, they inflamed the hostility of their partners the more they came to resemble them. Their early opponents had demanded of them that they become truly German. They had responded with enthusiasm, and their manifold contributions to German culture gave them an undeniable right to claim it as their own. For were not Marx and Freud and Einstein German thinkers, and Mahler and Schönberg German musicians? Were not Carl Sternheim and Jakob Wassermann German writers, and Max Liebermann and Emil Orlik German painters? And could not the same claim be made by persons of lesser achievement but equal dedication? As Golo Mann once wrote, the average German Jew, baptized or unbaptized, was German in his virtues, German in his vices, German in his dress, speech and manners, patriotic and conservative. There was nothing more German than those Jewish businessmen, doctors, lawyers, and scholars who volunteered for war service as a matter of course in 1914.

And yet all this accomplishment and devotion failed to bring them the acceptance they sought; and wealth and cultivation, which the Enlightenment had regarded as the keys to integration, were of no avail. "In the youth of every German Jew," Walther Rathenau wrote in 1911, "there comes a moment which he remembers with pain as long as he lives: when he becomes for the first time fully conscious of the fact that he has entered the world as a citizen of the second class, and that no amount of ability or merit can rid him of that status."

The case of Walther Rathenau is an instructive one, for he was, like Heinrich Heine, a disturber of the peace, one whose achievements were a provocation that brought the hatred of less gifted men down upon him. Unfortunately for him, he had neither the wit nor the joy in outraging the philistines that sustained Heine, nor did he possess Heine's superb self-confidence, which enabled him to admit his Jewishness without for a moment doubting his essential Germanness. In Rathenau's case, his Jewish heritage was something he honored by remaining true to the orthodox faith but of which he was, at the same time, ashamed. Conscious of his own abilities, he desperately wanted to have them recognized by the class least likely to understand him, the blond, blue-eyed Prussians whose fundamental opposition to intellectuality Heine had jeered at in *Germany: A Winter's Tale* but whom Rathenau idealized and sought to emulate.

The elder son of the founder of the Allgemeine Elektrizitäts-Gesellschaft (AEG), which became one of the largest industrial combines in Wilhelmine Germany, Walther Rathenau studied mathematics, physics and chemistry at the Universities of Berlin and Strassburg, receiving his degree in 1889 with a thesis on "Light Absorption by Metals." He then spent ten years of apprenticeship, first in an aluminum factory in Switzerland, and then as manager of an electrochemical works at Bitterfeld, near Leipzig. At the end of that time, it was clear that he had all the abilities necessary to succeed Emil Rathenau in the direction of AEG, for he combined practical and administrative skill with keen critical and analytical talents. But, as the English historian James Joll said in a brilliant essay on Rathenau, he always seems to have suffered from a misplaced sense of vocation, as if he felt that he could only rise above the limitations of his Jewish birth and his own self-doubt by purely spiritual accomplishments. He took to writing philosophical essays, which had some temporary success in an age interested in metaphysics, but, seen in retrospect, were dilettantish and intellectually pretentious, intended to impress rather than to enlighten.

He was also drawn to politics, despite his statement to a friend that external circumstances would militate against his success. "Being a Jew, a second-class citizen," he wrote, "I could not become a higher civil servant and, in peacetime, not even a lieutenant. I could have avoided these disadvantages by conversion, but then I would, I am convinced, have been condoning the breach of justice committed by the ruling classes." Even so, he was not immune to the challenge of political life. In 1907 and 1908, he accompanied the Colonial Secretary, Bernhard Dernburg, on tours of Germany's African colonies, and although Dernburg and others later became irritated over his importunities in asking for a decoration in recognition of his services, the memoranda that he wrote for the government after those trips were shrewd assessments of the colonial situation that did not hesitate to cast doubt upon German talents for empire-building.

It was during the First World War that Rathenau had his first real opportunity to serve his nation, and he demonstrated his abilities in the superb manner in which he organized and administered the War Raw Materials Department during the first years of the conflict. Despite the importance of his contribution to overcoming the dangerous shortage of strategic materials that had confronted Germany in 1914, he felt that his work had been resented both by the soldiers and the industrialists with whom he had had to deal and, when he resigned in 1915 to assume the presidency of AEG, he wrote to a friend: "Neither of the groups concerned can forgive me that I, a private citizen and a Jew, have done the State some service of my own accord, and I do not think that this attitude will change in my lifetime." This did not, however, cause him to withhold his services from the government. In the last years of the war, he gave his advice when it was asked for, particularly on economic questions, and wrote a series of reports that foresaw the kind of economic problems that would face Germany and her European neighbors when the war was over. His reflections upon these and his expert financial knowledge made him an indispensable man to the republican governments after 1919, and he served as a member of the German delegation to the Spa Conference on Reparations in 1920 and became minister of reconstruction in the cabinet of Josef Wirth in the following year.

At a time when the right-wing parties were spreading the stab-in-the-back legend and demanding an impossible resistance to Allied demands, Rathenau's willingness to undertake such sensitive assignments was courageous, the more so because he had the honesty to say publicly that Germany had no alternative to doing its utmost to carry out the terms of the Versailles Treaty, no matter how unpopular they might be. He became the strongest advocate of the policy of fulfillment, in the hope that this would in time persuade the Allies to moderate the treaty terms; and he devoted his considerable energies to negotiating with Western governments in order to advance this goal. "We must," he said in a speech to the German people, "find ways to bring ourselves together again with the world."

These exertions merely exasperated the resentful patriots, who regarded Rathenau's work as a continuation of the capitulation of 1918, which, they had convinced themselves, had been unnecessary and engineered by traitors, mostly Jews. It was inevitable, therefore, that when Rathenau was named foreign minister in February 1922 their reaction would be passionate. "Now we have it!" one right-wing paper wrote. "Germany has a Jewish foreign minister! . . . His appointment is an absolutely unheard-of provocation of the people"; and soon the murderous gangs of ex-Freikorps troopers were chanting:

> Knallt ab den Walther Rathenau,
> Die gottverdammte Judensau!

> [Shoot down Walther Rathenau,
> The Goddamned Jewish swine!]

The verse was a statement of intention. On the morning of June 24, 1922, as he rode down the Königsallee in Berlin, sitting in the open tonneau of his limousine, he was overtaken by a car carrying three young men, one of whom tossed a hand grenade into his machine while another shot him with an automatic pistol. He died a few hours later.

With the murder of Walther Rathenau, a border had been crossed, and Germany had entered a new and forbidding territory in which to be Jewish was more than a handicap or a social embarrassment; it was a danger and, not impossibly, a sentence to death. For Rathenau's only crime had been that he was a Jew who had dared not only to pretend that he was a German but to represent Germany to the outside world. His death caused a wave of horror in the land, but there is no doubt that many people privately considered it a not unjustified punishment. The obscene ravings of prewar anti-Semites had been given their first concrete expression. It was deplored but rationalized. The unthinkable had become thinkable. *Kristallnacht* was only sixteen years away, and the Final Solution was already beginning to take shape in the mind of the Führer of the National Socialist Party.

V

In 1975, thirty years after the Holocaust, the literary critic Hans Mayer, in an interview that dealt with his new book *Aussenseiter (Outsiders)*, was asked about statements in that book about contemporary German attitudes toward Jews. He answered: "The enmity toward the Jews is not much different, even though hardly any Jews live in Germany any more. This can be easily demonstrated by the fundamentally unsound relationship of the average German toward the phenomenon of the Jew and the state of Israel. First, there was the bad conscience, then the horribly artificial friendship for the Jews, the rejoicing over the victorious Seven Days War of the Israelis. Every 'progressive' bourgeois family in Germany wanted at some time or other to travel to Israel and to meet with Israelis. This enthusiasm soon became lukewarm again and ended up with the view that the Israelis were overdoing it, that they never learned, and that one had to admit there was lots to be said for the Arab point of view. The result is that hatred of the Jews—entirely in accordance with the example of Soviet propaganda—is differently expressed, as we already see in the case of part of the German student body and of average citizens: Of course, we have nothing against the Jews, 'only' against Israel and the Zionists. But, in the end result, this comes down to the same thing."

This is perhaps too drastically stated, although it is not hard to find evidence that seems to support it. That there is among some German intellectuals a tendency toward a kind of left-Fascism is undoubtedly true, and one of the characteristics of this has, as Mayer says, been an anti-Zionist attitude. It was noticeable in 1967, when the explosion in the universities coincided with the outbreak of war in the Near East, that radical student organizations in Heidelberg and other universities took the time from their local concerns to declare their solidarity with the Arabs on the grounds that they were fighting against imperialism and monopoly capitalism. A more blatant example of left-Fascism (although his supporters were quick to claim that it was nothing of the sort) was provided in 1978 by Rainer Werner Fassbinder in a play called *The Garbage, the City and Death*, in which one of the main characters was a "rich Jew," who was portrayed, as Joachim Fest said in an outraged article in the *Frankfurter Allgemeine Zeitung*, as "bloodsucker, speculator, swindler, murderer, and, in addition, as lascivious and vengeful," and in which one of the other characters was permitted to say, "They forgot to gas him. . . . I rub my hands when I think of the air going out of him in the gas chamber."

Offensive as it was, the Fassbinder play, which was printed but never produced, can probably be dismissed as an isolated case, a misguided attempt to *épater le bourgeois* and awaken people to what is happening to the modern city. As for the ambivalent attitude toward the Israelis, this is not unique to Germany; and it might reasonably be argued that the government of the Federal Republic, with the support of those "average citizens" to whom Mayer, without any evidence, attributed anti-Semitic feelings, has done more than most others to support the state of Israel. The president of the Jewish World Congress, Nahum Goldmann, who visited Germany in 1978 to attend services marking the fortieth anniversary of *Kristallnacht*, wrote shortly thereafter: "The generous attitude of the Federal Republic in matters of indemnification and reparations—unique in their extent and in the precedents that they created (to pay indemnities to a State that didn't exist in the Nazi period and reparations for noncitizens who suffered under the Nazis)—has done a great deal to normalize the wholly justified, mostly negative and often hostile attitude of the Jews toward post-Hitler Germany. There can be no talk of forgetting, and, between peoples, forgiveness has little meaning."

The question of forgetting—or rather of remembering—is, of course, crucial, and it would seem to be more important to inquire about collective German memory of the crimes committed against the Jews than to dwell longer on Mayer's generalized indictment. In August 1945, the philosopher Karl Jaspers gave an address in which he reminded his fellow Germans that "we did not go into the streets when our Jewish friends were led away; we did not scream until we too were destroyed. We preferred to stay alive, on the feeble, if logical, ground that our death could not have helped anyone. . . . We are guilty of being alive," Jaspers said, and he spoke of "our ineradicable shame and disgrace." How ineradicably was that shame to be felt by generations that had not participated directly in the execution of the Final Solution?

It is to the credit of the government of the Federal Republic and of the communications media and the West German theater and film industry that the memory of the inhumanities of the Nazi period has been periodically renewed, not only by commemorative services like the one that Nahum Goldmann attended, and by the preservation of the ruins of synagogues outraged and looted on *Kristallnacht*, but also by a series of notable television programs which documented the realities of the Final Solution and some memorable motion pictures like *The Diary of Anne Frank* and the Alain Resnais film *Night and Fog*, which were shown widely in Germany. German novels, particularly those of the members of Group 47, sought, like the inventor in Grass's *Dog Years*, to supply the postwar generation with spectacles that would enable them to see the true past; and there have been a number of powerful German plays that have dealt honestly with the persecution of the Jews. Notably effective in this last respect was Max Frisch's *Andorra* (1961), which told the story of a young man who was taken to be a Jew, although he was not, and who was first ostracized, then physically mistreated, and finally tortured and killed by his fellow citizens. Given its première in the Schiller Theater in Berlin, with the late Klaus Klammer and Martin Held in the leading roles, this was a deeply moving, and doubtlessly, for many spectators, painful experience, particularly because of the author's device of having the characters in the piece appear singly before the audience, in short scenes that interrupted the flow of the action, to explain, in contrived arguments, why they were guiltless in the fate of the victim.

It is ironical that all of these commendable efforts to prevent Germans from forgetting the dreadful issue of the German-Jewish relationship were outdone by a commercial television film made in the United States and aired in the Federal Republic in four consecutive installments in February 1979, each program lasting for two hours and being followed by an hour of discussion based on telephone calls from the viewing audience. Entitled *The Holocaust*, the series told the story of what the Germans had done to the Jews by focusing its attention on the fortunes of two fictional families, the Dorfs, whose son Erik made his career in the Nazi Party and, as Heydrich's deputy, organized the mass destruction of the Jews, and the family of the Jewish doctor Weiss, almost all of whom are caught up and killed in the machinery of terror. Because of this technique, viewers were able to identify themselves with the story to an extent that had been impossible in the case of earlier historical and documentary presentations, and this was reflected in the increase of the size of the audience from installment to installment, from 32% to 41% of the total audience, and in Berlin 47%. All told, 20 million people saw all or part of the series, and 30,000 of them telephoned to their local stations, the great majority of them to ask serious questions or to offer materials that corroborated or amplified details of the story. Schools all over Western Germany held discussions of the film and the historical reality behind it, at the request of the students, and the Düsseldorf Central Office for Political Education responded by sending 139,530 information kits containing 56-page brochures on the Final Solution to teachers all over North Rhine Westphalia.

There is no doubt that the reaction to the Holocaust film was more impressive than Hans Mayer's arguments about anti-Semitism in the Federal Republic. Although some of those who telephoned the television stations were belligerent and wanted to know why it was necessary to revive unpleasant memories after more than thirty years, they were vastly outnumbered by those who were obviously shaken by what they had seen and wanted answers to troubling questions: about how much average Germans living before 1945 had really known about what was being done to the Jews; about the degree of responsibility that today's Germans must bear for past crimes; about the lessons to be drawn from the story of the Holocaust.

That such questions should be asked, particularly by young Germans, struck observers as being a healthy and a hopeful sign, a sign perhaps of willingness to accept a dreadful past as one's own, without evasion or attempted exculpation. In a reflective essay on the effects of the film and the questions raised by it, Gräfin Dönhoff wrote that perhaps the most difficult of the latter was that of the conclusions that young people should draw from the awareness of the frightful outcome of German anti-Semitism. She cited the answer given by Renate Harpprecht, who had been an inmate of Auschwitz and whose parents had been gassed there. She said, "One cannot choose one's people. In those days, I wished many a time that I was not a Jew, but then I became one in a very conscious way. Young Germans will have to accept the fact that they are Germans—this is a fate that they cannot escape."

7

Women

The history of women's struggle for equality in Germany was, at least in its early stages, similar in some marked respects to that of Jewish emancipation. As in the latter case, the hopes that women entertained during the period of the Enlightenment faded rapidly in the nineteenth century, and women came under attack as inferior beings who had no right to expect full integration in society. If the analogy cannot be carried further, it is because Germans who found it possible to conceive of a society without Jews could not comfortably imagine one without women. Even so, the offensiveness of some of the antifeminist rhetoric was not significantly different from that employed by the anti-Semites.

This was, of course, not a solely German phenomenon. Women were victims in all bourgeois societies, and their plight was no better in Victorian England than in Bismarckian Germany. What was unique to Germany was that the subordination of women was more stubborn and protracted than in the advanced Western countries. The progress made in all those countries after the First World War was reversed in the German case when the Nazis came to power in 1933; and, although the lost ground was regained after 1945, it would be difficult to argue that the German Federal Republic, in its first thirty years, achieved anything like complete social and economic equality between the sexes. In the 1970s in particular, progress was disappointingly slow, a circumstance that could be attributed in part to continued male resistance to women's claims but also to the atomization of the women's movement and the tactics of much of its membership, and perhaps also—although this was harder to estimate—to the historical ambivalence of women toward the idea of equality and their fear of its possible consequences.

I

The subordination of women had ancient roots in Germany and was sanctified by custom, religion and law. Tacitus, who admired the morality of the German tribes and praised their marriage customs, nevertheless pointed to the inferior position of the wife by noting that she was "reminded by the ceremony that inaugurates marriage that she is

147

her husband's partner in toil and danger, destined to suffer and dare with him alike both in peace and war," that German women "receive one husband, as having one body and life, that they may have no thoughts beyond, no further-reaching desires," and that, in case of dereliction, "punishment is prompt . . . and in the husband's power." In a tribal society of warriors, male children were more important than females, and this prejudice found expression in customary rules concerning property and inheritance and basic rights that were transmitted from generation to generation and were eventually written into legal codes and statutes. Legally, women were dependents with few rights of their own, under the complete control of their fathers before marriage and their husbands thereafter, bound to obey the commands of these male protectors or, in case of refusal, to be punished by them, if need be—as various modern territorial civil codes stipulated—by physical means.

The fact that the labors of child-rearing devolved upon the wife did not alter the fact that, in disputes concerning the children, the husband's word was final; and, in the case of his death, ancient custom, reinforced by law in most German states, compelled his widow not only to have a male guardian for her children, even when she was their sole source of support, but to suffer his administration of family property, including that part of it gained by her own efforts. In states where the right of primogeniture prevailed, a woman with living brothers could not inherit her father's estate, even if she were the firstborn child. Nor, as far as society as a whole was concerned, did she possess basic civil rights, for she was excluded from many public activities, could not be a member of any political association, and did not possess the right to express herself on government policy that might affect her very nearly.

These disabilities were reinforced by a deep-seated Christian prejudice against women that was based on the suspicion that, as essentially emotional rather than intellectual beings, they were more prone to fleshly lust and carnal behavior than men. In the middle ages, there were churchmen who doubted whether women could be considered as Christians at all and whether it might not be seemlier to exclude them from church membership and observances. Later, with a curious reverse logic, it was argued that religion was a necessary means of occupying women's attention and preventing their minds from turning to more harmful activities. But even this tolerance was for long years coupled with restrictions on the nature and extent of women's participation. As late as 1700, in Hamburg, it was considered improper for them to sing in church; and, in the middle of the nineteenth century, their appearance at public meetings of the Friends of Light caused, as we have seen, much unfavorable comment.

During the eighteenth century, both the subordination of women and the tendency to justify it by means of theories based upon their innate sinfulness or lack of intellectuality came under sharp attack. For one thing, the influence of Pietism, which in contrast to orthodox Lutheran-

ism gave women an opportunity for self-expression in religious observance, had far-reaching repercussions, not the least of which was a moderation of the patriarchal idea of the family. Eda Sagarra has written
that the encouragement Pietist circles gave to frank revelations of religious experience and feeling "contributed to the notion that women's
sensibility might be different from that of men, that they might have a
personality outside their families, or that a marriage might even . . .
be a partnership of equals rather than an extension of the father-daugh-
ter relationship."

This was an idea that was not lost upon the great writers of the German age of classical humanism. The female characters in Goethe's
Elective Affinities and *Wilhelm Meister* had more sophisticated minds
and more independent wills than the male-dominated women in *Götz
von Berlichingen* and *Faust I;* and in Schiller's poem "The Dignity of
Women," the poet sought to describe the complementary relationship of
the sexes, the male passionate, Promethean, insatiable in his hunger, the
female the warning voice of morality and moderation and, at the same
time, the transformer of harsh reality into grace and beauty.

> Ehret die Frauen! sie flechten und weben
> Himmlische Rosen ins irdische Leben,
> Flechten der Liebe beglückendes Band,
> Und in der Grazie züchtigem Schleier
> Nähren sie wachsam das ewige Feuer
> Schöner Gefühle mit heiliger Hand.

> [Honor women! They twist and weave
> Heavenly roses into earthy life,
> Braiding the joy-bringing ribbon of love.
> And in the disciplined veil of grace
> They vigilantly nourish the eternal fire
> Of beautiful feelings with a holy hand.]

At the same time, especially among the upper middle class, the wholly practical idea began to dawn that women might become more interesting wives and better mothers to their children if they were encouraged to develop talents that went beyond the domestic arts. Under the
influence of books like the Marquise de Lambert's *Nouvelles réflexions
sur les femmes* (1727), which was widely read in educated circles in
Germany, there arose a lively interest in women's education, which had
until this time been neglected. The so-called moral weeklies, periodicals
that began in the first part of the century to imitate English magazines
like *The Tatler* and *The Spectator,* attacked the idea that women were
incapable of intellectual activity and the contradictory but related notion that women who read serious books would become inefficient in
their other tasks. They portrayed women who restricted themselves to
domestic chores as stupid or selfish and urged young women in particular to broaden their capacities by reading and not to be discouraged

from this by custom or prejudice. The editors of these journals and of the first successful women's magazine, Gottsched's *Die vernünftigen Tadlerinnen (The Discerning Gossips),* which was founded in 1725, fell short of urging anything like professional education for women; it was not their intention to encourage women to compete with men on their own ground. The abstract aspects of the learned disciplines were not for them. They should become readers of history rather than historians; they should know a great deal but not *gründlich* (profoundly). Their goal should be, not *Wissenschaft* (scholarship) for its own sake, but cultivation and a finer sensibility.

There were people who were unwilling to place these essentially artificial limitations on women's intellectual development. Both the Pietist leader A. H. Francke, who founded a school for young women called the Gynaceum in 1706, and the educational theorist Johann Bernhard Basedow saw no limits to women's capabilities if formal education were made available to them, and, at the end of the century, Theodor Gottlieb Hippel, the president of the city of Königsberg and administrator of the territory of Danzig, went even further. In a work entitled *The Civil Improvement of Women,* Hippel argued that all of the supposed weaknesses and inferiorities of women were the result of man-made conventions and laws and called for a liberation through education that would not only change the very nature of marriage but entitle women to full civil rights and responsibilities.

That this need not be idle theory seemed to be proved at the end of the eighteenth century by the appearance of a group of cultivated and liberated women who set out, with a remarkable indifference to convention, to demonstrate their intellectual equality with men. Some of them, the leaders of the Berlin salons, have already been mentioned. In addition, four famous daughters of famous scholars aroused the imagination of the age. Dorothea Schlözer, the daughter of the Göttingen political scientist A. L. Schlözer, demonstrated such marked intellectual gifts as a young woman that her father's colleagues urged her to work for an academic degree, and she became a doctor of philosophy in 1787, on the fiftieth anniversary of the University of Göttingen. She later became her father's research assistant and collaborated with him on a book on Russian coins; she studied mining, went on field trips to the mineral deposits near Goslar in the Harz, and wrote an article about her findings; and finally, after marrying a man of means, she presided over a salon that was the intellectual center of the town of Lübeck. She had firm opinions about the relationship of man and wife and once wrote to a friend: "Women are in the world not merely to amuse men. They are human beings like men, and each is supposed to make the other happy. Anyone who wants only to be amused is a rascal, or he deserves a woman with a pretty face, with whom he will be bored in four weeks. Does a woman make a husband happy solely because she is his cook or seamstress? . . . Don't you think that what I have studied could satisfy a man?"

Even more liberated from customary ideas about woman's role were

Thérèse Forster, the daughter of the philologist Moriz Heyne, Dorothea Veit, the daughter of Moses Mendelssohn, and Caroline Böhmer, the daughter of the orientalist J. D. Michaelis. The wife of Georg Forster, who sailed around the world with James Cook on his second voyage and, after an unrewarding life as professor of natural sciences and man of letters, founded a short-lived republic in Mainz in 1792 and died in Paris during the Terror, Thérèse remained her husband's confidante and the recipient of his most intimate reflexions on politics and philosophy even after she had left him, during the revolutionary turmoil in Mainz, for another man. Dorothea Mendelssohn Veit also left her first husband in order to marry Friedrich Schlegel, and this union of superior spirits produced, among other things, Schlegel's novel *Lucinde* which titillated the prurient and shocked the sober-minded by the frankness with which it discussed intimate relations between the sexes and called for an end to the kind of culture that pandered to male preconceptions and prejudices. As for Caroline Michaelis, whose independent spirit and determination to experience everything her century had to offer can best be gauged from her incomparable letters, after living in quiet domesticity with her first husband Böhmer, she began a new life after his death, fell in love with a man who brought her into Georg Forster's circle in Mainz and then left her pregnant when the revolutionary tide began to turn, was captured by the Prussians when they retook the town, was rescued from imprisonment and social ostracism by August Wilhelm Schlegel, who married her and whose translation of Shakespeare greatly benefited from the union, and finally parted from him and became the wife of the philosopher Schelling.

These were talented and formidable women, each in her own way following the tenth commandment of Dorothea's friend Schleiermacher's *Catechism of Reason for Noble Women,* to "lust after men's education, art, wisdom and honor"; but their activities rather daunted some people who had in the past been advocates of the liberation of women from old prejudices. Schiller, for example, had a high regard for the intellectual potential of women and was, in his dramas *Maria Stuart* and *Joan of Arc*, to give convincing portraits of women as practitioners of power, but he nevertheless tended to the view that the domestic scene was, for the great majority, the normal sphere. In his poem "The Song of the Bell" (1799), a work that was much admired and interminably recited in the nineteenth century, he wrote of the German home:

Und drinnen waltet	[in which governs
Die züchtige Hausfrau,	the disciplined housewife,
Die Mutter der Kinder,	the children's mother,
Und herrschet weise	and rules wisely
Im häuslichen Kreise	in the domestic circle
Und lehret die Mädchen	and teaches the girls
Und wehret den Knaben	and controls the boys
Und reget ohn' Ende	and moves without pausing
Die fleissigen Hände	her busy hands
Und mehrt den Gewinn	and increases the profit

Mit ordnendem Sinn	with her sense of order
Und füllet mit Schätzen	and fills the fragrant
die duftenden Laden	drawers with treasures
Und dreht um die schnurrende	And turns the thread on the
Spindel den Faden	humming spindle
Und sammelt in reinlich	and gathers in the clean
geglätteten Schrein	smooth cupboards
Die schimmernde Wolle,	the shimmering woollens,
den schneeigten Lein,	the snowy linens,
Und füget zum Guten den	and manages all of this
Glanz und den Schimmer,	shining glory well,
Und ruhet nimmer.	and never rests.]

Caroline's comment on this poem ("We almost fell off our chairs laughing . . . about 'The Song of the Bell' ") was characteristic and would not have surprised Schiller, who thoroughly disapproved of Caroline, whom he called "Dame Lucifer."

Wilhelm von Humboldt, certainly a man of normally progressive views, seems also to have been unfavorably affected by the excesses of Caroline and the others, and, in general, to have had serious misgivings about how emancipated it was permissible or proper for women to be. Humboldt's involuted attitudes toward the other sex are instructive, since they were probably not unique to him. Their key may be found in a passage in his journal for July 18/23, 1789, written as he was on his way to Paris:

> Between Duisburg and Krefeld one crosses the Rhine by ferry. One of the workers on this ferry was a girl, extremely ugly, but strong, masculine, and a good worker. It is incredible how such a sight attracts me—any sight of a physically hard-working woman, especially from the lower classes. I find it nearly impossible to turn my eyes away, and nothing else so strongly stimulates my sexual feelings. This is a left-over of the first years of childhood. When my soul was first occupied with females, I always imagined them as slaves, oppressed by all sorts of toil, tormented with a thousand tortures, and treated in the most despicable fashion. I still have some feeling for such notions. I can still, as formerly, imagine whole novels with such contents. Only now they contain somewhat less poor taste and somewhat more probability than when I was younger. It continues to be of great psychological interest to me to go through these unwritten novels in mind, in chronological order. How this direction originated in me remains a mystery. On the one hand, such harshness, on the other such voluptuous indulgence. But I am sure that it has been the basis, coupled with the situations that came my way, for my whole present character.

This is almost devastatingly frank. Humboldt married one of the most attractive and accomplished women of his age, Karoline von Da-

cheröden, whose letters to him, particularly during the months when he
was a member of the Prussian delegation to the Congress of Vienna,
reveal a lively perception of foreign affairs and a gift for political analysis. Humboldt respected her greatly, and there are some indications
that he was a little afraid of her. Although he was himself given to
uninhibited extramarital sexual behavior (if we can believe the tales of
his nocturnal adventures with Metternich and Friedrich von Gentz during the interallied talks in Prague in 1813), it is unlikely that his marriage was characterized by the kind of intimate abandon that was recommended in *Lucinde* or that figured in his private fantasies, and it is
even more unlikely that he wished it to be. He would probably have
rejected the suggestion that he believed in St. Jerome's dictum that "he
who loves his wife too passionately destroys the marriage," but it may
well have represented his view. He did not wish his wife to be too sex-
ually liberated, and he seems even to have regretted that she was so
intellectually liberated. Indeed, in his last years, he carried on a long
correspondence with a woman called Charlotte Diede, whom he never
allowed to come and see him, and whose attraction consisted in a complete submissiveness to his will, as expressed in the moral homilies and
instructions for self-improvement with which he crowded his letters.
Charlotte was in a sense the wife that Karoline refused to be.

After the transition from the enlightened aristocratic world of the
eighteenth century to the bourgeois respectability of the nineteenth,
such hidden reservations about women with intellectual pretensions and
a determination to make themselves the equals of men became at once
more general and more explicit. There was no longer a place for either a
Dorothea Schlözer or a Caroline Michaelis. In an age that now ceased
to believe in the utility of women's education (there were no decent
secondary schools for women until the eve of the First World War), the
former would have been a freak, while the latter, in a world of blue laws
and moral censorship, would have been regarded as disreputable. The
view of Theodor Gottlieb Hippel, that women deserved a share in civil
responsibility, was repudiated indignantly by some of the century's most
esteemed thinkers, on the grounds that feminine activity in the public
sphere was unnatural and unwomanly.

The dramatist Friedrich Hebbel, for example, declared cryptically in
1836, "Woman is banned to the narrowest circle; when the flowering
bulb breaks its glass, it dies." In his play *Judith* (1841), he elaborated
on this by portraying the biblical heroine as a woman whose feminine
frailties defeated her public mission, an implied argument against political women, and, indeed, against women with any aspirations outside
the domestic sphere; and in 1844, in the contemporary drama *Maria
Magdalena*, he idealized in the form of his heroine devotion to family
and the most extreme kind of social conformity. In the same spirit, in
the second volume of *Parerga und Paralipomena* (1851), Arthur Schopenhauer wrote that notorious Chapter 27, "On Women," in which,
with much faint praise, he damned them as incapable of either mental
or physical achievement, of having a weak reasoning faculty and being
"inferior to men in point of justice and less honorable and conscien-

tious," of existing "in the main solely for the propagation of the species and [of not being] destined for anything else," of being bereft of any sensibility for music, poetry or fine art and "incapable of taking a purely objective interest in anything," and, finally, of being "by nature meant to obey," which, Schopenhauer wrote triumphantly, "may be seen by the fact that every woman who is placed in the unnatural position of complete independence, immediately attaches herself to some man."

Richard Wagner, who combined a disreputable private life with a fervent advocacy of conjugal love, wrote to Liszt in 1852 that, in creating the character Ortrud in his opera *Lohengrin,* he had meant to portray a woman who "does not know love. In this fact, everything, of the most fearful nature, is summed up. Her nature is political. A political man is repellent, but a political woman is a thing of horror. I had to portray this horribleness."

Finally, this shrill and, one feels, nervous and self-protective, offensive against the idea of female equality in all aspects of civil life reached its peak in Nietzsche's assault, in *Beyond Good and Evil* (1886), upon people who were of a different persuasion. "Of course," he wrote sarcastically, "there are enough imbecilic friends of women and destroyers of women among the learned donkeys of the male sex, who advise woman to de-humanize herself and to imitate all the stupidities on which the European man and European masculinity sickens—who would like to drag woman down to 'universal education,' indeed, to newspaper-reading and politicking." The antifeminist animus was encapsulated here in a general critique of society, but it was nonetheless blatant for all of that.

Opinions like these were representative of the general disposition of bourgeois society in the nineteenth century, which was hostile toward any extension of civil rights to women. At the same time, the egalitarian idea of the family, which Schiller had championed, gave way once more to the patriarchal model. In his essay *The Subjection of Women* (1869), which was translated and widely circulated in Germany, John Stuart Mill wrote, "Marriage is the only serfdom that is recognized by the law." This described conditions in nineteenth century Germany as accurately as it did those in England. German women were imprisoned in a contract that might give them privileges but guaranteed them no rights, and that they could break, for whatever reason, only at the cost of material deprivation and social contumely. Even when they had property of their own, the law did not protect it adequately against the depredations of stupid or larcenous mates, and one of the more unpleasant aspects of Schopenhauer's essay on women was his matter-of-fact assumption that, since women created no property, they should be given no rights over it.

If the great majority of German males viewed these conditions with complacency or with that bland sentimentality that led one Catholic notable in 1912 to say that woman should be content "to wield her gentle scepter" and create "that dear, intimate domesticity against whose firmly girt walls the raging storms of the outside world break in vain," there were some who were moved to protest. In 1878, the leader of the German Social Democratic Party, August Bebel, wrote a book called *Woman and Socialism* which went through fifty-nine editions in the next fifty years. In a circumstantial analysis of the position of women in contemporary society, Bebel elaborated on a point made but not developed in Marx's *Communist Manifesto* of 1848, namely, that bourgeois marriage was at bottom a mere form of exploitation, a fitting reflection of a society that overworked and underpaid women in industry and domestic service and forced them into prostitution. Bebel criticized the prevalent assumption that women were intellectually inferior to men and the tendency to use this as an excuse for failing to provide adequate facilities for women's education, and he argued that woman had a right to be "a co-equal individual in her relationship to man and . . . the mistress of her own fate," choosing "as fields of activity areas that correspond[ed] to her wishes, inclination and temperament and . . . employed under the same conditions as men." Bebel's view was that none of this could be accomplished within the framework of the present society but must be the result of a thoroughgoing social revolution, and he called upon women to agitate for the right to vote as a necessary prerequisite to this.

With equal moral indignation, but with greater literary force and grace, the greatest novelist of the Bismarckian and Wilhelmine years, Theodor Fontane, attacked the victimization of women in his country, a problem that preoccupied him to such an extent that women were the main characters in twelve of his fourteen novels. This was not because Fontane held theoretical or doctrinaire views on the subject of women's rights, although he was aware of the arguments of Mill and Bebel, but rather because his own observations of German life convinced him that the current condition of women was a distressing commentary on the moral state of the country.

Fontane's approach to the problem was illustrated by his reaction to the protests against the serialization of his novel *Irrungen, Wirrungen* in 1887. This is the story of a happy love affair between a young nobleman and a daughter of the people, both of whom know that the norms of society will not permit it to last and are reconciled to that fact. The heroine of the novel was one of Fontane's most fully realized, and most positively Prussian, characters, as her lover recognized when he said that her character was one of "simplicity, truthfulness, and naturalness" and that she had "her heart in the right place and a strong feeling for duty, right, and order." Nevertheless, during the serial publication of the novel in the *Vossische Zeitung,* members of the Prussian aristocracy bombarded the newspaper with letters, demanding to know when "the dreadful whore's story" was going to be terminated.

Fontane reacted strongly. In a letter to his son, he wrote, "We are up to our ears in all sorts of conventional lies and should be ashamed of the hypocrisy we practice and the rigged game we are playing. Are there, apart from a few afternoon preachers into whose souls I should not like to peer any educated and decent people who are *really* morally outraged over a *Schneidermamsell* who is having an unsanctioned love affair? I don't know any. . . . The attitude of a few papers, whose yield of illegitimate children well exceeds a dozen (with the chief editor having the lion's share) and which are now pleased to teach me morality, is revolting!"

It was these hypocrisies that Fontane attacked in his novels, exposing the double standard of morality that tolerated infidelity and sexual license on the part of the male but outlawed women who acted similarly. This theme he developed particularly in his finest novel, *Effi Briest*, the story of a young woman who is married to an older man, who treats her with affection but as a child who must continually be taught lessons or reproved for mistakes. In a search for a moment of tenderness, she has a brief affair with another man. This is discovered by her husband six years later and, despite his love for his wife and his knowledge that the affair was meaningless, he kills the lover in a duel and leaves his wife, taking their child from her. The wife is subsequently abandoned by all of her friends and even by her own parents and, under this treatment, sickens and dies. The vindictive power of society against those who violated its conventions fascinated Fontane, who dealt with this theme also in his novel *L'Adultera*, in which the heroine, Mélanie van Straaten, is, however, strong-minded enough to defy social censure and, if not to defeat it, at least to survive.

In two of his most interesting, if least read, stories, *Quitt* and *Cécile*, Fontane described, with a cold disgust, the practice of the upper classes of educating their daughters only in such things as would make them attractive to men and secure them good marriages. This he regarded as shameful and degrading, since it deprived women of the opportunity for full development of their talents and depersonalized or reified them by turning them into commodities on the male market or, as was the case in *Cécile*, into odalisques.

Finally, Fontane challenged the basic assumptions of a society that was male-dominated and fed its prejudices by taking as gospel the views of people like Hebbel, Schopenhauer and Wagner on feminine inferiority. In the relationship between Mélanie and Rubehn in *L'Adultera*, between Stine and Waldemar in *Stine*, between Lene and Botho in *Irrungen, Wirrungen*, and between Mathilde and Hugo in *Mathilde Möhring*, it is the woman who is the stronger partner, the more resilient under the pressures of society, and in every sense the educator of the man. The last of these novels is the story of a plain but intelligent woman of the lower middle class who marries an attractive young man of good family but little power of concentration and will and, through her own energy and drive, gets him through his examinations, secures a job for him as *Bürgermeister* (mayor) of a small provincial town, and lays the basis for a brilliant career for him by her sage counsel and her ability to ingratiate herself with the local notables. It has been said that, in his protagonist, Fontane succeeded in creating a woman of the twentieth century rather than of his own, and that none of his other women possess so many qualities, positive and ambiguous, that point to the future. If this was so, it was also true that Mathilde Möhring reflected the basic predicament of women in Wilhelmine society, for she was allowed to profit from the fruits of intellectual energy and social and political skills only as long as her husband was present to take credit for them. After his death, she was forced to return to the station out of which she had lifted herself and him and to begin all over again, which, indomitably, she proceeded to do.

Upon the bulk of middle class opinion, the criticism of Bebel and Fontane had little effect. The very fact that the former was a Socialist prevented his analysis from touching bourgeois hearts and minds. As for Fontane, his reputation rested upon his ballads and his *Wanderings Through Mark Brandenburg* rather than his novels, and those who read the latter reminded themselves that he was a good Prussian who was, after all, simply telling stories. His powerful and profoundly critical novels were thus digested by the middle-class reading public with no deeper discomfort than an occasional twinge of moral outrage over his frankness in dealing with relations between the sexes.

II

In this masculine society, there was for a long time nothing that could properly be described as a women's movement—that is, an organized effort to relieve the various kinds of subordination from which women suffered. In the 1840s, to be sure, the literary movement known as Young Germany was interested in the kind of sexual liberation preached in *Lucinde*, but the Young Germans pursued so many diverse objectives that nothing much came of this. The same could be said of the efforts of individual writers to call attention to women's problems, like the society novelist Countess Ida von Hahn-Hahn and Luise Aston, whose book *My Emancipation, Censure and Vindication* made a mild sensation in 1846. These isolated cases had no sensible effects.

In the period before the revolution of 1848, there were, nevertheless, some notable women activists, like Bettina von Arnim, the sister of the poet and fabulist Clemens Brentano and the wife of Achim von Arnim, who had collaborated with Brentano on the collection of folksongs known as *Des Knaben Wunderhorn (Youth's Magic Horn)*. Bettina combined all of the domestic virtues (her governance of the Arnim household would have aroused the admiration of the author of "The Song of the Bell") with a desire "to be a part of everything that is in the world at the same time as I." After her husband died in 1831, she moved to Berlin and won respect as a writer with two letter-novels, *Goethe's Correspondence with a Child* (1835), from which she acquired her nickname *Das Kind*, and *Die Günderode*, which commemorated her friend Katherine von Günderode, an accomplished poet who had taken her own life because of an unhappy love affair.

Bettina's salon in Berlin acquired some of the fame that had once attached to Rahel's, but she was not content to be a social lioness and turned her attention increasingly to the problems of the vulnerable and the deprived. During the great cholera outbreak of 1831 (which took the lives of, among others, Hegel and Clausewitz), she organized medical care for the poor of Berlin and was appalled by the misery she found in the already well-developed slums of the city. After the accession of Frederick William IV, an event that was mistakenly regarded as the beginning of a period of liberal reform, Bettina wrote a remarkable book called *This Book Belongs to the King* (1843) in which she gave a detailed description of the colony of unemployed and paupers called the *Vogtland* that had grown up around the Hamburg Gate in Berlin and attacked the churches and the royal bureaucracy for having done nothing to check the progressive social decay caused by the Industrial Revolution.

This appeal to Frederick William to become a king of the common people was not successful, and the authorities confiscated a digest of the book as subversive. This did not prevent Bettina from writing an account that exposed the wretched conditions of the Silesian weavers, although this work too was a victim of the censors. In 1848, she stood on the side of the working class, and her efforts in behalf of the inhabitants of Prussia's Polish districts made her unpopular both with the King's party and with the liberals.

No less indomitable a champion of democracy was Emma Siegmund, who became the wife of the poet and revolutionary Georg Herwegh. The daughter of wealthy Berlin parents who were converted Jews, she devoted her youth, with an assiduity resembling that of Dorothea Schlözer, to an intensive study of history, foreign languages, music and painting; but after 1842, when she met and married Herwegh, she lived and breathed politics, moving to Paris, where she and her husband became friends with Karl and Jenny Marx, Heine and the popular poet Pierre-Jean Béranger, Liszt and George Sand. When the revolution of 1848 came, Emma Herwegh lived up to the promise that she had made in an early letter to her husband: "We will show what two people can do who are sworn to the same flag. . . . No person's strength is too slight to set the great wheel in motion. Inspiration has mighty powers and awakens them also in women." The painter Anselm Feuerbach once sketched Emma Herwegh as a Germanic woman driving wavering warriors back into the fray. In the struggles of 1848, her role was not much different, and in the days when all the high hopes collapsed, she fought at her husband's side, revolver in hand, as a member of the Badenese Legion, and then fled into exile in England. Here her political activities did not cease. She had intimate contacts with the Italian secret revolutionary society called the Carbonari and, in 1857, helped Felice Orsini escape from the dreadful Austrian prison in Mantua known as St. Giorgio by sending him a book with two saws inserted in the binding and by planning his escape route. She became an ardent Garibaldian, translating the Italian patriot's memoirs in 1860, was a bitter foe of Napoleon III and, after his defeat by the Prussians, became an equally determined enemy of Prussian militarism.

Neither Bettina von Arnim nor Emma Herwegh thought it important to work for women's rights. Their attention was focused on the general political and social problems of their age, which, they thought, democratic revolution would solve. If they took the time in their busy lives to think of specifically feminine grievances, they probably assumed these would disappear when that revolution was triumphant. This was doubtless naive. There is more than enough evidence to indicate that, even had the events of 1848 effected a decisive change in the German political situation, the position of women would not have changed significantly. In the debates of the Frankfurt Assembly, the male parliamentarians (there were no women delegates to the body that aspired to write a new constitution for Germany) didn't raise the question of women's rights at all, and the Fundamental Rights of the German People, drafted by the Assembly, was silent on the subject.

This omission was not forgotten by the woman who became the founder of the first organized movement for the rights of her sex. Luise Otto, the daughter of a Saxon civil servant, began her career as an aspiring writer and, in the 1840s, under an assumed name, wrote two novels, *Ludwig the Tapster* and *Castle and Factory*, which in their social criticism deserve comparison with the contemporaneous novels of Elizabeth Gaskell. Her study of economic conditions in Saxony opened her eyes to the fact that women were the most exploited members of the working class; and, in 1848, with a forthrightness and explicitness that was extraordinary for the times, she appealed to German workers, in a letter to the *Leipzig Workers News* and in a speech to an All German Workers Congress in Berlin, to include the protection of women's rights in their demands, reminding them that prevailing conditions in industry were contributing to family disintegration and prostitution. Her audience was unresponsive, and she drew the conclusion that "men can give us only limited aid" and that women themselves must henceforth take the initiative.

The political reaction that was prevalent in all German states in the decade after the revolution was unpropitious for any organized movement, but in the 1860s, as the unification issue revived political agitation for many causes, Luise Otto-Peters (in 1857 she had married the radical democrat Karl Peters, who had been imprisoned for seven years for his share in the fighting in Baden) took up the fight again and in 1865 founded a Women's Educational Union to promote the idea that women should have the right to work and to an education as a matter of principle. Later in the year, as a result of her efforts, a convocation of women's groups led to the founding of the General German Women's Association. This organization, which had 9000 members as early as 1870, became, under the leadership of Otto-Peters's disciples Helene Lange and Auguste Schmidt, the spearhead of the middle-class women's movement in the Bismarckian and Wilhelmine periods and the directing force in the Federation of Women's Associations, which was founded in 1894, when the proliferation of local and special women's societies made amalgamation seem advisable.

It was characteristic of the bourgeois movement that, as the years passed, it tended to become increasingly conservative in its objectives, shifting from the impulse toward democratic reform that had animated its founder to an emphasis on amelioration of existing conditions rather than fundamental change. Perhaps this was because it was influenced both by the prevailing nationalism of the age and by the tactics of the German liberal parties, where it had some sympathizers. In any event, both Helene Lange and her secretary Gertrud Bäumer, who became the head of the Women's Federation in 1910, believed that it was more important for women to prove that they were loyal and competent subjects who could perform useful services to the nation than to concentrate their efforts on gaining rights for themselves. Even the right to vote seemed to them to be relatively inessential. Although Hedwig Dohm, whose political ideas had been formed during the struggles of 1848, had declared as early as 1872 that the "beginning of all true progress in the woman question . . . lies in woman suffrage" and in 1876 had cried, "What is a negro? What is a Jew? What is a woman? . . . Oppressed People. Oppressed by whom? By their brothers who are stronger than they," it was not until 1902 that this was accepted, reluctantly and ambiguously, as an objective by the Federation. In most middle-class women's societies before then, the emphasis had been on character-building and self-help, on educational reform to prepare women to be better wives and mothers, and on charitable and welfare activities, like the establishment of kindergartens, homes for unmarried working women, and recreational centers to protect single working women from big-city vice.

There were more radical tendencies within the bourgeois movement, and at the turn of the century these were represented by the *Mutterschutz* League, which focused more directly on the male-female relationship, demanded that women be given the same right to determine their personal lives as men, and campaigned for such things as the dissemination of knowledge about contraception, the recognition of marriage without benefit of clergy, and government support for unmarried mothers. These demands, which were in excess of anything in the programs of women's associations in Great Britain and the United States, aroused so much indignation in the general public that after 1908 they were virtually repudiated by the Women's Federation. In the last years before the war, the policy of that organization became increasingly moderate and supportive of the status quo, Gertrud Bäumer stating explicitly in her speeches that it was the duty of women to strive in their own way to promote national strength and reduce social conflict and that their goal should be not "formal equality but [to bring] the equally full and rich influence of all female values on our culture."

In the years that followed the publication of Bebel's *Woman and Socialism*, a strong Socialist women's movement had grown up, affiliated with the Social Democratic Party and the trade unions. Its leaders focused their attention on practical tasks, such as educating women workers to the realities of their position in the labor force and agitating for the eight-hour day, the prohibition of work in jobs detrimental to women's health, maternity and health insurance, female factory inspectors, and similar objectives, and at all times urging the importance of votes for women in trade councils and local and national government. Between this movement and the middle-class one there was, for reasons of ideology and class, little possibility of collaboration. When Lily Braun, a nobleman's daughter who had become a Socialist out of humanitarian conviction and who rejected both the historical materialism and the class bias of the party, called for a Socialist-led women's movement that would cut across class lines, work for specifically feminine objectives, and try to alleviate some of the consequences of the decay of the family by practical reforms like home cooperatives, she was assailed by her party comrades for failing to understand the class struggle and for other sins of deviation. Klara Zetkin, an influential member of the party's left wing, declared, "Feminist ideas are a great danger to the German Social Democratic Women's Organization. . . . There is no community among women as a whole." In Zetkin's view, and it was the majority one, there could be no trafficking with the class enemy, nor should good Socialist women place their feminist objectives above the general aims of the party. Their grievances would disappear when the classless society was attained.

Despite its large membership (the bourgeois Women's Federation spoke for about 300,000 women in 1912, and the Socialist Women's Organization was larger), the women's movement was badly split before 1914, and the effect of the war was to weaken and divert what strength of purpose it possessed. The acquisition of political rights for women was not, therefore, the result of pressure or persuasion brought to bear by any of the groups that have been mentioned here, but rather of military defeat and the collapse of the German Empire.

III

In all countries, the First World War weakened old orthodoxies and authorities and, when it was over, neither government nor church nor school nor family had the power to regulate the lives of human beings as it had once done. One result of this was a profound change in manners and morals that made for a freer and less restrained society. Women benefited from this as much as anyone else. Time-worn prescriptions concerning what was or was not proper behavior for them no longer possessed much credibility, and taboos about unaccompanied appearances in public places, or the use of liquor or tobacco, or even premarital sexual relationships had lost their force. All of this was as true in Germany as it was in England and France; and, during the years of the Weimar Republic from 1919 to 1933, women were no longer as vulnerable to the tyranny of society as they had been in Fontane's day.

With this new freedom came new accomplishment. The role of women in the cultural activities of the Weimar period was prominent, and it is impossible to believe that the Republic's brief existence would have been so exciting and productive without the work of Elisabeth Bergner, Tilla Durieux, Fritzi Massary, and Trude Hesterberg in the theater, Sigrid Onegin and Frida Leider in the opera, Mary Wigman in the dance, Else Lasker-Schüler, Gertrud Le Fort, Mechtilde Lichnowsky and Vicki Baum in literature, and Ricarda Huch in history.

Moreover, the road was now open to distinguished performance by other women, for the old prejudice against higher education for women had been forced to give way. One of the most notable accomplishments of the Republic was the raising of the status of secondary education for women, a reform promoted by the Reich School Conferences of 1920–1923. Since the universities had finally recognized the inevitable and opened their doors to qualified women during the war, the improvements in the lower schools meant that female admissions rose sharply, and that circumstance was reflected in turn in the numbers of women who now stormed the barricades of the professions or made their way in the less tradition-bound academic disciplines like psychology, sociology and—the choice of one of Vicki Baum's heroines—chemistry.

These gains lasted at least until the Nazis took power in 1933. Less permanent—and their impermanence may to some degree have contributed to the rise of Nazism—were the political and economic gains registered in 1919.

As a result of the November revolution of 1918, which toppled the Imperial regime, and the acceptance of a republican constitution a year later, German women received the right to vote. It was expected, particularly in view of the enthusiasm with which women initially responded, that this would lead to an appreciable extension of women's rights. Nearly 80% of all eligible women voted in 1919; nearly 10% of the National Assembly and between 5% and 10% of the state legislatures were women; and it seemed inevitable that this would bring legislation that would equalize wages, improve working conditions for women and effect other long-delayed reforms.

In fact, nothing of the sort happened. Confronted with an entirely new political situation, no political party at the war's end had dared express any doubts about women's rights. From the left-wing Socialists to the Conservatives, they had all supported the grant of suffrage to women, and each of them had sought to attract as many of the new voters as possible by including women on its party list and even in its executive. But this did not mean that they were happy about the change. Some of the men who controlled the parties were, in fact, deeply troubled by it and recognized that male voters shared their doubts. The Democratic Party, which in the spectrum of party politics stood originally toward the left, distributed to its constituents a flyer that read:

> Are you, whose word counts in the family, content with this new franchise? You need not alter your position in your family circle! Remain what you were and what you are, but bring your wife and daughters along with you to vote, even if

it is not your custom to discuss politics with them. . . . You
must become their political educator.

In the same spirit, the party executives saw to it that power in their
organizations was left in male hands; and, as time passed, women
received a decreasing share of party offices and influence. This was true
even of the Social Democratic Party, despite the fact that the number of
women party members increased from 15.8% in 1924 to 23% in 1930. In
no party did women ever fill more than 10% of the leading positions, and
at the local level the percentage was between 1% and 2%.

The competence of the 111 women who served in the German Reichstag between 1919 and 1933 was undoubted; their work, particularly on
parliamentary committees on population, legal and educational questions, and social welfare, was valuable; and their courage was extraordinary. In 1933, the Social Democrat Klara Bohm-Schuch did not hesitate to protest to the president of the Reichstag, Hermann Goering,
about the storm troopers' mistreatment of the municipal deputy Maria
Jankowski and to demand punishment of the guilty parties. Goering's
answer was to have her arrested and interned, an experience that caused
her death in 1936. Of the whole body of Weimar woman parliamentarians, four committed suicide after the Nazi takeover, thirteen were arrested and ten sent to concentration camps, and fourteen had to go into
exile.

There is no question that the presence of these women in the Reichstag had some positive effects upon the position of German women in
general, but certainly not as much as one might have expected. They
soon found that the political parties were not prepared to fight for any
extension of women's rights that might threaten male prerogatives.
When the chips were down, not even the Social Democratic Party voted
for equal pay for equal work, or for equal job security and working
conditions. Statutes that discriminated against women in family governance and property rights went uncorrected. And, on occasion, the male
Reichstag members showed a startling tendency to revert to prewar
moral attitudinizing and to gestures that seemed to say that, if women
wouldn't stay at home where they belonged, they deserved no consideration. Legislation to protect unmarried mothers from disqualification
for the public service was defeated in the Reichstag, as were efforts
to protect working mothers and to improve health care for their
children.

It is possible that disenchantment with the meager results of the
acquisition of voting rights had something to do with the fact that, in the
last days of the Republic, women voters turned increasingly to the conservative parties, and particularly to National Socialism. More important, probably, was the Depression, which strengthened latent doubts
about the advantages of emancipation. That women had mixed feelings
about equality was noticeable even in the prewar period. As the novelist
Gabriele Reuter once wrote, even those who aspired to a life whose
horizons comprehended more than marriage and family sensed that the

costs of wider freedom might not be negligible, "that the taste of that seductive fruit of knowledge [might] exclude [them] forever from the paradise of [their]innocence and all the blessed happiness of blindness." And of course there were many—indeed, the great majority—who had no such aspirations. In 1919, these women did not regard the right to vote as a victory. An electoral pamphlet of the Evangelical Women's Federation stated in that year: "Evangelical women in their great majority did not strive after the female franchise. Now that it is given to them, they must exercise it as a duty imposed upon them"; and an appeal addressed to Conservative women spoke of the vote as "the unwished burden" that had been "laid on" women. It was noticeable that many were unwilling to carry the new load, and that the number of women who took the trouble to exercise their franchise decreased from election to election.

On the other hand, once the National Socialist Party had recovered from the debacle of 1923, it always attracted a respectable number of female votes and, after September 1930, when the party increased its popular vote from 809,000 to 6,400,000, women voters constituted a large part of that total. Despite the fact that the NSDAP was consistently reactionary on all questions relating to women from employment to education, that it had no women in its executive organization or its Reichstag delegation, and that it made no bones about its blatant philosophy of male superiority, it attracted women voters because it promised to restore the position of the home and the family in a society whose growing economic troubles threatened them and to restore the dignity that was properly woman's, as helpmate and supporter of her husband and as German mother, assuring the future of the Germanic race. It has often been said of Adolf Hitler that the key to his success as an orator was his ability to make every one of his auditors the hero of the German drama, and women were by no means immune to this hypnotic power. When the Führer talked of the divided but complementary worlds of man and woman, the former the struggle for State and community, the latter "a smaller world . . . her husband, her family, her children and her home," his words seemed to define and ennoble the natural vocation of women and to invest it with patriotic purpose. This would doubtless not have been so compelling had the Depression not denied to so many women the comforts of that smaller world and left them feeling unfulfilled and insecure.

Hitler's response to the help women gave him in his conquest of power was to defeminize the whole of the public service as well as the agencies that supplied it with talent. Women in the federal and regional bureaucracies and the courts and in the legal and medical professions were dismissed or pressured into resigning. There was a reduction in the number of women teachers at all levels; curricula in girls' schools suffered modification to place greater emphasis upon domestic sciences; the number of women students in universities shrank radically. At the same time, in order to encourage social sharing as a means of overcoming the Depression, working women who had fathers or brothers with jobs were asked to surrender their own.

In return, however, the Nazi State offered a number of rewards to women who were willing to leave the labor force in order to get married and raise a family: marriage loans, tax allowances, maternity benefits, provision for the education and vocational training of older children, health services, and other inducements, including the psychological bonus of being publicly praised for their services to State and race. This last reward was not negligible. The propaganda that appealed to the warlike instincts of the Germans, calling upon them to awaken and break the ring of their enemies, made the German *Frau und Mutter* a warrior too; and the continued loyalty that millions of women (the National Socialist *Frauenschaften* claimed 7 million members) showed to Hitler to the bitter end testifies to the pride that they took in the assignment.

Even in so cursory a treatment of the relationship between women and National Socialism, two additional observations have to be made. The first is that there were also many women who did not venerate Hitler or delight in serving him, but were either part of that negative opposition to the regime that was known as the Inner Emigration or members of active resistance groups. How many of the former there were will never be known, nor is it possible to estimate the effectiveness of their only weapon—the withholding of their energies, as far as possible, from any enterprise that might benefit the regime—although it is likely that it was not inconsiderable. Among the latter, not a few gave their lives, among them Elisabeth von Thadden, a member of the oppositional Confessing Church, Johanna Kirchner, who worked tirelessly to help Hitler's victims escape and to find support for German exiles, Maria Terwiel, who cooperated with the resistance group of Captain Harro Schulze-Boysen, disseminated subversive materials, and procured forged papers for Jews, Sophie Scholl, who with her brother and a small group of fellow students and teachers in the University of Munich, tried to awaken people to the enormity of Hitler's actions and, in the words of one of the flyers that she broadcast, "to promote a renewal of the sorely wounded German spirit." To paraphrase a poem by Georg Herwegh,

> While the masses of the people
> Formed a lane, as usual, for the ruler,
> They cried,
> "Make way for freedom!"

In the second place, it is not unlikely that the Nazis' ideological and biological prejudices about the role of women in society hastened their defeat in the war. Albert Speer, Hitler's minister of armaments and munitions from 1942 to 1945, repeatedly urged the total mobilization of women for war production on the ground that they would be better workers than foreign laborers. In April 1943, his pleas encountered the sharp opposition of Fritz Sauckel, the commissioner of manpower, who persuaded Hitler that factory work would inflict physical and moral harm upon German women and damage their psychic and emotional life and possibly their potential as mothers. Later in the year, when

Speer returned to the charge, the *Gauleiter* protested to Hitler in a body, and the request was once more denied. According to Speer's calculations, the mobilization of the 5 million women who were capable of war service but were performing none would have released 3 million male workers for military service. Such an accretion of strength might well have altered the result in Africa or at Stalingrad, although it is doubtful that it would have prevented the ultimate defeat and collapse of the Nazi war effort.

IV

In 1968, at the height of the university agitations in Berlin, women members of Students for a Democratic Society (SDS), tired of duplicating messages of protest that never mentioned women and of sitting through interminable discussions in which their own grievances were never raised, suddenly rebelled, crying, "Comrades! Your meetings stink!" They were outraged by the discovery that, even within a group protesting against inequality, injustice and exploitation, the male leadership was proving to be just as indifferent to women's concerns as men in society at large, an indication that the inferior position of women would be as pronounced in the brave new world that the SDS was trying to create as it was perceived by them to be in the Federal Republic.

Legally, of course, such inferiority did not exist in the Bundesrepublik. When the rubble to which Germany had been reduced by Allied bombing had been cleared away, and the process of denazification completed to the satisfaction of the Occupying Powers, and political sovereignty granted to the West Germans, the Basic Law of their new Republic stated clearly in its third article: "Men and women have equal rights." This was regarded in 1949 as being the completion and full realization of the process begun in 1919 with the grant of women's suffrage. It was a legal order to cease and desist, to eliminate once and for all any kind of restriction, in any field of activity, on women's rights relative to men's. But, of course, the effectiveness of laws depends upon how they are implemented, and the full implementation of Article 3 had not been achieved by 1959, when the Godesberg Program of the Social Democratic Party protested against the lack of progress made during the past ten years, or by 1968, when the angry women marched out of the SDS meeting, or by 1980, when the Bundestag passed a law declaring its adherence to the European Community's normative declaration of 1976 on equality, remuneration and benefits and was immediately attacked for making an empty gesture.

That there had been improvements in the position of women was doubtless true. The change in manners and morals, begun in the Weimar Republic and interrupted in the Nazi period, had been resumed, accelerated now by television and by closer contact with Western countries, and profoundly changing the way people looked at family arrangements. There was little place for old orthodoxies and patriarchal notions in a society in which, in 1971, 92 out of 100 unmarried women under thirty years of age (as opposed to 24 out of 100 in 1967) said that they would be willing to share an apartment with a man without being married to him. The new freedom was gradually reflected in law. Women's right to possess property of their own was assured by statute; and new regulations on marriage and the family not only abolished Paragraph 1356 of the Civil Code, which had defined housework as the woman's duty, but modernized the marriage contract by stipulating that family roles were to be defined by mutual agreement and by protecting women's property and family rights in case of divorce. Critics pointed out that the new marriage, family and divorce law of 1977 was far from perfect and that lawyers could easily interpret the clauses concerning the wife's right to be employed outside the family in such a way as to prevent her taking a position that might jeopardize the smooth running of family affairs (maintaining, perhaps, that wives could not be flight attendants, although husbands could be pilots). But there was no doubt that, in the private sphere, women had more legal protection against mistreatment than ever before.

In the world outside the home, this was far less true. Despite all the brave words of politicians, it was easy to prove that women did not enjoy equal opportunity in employment in the Federal Republic and that the number of positions held by them in the public service and the professions was disproportionately small. Representation of women in the Bundestag reached its highest point—9.2%, less than the 10% of the National Assembly in 1919—in 1957 and fell steadily thereafter, to less than 7% in 1980; and this was true also of their membership in the parliaments of the separate states. The number of women lawyers in 1980 was ten times what it was in 1925 and three times what it was in 1933, but this wasn't saying much, for the respective figures were 5%, .5% and 1.5%. The number of doctors had increased fourfold since 1933 but amounted to only 20%.

In the world of business, the situation was even worse. Theoretically, management positions were open to qualified women, but the principle of tokenism clearly prevailed, and most women found themselves shunted off into inferior positions even when their qualifications were as good as those of their male competitors. Laws concerning discrimination were neither as explicit nor as punitive as in the United States; it was difficult and costly for women to prove discrimination and, in most cases, they could not count on union support unless they were already employed. As Germany's largest women's magazine, *Emma*, said, the result was that women "got only what men left, the crumbs that fell from the table." Realization of this had depressing effects on enrollments in government-supported professional training programs for women, which fell by 50% between 1975 and 1976.

It was not inaccurate to talk of a progressive disqualification of skilled women workers. Women who were trained as bookkeepers, accountants and secretaries found themselves threatened increasingly by data-processing machines and other forms of rationalization. Meanwhile, the great majority of working women were assigned to those positions that required the least skill, mental exertion and personal initiative, were the worst paid, and were the most vulnerable to economic recession. Sixty-three percent of all workers on assembly lines, for example, were women, and these were generally the first to be let go in time of slowdowns and, once unemployed, were the most disadvantaged in the search for new positions. In hard times, the job market was dominated by the traditional male prejudice that women really didn't need jobs at all; and in 1978 this was reflected in the fact that although women constituted only 40% of the working force, 54% of the unemployed were women.

It was clear that some of this inequality of treatment (particularly in the matter of unemployment) was due to the fact that women workers were in general less well trained, less mobile, and more concentrated in especially crisis-prone activities; but these special circumstances could not explain away the discrimination in pay and promotion and other areas, which was in large part the result of decisions made in male-dominated employment agencies, unions and executive boards. In the economic sphere, it appeared that the explicit requirement of Article 3 of the Basic Law had not persuaded these bodies to change their traditional views. In 1980, Eva Rühmkorf, director of the Hamburg Senate's Office for the Equalization of Women, said, "I'm afraid we'll still have to wait hundreds of years if we think that we can improve the situation of women by changes in the consciousness of men," adding that only legal compulsion and monetary fines for discrimination would be of any use.

Why were women themselves incapable of mounting a movement of protest to change these conditions? The answer seems to lie in the divided focus of the kind of activist-minded women who in the past had formed the backbone of the militant feminist organizations. In the first place, disillusionment with the progress made toward emancipation during the Bundesrepublik's first two decades, and a more general disenchantment with the values of capitalist society, led many women, during the violent phase of the university revolution, into radical political activity, which they followed with various degrees of intensity, the most unconditional of them becoming in the end part of the terrorist scene. Women like Gudrun Ensslin and Ulrike Meinhof were in the tradition of Emma Herwegh and the murdered revolutionary of 1919, Rosa Luxemburg, rather than fighters for women's rights, and, in the end, their activities probably hurt the women's cause.

In the second place, many other women devoted their energies to a radical feminism that sought to attack male dominance in the sexual sphere by means of an emancipation of the body and an assertion of womanliness. The original appeal of this shift in direction, which was reminiscent of the prewar *Mutterschutz* movement, was apparent in 1972 in the nationwide campaign against Paragraph 218 of the Civil Code, which placed stringent inhibitions upon abortion, and in the euphoric mood of the first national Women's Congress in Frankfurt, which was the high point of that campaign. But, as the author Lottemi Doormann pointed out in 1979, that was the last truly representative congress of women, for the feminist movement soon fragmented until there were 140 different women's groups, few of which found it possible to agree either on objectives or tactics, many of which carried their war against men to ridiculous extremes—turning feminism, in her words, into "an expedition into the irrational"—and some of which elevated lesbianism into their ideal. This amounted to a form of self-banishment into female ghettos, and it was a wasting of energies that might properly have been used to protect women's rights at a time when the chances of employment were worsening and when local and national agencies were reducing expenditures for kindergartens, daycare homes and playgrounds, all of which hit directly at the working mother.

Progress toward equality for women in the Federal Republic would seem, therefore, to have been handicapped as much by the tactics of women's groups as by the traditional reluctance of men to give up the material and psychological advantage that they have always enjoyed. Moreover, just as the extreme tactics of some of the advocates of the the Equal Rights Amendment in the United States had the effect of arousing the opposition of many women to that proposed legislation, so did the activities of the Ulrike Meinhofs on the one hand and the radical feminists on the other reinforce the doubts of many German women about the social and moral costs of equality.

Official statements from the German Democratic Republic often claim that, with respect to women's rights, the DDR is considerably more advanced than the Federal Republic. They point out that the constitution guarantees equality of the sexes in all spheres of social, State and personal life and stipulates that "the advancement of the woman, particularly in professional qualification, is a mission of society and State" and cite data to show that every third member of the Peoples Chamber (as of 1974) was a woman, as well as every fifth mayor, every fourth person in a supervisory position in State-owned industry, every third chairman of an agricultural collective, every fifth school director and every third judge. They argue that equal pay for equal work is not only laid down in the constitution but is a reality, and that working women have a wide range of social benefits.

This would be more impressive if these preferments were open to women on some other basis than party loyalty in a one-party State. The problem in East Germany is not that women are not equal to men (although, if we knew more about family conditions in the DDR, we might discover that that was true also), but that, given equal talent and qualifications, all women do not possess the same rights as other women. There is more than enough data to show that professing Christians cannot expect the same treatment as women with more conformist minds, and religion is not the only disability. When ideological conformity is the determinant of appointment to public office, of educational opportunity and of job assignment, as it is in the DDR, comparison with other systems, with respect to the rights of women or anything else, becomes impossible.

8

Professors and Students

Perhaps no institution in modern Germany has been more resistant to change than the university and, until the 1970s, more successful in preserving its traditional forms of internal governance. After the Second World War, there were people who remembered its authoritarian anti-republican stance during the Weimar period and who talked of the necessity of a basic reorganization and democratization of the university structure, and some experiments were actually made in this direction. This was true in the Free University of Berlin, for instance, which was founded in 1948, when students and young faculty seceded from the old Friedrich Wilhelm (now Humboldt) University on Unter den Linden in the Soviet sector and, with American aid, relocated in Dahlem in the western part of the city. This new foundation began as a collaboration between professors and students, and the latter were admitted to all committees and were given a voice in the appointment of all new faculty. But after a few years, restrictions were imposed on this system of parity, and the rights of the students in university decision-making gradually disappeared. In 1962, when one of the original founders of the Free University described to Frederick Burckhardt of the American Council of Learned Societies how hard it was to persuade the various university institutes even to consider innovative proposals, Burckhardt exploded, "My God! In 1948 we thought we were helping you found the most democratic university in the world, and here you are back in the days of William II!"

The principal force of resistance to change was the university professoriate, or more particularly the full professors (*Ordinarien*) and associates (*ausserordentliche Professoren*). A mere 5000 in number in the late 1960s, these faculty members had every reason to be satisfied with conditions as they were. As servants of the State, they had secure tenure, incomes which, when one added together annual stipend, housing allowance, student lecture fees (a healthy increment unknown to the American system), fees for private speaking engagements, and *per diem* for government assignments, could range well above 70,000 DM, and handsome pension arrangements. In an informative article in *Der Spiegel* in February 1968, they were described as being enthroned "with their 300,000 students far beneath them, at the peak of a hierarchically constructed pyramid of positions, ruling over junior assistants, assistants, *Dozenten*, senior assistants, professors without chairs, scientific advisers, section heads, academic advisers, custodians, *Prosektoren*, *Konservatoren*, auditors, lectors, librarians, student advisers, workers and staff." They defined what was to be taught and what was to be the subject of research in their institutes and seminars; they determined how subjects were to be studied and how students were to be examined; and, most important, they decided who was to be allowed to teach and do research.

Since the average age at which a scholar won a chair was 53.6 years, and since by that time he was heavily committed to his own research and related activities, it was only natural that there would be few "young Turks" among the professoriate. In general, the professors tended to approve of the status quo, questioning neither the effectiveness with which the university served the needs of society nor the way in which those needs were defined by government, industry, press and public opinion. Within the university, they held to old routines because they were comfortable and opposed innovation because it was disruptive and time-consuming. To suggestions that a more democratic structure was the only way of ensuring that the university would keep up with change and was necessary in order to strengthen democracy in the country, they were generally unresponsive.

The student movement of the 1960s and 1970s came as a challenge to, and indeed a nationwide assault upon, this conservatism. When this confrontation took place, public opinion ranged itself, for the most part, on the side of the professors. There were, as we shall see, adventitious reasons for this (the violence of the tactics of some student organizations) and ideological ones (the role of Communist organizations in the leadership of the student movement after the middle of 1967), but there were also historical ones. The German people have always had an inordinate respect for their professors—opinion polls in the fifties and sixties regularly showed them as being more admired than bishops, ministers of state, general directors of business concerns, military commanders, and other dignitaries—and the sudden appearance in the press of pictures of students breaking into meetings of academic senates and—in one famous case—marching in front of an academic procession with a sign reading, "Under the gowns, the mustiness of a thousand years," shocked and outraged them. At the same time, the spread of university disorders led them to revert, in a curious way, to a historical prejudice about the limits of the freedom that university students should have while *in statu pupillari* and, when they did so, they tended to forget the unfortunate results that that prejudice had had in their country's past.

I

Professors were not always the exalted persons who have been described above. In the seventeenth century, particularly in some of the smaller universities, they were often little better than innkeepers, supplying beds and meals to students, and selling them wine and beer in addition to information about whatever branch of learning they professed. Far from possessing the respect of their fellow citizens, they were often seen as figures of fun and, in the moral weeklies of the early eighteenth century, were portrayed as vain, contentious and quarrelsome eccentrics, wearing dirty linen and uncombed wigs, unversed in the usages of polite society, and incapable of speaking coherently about anything except their own specialty, which was generally so esoteric as to be irrelevant to the practical concerns of life.

But that was in a period in which the medieval universities were in full decline and before the birth of the first modern universities, Halle (1694) and Göttingen (1737) had reversed the process. Halle, with professors like A. H. Francke, Thomasius and Christian Wolff, and Göttingen, with its distinguished law faculty, not only attracted members of noble and wealthy middle class families, who later boasted of the famous men they had studied under, but set standards that were emulated by other universities, which now began to expect their faculty to have more than a local reputation. By the end of the eighteenth century, professors had acquired a new nimbus of authority and a prestige that their students recognized by making them the recipients of *Fackelständchen* or musical serenades, like the one that Goethe participated in in Strassburg in 1771 in honor of the historian Johann Daniel Schöpflin, a professor of the new style, author of the renowned *Alsatia illustrata* and other works known and admired throughout Germany.

During the first half of the nineteenth century, when the German middle class still cherished the hope of achieving national unification on the basis of constitutional liberty and parliamentary government, the professors were in the vanguard of the movement. The works of the political scientists Karl Theodor Welcker and Karl von Rotteck, who advocated the introduction into Germany of principles similar to those of the French constitution of 1830 and who played an active role in the parliamentary life of southern Germany, were read and discussed all over the country. Even more famous were the so-called Göttingen Seven, who in 1837, when the new ruler of Hannover, Ernst August, abrogated the constitution that his predecessor had granted to his people, refused to retract their oaths of allegiance to that document as they were ordered to do. These scholars, who included the historians Georg Gottfried Gervinus and F. C. Dahlmann and the brothers Grimm, who collected the famous *Fairy Tales*, announced that they were bound by their oath and added, "The whole success of our activity depends no less on our personal honor than on the academic integrity of our teaching. If we should appear to our students as men who take their oath lightly, there would be an end to any good we might be able to accomplish by our teaching."

Ernst August was unmoved and, despite their distinction, charged them with "revolutionary and highly treasonable activity," dismissed them from their posts and tried to have them tried for high treason, and, failing that, expelled them from the realm, saying engagingly, "Professors, whores and ballet dancers can be had anywhere for money." He came to regret this for, wherever there were elected chambers in Germany, there were public protests of his action, and the welling up of sympathy for the exiled professors was so great that the Hannoverian ruler grumbled, "If I'd only known all the trouble those seven devils were going to cause me, I'd never have interfered in the matter at all."

It was not surprising that when the revolutions of 1848 came and elections were held for the first National Assembly in Frankfurt, professors should bulk large in its membership, a fact that attracted attention in countries where scholars were not held so highly in esteem and, in England, led the irreverent Benjamin Disraeli to speculate about "the fifty mad professors in Frankfurt" and all the unrealistic things that they might attempt to do. In fact, their exertions in the Assembly were not productive of much that was positive or permanent, and the ultimate failure of the revolution, which led to a marked diminution of liberal hopes and a gradual abandonment by the middle class of constitutional ideals in favor of force and realism, resulted also in a general retreat of the professoriate from the political arena and a withdrawal into the world of scholarship.

Here their triumphs were undeniable. It was during the second half of the nineteenth century that the German universities, in accordance with the ideals enunciated by Wilhelm von Humboldt, the founder of the University of Berlin in 1809, became the homes of scholars dedicated to *Wissenschaft* (pure learning as opposed to utilitarian skills) and *Bildung* (the cultivation of the whole person) and were known around the world for their accomplishments. If the natural scientists led the way, with people like Justus von Liebig in chemistry, Karl Friedrich Gauss in mathematics, Wilhelm Weber and H. L. von Helmholtz in physics, and Rudolf Virchow and Robert Koch in medicine, the humanities could boast of historians like Leopold von Ranke and Theodor Mommsen, philosophers like Karl von Hartmann, Kuno Fischer, Edmund Husserl and Ernst Cassirer, philologists like Ulrich von Wilamowitz and Ernst Curtius, pioneers in psychology like Wilhelm Wundt, and trail-blazers in sociology like Ferdinand Tönnies, Georg Simmel and Max Weber. From the deserved fame of these giants, lesser minds were permitted to profit also, and it was in this period that the glorification of the German professor as such began. At the end of the century, there was a plethora of novels about university life, in all of which the professor appeared as a figure of infinite wisdom and nobility. Thus, in Paul Grabein's *In Jena, ein Student*, the protagonist listens to a lecture by a senior professor as if participating in a religious rite.

> While the elderly scholar spoke, in his warm-hearted inspired manner and with shining eyes, his worthy head was illuminated by the warm sunshine that came through the window like an aureole. A solemn pure feeling came over Helmuth.

He felt in this hour as if he were standing in the Holy of Holies of *Wissenschaft*, and with happy pride he felt the consciousness of being himself called one day to be a priest in this temple.

This was, to be sure, a scene from fiction. But its equivalents can be found easily enough in real life (during the Weimar period, the Prussian minister of education, Carl Heinrich Becker, described the university as "the Castle of the Grail of pure scholarship" and the professors as "its knights, fulfilling their holy service"); and it represented a respect for the professoriate that was, at the very least, idealized.

It is worth noting that, in place of the liberal activism that had been admired in the pre-1848 professors, *Weltfremdheit*, an odd word that means ignorance of the ways of the world, with connotations of distractedness and absentmindedness, was considered to be a respectable and even endearing trait of their successors. There was doubtless something attractive about the figure in Kurt Tucholsky's verse:

> Er ging durch alte Winkelgässchen
> im schlappen Hut, in faltigem Rock.
> Ein kleines Bäuchlein wie ein Fässchen
> . . . nicht jung mehr . . . graues Stirngelock . . .
> Vergass er auch sein Regendach,
> man raunte: "Der versteht sein Fach!"
> Ein stilles, manchmal tiefes Gewässer:
> der alte Professor.

> [He goes through narrow winding streets
> In slouch hat and wrinkled coat.
> A little belly like a small cask
> . . . no longer young . . . a gray forelock . . .
> Even though he forgot his umbrella,
> it's whispered, "He knows his specialty!"
> A still water, but often deep,
> the old professor.]

But, as the historian Theodor Mommsen once said, there was surely something wrong about a country in which *Weltfremdheit* was praised more highly than political awareness, and where, when the rare reversion to earlier ideals took place and a professor became a candidate for a provincial parliament or for the Reichstag, people said, "How could a man with better things to do busy himself with politics?" Mommsen noted that it was not unusual for professors to cultivate *Weltfremdheit* and wrote bitterly, "It is the worst of all mistakes, when someone takes off the citizen's coat in order not to compromise the scholar's nightgown."

In reality, of course, the attitude that caused Mommsen's complaint amounted to acquiescence in the status quo and, on occasion, when prompted by authority, a not unpolitical defense of it. Despite their insistence that they were independent searchers for the truth, the professors were State servants, and their universities were increasingly beholden to the government for the funds necessary for laboratory and other equipment, adequate library resources, new buildings and research and travel funds. Insensibly, this dependence tended to erode the academic freedom that was supposed to be the distinguishing characteristic of the German university system. No matter how strongly they might feel about it, professors could not be counted upon to protest strenuously and *en masse* against an appointment that was imposed, as sometimes happened, by a regional ministry of education. Nor, in an age in which the Imperial government was increasingly concerned about subversion and the growth of Socialism, were they likely to speak out on controversial social and political issues themselves or to object when scholars who did so and whose views were considered by the government to be dangerous to the State were denied promotion to chairs. After all, the Berlin philosopher Friedrich Paulsen once wrote, the State had a right to expect that the sciences would recognize and prove its reasonableness and necessity. "If they do not wish to do this, their work appears as a dangerous subversion of the existing order. Measures against them seem much more possible and justified because the institutions for scientific research are not only created and maintained by the public powers but are also designated for the instruction of the future officials of State and Church. How should they be allowed to work on the loosening of the foundations of precisely the existing order whose preservation is their office and calling?"

There were, of course, professors like Mommsen and the economist Lujo Brentano who fought against palpable breaches of academic freedom and against the increasing conformity of the faculties, but they did not always receive strong backing from their colleagues. In some cases, this was because of timidity, in others because of calculation and self-interest, for conformity had its occasional rewards, and many professors hoped that demonstrated loyalty would bring them titles and preferments. Others took the same road, not out of fear or ambition, but because they were concerned about the social, political and moral results of industrialism and wanted to reinvigorate older national and cultural values. Those who felt this way were apt to become strong supporters of those national policies that seemed to promise to check the advance of materialism and Social Democracy and what they considered to be cultural degeneration. In surprising numbers, they ended by acclaiming the expansive naval policy of Grand Admiral Alfred von Tirpitz (apparently because they hoped, as he did, that navalism would be an effective antidote to Socialism because of the national pride that it would inspire), the adventurous colonial policy that complemented it, and the dynamic but generally irresponsible foreign policy that was associated with the names of William II and Bernhard von Bülow.

By 1914, the German professoriate had become, as one of its members once said, the intellectual bodyguard of the Hohenzollern dynasty, and they proved it during the conflict that broke out in that year. Uncritical of the forces that had caused the war, they were even more so of their government's attitude toward the aims of the war effort. In 1915, 352 of the country's most distinguished professors, including Ulrich von Wilamowitz-Moellendorf, Eduard Meyer, Otto von Gierke and Adolf Wagner (but not Hans Delbrück, Max Planck, Albert Einstein, Max Weber, Ernst Troeltsch or Friedrich Meinecke), signed their names to a Declaration of Intellectuals that announced that it would be reasonable and just for Germany to acquire Belgium, France's channel coast and all of its important mineral areas, Courland, the Ukraine, and extensive colonial territories as the price of its exertions; and in the last year of the war the numbers of university scholars who were members of the right-wing and unregenerate Fatherland Party, founded in 1917 to fight against the Reichstag's Peace Resolution, swamped the few who, feeling the shadow of defeat draw nearer, tried desperately to persuade the government to moderate its expectations and seek peace by negotiation. When the front collapsed in 1918, the majority of the country's professors were as thunderstruck as those nationalist politicians in the Reichstag who had trusted in Ludendorff's military genius and persisted in believing in victory and lucrative annexations long after any hope of them had disappeared.

There was a considerable amount of feeling after the First World War, as there was to be after the Second, that the professoriate had employed their talents to encourage the most destructive forces in German society and to stifle the kind of critical self-analysis that might have averted the catastrophe. Surely the time had come, people who felt this way argued, for a new kind of university system with more democratic recruitment and internal governance. Had plans for such a reform been developed, they would have had to run the gauntlet of religious sectarianism and the particularistic interests of the various *Länder*. In fact, however, no serious reform effort materialized, the humiliation of postwar occupation and control by the victorious powers being enough to make any attempt to introduce democratic values seem to be unpatriotic. The professors retained their monopoly of effective power over the internal affairs of the university and, since the government of the new Republic had too many other problems to allow it time to exercise as strict a supervision over the universities as its Imperial predecessor, they were able to shape appointments and promotion policy after their own preferences. These were the reverse of democratic, for the views of the majority of the professoriate had not been altered by the fall of the Empire, and they remained unregenerate conservatives and monarchists, as much on the *qui vive* for subversives and Socialists as if the Kaiser were still on the throne. It is significant that the philosophers Ernst Bloch, Georg Lukács and Walter Benjamin, scholars of unquestionable distinction, were denied the right to teach at universities in this period, presumably because they were Marxists.

For the Weimar Republic, which paid their salaries, the professors had nothing but contempt, which deepened into hatred when the inflation, which they were quick to blame on the new democracy, reduced government appropriations for higher education, sharply cut funds for library purchases, and greatly diminished their real income, which had been seven times that of an unskilled worker before the war and was now only about twice as much. They used their university lecterns to inveigh against the Republic, a practice in which the natural scientists and professors of medicine were as vituperative as the historians and the professors of literature. In doing this, there is no doubt that they contributed to the antidemocratic tendencies of their students. But if they had hoped to persuade their auditors to join with them in an effort to turn the clock back and restore the monarchy, they were betrayed once more by their essential *Weltfremdheit*. To university students in the late twenties, the political opinions of most of their professors amounted to reactionary nonsense. Their ears were attuned to other appeals, and they were already beginning to join the ranks of Adolf Hitler.

When the Nazi revolution came, however, the professors rallied to it with little hesitation. In the University of Munich, professor of theology Joseph Pascher remembered, there were a few faces that betrayed concern and even terror, but there were also "throngs of shining faces in which one could see from a distance the hope in a thousand-year Reich of Germans." In the University of Freiburg, the philosopher Martin Heidegger, in his inaugural address as *Rektor*, admonished his colleagues to recognize in Adolf Hitler the leader whom destiny had called to save the nation. In another *Rektoral* address in Regensburg, Professor Götz Freiherr von Pölnitz proclaimed the accession of Hitler as the "hour of victory" for his countrymen; while in Tübingen the professor of *Volkskunde* (folkloric studies), Gustav Bebermeyer, announced, "Now the great wonder has occurred. The German people has arisen!"

These cries of rapture were not stilled when, in April 1933, a new Law for the Restoration of the Civil Service forced the dismissal of all teachers of Jewish blood or oppositional tendencies, some 1684 scholars, representing 15% of the national total, and including 32% of the faculty of the University of Berlin. From this bloodletting, which was made more serious when many people who realized that serious work would be impossible under the Nazis resigned voluntarily, the German universities were not to recover until well after 1945. In science alone, the loss was irreparable, for nearly all of the members of the Max Planck institutes left their posts, and in disciplines like history the best of the younger generation made haste to seek positions in Great Britain and the United States. But the majority who remained in Germany were undismayed, partly no doubt because they were now offered unexpected opportunities for advancement, for which many of them began to compete with every kind of byzantinism and intrigue and denunciation of colleagues. In November 1933, the professors of the University of Leipzig issued a declaration of loyalty to Adolf Hitler and the National Socialist State, and in the months that followed, scholars tumbled over each other in attempts to make their disciplines conform to the ideology of their new masters. Germany's most distinguished political scientist, Carl

Schmitt, had already shown some dexterity in devising theories of law that proved that everything that Hitler did was justified by a higher morality (or what Schmitt once called "the superiority of the existential situation over mere normality"). Other scholars proved almost equally adept in discovering "National Socialist physics" or "Germanic philology" or "National Socialist genetics," to say nothing of the variants of *Volkskunde* and racial theory that proliferated in university institutes.

It cannot be said that the Nazis rewarded, or even recognized, all this zeal. In general, they had contempt for the universities and the people who taught in them. Hitler himself had such an ingrained distrust of intellectuals that he was indifferent even to the importance of the university as a training ground for the technicians whom his regime, with its projected armaments and synthetics program and its dream of a successful conquest of Europe, would sorely need. He had neither understanding nor sympathy for other university functions, such as promotion of basic research and work in the humanistic disciplines. His thinking about universities, indeed, was so primitive that he made no attempt, and gave his minister of education no authority, to develop a systematic policy concerning them, simply leaving them to the mercies of the *Gauleiter*. What they could expect from these Old Fighters of the party was illustrated by a speech of the Jew-baiting *Gauleiter* of Franconia, Julius Streicher, in which he asked a group of university teachers, "If someone put the brains of all of the professors in one pan of a scale and the brain of the Führer in the other, which pan, do you think, would sink?"

During the twelve years of the Nazi regime, the professors lost control over not only appointments and promotions but course content, examinations, and admissions policy as well. Under uniformed *Rektors*, who now bore the title "Führer of the University," they were a faithful reflection of the new society, with a great deal of marching and foot-stamping and Heil-Hitlering but few signs of intellectual or spiritual energy. As institutions, the universities showed a marked decline in every respect, partly because of the ideological debauching of the curriculum, in which many of the professors had concurred, and partly because party demands upon students at all levels rendered the traditional school-leaving certificate meaningless and brought to the universities students who were incapable of doing seminar or laboratory work, who showed no competence in foreign languages, and who had to devote their first semesters to remedial work.

To this sorry pass, the university had been brought in some part by the innate conservatism, *Weltfremdheit*, and conformity of the professoriate. Because of this, as well as of their open avowal of Nazi principles, it was understandable that 4000 university teachers lost their positions after the defeat and collapse of National Socialism in 1945. Unfortunately, not all of those who retained their positions or acquired chairs in the universities that were reestablished after the war had divested themselves of traditional prejudices and ways of thought. That was one of the reasons for the student movement of the 1960s.

II

That movement and the tension it brought between university youth and civil society were by no means unprecedented. Since the eighteenth century, there had generally been a state of latent friction between the students and the burghers, and periodically this became acute. The relationship is worth considering for the light it throws upon Germany's political and social development.

When he was an old man, the poet and novelist Joseph von Eichendorff, in an essay called "Halle und Heidelberg," painted a highly idealized portrait of student life at the end of the eighteenth century, in which he paid particular attention to the antagonism between the students and the ordinary citizens of the towns in which they studied and the frequent brawling between academicians and handicraft apprentices.

> Valor ever ready for battle was the cardinal virtue of the Student. . . . When the apprentices let themselves be seen on the *trottoirs* or dared sing student songs, they were at once beaten till they fled. Were they, however, in an all too apparent majority, then sounded the battle cry *Burschen heraus!* Without asking for cause or occasion, half-clothed students with rapiers and clubs poured out from every doorway. . . . The improvised fray grew. . . . Thick clouds of dust covered friend and foe, the dogs barked, the bailiffs thrust their staves into the contorted mass, and the fight rolled on in the middle of the night through street and lane, as timorous nightcaps poked out of the windows . . . and here and there a maiden's curly head was visible in shy curiosity behind the leaded panes.

Contemporary observers were apt to take a less romantic view of these nightly *Krawalle* and to feel that student life was little more than debauchery and depravity. This was a reasonable enough conclusion in an age in which universities were distinguished from one another less by their academic reputation than by the tone of their corporate student life, when Jena and Wittenberg were considered preeminent for the amount of beer drunk and skulls broken by their scholars, Marburg for the number of duels fought, and Leipzig for student licentiousness. In Tübingen in the eighteenth century, the workers and peasants of the lower town and the inhabitants of the *Judenviertel* were bedeviled by student foolery that often took ugly forms, the disturbance of popular festivities, incursions into wedding ceremonies, assaults on Jewish shops, and other outrages. The student was a *Bürgerschreck*, a terror to the bourgeois. He regarded the townspeople, whom he called *Philister* (philistines) as his inferiors and treated them with condescension and good-natured contempt and a total disregard for their human rights. This is more than adequately documented in the songs sung during the festal meetings of student fraternities and orders. If one leafs through collections of eighteenth and nineteenth century *Studentenlieder*, one finds song after song that states unambiguously that the students, as a superior caste, have a right to expect deference, and even admiration, from the townspeople.

> And if we kick over the traces now and then,
> Who is going to deny us that?
> That's just our nature.
> So to the Devil with all your preaching!
> Keep quiet, Philistines!

The world of the philistines generally put up with these abuses for economic reasons. A merchant who supplied beer to student associations was not apt to preach temperance, nor were tailors, armorers, farriers, and other tradesmen likely to allow their grievances to get in the way of their material advantage. As for those classes from which the students were drawn—the nobility, the civil service, the clergy and the wealthy bourgeoisie—they were tolerant of their escapades and excesses, regarding them, indeed, as a healthy means of allowing the young to get rid of their natural tendency toward violence and wantonness before they took up their responsibilities as members of the ruling elite.

In addition, among the upper and upper-middle classes of society, there was a widespread feeling that the *Verbindungen*, in which a large part of the student body was enrolled, the color-bearing fraternities with their long history and vigorous traditions, were, as Friedrich Paulsen wrote late in the nineteenth century, "a kind of preparatory school for public life [which] develop a capacity for self-control and government." Despite their absurd rituals and the floods of beer that accompanied their formal activities, they taught their members a respect for tradition and order and hierarchy and, through the perpetuation of the duel and the court of honor, inculcated a sense of honor that was indispensable to a future ruling caste.

There was, however, one limitation, and that was drawn, as Heinrich von Treitschke wrote in a famous chapter in the second volume of his *Deutsche Geschichte*, when "the old terror of the domesticated townsman for the students who used to beat up the night watchman clothed itself in a political dress." Whenever organized student activity seemed to be aiming at fundamental changes in the political status quo or to be bent on subverting the existing social order, the reaction of the propertied classes and the authorities was prompt and severe. This was true in 1792, when Professor Gottfried Hufeland's lectures on the new French Constitution agitated the students of Jena, who began to make speeches about the light of philosophy awakening mankind from its "bestial slumber" and elevating Reason to the throne of Law. When these outbursts gave way to concrete demands for greater university autonomy and student participation in university governance, Grand Duke Carl August of Weimar despatched troops to Jena and arrested the ringleaders.

A better-known illustration is afforded by the history of the Allgemeine Burschenschaft, a movement that had more clearly articulated aims and a wider political scope. Originating also in Jena, among students who had participated in the war of liberation from Napoleon, the Burschenschaft aimed at replacing the traditional student orders with an interuniversity organization that would devote itself, not to the perpetuation of outworn traditions, but to the moral and political regeneration of Germany and the cause of national unity. The movement spread rapidly and reached its height in 1817 in a national assembly of *Burschen* at the Wartburg Castle near Eisenach, where student orators made patriotic speeches and attacked princes who were considered to be uninterested in national unification and constitutional reform, and where there was a formal burning of reactionary books and symbols of despotic authority.

The Wartburg ceremony had an exciting effect upon constituted authority. At the conference of Aix-la-Chapelle in 1818, a member of the Russian delegation, in language that would not have seemed strange in some German newspapers in the late 1960s, described the German universities as "repositories of all of the errors of the century," and the Prussian minister of police echoed him by charging that Jena was a breeding place of Jacobinism. The sentiment for repression was strong even before Karl Ludwig Sand, his head muddled by the doctrines of a radical offshoot of the student movement, murdered the dramatist and sometime Russian agent August von Kotzebue, in the foolish expectation that this would liberate Germany from reaction. After that deed, the Austrian Chancellor Metternich persuaded the German princes to accept the Carlsbad Decrees, which imposed rigid controls on university teaching and student activity and dissolved the Allgemeine Burschenschaft.

In the years that followed, the period sometimes known as the *Demagogenverfolgung* (the persecution of the demagogues), the German governments sought, with varied degrees of energy, to suppress radical political activity in the universities, and all student societies came under close supervision. Yet this concern over student politics was always excessive. Even at the height of its strength, the Allgemeine Burschenschaft was never as comprehensive as its name implied and could not claim to speak for all, or even most, students. After its suppression, there was never again anything approaching a united student movement, for although the Burschenschaft revived in the late 1820s it was, and remained, a shadow of its former self and was moreover only one of several corporations competing for student support. In the agitations that followed the French Revolution of 1830 and again during the revolutions of 1848, student organizations played a very minor role, and as Germany moved toward unification the great majority of the student body became steadily more conservative. In the Bismarck and Wilhelmine periods, the political tone of the universities was set by the aristocratic student Corps and by the Burschenschaften, now virtually indistinguishable from the Corps in their loyalty to the Crown and their abhorrence of subversion, while the majority of unaffiliated students,

Brotstudenten who did not possess the means to belong to a fraternity, were too absorbed in their studies to have political views. A French observer wrote in 1906 that one could not talk with German students without being touched by their ignorance and disturbed by their indifference, and he added that it looked as if the government encouraged the student corporations precisely because their social activities kept their members away from politics.

From the 1880s onward, the corporations also fell under the influence of anti-Semitism, as a result of the establishment and activities of the Kyffhäuser Verband der Verein Deutscher Studenten (VDS), a hypernationalist and monarchist movement, *Völkisch* and Germano-Christian, and bent on purging the nation of alien influences. The VDS focused its propaganda upon the older corporations, pressuring them to make anti-Semitism part of their official programs. Its success was notable, the Burschenschaften, for example, ceasing to admit Jews to membership in 1906.

All of this—coupled with the fact that students came overwhelmingly from upper middle class and aristocratic families—explains the antirepublicanism of the majority of the students during the Weimar period. It has been estimated that 56% of the male students of the universities were enrolled in these years in color-bearing fraternities—Corps, Burschenschaften, Catholic and Protestant *Verbindungen*, and other orders. Their opposition to the Republic was not generally expressed actively, although in 1929 the VDS and the Burschenschaften joined the Nationalists, the paramilitary veterans' organization called the Stahlhelm, and the Nazis in calling for a referendum on the Young Plan and the punishment of the ministers who had accepted it, because the plan, while reducing the burden of reparations, reaffirmed the German obligation to pay; and although the same student organizations were zealous in promoting anti-Semitism in the universities. In general, the Corps students remained true to their traditional abstention from politics, devoting themselves to social activities, in which beer and saberplay still occupied a large place; but the Republican government could derive little satisfaction from this, since the Corps students, reflecting the inflexible monarchism of their parents and their alumni, were a silent opposition. After all, the Weimar Republic needed all the friends it could find. When a large part of the student body, with the open approval of some of the country's most prestigious professors, withdrew into what has been called "the pleasant twilight of an idealized past," while many others were seduced by the advice of self-proclaimed preceptors of youth like the right-wing Hans Zehrer with his slogan *Draussenbleiben!* ("Remain uncommitted!"), this represented a serious weakening of the embattled democracy.

To the most unconditional of the Republic's foes, this was not enough. In 1927 Adolf Hitler said:

> In the midst of this mighty struggle of our people, we see the young members of the German intelligentsia wandering

about, completely bereft of goal or plan, or gathering together on a platform that once led to their fathers' destruction. What we need today is not "beer-honorable" fortitude
but political striking force . . . not the *Studiosus* of yesterday . . . but the man who is lithe as a greyhound, tough as
leather, and hard as Krupp steel. A new type must arise
whose value is not measured by his ability to hold beer, but
by his sobriety, the way he withstands hardship, and the fanaticism of his assault upon the enemies of life wherever they
may be.

The Nationalsozialistischer Deutscher Studentenbund, founded in
1926, was designed to produce that kind of student and to direct his
energies into effective political channels; and within five years of its
founding, this body, which was led by Baldur von Schirach, a student
who failed to get his degree and was contemptuous of the true purposes
of a university, was the strongest political force among German students, claiming the support of more than half of the student body and an
absolute majority in the student representative organizations (ASTAs)
of twelve universities and pluralities in at least eight more. The world
depression was doubtless the most important of the forces that turned
German students to the NSDStB, for it threatened a social group that
was accustomed to think of itself as the elite of the future with unemployment and loss of status. The belated realization that the monarchism favored by their parents and professors was no viable alternative to the present system was also important; and so certainly was
National Socialism's appeal to their idealism and their rage and their
youthful combativeness, and the urgent encouragement it gave to them
to save Germany by striking out at its enemies, not with words, but with
fists and clubs and knives. To the Nazis the approved model was once
more, as in the eighteenth century, the Student as *Bürgerschreck*, his
target in this case being not the deferential *Philister* of old, but the
Communists, the Socialists, the supporters of the Young Plan, the followers of the Center Party's leader, Heinrich Brüning and, above all,
the Jews.

The response to this siren call was as remarkable as the brutality of
the Nazi-mobilized students was frightening. Led by the *Burschenschaften* and the VDS, the corporations carried terror into the lecture
halls of liberal professors all over Germany, while thousands of other
students enrolled in the SA and were soon happily beating up defense-
less people in the streets and hurling bricks through the windows of
Jewish shops. Among the jubilant throngs that marched down the Wilhelmstrasse on the night of January 30, 1933, and hailed Hitler as the
new Reichskanzler, becapped fraternity members were prominent, and
the German Burschenschaften were quick to announce that "what we
have for years longed and striven for, what we have, in the spirit of the
Burschenschaft of 1817, nurtured . . . year in and year out, has now
become fact." To celebrate the "Revolution of the German Spirit," they

promptly formed a "Student Combat Group 'Against Un-German Influences' " and, on May 10, 1933, in front of the university on Unter den Linden, they burned 20,000 books that were considered to be politically and morally un-German. These were all by German authors.

The contribution that students made to the destruction of the demoralized democracy was one of the saddest chapters in the history of the German university, but it should be remembered that the naive acceptance of Nazism was the result of a century of systematic discouragement of student reform movements and the deliberate fostering of political indifference by regional governments. The burning of the books by the *Burschen* in 1933 was an ironical perversion of the Wartburg ceremony of 1817; it was the price paid for the Carlsbad Decrees mentality.

III

During the late 1960s and the early 1970s, German universities were the scene of violence and disruption that was strongly reminiscent of the activities of the NSDStB in 1931–1933. How this came about was a tragic story that threw new light upon the resistance of the universities to change and seemed for a time to cast doubt upon the depth of democratic conviction in the German Federal Republic.

These troubles had their origins in two distinct sets of circumstances. In the first place, after 1960 there was a marked increase in the number of students attending universities in West Germany from less than 300,000 to something in the neighborhood of 900,000 by 1978. This growth was balanced by an increase of the numbers of professors, *Dozenten*, and academic staff, but in such a way that the burden of teaching fell increasingly on the last group. These *Assistenten*, although more and more frustrated by their inability to give proper attention to the needs of the masses of new students, were nevertheless in no position to correct the situation, for their status was low and their power in the university institutes negligible. Their feelings were, however, shared by the more activist members of the student body, who began to agitate for structural reform. In 1960, the Berlin branch of the Students for a Democratic Society (SDS) called for a democratization of the university that would substitute American-style departments for the hierarchically structured seminars and institutes, replace the large lectures with small reading-groups and tutorials, establish interdisciplinary departments for the study and solution of current social problems, and introduce a tri-parity system (*Drittelparität*), with equal voting rights for professors, academic staff and students, on all university committees and organs of governance. This model of reform received the support of student groups and ASTAs at other universities.

In the second place, many university students became affected by the cultural pessimism discussed in an earlier chapter and were concerned over the growing conformity and the lack of any organized opposition to prevailing tendencies in the country. In their view, the worst elements of the German past were reasserting themselves, the values of the market-place were dominant once more, militarism was reviving and the country was becoming involved in imperialistic activities, like support of the American war in Southeast Asia, former Nazis were becoming socially acceptable again—even the Social Democrats had so far forgotten their tradition that they were willing to serve in a government headed by one of them (the Kiesinger-Brandt Great Coalition of 1966)—and the universities were being turned into bureaucratic organizations whose purpose was to turn out conformist servants of a system that was ceasing to be democratic. Like the members of the Burschenschaft movement of 1817, they felt that university reform and reform of society must go hand in hand and that the university had a duty to study current social and political problems in order to enlighten the public about threats to democracy. Student groups began to concern themselves with this task, and a prominent part in this was taken by the SDS, which had originated as the student movement of the Social Democratic Party but had broken off that affiliation in 1959, when the SPD gave up its Marxist tradition and became a mass party appealing to all citizens. Starting in 1964, the SDS in Berlin held teach-ins on apartheid in South Africa, the Vietnam War, and political repression in Iran and began also to organize demonstrations and street actions in order to seek popular support for their opposition to German involvement in imperialistic ventures in other parts of the world.

The movement for reform within the university might have made progress if a coalition of professors, academic staff and students had applied themselves to the issues seriously and urgently. But such a coalition was never formed, largely because, as Henry L. Mason suggested in an article in 1974 in the *Bulletin of the American Association of University Professors*, "the full professors still did not care to admit that their traditional privileges would have to be curtailed, or because the professors happened to be bad campus politicians without the talent for coalitions with other components." This professorial foot-dragging and the stonewalling of university and government administrations increased the frustration of those who felt that change was urgent and deepened the pessimism of those who saw democratic procedures threatened.

Simultaneously, the political activity of student groups elicited a strongly negative reaction among the public that was partly the reflection of Cold War thinking (so that opposition to the Vietnam War seemed to many to be Communist-inspired) and partly the result of the influence of the newspapers of the Axel Springer consortium, which controlled 32.7% of the West German press and had since the mid-sixties been spreading the view that the universities were being taken over by the left. In Berlin, student demonstrators against Vietnam were often shouted down by angry onlookers who urged them to emigrate to the DDR; and in April 1967, when a group sought a confrontation with Hubert Humphrey, the Vice President of the United States, who was visiting Berlin, the criminal police arrested eleven of them on the ground that they were planning to throw bombs at him, which, the press explained in the days that followed, had been provided by the Chinese embassy in East Berlin. The "bombs" were subsequently proved to be sacks filled with dry tapioca, but this did not silence the press, which was filled with attacks on *"pubertäre Weltverbesserer"* (half-baked world-improvers) and demands that "left-radicals" be cleared out of the Free University.

It was in this tense atmosphere that the late Shah of Iran paid a state visit to West Berlin on June 2, 1967, and, after a day of sight-seeing and formal receptions, was taken by his hosts to a performance of *The Magic Flute* at the Deutsche Oper. A large body of students gathered in front of the opera house to hoot at the official party, and objects were thrown, and there were scuffles with the police. This might have passed off as harmlessly as the Humphrey visit had not the police president, after the Shah's party was safely inside the theater, ordered the police to charge the demonstrators. As a result, forty-seven people were injured, some of them seriously, and one student, Benno Ohnesorg, was killed by a bullet from a police revolver.

The death of Ohnesorg marked the beginning of the taking over of the student movement by extremist forces. This might still have been prevented if the university administration and the professoriate had acted vigorously to bring things under control. On June 5, 1967, seventy-one writers and artists, including Hans Magnus Enzensberger, Hans Werner Richter and Günter Grass, issued a statement accusing the Springer press of having inflamed public opinion, criticized the city authorities for having declared the students culpable without holding an investigation of events, and called for a parliamentary inquiry into police irregularities (the use of plainclothes policemen, including some of the Shah's personal security men, against the crowds) and brutality. Nothing similar came from senior members of the university. When thirty-four students of the Meinecke Institute (the history department) of the Free University drafted a resolution pleading for an end to mutual denunciation and vituperation and asking for a circumstantial investigation of the events of June 2 and continued effort to secure university reform without allowing recent events to prejudice it, only one of the professors, the author of this book, was willing to sign it; and in the assembly that was held in the Institute to discuss the resolution, when a student asked why the professors didn't pay some attention to what was going on in the world around them, the *Ordinarien* marched out in a body, one of them imperiously beckoning his Assistants to follow him. The moderate students, abandoned by those with whom they might have worked for a viable reform of the university structure, were powerless now to prevent the capture of the reform movement by groups that had no interest in, or respect for, the true purposes of the university but wanted to use it as a base for their own ideological experiments and for attacks upon society.

What happened in Berlin was repeated in other universities and was compounded in most cases by belated and clumsy attempts by regional governments to control the situation by incompetently drafted and unworkable statutes, which allowed alliances between radical student representatives and academic staff, sometimes augmented by janitors and cleaning women who were enfranchised in the name of democracy, to outvote the professors on matters vital to academic respectability and integrity. The universities now entered a long period in which "action groups" and "Red Cells," sometimes indoctrinated and financed in the German Democratic Republic (where the universities were completely controlled by the SED and where neither professors nor students had any freedom to boast about), prowled through the departments, breaking up lectures, restructuring seminars and colloquia that had no relevance to the realities of the world as they saw it, changing the rules for examinations, and homogenizing all subjects into one endless disquisition on *"Faschismustheorie."* In this destructive work, a bewildering number of radical groups participated, ranging from Stalinist DDR sympathizers to the so-called *Chaoten*, who paid lip-service to Maoist principles. At no time did they speak for the majority of students, who, like the *Brotstudenten* of old, tried as best they could to get an education despite the continual disruptions and strikes; but it is probably true that, just as the corporations of the Wilhelmine and Weimar periods provided some kind of security for incoming students, so did Marxist student organizations perform this function for some students who were disoriented and insecure and without proper academic guidance in the mass university.

As this radicalization proceeded, and as other outrages occurred that could be laid at the doors of the universities (the setting afire of a Frankfurt department store by Andreas Baader and Gudrun Ensslin in 1968, as a protest against the consumer society and a demonstration to the bourgeoisie of what the Vietnam War was like, and the forcible freeing of Baader from detention by Ulrike Meinhof and two accomplices in 1970, during which they fatally wounded an onlooker), there was a hardening of public attitude and a demand, from rightist politicians and some churchmen and the press, for retaliatory measures. In 1972, the SPD-FDP coalition, anxious lest their policy of opening up new connections with Eastern Europe (*Ostpolitik*) be jeopardized by imputations of softness on domestic subversion, yielded to this pressure. A meeting between the Chancellor, Willy Brandt, and the ministers of the interior of the separate states resulted in an agreement which stipulated that civil servants were obliged, in their official and private lives, to defend the democratic order in the spirit of the Basic Law and that henceforth candidates for civil service positions who engaged in activity inimical to the constitution would not be accepted and those who belonged to organizations that had anticonstitutional aims would be regarded as doubtful cases and would probably suffer the same fate.

Since most university students, at least on the humanities side, were working for degrees that would qualify them for government service, either as teachers or as officials in state administrations, this so-called *Radikalenerlass* applied directly to them. To the leaders of the radical groups, it was of course of little concern, for they had long since given up any thought of government employment. But for many students, who had been swept up in radical causes for a time or who had participated in demonstrations without much calculation, it represented a serious threat to their careers, particularly after it became clear that some of the state and local boards who administered the regulation and examined candidates did so vindictively and without any attempt to consider special circumstances. Appalled by some of the results, the SPD sought to modify the statute by an amendment providing that membership in an organization should not be enough in itself to disqualify a candidate, but this was rejected in the Bundesrat (Federal Council). Indeed, after former university activists began in the mid-seventies to engage in acts of terrorism, there was pressure to supplement the *Radikalenerlass* by legislation against "sympathizers" in the university, on the dubious grounds—advanced by, among others, the German Catholic Bishops Conference—that "the terrorists acquired their ideological ammunition" in the universities. By 1978, the political atmosphere had been poisoned by a *Demagogenverfolgung* as intensive as that of the 1820s; and the national magazine *Stern*, pointing out that "millions of young people had been examined about their political views and over 4000 rejected," wrote that "the Bundesrepublik is on its way back to the authoritarian State that regards its citizens first and foremost as security risks."

Things didn't come to that point for a number of reasons, the most important of which may have been press revelations concerning the Nazi past of one of the most determined advocates of new measures of repression, the prime minister of Baden-Württemberg, Hans Filbinger, which had the effect of shocking people into changing their perspective. By the end of the seventies it was generally realized that the fears of subversion had been exaggerated; and inside the universities the radical movement had lost its confidence in its ability to force the collapse of the capitalist system and was losing its followers rapidly.

Meanwhile, new forms of university governance had begun to work reasonably well, aided by the gradual recognition of the wisdom of a decision of the Federal Constitutional Court in May 1973. This accepted the model of the Group University, in which academic staff and students shared in the decision-making process, in preference to the old *Ordinarien-Universität*, which the justices were convinced was too authoritarian and had proven unsuitable for integrating the academic staff that had to do most of the teaching. The court ruled, however, that the special position of the professors must be recognized and that, in university organs, they should have at least half the votes in matters affecting teaching and that the "functionability" of the university must be guaranteed in case of deadlock. In questions of research and appointments, the professors were to have more than half of the votes. University administrations were now headed by elected presidents serving usually for seven years and provided with large staffs instead of by short-term *Rektors*, as in the old days. This represented an additional diminution of the power of the *Ordinarien*, but, in the new Group University, it was an assurance of functionability.

Thanks to these changes, the universities were back at work, performing their normal tasks of teaching and research. Unfortunately, during the ten years in which professors and students were engaged in a conflict made more difficult by the interventions of politicians, press and public opinion, important problems had been neglected. Perhaps the most pressing of these at the end of the seventies was whether the old idea of the elite university serving chiefly as an agency for providing society with civil servants and teachers and professional men and women was viable any longer. Leaving aside the question of whether, with a student population that now exceeded 900,000, it made any sense to talk in terms of an elite, it was becoming apparent that there were more candidates for government and teaching jobs than society needed. In 1978, the Senator for Scholarship and Research in Berlin, Peter Glotz, pointed out that 10% of the student body was dropping out each year and that a continuation of this would create a politically volatile academic proletariat, which would not be good for German democracy. It was clear that the time had come to extend university reform to more than governance and to begin to think of ways of training the inflated student population, not for positions that no longer existed, but for tasks that democratic society needed to have done.

9

Romantics

In Ludwig Tieck's novel *Franz Sternbald's Wanderings,* a young painter leaves the studio of his master and goes out into the world, with no very clear objective in mind. In the course of his journeying, he passes through a great wood, in which "all the trees seem to call after him, and apparitions to emerge from behind every bush, seeking to detain him," so that he "reels from one memory to another and loses himself in a labyrinth of strange feelings." He comes upon a clearing and is overwhelmed by a feeling that somehow, in his youth, he has been there before and that on that occasion something significant occurred that he cannot quite remember. "In the drunkenness of his feelings, he hears again the melody of a forest horn and cannot contain himself for sadness, the pain of memory and sweet undefined hopes." He cries:

> Am I mad, or what is happening to this foolish heart? What invisible hand plucks all the strings of my being, at once so tenderly and so terribly, and scares out from their hiding places all the dreams and magic appearances, all the sighs and tears and forgotten songs? Oh, I feel it in myself that my spirit strives after something that is more than earthly and is granted to no man. With magnetic force, the invisible heaven draws my heart to itself, and mixes up together all my premonitions, all the joys that have been wept over and forgotten, all the impossible ecstasies, all the unfulfilled hopes.

It would be difficult to mistake this for anything but what it is, an example of early nineteenth-century German Romantic prose. All the ingredients are there: a sentient nature whose components have the power to invite and to warn; the distant horn that awakes memory and desire; the young man in a limbo between past and future, his mind a tumult of inexplicable regret and undefined longing, of premonitions of unfulfilled individuality and lost identity; and that peculiarly German sense of inwardness, or remoteness from reality, of intimate community between self and the mysterious forces of nature and God. It was these characteristics that gave German Romantic literature its peculiar attractiveness to foreigners, particularly to the French, who, from Mme.

de Stael's time onward, found its marked contrast with the precise rationality of their own literature both charming and reassuring, since a literature that was at once so unworldly and so intent upon plumbing the psychological depths of the individual could only indicate that the Germans were destined to be an interesting, indeed exotic, people, but one that would not be likely to develop the kind of coherence and collective strength that would make them troublesome neighbors.

This was a complacent and dangerously uncritical view, as Heinrich Heine once wrote in an attempt to warn his Gallic friends. Beneath the combination of archaicism and *Schwärmerei* that seemed to define Romanticism for the foreigner were forces of terror and violence and death. The posthorns in the night that called Eichendorff's hero to his lonely window and made his "heart burn in his bosom" were to take on more sinister tones as the years passed, and to arouse more dangerous passions. In time, the French came to see Romanticism as the *malaise allemand* and to recognize its influence in the rise of Adolf Hitler. We need not stop with Hitler, for it has assumed recognizable and distressing forms in contemporary Germany.

I

Romanticism began in the years between 1770 and 1830 as a protest of youth against the standards of their elders. In literature and the arts, it was a revolt against classicism, which seemed to the rebels to stifle all that was creative and spontaneous in artistic expression; it was, as Nietzsche once wrote, "a barbaric and enchanting discharge of ardent and gay colored things from an unrestrained and chaotic soul, . . . an art of exaggeration, of excitement, of antipathy to anything regulated, monotonous, simple and logical." In a more general sense, it was a reaction against the rationalism and systematic thinking of the eighteenth century, and particularly against the Enlightenment's deification of the intellect, its utilitarian prejudice, which rejected the claims of tradition and prescription in favor of those of efficiency and relevance, and its optimistic belief in progress. The Romantics preferred the fullness and incoherence of life to the mathematical order of the *philosophes;* they turned from the prim elegance of the French garden to the tangled mysteries of the German forest.

Because it was a movement of youth and of protest, Romanticism was marked by a high degree of emotionalism and excess, but it was not as formless and disordered as the actions of some of its representative figures made it appear. In general, the Romantics were convinced that life had dimensions that could not be comprehended by scientific analysis and that instinct was a better guide to the deeper truths than reason. In contrast to the *philosophes'* insistence on modernity and their orientation to the future, they venerated the origins of things and were fascinated by history and such keys to its secrets as the folksong and the fairy tale.

It is not surprising that, when they thought about politics at all, their views should have been conservative and that some of their leading figures—Friedrich Schlegel for one—should have ended their careers as agents of Metternich. But, in general, their conservatism was curiously anachronistic and often wore the trappings of a remote past or an imagined one. The Romantics were essentially unpolitical people, for they understood neither the issues of their time nor the process by which viable solutions were found for the problems of contemporary society. Such things held no essential interest for them, because they did not recognize that society had legitimate claims upon the individual. In the place of the Enlightenment's belief in the recognition of individual rights within the framework of a community of law and obligation, they placed their own cult of individuality, the right of the superior individual to realize his potential even at the expense of society's laws and conventions. It was no accident that so many of the Romantics were preoccupied with Genius or that this "Genius-fever," as Goethe called it in his memoirs, sometimes assumed absurd forms, being used to explain and excuse any eccentric behavior and to dignify the inadequacies of untold self-styled intellectuals and artists.

For this emphasis upon individuality, Goethe himself was largely responsible, for, despite his frequent criticisms of the Romantics in his last years, he was, in a true sense, their father. No single book had greater influence upon the first Romantic generation than his novel *Wilhelm Meister's Apprenticeship,* the story of a young man who left a comfortable life and promising career to go out into the wide world, and who was so transformed by the experience that, when he returned, a friend said, "You remind me of Saul, the son of Kis, who went forth to seek his father's asses and found a kingdom." Goethe's emphasis in that great work upon his hero's *Bildung*—that is, his growth as an individual—rather than upon the realities of human existence, indeed, his poeticization of life itself, had a pronounced effect upon the world view of the Romantics. It was due to his influence that so many of the characters in their books went on journeys, not in order to see the world or to learn how other people lived or to acquire new skills, but rather to discover themselves, to complete their identity.

Because of the importance of the journey to self-fulfillment, it tended to assume a mystical or quasi-religious significance, and Romantic wayfarers often thought of themselves as being in the grip of forces beyond their control, which expressed themselves in *Sehnsucht,* that irresistible longing for something sensed but not known, that yearning after distant but undefined gratifications, from which they all suffered. Thus, the protagonist of Joseph von Eichendorff's *The Life of a Good-for-Nothing* is suddenly overcome by "all the old melancholy and joy and great expectation" and finds himself compelled to "go forth from here and ever forth as far as the sky is blue." Thus, in the most famous of the early Romantic novels, and the one in which the symbol of Romantic longing was invented, Novalis's Heinrich von Ofterdingen sets forth on his travels after a meeting with a mysterious stranger and a sleepless night during which he lay restlessly on his cot and thought of the stranger and his stories. It isn't the treasure that has awakened such an indescribable longing in me, he said to himself; far from me any trace of greed: but the Blue Flower I long to see. I can't get it out of my mind, and I cannot rhyme or think of anything else. I have never felt this way before: it is as if I had dreamed of it heretofore, or as if I had fallen asleep in another world, for in the world in which I am used to live who would have worried about flowers, and precisely of such a peculiar passion for a flower I have never heard.

The world that these Romantic heroes traveled through was not the humdrum world that the ordinary citizen lived in, the world of nagging problems that required patient attention, but a poetical world of fantasy and wonder. In it the rules of logic did not apply; the unexpected meeting and the solution that defied rationality were normal; and even the appearances of life became what the imagination made them. The prosaic details of Italian geography meant nothing to Eichendorff's Good-for-Nothing when his eyes first fell upon Rome. It was a dream city rather than the real one that he saw.

The night had already long since fallen, and the moon shone splendidly, as I finally came out of the woods on a hill and all at once saw the city before me in the distance. The sea gleamed from afar, the heaven in its vastness sparkled and twinkled with countless stars, and there below lay the Holy City, of which one could distinguish only a long streak of mist like a sleeping lion on the silent earth and the mountains standing by like dark giants to watch over him.

More often than not, their road led, as it did in Franz Sternbald's case, to the wood, the German wood, the home of those fairy stories that the Romantics collected so eagerly, the refuge from the cares of city and town. This was their true spiritual habitat, as Bogumil Goltz wrote in the 1860s. "Of all of nature's scenes," he said, "it is the wood in which all of her secrets and all of her favors are found together. . . . What the evil, over-clever, insipid, bright, cold world encumbers and complicates, the wood—green, mysterious, enchanted, dark, culture-renouncing but true to the law of nature—must free and make good again. Whoever has a heart in his body must regret that he cannot stay in the wood and live on berries."

And yet it was a sinister wood. The children who lived on berries found themselves soon in the witch's house. When the forester Max, in Weber's *Der Freischütz,* went into the wood, seeking a spell that would restore his skill as a marksman, it was not long before he was under the dominion of Samiel, the Black Ranger. Hunding's cabin was in the wood, and the place where he slew Siegmund, and so was the glade where Siegfried fell to Hagen's spear. When the twilight fell in the woods, the hour of dread began, as in Eichendorff's poem:

Dämmrung will die Flügel spreiten,
Schaurig rühren sich die Bäume,
Wolken ziehn wie schwere Träume—
Was will dieses Graun bedeuten?

Hast ein Reh du lieb vor andern,
Lass es nicht alleine grasen,
Jäger ziehn im Wald und blasen,
Stimmen hin und wieder wandern.

Hast du einen Freund hienieden,
Trau ihm nicht zu dieser Stunde,
Freundlich wohl mit Aug und Munde,
Sinnt er Krieg im tückschen Frieden.

Was heut müde gehet unter,
Hebt sich morgen neugeboren.
Manches bleibt in Nacht verloren—
Hüte dich, bleib wach und munter!

[Twilight begins to spread its wings.
The trees bestir themselves with a shudder,
Clouds gather like oppressive dreams—
What does this dread signify?

If you like one roe more than others,
Let it not graze alone.
In the woods, hunters sound their horns,
And the sound dies as they wander on.

If you have a friend here on earth,
Trust him not at this hour.
Though his eye and tongue are friendly,
He plans strife in deceitful peace.

What sinks down weary today,
Will rise newborn tomorrow.
Much remains lost in the night.
Guard yourself! Be vigilant and wary!]

The terror that lurked beneath the surface was an essential part of the Romantic world, and perhaps the most important part. Thomas Mann once wrote that, when he thought of Romanticism, it was not the happy wandering or the *Volkslieder* or the fantasy or the dreamy longing that came to his mind but rather the dark side, which came from the eager submission of the Romantic intellectuals to the elemental forces that stirred behind the trees at night. Romanticism seemed to him to be "a dark powerfulness and piety . . . an ancientness of soul that feels close to the cthonic, irrational and demonic powers of life. . . . [It] is far from being a sickly sentimentality. It is the deepness that at the same time feels itself as strength and fullness, a pessimism of honesty that holds with being, with the fundamental, and with history against criticism and meliorism, in short, with power against the spirit."

This may seem an exaggeration that attributes too much meaning, and too profound a significance, to what one might gather, from reading the tales of E. T. A. Hoffman and Adalbert von Chamisso, was nothing more than a curiosity about the supernatural. Yet there was undeniably something unhealthy about the Romantics' preoccupation with a world that lay beyond the confines of our own, in which good and evil spirits moved and in which all the real answers and solutions were to be found. It denoted, if nothing else, an abdication of responsibility for the problems of actual existence. And even more troubling was the fascination with death that was so pronounced among the first Romantic generation. The most elemental of all powers and the ultimate solver of all problems, Death was omnipresent in Romantic prose and verse, walking the highways and talking with ordinary persons in the Tales of the brothers Grimm, coming to the brave Kasperl of Brentano's story in his sleep and warning him of his approaching end, speaking to the forsaken lover in Schubert's "Die Winterreise" through the leaves of the linden tree

> Komm her zu mir, Geselle
> Hier findst du deine Ruh!

and to the broken-hearted apprentice in "The Beautiful Miller's Daughter" through the murmuring of the brook

> Wanderer, du müder, du bist zu Haus,
> Die Treu ist hier, sollst liegen bei mir
> Bis das Meer will trinken die Bächlein aus,

whispering seductively to maidens in the full bloom of their beauty

> Gib deine Hand, du schön und zart Gebild!
> Bin Freund und komme nicht zu strafen,

and imperiously to the child in its father's arms

> Ich liebe dich, mich reizt deine schöne Gestalt;
> Und bist du nicht willig, so brauch ich Gewalt!

and touching the mind of the proud horseman of Wilhelm Hauff's verse

> Morgenrot, Morgenrot,
> Leuchtest mir zum frühen Tod?
>   Bald wird die Trompete blasen.
>   Dann muss ich mein Leben lassen,
> Ich und mancher Kamerad.

Goethe, who once said that the Classic was healthy and the Romantic sick, may have been thinking of this insistent familiarity with Death, who, once called by name* and invited into the light, was not easily expelled again. In Romantic literature and thought, from the eighteenth to the twentieth century, he was never far away. Willing submission to him was, for example, the theme of Wagner's Romantic operas, particularly *The Flying Dutchman* and *Tristan and Isolde,* and found striking expression in a letter from the composer to a friend in 1854, commenting on his conception of Wotan in the Ring Cycle, in which he said, "We must learn to die, and indeed to die in the most complete sense of the word." This dominion of Death over the Romantic temperament is perhaps the major theme in Thomas Mann's *The Magic Mountain,* and the climax of his hero's *Bildung* comes when he frees himself from it.

Associated with this mortuary obsession was an apocalyptic strain and an idealization of violence that prefigured coming events in the most ominous way. When Romantic literature touched upon the world of politics, as it did in the dramas of early Romanticism—Johann Heinse's *Ardinghello,* for example, Schiller's *The Robbers,* and Friedrich Klinger's *Storm and Stress*—its protagonists were men of passion and violence who were rebels against society's norms and laws. "Put me at the head of an army of real men like myself," boasts Schiller's Karl Moor, "and we will make Germany a republic compared to which Rome and Sparta will look like seminaries for girls!" The Romantics approved. The corollary of their faith in the miraculous was a belief that change was best effected by violent means. Such was their innocence in social and political affairs that, on the rare occasions when their minds lighted upon ideas for improving society, they rather hopelessly concluded that these could be actualized only by means of revolution.

This tendency was doubtless rooted in their fundamental pessimism, which was apt to take the most catastrophic forms. In Tieck's notes on Novalis's plans for the conclusion of his novel *Heinrich von Ofterdingen,* he indicated that the *dénouement* and fulfillment of the poet's wanderings would be a great war. Tieck wrote cryptically:

> Human beings must learn to kill each other. That is nobler than falling through destiny. They seek death.
> Honor, fame, etc. are the warrior's pleasure and life.
> In death and as a shadow, the warrior lives.
> The desire for death is the warrior-spirit. Romantic life of the warrior.
> On earth war is at home. There must be war on the earth.
> War songs. Oriental poems. Song at Loretto. Contests of the minstrels. Transfiguration.

Joseph von Eichendorff's *Intimations and the Present* (1815), a fine novel and an accurate reflection of Romantic thought and attitudes,

---

*When Reich President von Hindenburg was dying, he asked his doctor, "Is Freund Hein here?" The doctor answered, "Not yet, but he is near."

concludes on the same apocalyptic note. As the two friends in the story part, one to go off to the New World, the protagonist declares:

> It seems to me that our time is like this deep uncertain dusk.
> Light and shadow, in great masses, are struggling against
> each other, powerfully but with uncertain issue, and dark
> clouds, heavy with fate, are moving in between, uncertain
> whether they bring death or blessing. The world lies below in
> broad, dully silent expectation. Comets and strange portents
> show themselves once more in the heavens. Spirits wander
> again through the night, fabulous sirens plunge, as if before
> approaching storms. . . . Everything points, as with a bloo-
> dy finger, in warning of a great unavoidable misfortune. Our
> young people will enjoy no careless, easy play, no happy
> peace like our fathers. The earnestness of life has seized us
> early. We were born in struggle and in struggle we will go
> down, conquered or in triumph. For out of the magic incense
> of our making a ghost of war will materialize, armored, with
> the blanched face of Death and bloody hair.

Such dark dreams were to touch other minds as the nineteenth century wore on its way and the twentieth approached. To the Romantic
temperament, often baffled and frustrated by the limitations of ordinary life, the vision of a universal holocaust was often a comforting one,
a transfiguration, a promise of escape and vindication.

II

Romanticism as a literary movement came to an end in the 1830s,
when it was superseded by a more realistic and socially critical literary
avant-garde called Young Germany. But this did not mean that its ideas
and habits of thought disappeared. Throughout the next 150 years,
these continued to influence prominent writers and intellectuals and,
more generally, to color German attitudes toward political and social
questions, and there were times indeed when they became so pervasive
that they had significant effect upon the course of politics in the country, as was true before 1914 and again before 1933.

Sociologically, Romanticism was always—as the sociologist of literature Leo Lowenthal has suggested it was in its first phase—an essentially bourgeois movement, and politically it was an escape from the
bourgeois dilemma of powerlessness. Thus, it was significant that the
years in which Romanticism appeared to have run its course were the
years 1830–1848, when bourgeois self-confidence was at its height, and
when the German middle class had every expectation of seizing political
power, as the middle class had succeeded in doing in France in 1830 and
in England in 1832. But the failure of the revolution of 1848 destroyed
these hopes and did serious and permanent damage to middle-class
amour propre and self-confidence, and in the subsequent period escapism and regressive behavior became the order of the day.

After the debacle of 1848 (and such reaffirmations of that disaster as the renewed defeat of liberal hopes in 1866 and 1879), the educated middle class was effectively barred from any responsible share in the governing of their country and was relegated to the uninspiring occupation of making and spending money. This empty existence affected many of its members with the same *horror vacui* that Dolf Sternberger tells us, in his book on nineteenth century style, determined their taste in interior decoration. In the latter case, they sought to hide every inch of vacant wall with tapestries, pictures, easels, vases, weaponry, trophies, skins, stuffed eagles and peacocks, dried plants, painted plates, and books. The vacancy in their lives they sought to escape by means of fantasy.

During the second half of the nineteenth century, such escapism took various forms. Perhaps the two most innocent of them were the vogue of Wagnerian opera and the popularity of the work of Karl May.

"No matter where one goes," Karl Marx wrote to his daughter Jenny in 1876, "one is now plagued with the question 'What do you think of Richard Wagner?' " Marx was obviously puzzled by the crowds of people who streamed toward what he called "the Bayreuth fools' festival of *Staatsmusikant* Wagner," and he was perhaps annoyed, although he did not say so, that they should be so much more interested in the muddled Socialism of the *Ring* cycle than in the scientific model that he offered in his own writings. We can understand his irritation over what must have seemed to him to be a deplorable example of the aversion of the German people to rational argument.

Certainly it was not rationality that Wagner offered them in his last works. The motivation of many of the characters in the *Ring* dramas have baffled generations of critics and have led one distinguished philosopher of music to dismiss them as "painted marionettes"; and the argument of the plot of *Parsifal* is even more perplexing, since it is difficult to determine what sin the hero, the "pure fool who understands through pity," could possibly have commited that demands such drastic atonement. But these weaknesses—which, like Wagner's insistence on his own genius and the disregard for convention that marked his personal life, are to be explained by his quintessential Romanticism—were offset by another gift that showed his oneness with the Romantic spirit. He once told his wife, Cosima, after they had been reading E. T. A. Hoffmann's *The Golden Pot,* that the greatness and profundity of Hoffmann lay in the fact that he thought of the real world as being populated with spirits and regarded the world of fantasy as "the truly real" as far as he was concerned. Wagner might have been speaking of himself, for certainly it was his ability to make the world of dream and myth credible that explained his powerful appeal to his audience.

He accomplished this largely, of course, by means of music, the true language of Romanticism. It is unlikely that his audiences worried over, or even noticed, the inconsistencies of the plot or the author's opaque philosophizing when they were under its spell. It was a music that had the power to dissolve reality and to induce an almost narcotic state of receptivity to suggestion. The music critic Eduard Hanslick, after the premiere of *The Master Singers of Nuremberg* in 1860, described it as a kind of sickness, a judgment that Nietzsche, who in the end came to find all Romantic music psychologically intolerable, amplified in a passage in *Beyond Good and Evil* that deserves to be quoted at some length. Explaining the effect of the overture to *The Master Singers* upon German listeners, Nietzsche said that the music had

> fire and spirit and at the same time the flabby fallow skin of fruit that becomes ripe too late. It flows broad and full, and suddenly there is a moment of inexplicable hesitation, like a gap that springs in between cause and effect, a pressure *[Druck]* that makes us dream, almost a nightmare *[Alp-druck]*. . . . All in all, no beauty, no south, nothing of the south's fine luminescence of sky, nothing of grace, no dance, hardly a will to logic; a certain bluntness, which is even underlined, as if the artist wanted to say to us, "It is part of my intention"; a heavy drapery, something voluntarily barbaric and ceremonious; a flaunting of esoteric and dignified jewelry and lace; something German in the best and worst sense of the word; something, that is, in the German manner, complex, formless and inexhaustible; a certain German mightiness and overfullness of soul, which is not afraid to hide under the refinements of decay—which perhaps feels at its best there; a really genuine symbol of the German soul, which is at once young and aged, overripe and overrich with respect to the future. This kind of music best expresses what I think of the Germans: they are of the day before yesterday and the day after tomorrow—they have no today.

The relentless insistence that Nietzsche sensed in this music, which had the power of giving a compelling verisimilitude to the dream landscapes that it projected, was even more notable in the prelude to *The Rhine Gold,* in the astonishing passage in which figurations on the chord of E flat were prolonged for 136 bars in order to simulate the movements of the river and to create the mood in which the mighty drama of greed and betrayal began, and again in the prelude to *Parsifal,* where the extraordinary slowness of the pulse, in stark contrast to the tempo of modern life, and the somnambulistic inwardness of the music created a mood of vulnerability to the mysterious and the wonderful.

When they were in this mood, audiences found in Wagner's contrived and improbable medieval Nuremberg a dream of their own youth, like the one of which Hans Sachs and his friends sing on the morning of the tournament

> . . . ein schöner Morgentraum
> dran zu deuten wag' ich kaum

[. . . a beautiful dream
which I hardly dare to interpret]

and in the fustian world of gods and heroes, a mythic representation of
their own uniqueness and nobility of spirit as well as of their kinship
with the secret powers and principalities of the universe. What drew
them to *Parsifal,* it would be more difficult to say. Perhaps the sultry
combination of eroticism and religiosity, as when Parsifal, a Schopen-
hauerian Tristan in the ultimate stage of transcendence, repulses the
seductions of Kundry:

> Die Lippe, ja . . . so zuckte sie ihm;
> so neigte sich der Nacken,—
> so hob sich kühn das Haupt;
> so flatterten lachend die Locken,
> so schlang um den Hals sich der Arm;
> so schmeichelte weich die Wange;
> mit aller Schmerzen Qual im Bund,
> das Heil der Seele
> entküsste ihm der Mund—
> Ha—dieser Kuss!
> Verderberin! Weiche von mir!
> Ewig, ewig von mir!

> [These lips, yes—they trembled thus for him,
> just so inclined the neck,
> thus boldly did the head lift itself,
> thus fluttered the laughing locks,
> thus wound the arm around his neck,
> thus teased the soft cheek;
> allied with the torment of all pain,
> the mouth kissed from him
> the salvation of his soul!
> Ha—this kiss!
> Destroyer! Away from me
> For ever and ever, away from me!]

But Ernst Bloch has pointed out that Wagner's fable is part of the world
of the *Märchen*—the fairy tales that are so near to the German soul,
and that this relationship may be the compelling factor. "Kundry still
lives on fairy-tale-like as the good-natured imprisoned wife of the man-
eater or as the devil's grandmother. The fairy-tale 'Table, Cover Thy-
self!' still holds for us the whole myth of the Grail, the thieving landlord,
the club out of the sack or the holy lance, the ass Bricklebrit or the
Moon Grail, and the Table-Cover-Thyself the genuine, the supreme
Sun Grail itself."

The perfect Wagnerite was thus provided with a temporary escape
from the perplexities and frustrations of contemporary life into the lost
world of childhood. That this was perhaps the real answer to Karl

Marx's irritable question and the basic reason for the vogue of Wagnerian opera in the nineteenth century is supported by the fact that the most popular German opera after Wagner's death was written by one of his closest associates during the composition of *Parsifal*, was strongly influenced by his musical technique, and made no attempt to disguise its fairy-tale components. This was Englebert Humperdinck's *Hansel and Gretel*.

A different kind of escape, one that led into an imaginary life of adventure in exotic places, was offered to his readers by Karl May, who has been called the most successful writer in the German tongue, a distinction based on the fact that, when he died in 1912, 1.6 million copies of his books had been sold, a figure that increased fourfold by 1938 and seven times again by the end of the 1970s. Born in a weavers' community in the Erzegebirge that had been impoverished by the coming of industrialization, May's personal life was a constant flight from the hard realities of the world of labor and poverty which he called, in his memoirs and in his last novel, Ardistan. Encouraged by his father, he acquired the skills necessary to qualify him for admission to a teachers seminary, and in 1861 he became an assistant in a school in Glauchau. But his excessively high opinion of his own abilities made him impatient with what seemed to him to be an unrewarding profession; and, after he had committed a series of petty thefts (he shared with the early Romantics and with Wagner the belief that society's rules did not apply to genius), his name was stricken from the roll of the state educational service.

Lack of regular employment merely stimulated May's fantasy. He began a short but variegated career as confidence man and petty swindler, posing alternately as an oculist, a seminarist, an engraver, a Police Director von Wolframsdorf, a Dr. Heilig, and—after being arrested and escaping —"the natural son of the Prince of Waldenburg," and a Martinique planter's son on the Grand Tour, using these impersonations to bilk the unsuspecting out of small sums. In 1870, he was arrested again and sentenced to four years in prison, an event that forcibly redirected his energies and changed the nature of his role-playing. It was in prison that he became a writer.

There are some indications that he intended at first to revenge himself on society by exposing its injustices in a series of novels of social criticism, but he did not persist in this. In his youth, he had been fascinated by penny-dreadfuls with titles like "Emilia, the Walled-In Nun" and "Bellini, the Bandit Who Deserved Admiration," and it was to this genre that he turned, almost immediately demonstrating imagination and inventiveness. After his release from prison, he wrote short stories and serial novels for the weekly journals of a Dresden publisher, registering his first great success with a rambling and disconnected story called *The Little Wood Rose* [*Das Waldröschen*], in which, for entirely improbable reasons, a doctor from the Rhineland named Sternau finds himself involved with ravening tribes of Comanches, bands of Mexican renegades, poisoners, murderers, kidnappers of children, and false dukes, and demonstrates Herculean powers of strength and agility and a variety of skills that are hardly appropriate to his profession. This was followed by four other novels in serial installments, *The Love of the Uhlan, The Lost Son, German Hearts, German Heroes,* and *The Road to Fortune,* all in a style that combined the worst features of Alexandre Dumas, Eugène Sue and German sentimental novelists like Eugenie Marlitt, and all sacrificing character development and logic of construction to movement and violence. (The characters of *German Hearts, German Heroes* start their adventures in Istanbul but move on to Tunis, Egypt, Arkansas, Arizona and Siberia before their difficulties are resolved and they can return to Germany; and in *The Little Wood Rose,* whose locale shifts from Spain to Mexico to the Far East, it has been estimated that 2293 persons are killed or physically assaulted in the course of the story.) But no one objected to this, and the popularity of these stories encouraged May to give up the installment novel and to turn to the more tightly constructed works upon which his fame chiefly rests, the adventure stories about the American West, like the three-volume *Winnetou* and the two-volume *Old Surehand,* and the novels about eastern Europe and North Africa, like *The Gorges of the Balkans, The Land of the Mahdi,* and *The Empire of the Silver Lion.*

May was a one-man dream factory, in an age that did not yet know cinema, radio or television, and he was both aware and proud of the function that he performed. In an interview in 1898, he said, "Everyone lives in such a way that nothing very extraordinary can or should ever happen to him. Our European *Bildung* is of such a nature that chance, the happening, adventure, surprise are completely excluded. The life of any person in school and home, in office and profession, in marriage and society is fixed and must not give itself to extravagance. In the case of the slightest deviation from the philistine course, a hundred forces come together to suppress that alien element." His books were intended to break throught the shell of convention and to appeal to the suppressed fantasy of the ordinary German.

In order that they should do so effectively, May saw to it that his heroes, whether they called themselves Old Shatterhand or Kara-ben-Nemsi, whether they wore skins and moccasins or turbans and robes, were Germans, who came from recognizable German towns and intended to return to them. They possessed all of the virtues that Germans were taught in church and school, but they were placed in situations in which those qualities could find fuller expression and achieve more impressive results than in counting house and factory. They conquered the far places of the world, they resisted the intractability of the elements, they shared the lives of the noble—and sometimes less than noble—savage, they protected the innocent from the vicious, they freed captives from unjust imprisonment, they reunited lovers, they re-formed shattered armies and regained the stricken field. In whatever enterprise was afoot, May's heroes were the natural leaders. In his first appearance on the American frontier, Old Shatterhand was regarded as a greenhorn, but he soon demonstrated his mastery with rifle and pistol, defeated the deadliest knife-fighter of the Kiowas in single combat, and showed a facility in taming wild horses, strangling dangerous beasts with his bare hands, planning attacks on enemy camps, and practicing the arts of survival in forest and prairie that was equaled only by his Indian friend Winnetou.

These gifts May's heroes used with moderation ("I guard my own skin when I am attacked," says the hero of *Through the Desert*, "but I kill no one unnecessarily") and never for show or reward. Their compensation was moral rather than material ("A little bit of heroism like that," says a character in *The Empire of the Silver Lion*, "pays for itself inside!"), and in general they were nobler in their motivation than their rivals and antagonists. This was particularly true in their dealings with peoples who were looked down upon by Caucasians. Old Shatterhand greatly preferred Indians to most of the white men whom he met, and tried to protect them from exploitation and corruption by white traders; and in *German Hearts, German Heroes* the Turkish princess Emineh is moved by the services of her German friends to contrast their behavior with that of other foreigners, saying, "Only the German is trustworthy. . . . He comes as a friend and offers what he himself possesses in a high degree: intelligence without arrogance."

As a dispenser of fantasy to a public bored with the monotony of everyday life, as well as to such diverse outsiders as Albert Einstein and Adolf Hitler, each of whom later admitted that he was among his most avid readers, May was successful partly because of his extraordinary fidelity to detail in his descriptions of lands he had never seen (German travelers to the Great Plains sometimes claimed that they recognized the landscape from their memory of *Winnetou*), but certainly more because of the dream elements in his narrative, which made anything and everything possible. May's persuasiveness was doubtless due also to the fact that he believed in the dreams himself and, in the mid-nineties, abandoned himself to them, claiming publicly that he himself was Old Shatterhand and Kara-ben-Nemsi, that he commanded 2100 languages and dialects and had traveled to all the distant lands and experienced all of the adventures described in his books. In his last years, his thinking became increasingly mystical and, like another Heinrich von Ofterdingen following the Blue Flower, he journeyed in his mind toward the exotic realm of Djinnistan where he was sure that the ultimate secrets of the universe would be revealed to him and he would learn how to free the world from industrialism and materialism.

III

These evidences of bourgeois escapism were relatively innocuous, not least of all because they were discontinuous, it being impossible to spend all one's time sitting in opera houses or reading novels. It was a long time before a significant part of the middle class sought in a more determined way to leave the real world for what they hoped would be a better one and, in doing so, succumbed to those darker aspects of Romanticism that have been alluded to above, the forces of irrationality and violence and death. That was to happen only after the First World War, when their economic difficulties made them fear that the bourgeois epoch and its values were coming to an end and that they were confronted with a crisis that made a radically new ideology imperative.

But even before the First World War there were strong intimations of a revival of Romantic ideas and prejudices. These were manifest in a burgeoning antimodernity and cultural pessimism that became particularly insistent during the Wilhelmine period, made some contribution to the coming of the war, and survived it in more virulent, and, tragically, more seductive forms.

The pioneers of this new Romanticism were W. H. Riehl and Paul de Lagarde, the first a social geographer and professor at the University of Munich, the second an embittered eccentric whose cranky essays about the state of German culture struck chords of deep uneasiness in the psyche of the educated classes. Both men were convinced that the efflorescence of science and industry represented a misfortune for their country, which had caused it to lose its moral and cultural moorings, so that it was now adrift on a sea of relativism and materialism. Only a return to older, more fundamental values could save its soul.

For Riehl, such values were to be found in the life of the peasantry. This was not a new idea, being rooted in the belief of many of the early Romantics that the peasantry, because of its intimate connection with nature, was the most genuine embodiment of native German culture, that is, of a culture free of artificiality and foreign derivatives and rooted in the life of the people. Riehl, the first scholar to elevate folklore to the level of a social science, made the idea of a *Volkskultur* the basis of a cultural philosophy and a program of conservative social policy. As early as the 1850s, in an essay on the structure of German society, he was declaring that "the peasant is the German nation's future," and he later amplified this in language that was replete with Romantic antagonism to modernity. He wrote:

> In the peasants the practical statesman can mobilize living
> history against an educated younger generation that has lost
> its historical sense; he can mobilize a living realism against
> the abstract ideas of the litterateurs; he can mobilize the last
> elements of nature against an artificial world; in the peasan-
> try he can bring the power of community and mass to bear
> against a cultivated society that is distracted to the point of
> being without objective and, as individuals, denatured and
> degenerate.

It is to Riehl's writings, which were prolific and widely read, that we can trace the origins of that *Völkisch* strain in German thought that became increasingly strong in the last years of the nineteenth century, as well as the beginning of the antiurban prejudice that was associated with it. Romanticization of the peasantry and hatred of the city were constant ingredients in the writing of publicists like Heinrich Söhnrey, who saw in the shift of population from country to town a symptom of national degeneration and wrote:

Bauernfaust und Bauerngeist
Ob auch selten man sie preist
Sind des Staates Quell und Macht
Sind die Sieger in der Schlacht
Wohl dem Staat, der das bedacht.

[Peasant fist and peasant spirit,
Although one rarely praises them,
Are the State's health and power,
Are the victors on the battlefield.
Health to the State that keeps that in mind!]

Novelists like Emil Strauss, Hans Friedrich Blunck, Ludwig Ganghof-
er, and Ernst Wiechert elaborated on the same theme, as did the poet
Rainer Maria Rilke, whose *Book of Hours* [*Stundenbuch*] (1899–
1903) portrayed the city as the center of materialism and depravity,
whose inhabitants

nennen Fortschritt ihre Schneckenspuren,
und fahren rascher, wo sie langsam fuhren,
und fühlen sich und funkeln wie die Huren
und lärmen lauter mit Metall und Glas

[name their snails slime progress,
and travel more quickly where they carry slowly,
and feel themselves and sparkle like whores
and make louder noises with metal and glass]

and expressed the conviction that the guardians of the values that could
make Germany great and powerful again were to be found in the fields
and the villages

und in den Tälern, stark und vielgestaltig,
ein Volk von Hirten und von Ackerbauern.

[and in the valleys, strong and many-formed,
a people of herds and farmers.]

In the most famous of the peasant novels, Hermann Löns's *The Were-
wolves* (1910), the story of a peasant community learning to survive
during the horrors of the Thirty Years War, an additional and ominous
note was struck: namely, that it was only in the *Volk* that one found the
simple heroism needed to meet great crises and the willingness to go to
the limits of brutality and terror when necessary. Such actions, one of
Löns's peasants describes as "terrible, but beautiful."

The theme of heroism was also central to the writing of Paul de
Lagarde, whose essays, under the title *German Writings* (1878), were a
prolonged attack upon a culture in which industrialization, urbanization
and preoccupation with material things had stifled the spirit, in which

religion had become an empty fetishism and education been corrupted by the desire to teach the masses instead of training an elite for future tasks, in which even the language was in a state of decay, and in which creativity had given way to mediocrity and the joy of life to discontent and boredom. "Better to split wood," Lagarde cried, "than to continue this contemptible life of civilization and education; we must return to the sources [of our existence], on lonely mountain peaks, where we are ancestors, not heirs."

Here was the familiar Romantic antagonism (somewhat more disguised than it was to be among some of Lagarde's followers) to rationality and progress; and it was accompanied, as it had been among some of the early Romantics, by the conviction that the present crisis could be overcome only by violent means. A bitter enemy of liberalism because of its flexibility (which he regarded as lack of principle), its cosmopolitanism, and the number of Jews who belonged to liberal parties (for he was a virulent anti-Semite), Lagarde took the line that it was an alien philosophy that was subverting the individuality of the German people and draining it of its virtue and virility. He repeatedly intimated that war might be the only means of freeing the country of this incubus and the cultural ills that it encouraged. Indeed, he idealized war and expressed the view that it was the means by which a nation gained—and could presumably regain—strength, vitality and dedication.

Riehl's agrarian Romanticism and Lagarde's cultural pessimism found new expression in the enormously successful book of Julius Langbehn called *Rembrandt the Educator*, which appeared in 1890. This incoherent, illogical and often confused book, tricked out with spurious scholarship and bad imitations of Nietzsche's aphoristic style, had relatively little to say about its subject, who was employed by the author only as a symbol of the vitality, creativity and individuality that he felt were being destroyed by the forces of modern science, egalitarian education and technology. Langbehn's basic theme was that Germany was a riven nation, in which the ideals of contemporary culture were in sharp opposition to authentic German values that could still be found among the peasantry, the last undefiled element in society, the true incarnation of the *Volk*. The task before Germany—or rather before German youth, for Langbehn despaired of their elders, who had tolerated the developments that had liberalized and Judaicized and technologized the country, and appealed directly in his book to "the uncorrupted, un-miseducated and uninhibited youth"—was to "raise the German *Volksthum*," to restore the organic community, which would lead to a resurgence of individuality and a rebirth of art and a truly Germanic culture.

How this was to be done Langbehn did not make clear, although his contemptuous rejection of reason leads one to infer that the change would be effected by will and, in all probability, by violence, since his aim was not the reform but clearly the annihilation of modern society. His book was, in fact, a Romantic manifesto against the nature, and even the tempo, of contemporary life and an appeal for a return to an existence that would be simpler, more spontaneous, and guided by intuition rather than by rationality. But the new life would not be a passive one. The reunited *Volk* would have a leader, a "secret emperor," who would be the true unifier and embodiment of the national culture and, under his leadership, Germany would assume her rightful position as the leading world power. Langbehn wrote matter-of-factly that the precept that "the best shall rule applies to peoples too, and that is why the Germans have a calling to world domination."

Behind the incoherence, then, as always in products of the Romantic temperament, was the longing. As Fritz Stern has written in his admirable analysis of *Rembrandt the Educator*, "the book was dominated by a consistent aspiration toward a form of primitivism which, after the destruction of the existing society, aimed at the release of man's elemental passions and the creation of a new Germanic society based on Art, Genius and Power."

It would be hard to say, with any hope of exactitude, how pervasive the cultural pessimism that was characteristic of the new Romanticism was in Germany before 1914. That Lagarde was widely read has already been mentioned, and the fact that Langbehn's book went through thirty-nine editions in its first two years is surely not without significance. There is no doubt that the views of these authors contributed in some part to the growing feeling of uneasiness in the decades before the war, the sense that the Empire had not lived up to its great expectations, that the political system had reached a condition of stalemate, and that none of the high ideals meant much anymore. This pessimism was reflected in the premonitions of doom that marked the work of writers like Frank Wedekind, Carl Sternheim and Heinrich Mann, and of the poets and painters of the first phase of Expressionism, and there is no doubt that it influenced both the decision to go to war and the popular mood that accepted that decision.

It may seem odd to add the name of Theobald von Bethmann Hollweg, Germany's Chancellor in 1914, to our catalogue of Romantics, but it is difficult to read the diary of his secretary Kurt Riezler without feeling that his policy was in part determined by his growing despair about what he considered to be alarming signs of spiritual degeneration in political, intellectual and private life, and by a feeling that war might have a purgative and regenerative effect. Certainly it was the Romantic in Bethmann who told Riezler that his policy was "a leap into the dark and the heaviest duty." And perhaps it was the unconscious feeling, also Romantic in its origins, that the time had come for violence to be given its chance at the problems that reason could not resolve that accounts for the enthusiasm with which the outbreak of war was greeted by both the politically knowledgeable and the mass of the people.

The fact that violence did not, in fact, solve Germany's problems but merely compounded them did not check the tendencies of thought that had encouraged its use. The tragic years of the Weimar Republic saw an extraordinary growth of political Romanticism. Bitterly resentful of the military defeat and the terms of the Versailles Treaty, and contemptuous of those republican leaders who were trying with patient desperation to build a viable democracy in the face of unending crises, the bright young men who gathered in the offices of Otto Diederich's journal *Das Gewissen* or in the Juni-Club of which Arthur Moeller van den Bruck was a charter member, the Rudolf Pechels and Otto Strassers and Oswald Spenglers, the eager academicians who were members of Hans Zehrer's *Tat*-Circle, the Ernst Jüngers and Martin Heideggers and Carl Schmitts—the whole *Tohuwabohu* of the New Right—jeered at their efforts and called for new revolutions and new and more glorious incarnations of the *Volk*. It is possible that the economic and political problems of the Republic, however intractable they appeared, might have been amenable to rational solution, but these intellectuals refused to place their undoubted talents at the service of reason. Wilhelm Stapel, one of the most gifted writers of the right-wing intelligentsia, rejected the very thought of logical and analytical approaches to society's ailments, and wrote:

> More important than all the vivisection of intellectualism is the growth of a national myth, a myth that is not sweated out of the nerves, but one that blossoms forth from the blood. For it is not rationalism but myth that produces life. It is comprehended in *Bildung*. It is the sense and content of our time. For that reason, there is enmity, and there must be enmity, between nationhood (*Volkheit*) and intellectualism. *Volkheit* is faith and growth. Intellectualism is scepticism and barrenness. The spirit (*Geist*) is in the *Volkheit*; in intellectualism there is only calculation.

There was a great deal about myth and the call of the blood in the utterances of these people, from Rudolf Pechel ("Blood in its incorruptibility is the true intermediary between spirit and deed. In it lives the deepest sense of our myths, our sagas, and fairy tales. In it speaks the German woods and streams") to Gerhart Hauptmann ("I feel the event [Hitler's seizure of the Sudetenland] in my blood"). There were also many angry echoes of the cultural criticism of Lagarde and Langbehn, and much cloudy talk about the requirements of a truly *Völkisch* culture. And there was always the expressed readiness to reject the Weimar Republic and all its works for some undefined but splendid dream world of the future. Thus, in 1931, Franz Mariaux, in a work entitled significantly *The Junk Heap*, spoke of "the great drunkenness of madness (*Wahnsinnsrausch*)" in which the old world would be destroyed and new life be born.

Rausch was a favorite word of these Romantics. Ernst Jünger used it to describe the state of exaltation that came upon the warrior in battle, and Martin Heidegger was to explain Germany's turning to Hitler as a "drunkenness of destiny (*Schicksalsrausch*)." But drunkenness is always an unpredictable state, and decisions made while in this condition do not always turn out well. It was all very well for Jünger, who once boasted that it was a privilege to participate in the intellectuals' high treason against reason, to explain cheerfully, in words that testified to that idealization of violence that so many of the unpolitical aesthetes professed, that "the true will to combat, the real hate, takes pleasure in everything that can destroy the enemy. Destruction is the only means that is appropriate to [our movement]. The first part of its task is anarchic in nature, and whoever acknowledges that will, in this first part of the way, welcome everything that can destroy." But what was supposed to come next? The Romantic nationalists were hard put to it to explain the nature of their postulated brave new world. Mariaux, for example, could only write: "New dreams of a Reich overwhelm us. . . . It comes again. It gives birth to itself. New faith: old faithfulness. New myths, unclear, uncertain: old mystic final certainty"; and Moeller van den Bruck, who coined the term the Third Reich in his book with that title in 1925, was no more explicit when he wrote: "German nationalism champions the Final Reich. This is always promised and it is never fulfilled. It is perfection that can only be achieved in imperfection. . . . But there is only *the* Reich. German nationalism fights for the possible Reich." One is reminded again of the Blue Flower, always sought after by Romantic heroes but never very clearly defined in their thoughts and rarely, once they had caught up with it, what they thought it would be.

In 1930, shortly after Hitler's first great electoral victory, Thomas Mann sought to remind the German middle class of the danger of escapism and unstructured *Sehnsucht*. In this "Appeal to Reason," as he called it, he warned them against alliances with "the unknown, the dynamic, the darkly creative . . . , the obscurity of the soul, the sacredly fertile underworld." He continued:

> It may seem daring to associate the nationalism of today with the ideas of a romanticizing philosophy, and yet the connection is there . . . [and serves] to support . . . the National Socialist movement from the spiritual side. . . . We find here a certain ideology of philologists, a romanticism of professional Germanists, a superstitious faith in the Nordic—all emanating from the academic professional class, and the Germans of 1930 are harangued in an idiom of mystical philistinism and high-flown tastelessness with vocables like "racist," *völkisch*, *bündisch*, "heroic," which give the movement an ingredient of cultured barbarism more dangerous and more remote from reality, flooding and clotting the brain more grievously, than the *Weltfremdheit* and political romanticism that led us into the war.

The relationship that Mann saw was lost on the political Romantics themselves. They had no high regard for Hitler (indeed, some of them were openly contemptuous of him) and no intention of helping him to power. But, as one of their number, the brilliant political scientist Carl Schmitt, said in 1919, "Everything romantic stands in the service of other unromantic energies." The sheer energy of the literary activity of the political Romantics impressed the educated middle class, and especially academic youth, and helped both to weaken their confidence in the democratic system and to strengthen their latent tendency to escapism. The beneficiary of their work was Adolf Hitler, who showed no gratitude for their services and whose Third Reich did not in the slightest way resemble that of their dreams.

IV

Until the late 1960s, the German Federal Republic was largely free of the kind of political Romanticism that had helped to discredit its predecessor, but this ended with the coming of the student movement in the universities, and in the years that followed many of the characteristics of the older Romanticism became evident in the proliferation of anarchist groups in the universities and the large cities and, in the 1970s, in the growth of terrorism and the activities of the Baader-Meinhof gang and the Red Army Fraction.

The common basis for both movements, aside from the fact that their members, like those of previous Romantic movements, were largely recruited from the well-to-do middle class, was a profound cultural pessimism that was even more uncompromising than that of Lagarde and Langbehn in its condemnation of the results of modern science and industry. They saw the Federal Republic as an example of a society given over to consumerism and commercialized culture, in which the universities were debased into being suppliers of bureaucrats, technocrats and apologists for the system while science devoted itself to devising weapons of mass destruction in order to protect the established order. While many persons who shared this critical view tried to correct the conditions they deplored by joining citizen reform groups, or becoming active in the major political parties, or turning to Communism in the belief that the way to effect a change was by way of a systematic conquest of the infrastructure of society, that is, by "the long march through the institutions," a significant portion of the student population of the sixties and seventies—the figure has been placed as high as 10% to 15%—entered what may be called an anarchist subculture, while a much smaller group, led at the beginning by the group that formed around Andreas Baader and Ulrike Meinhof, took the road of violent confrontation with the existing society.

Among the various anarchist groups—Maoists, Mescaleros, Spontis, City District Indians [*Stadtteilindianer*], inhabitants of communes and collectives, and the like—there were wide variations of style and policy. But they were alike in three respects, that were characteristically Romantic. The first was their flight from the real world into one of their own creation. Tilman Fichter and Sigward Lonnendonker have written:

The average City District Indian wakes up in the living collective, buys his morning rolls in the local bakery and his

Müsli in a macrobiotic Mom-and-Pop store, reads [local leftist sheets like] *Pflasterstrand, Info-Bug*, and *zitty* with his
breakfast, goes to work—unless he is a zero-work freak—in a
self-organized small business or in an "alternative project";
every five days he must supervise a storefront day care center. He has his "duck" patched up in a leftist auto repair
shop, in the evening sees "Casablanca" at the Off-Kino, can
be found afterwards in a tea room, a leftist pub, or a music
bar, and goes to bed with something from the bookstore collective. There are doctors' and lawyers' collectives in the
ghetto too, and consulting offices for women and for women's
and men's groups. The whole content of life is to a large
extent covered. . . . At the same time, communication is
active compared with that which average citizens normally
engage in. With such citizens, however, city district Indians,
antiauthoritarian students and Spontis come into contact
only when they have to, for example, with the police during a
raid. In West Berlin and Frankfurt, there are participants in
the scene who are proud of not having exchanged a word with
anyone on the outside for two and a half years.

In the second place, the anarchist groups, whether "flipped out" or
not, had—and here the contrast with Socialist and Communist student
groups was marked—a pronounced hostility toward theory and a strong
belief that the instinct of the *Basis*, the collective, is a sounder guide to
action than reason. In discussions with other groups, Spontis were
known to say that any one who used the word dialectic violated solidarity; and an anarchist pamphlet, complaining about *Wissenschaft* because it separated theory and practice, stated that, "If anyone comes at
me with Bloch, Marx or Freud, I'll break his skull!" This open contempt
for reason had been a Romantic characteristic since the Enlightenment.

Finally, the anarchist groups were like the political Romantics of the
Weimar period in being much clearer about what they disliked in the
Federal Republic than about the nature of the society that they thought
should replace it. This was admitted by their first leader, Rudi
Dutschke, when he said, at the height of the student rebellion, "The
whole emancipation movement is suffering from the fact that it has not
yet created a picture of a concrete utopia." In place of a grand vision,
they had nothing to offer except the suggestion that society would be
better off if it were decentralized and transformed into a mass of voluntary collectives, an alternative that did not inspire the average citizen
with confidence.

All these Romantic characteristics were shared by the terrorists,
whose flight from the real world was, however, more drastic and whose
repudiation of reason more deliberate and considered. We need not
involve ourselves here in the complicated question of why disgust with
the world of materialism and plenty should make nineteen-year-old Su-

sanne Albrecht ("I'm tired of all this feeding on caviar [*Kaviarfresserei*]") act as an accomplice in the murder of her parents' friend the president of the Dresdner Bank, Jürgen Ponto, or what forces made Gudrun Ensslin and Ulrike Meinhof, intelligent and sensitive women with social conscience, throw their lot in with Andreas Baader, a man of coarse intelligence who prided himself on being a man of action and who persuaded himself that if he burned down a department store it would help liberate Germany from imperialism, consumerism and sexual repression. What is important to note is that the idealization of violence that was characteristic of the political Romantics of the 1920s was not only adopted by these middle-class rebels in the Federal Republic but made more consequential. For, if the terrorists had a guiding principle, it was that the use of the ultimately irrational weapon, violence, directed randomly at individual targets, would infect society with such unreasoning fear and anxiety that it would become paralyzed and inoperative and therefore ripe for a revolution that would destroy the false democracy and create a new society in the interest of the people and the working class.

The chance of this happening in a society that was prosperous and well-organized, and in which most people, including the real, as opposed to the idealized, working class, regarded these political Romantics as common murderers, was not great. But as the terrorism continued—and between 1970 and 1978, 28 people had died as victims of it, 107 had narrowly escaped murder attempts, 93 had been wounded in bombings and shootings, 162 had been taken as hostages, 10 cases of arson had caused heavy damage, 25 bombings had occurred, and 35 bank robberies had caused losses of 5.4 million D-marks—there was another danger, and that was that public exasperation would lead to security measures that would seriously weaken the legal protection and basic rights of individuals. The violent course of terrorism was accompanied by oblique suggestions from certain quarters that it might be a good idea to curtail democratic rights and principles in order to combat it. If that happened, or course, the new political Romantics would have proved to be as destructive as the old.

10

Literature and Society

In the 1950s and 1960s, it became commonplace to talk of West Germany's recovery from the ravages of the Second World War in terms of a *Wirtschaftswunder* or economic miracle. Less attention was paid to the parallel recovery of the spirit, which manifested itself in a remarkable literary renaissance. It is true, of course, that after the deadening banality of twelve years of National Socialist culture, almost any sign of new literary vitality would have attracted attention; but what happened in West Germany after 1945 exceeded any normal expectation and rivaled in energy and accomplishment the achievements of the Weimar Republic. This was recognized almost as quickly outside Germany as in the country itself. Publishers began to vie for the rights to German novels, and theaters in London and New York began for the first time in a generation to plan productions of new German plays.

The salient characteristics of the new novels were their contemporaneity, their attention to political and social problems, and their forthrightness in taking a position on issues of the day. This was in marked contrast with the traditional tendencies of German literature, which—partly because of Germany's long retarded political unification and economic modernization, and partly because of a stubborn convention that regarded philosophical and spiritual values as the only worthy subjects of literature—had generally been marked by provincialism and a pronounced distance from the problems of everyday existence. There were, of course, writers who were exceptions to this tendency—one thinks of Theodor Fontane, whose novels about the dilemma of women in the nineteenth century have been mentioned above, and of Heinrich Mann, who wrote stories that were biting analyses of the sociopolitical structure of the Wilhelmine Reich—but they were greatly outnumbered by those who continued to be so parochial in their outlook that their works were of little interest to the non-German reading audience or so abstract in their preoccupations as to be incomprehensible to it. This explains why it was that, even in the days of the Weimar Republic, so few German writers were known to the outside world, the notable exceptions being Thomas Mann, whose novels *Buddenbrooks* and *The Magic Mountain* had won him a relatively small but discriminating audience, and, at the opposite extreme, the enormously successful purveyor of

213

sentimental *Kitsch*, Vicki Baum, who gained access to foreign audiences as a result of the star-studded motion-picture version of her novel *Menschen im Hotel (Grand Hotel)*. The novels of such a powerful writer as Alfred Döblin were simply too abstract and philosophical, "too German," for Western taste.

That situation changed markedly after 1945, although this was true for a long time only with respect to the literature of West Germany. In the German Democratic Republic, the efflorescence of talent and the awakening of a public conscience on the part of writers might have been as remarkable as it was in the Bundesrepublik had it not been for the political conditions under which creative artists had to work. The constant surveillance and the pressure for ideological conformity had such restrictive effects that even a writer like Bertolt Brecht, whose eminence brought him a greater degree of latitude than was enjoyed by his colleagues, seemed to lose his creativity and never wrote a major work after he had taken up residence in the Soviet zone. The State-imposed censorship had the general result of discouraging the kind of social and political criticism that marked the literary production of West Germany, while at the same time imposing upon the literature of the DDR a new form of parochial narrowness and abstractness.

I

The rebirth of German literature after the cultural hiatus of National Socialism can with some justification be assigned to the year 1947, when two former POWs, Hans Werner Richter and Alfred Andersch, began to invite young writers to come together and read their works to each other, criticizing what they heard. This was the origin of Group 47, which became the liveliest force in German letters for the next twenty years, which is not surprising when one considers the extraordinary talents who became associated with it: the prose writers Ilse Aichinger, Gerd Gaiser, Günter Grass, Wolfgang Hildesheimer and Siegfried Lenz; the poets Ingeborg Bachmann and Hans Magnus Enzensberger, the dramatists Uwe Johnson and Günter Eich; and the critics Carl Amery, Hans Mayer, Walter Jens, Walter Höllerer, and Marcel Reich-Ranicki.

These writers did not form a group in any organized sense, for they were bound together by no single aesthetic canon and, although most of them might have been described as vaguely leftist in their attitudes on public issues, held diverse political views. They represented an impulse rather than a movement. They were convinced that German literature had been subverted and corrupted during the twelve years of Nazi rule, and they were determined to re-create it on a new basis so that it would henceforth yield to no compulsion except the inner drive of the artist and would, at the same time, show a critical awareness of the problems of contemporary society and a desire to help in their solution.

It was inevitable that these writers should feel compelled to come to terms with the Nazi experience, but, when they did so, they avoided the metaphysical and oversymbolic approach that characterized the postwar novels of older writers like Elisabeth Langgässer (*The Indelible Seal*, 1947; *The Quest*, 1950) and Hermann Kasack (*The City Across the River*, 1947) and sought to confront the past with directness and explicitness. Thus, of all the postwar writings on the Holocaust, none had the controlled intensity of Paul Celan's poem "Death Fugue" (*"Todesfuge"*) with its moving insight into the minds of the victims of the extermination camps:

> der Tod ist ein Meister aus Deutschland sein Auge ist blau
> er trifft dich mit bleierner Kugel er trifft dich genau
> ein Mann wohnt im Haus dein goldenes Haar Margarete
> er hetzt seine Rüden auf uns er schenkt uns ein Grab in der Luft
> er spielt mit Schlangen und träumet der Tod ist ein Meister
>   aus Deutschland
> dein goldenes Haar Margarete
> dein aschenes Haar Sulamith

> [death is a master from Germany his eye is blue
> he strikes thee with leaden bullets he strikes thee exactly
> a man lives in the house thy golden hair Margarete
> he sets his hounds on us he bequeaths us a grave in the air
> he plays with serpents and dreams death is a master
>   from Germany
> thy golden hair Margarete
> thy ashen hair Sulamith]

Thus, to take another example, none of the many essays on guilt that were written in this period had the damning finality of Hans Magnus Enzensberger's "Defense of the Wolves Against the Lambs" (*"verteidigung der wölfe gegen die lämmer"*), which laid the responsibility for the crimes and injustices of contemporary society upon those who were complacent or cowardly enough to tolerate them.

> gelobt sein die räuber: ihr,
> einladend zur vergewaltigung,
> werft euch aufs faule bett
> des gehorsams. winselnd noch
> lügt ihr. zerrissen
> wollt ihr werden. ihr
> ändert die welt nicht.

> [praise be to robbers: you,
> asking to be raped,
> throw yourselves on the lazy bed
> of obedience. While you still whimper,

you lie. To be torn
is what you want. You
don't change the world.]

The prose writers showed the same uncompromising bluntness. Heinrich Böll's "Wanderer, When You Come to Spa . . . ," the story of a quadruple paraplegic, and Bruno Werner's novel *The Slave Ship (Die Galeere)*, which culminates with a description of the destruction of Dresden, caught in shattering detail the ultimate horror at the end of the National Socialist dream. It was characteristic of these writers and their colleagues that they were descriptive rather than reflective and that they told stories that recalled the past in its detail rather than smothering it in moral generalizations. They sought always to emphasize the true meaning of what had happened to their country by demonstrating its causes and effects in the lives of real people in real places. Günter Grass wrote not about National Socialism as a German phenomenon but about what it was actually like in Danzig; the locale of Böll's stories, and his novels about the continuing influences of National Socialism in the Bundesrepublik, like *Billiards at Half-Past Nine* and *The Clown*, was Cologne. The regional approach was effective. When Siegfried Lenz, in *The German Lesson (Deutschstunde)*, described the way in which personal and family relations in a remote village on the coast of Schleswig were affected by the cultural dogmatism of Nazi ideologues in Berlin, or—to take an example from the seventies—when Walter Kempowski, in *Tadellöser und Wolff* and *Uns geht's noch gold*, showed how the triumph and decline of National Socialism was reflected in the fortunes of a Rostock merchant family, their fictional accounts possessed a verisimilitude which, combined with the power of the artistic imagination to seize upon the salient detail, did more to bring the meaning of National Socialism home to the reader than most scholarly reconstructions.

The weakness of the technique employed by many of the older novelists had been that, by investing Nazism with mythic qualities and by describing it, as some of them did, as a peculiar German destiny, they tended to enhance its stature. This was particularly true of Thomas Mann, who, because he had no direct experience of the actuality of life under the Hitler regime, chose, in Michael Hamburger's words, "to demonize it in *Doktor Faustus* [his novel about National Socialism] and so paid a paradoxical tribute to its perverse appeal." This was little to the taste of their successors, among whom Günter Grass proved to be the most effective disperser of this nimbus of mystery and fate. In three brilliantly conceived and splendidly executed novels, *The Tin Drum (Die Blechtrommel), Cat and Mouse (Katz und Maus),* and *Dog Years (Hundejahre)*, he set about the task of demonstrating the banality and shoddiness of the Nazi movement by deliberately demythologizing it.

In Grass's novels, there was nothing either heroic or diabolical about the Nazis. They were bogus strongmen whose posturing was always comic to the clear-eyed observer (like the dwarf Oskar in *The Tin*

Drum, whose inspired drumming had the power to dissolve their martial demonstrations into sentimental disorder) and who shriveled into ludicrous nakedness when one stripped them of their medals and decorations (as the swaggering war hero in *Cat and Mouse* does when Grass's comic protagonist Mahlke steals his *Ritterkreuz* (Knight's Cross).) Essentially, they were as insubstantial as the animated scarecrows that Eddi Amsell, in *Dog Years*, programs to strut and salute in ordered ranks, or they would have been, had they not been supported by pathetic *Kleinbürger* (petty bourgeois) who liked to dress up in uniform, like the grocer Matzerath in *The Tin Drum*, of whom Oskar says:

> Little by little Matzerath pieced together the uniform. If I remember right, he began with the cap, which he liked to wear even in fine weather with the "storm strap" in place, scraping his chin. For a time he wore a white shirt and black tie with the cap, or else a leather jacket with black armband. Then he brought his first brown shirt and only a week later he wanted the shit-brown riding britches and high boots. . . . Each week there were several occasions to wear the uniform, but Matzerath contented himself with the Sunday demonstrations on the Maiwiese near the Sports Palace. But about these he was uncompromising even in the worst weather and refused to carry an umbrella while in uniform. "Duty is duty, and schnaps is schnaps!" he said.

It was the incorrigible Romanticism and the hidden resentments of people like Matzerath that made them respond to the appeals of the Nazis, and it was their confused conviction that duty was its own imperative regardless of its object that transformed them into brutes who could convince themselves that they were doing something admirable and noble when they were breaking up a Jewish toy-merchant's shop and defecating on his rugs. And it was the collective stupidity that was ready to believe in the patently impossible that sustained the Nazis. The dwarf Oskar says, in a passage that reveals his creator's anger at the established churches for having encouraged this foolish faith:

> An entire credulous nation believed, there's faith for you, in Santa Claus. But Santa Claus was really the gasman. I believe—such is my faith—that it smells of walnuts and almonds. But it smelled of gas. . . . Credulous souls . . . believed in the only-saving gas company which symbolizes destiny with its rising and falling gas meters and staged an Advent at bargain prices. Many, to be sure, believed in the Christmas this Advent seemed to announce, but the sole survivors of these strenuous holidays were those for whom no almonds and walnuts were left—although everyone had supposed there would be plenty for all.

II

The Nazi experience challenged German writers to penetrate and reveal its meaning, but it also had another effect: it made them sensitive to any government action, or any tendency in the everyday life of German society, that appeared in any way to threaten individual freedom or to forecast a return to an authoritarian regime. In 1949, when the government proposed a law against pornographic literature (the so-called *Schmutz- und Schundgesetz*), the German branch of the international writers association PEN organized a vehement protest, and Erich Kästner, a highly respected author of the Weimar generation, reminded his countrymen that similar legislation in the 1920s had made unsophisticated people suspicious of literature and had thus prepared the way for Hitler's book-burnings and exhibitions of "degenerate art." "The story of the Trojan horse is well known," Kästner wrote. "This law is a new Trojan horse." It was filled with reactionaries of various stripes and with politicians who were incapable of solving the real problems of the day and hoped to divert people's attention from their failure by a law that would ostensibly protect German youth. "At last, the poor young people will be unable to buy dirty pictures at newspaper kiosks and will take their money to the savings banks, so that the banks will have liquidity and can advance credits, and workers will be employed and refugees will find decent lodgings, and those returning from the wars will get jobs as bank tellers! Oh yeah?"

In the years that passed, whenever an issue was posed that was reminiscent of the evil past or seemed to threaten its return, individual writers and organizations like PEN and Group 47 could be counted upon to speak up. This was true, for example, when regional governments in the fifties proved lax in preventing the dissemination of neo-Nazi literature, when the Adenauer government decided to accept membership in NATO and to meet the obligations of the alliance by raising a contingent army, when the government in 1962 attempted to take punitive action against the news weekly *Der Spiegel* for alleged breaches of State security, and, as we shall see, when legislation was passed in the seventies to control dissent by establishing political requirements for admission to the civil service.

To an extent unknown in the past, German writers acknowledged their responsibility to participate in the politics of their community. No theme was more frequently found upon the agenda of writers' conferences in places like Bad Boll and Tutzing than that of Engagement; and, if there was rarely any agreement concerning the forms that engagement should take, there were repeated declarations to the effect that the so-called Inwardness (*Innerlichkeit*) that had in the past been considered the mark of the true *Dichter* had had dangerous effects upon Germany's political development, and that Hitler had been the only beneficiary of the neutrality of the majority of the writers of the Weimar period, the Expressionists, who either professed contempt for politics, like Franz Werfel, or said that it was none of the writer's business, like

Gottfried Benn, and the New Objectivists, whose cynicism and lack of perspective had led them to attack the defenders of freedom as violently as its enemies. The *Parole* for the new generation of writers was given by the dramatist Günther Weisenborn in 1946, when he said, "The time of silence, of secrets, of whispers is past. We can speak. We must speak." Indeed, they felt that the very fact that theirs was a free profession made it particularly important that their views be heard. In 1966, Walter Jens wrote, "The German writer of our day, representing no class, under the protection of no fatherland, allied with no power, is . . . a three-fold lonely person. But it is precisely this position between the poles, this freedom from ties, that gives him a terrible, unique opportunity to be free as never before." And, with reference to the growing pressure for conformity that had come with the Cold War, Jens continued, "In a moment when blind obedience rules, the No of the warner, the Erasmian hesitation, reflection and Socratic caution are more important than ever . . . and this particularly in a country where Yes has always meant more than No, Government more than Opposition, the attacker more than the defender."

Among the many who spoke out in this spirit, often on questions and in ways that brought bitter public criticism down upon their heads, three deserve special mention: the poet Enzensberger and the novelists Grass and Böll.

The desire of all three was a society of free people determining their own destinies, and all of them found that this ideal was threatened in the world that emerged in the second half of the twentieth century. Enzensberger, a Socialist whose views corresponded to those of the early Marx, believed that the danger lay in the failure of the kind of revolution that Marx had envisaged—one that would have changed the material existence and consciousness of human beings and given that change effective political form—to materialize. Instead, society had moved from competitive capitalism to what Enzensberger called late capitalism (*Spätkapitalismus*), and this now characterized both of the opposing world systems, which, despite their ideological coloration, were essentially identical. This was evident in the fact that the irrationalism that Marx had said was characteristic of capitalism was present in both in magnified form, that the stupidity of their ruling classes became daily more evident in the self-destructive nature of their policies, and that any proposed change in either system was regarded as threatening and consequently impermissible. In both systems, productivity had become an end in itself without any reference to human need and social purpose, and the legitimacy of this situation was insisted upon by the instrumentalities of the State, which became increasingly authoritarian, and was defended by a press and publishing industry that reflected its philosophy. The salient feature of the Western, as of the Soviet, system was its essential inhumanity, indeed, its contempt for the human beings that it destroyed in the process of sustaining itself. In 1957, Enzensberger described the process in a poem called "*bildzeitung*," in which he attacked the practices of the most successful of the daily newspapers published

by the Axel Springer press. Addressing himself to that paper's readers,
Enzensberger wrote:

> du wirst reich sein
> markenstecher uhrenkleber:
> wenn der mittelstürmer will
> wird um eine mark geköpft
> ein ganzes heer beschmutzter prinzen
> turandots mitgift unfehlbarer tip
> tischlein deck dich:
> du wirst reich sein
>
> . . .
>
> auch du auch du auch du
> wirst langsam eingehn
> an lohnstreifen und lügen
> reich, stark erniedrigt
> durch musterungen und malz-
> kaffee, schön besudelt mit straf-
> zetteln, schweiss,
> atomaren dreck:
> deine lungen ein gelbes riff
> aus nikotin und verleumdung
> möge die erde dir leicht sein
> wie das leichentuch
> aus rotation und betrug
> das du dir täglich kaufst
> in das du dich täglich wickelst.
>
> [you will be rich
> coupon puncher clock paster
> when the center forward Will
> is identified for a mark
> a whole army of soiled princes
> Turandot's dowry a sure tip
> table cover thyself
> you will be rich
>
> . . .
>
> [and you and you and you
> will surely perish
> from wage-cuts and lies
> richly, powerfully debased
> by musterings and malt-
> coffee, beautifully dirtied with penal-
> certificates, sweat,
> atomic muck:
> your lungs a yellow reef

of nicotine and slander
may the earth lie lightly on you
and the shroud
of rotation and betrayal
that you daily buy for yourself
in which you daily wind yourself]

This process had already gone so far that it could be reversed only by revolutionary means. Enzensberger placed his hope in the ability of the masses to recognize the irrationality of the system that was enslaving them and to learn gradually to transform its manipulative techniques into means of action and liberation. To accomplish this, they would need leaders, and, while it was true that new societies were rarely built by poets and novelists, nevertheless writers and other intellectuals and the student rebels in the universities were indispensable in the educative process, not least of all in the systematic attack that had to be made upon the mass media that were the establishment's most effective defensive instruments. The goal was a transformation of society by means of a redirection of its energies and instrumentalities, an "*Umfunktionieren*," in the interest of freedom.

The novelist Grass did not entirely disagree with Enzensberger's view of current tendencies in the Bundesrepublik, and those portions of his first major novels that dealt with the years after 1945 included incisive criticism of the tendency of the new ruling class to seek a refuge from the past in material pleasure (the onion-cellar scene in *The Tin Drum*) and of the manipulations of its press lords and industrial tycoons (the mealworm scene in *Dog Years*). But, as Jochen Steffen pointed out in a useful comparison of the political views of the two writers, Grass was too much the eighteenth century rationalist to accept Enzensberger's revolutionary prescription with any patience. More specifically, his view was that the engagement of the writer should have the practical purpose of criticism and reform, and that this was best accomplished, not from the lofty eminence from which German intellectuals had usually preferred to view the turmoil of everyday life, or even from that abstract theoretical plane that Enzensberger occupied, but by means of actual participation in the democratic process.

In the history of German literature, Grass was something new, a writer of major stature who became an active supporter of a political party and played an important role in spreading its message to constituents, as he did during the campaign of 1969, when he traveled the length and breadth of the Republic, visiting sixty electoral districts and making more than ninety speeches for the Social Democratic Party. Why, he asked himself in the *Tagebuch* that he later incorporated in his book *The Diary of a Snail*, did he consider it important to travel through Münsterland and Franconia talking about dull subjects like property taxes and the right of workers to share in factory management (*Mitbestimmungsrecht*)? In the first place, because—although this was hardly a declaration that would make people throw their caps in the air—he was "a Social Democrat because Socialism without democracy is worthless to me and because an unsocial democracy is no democracy." Second, because he believed that progress toward democracy was made on the hustings and in the party councils and in parliament, and it was slow, indeed, snail-like. Writers, who tended to be impatient idealists, would have to face up to that fact. In any case, Grass added bluntly—perhaps with a thought to "the merry Enzensberger," who had spent the electoral campaign in Cuba, doubtless discoursing on loftier themes—"I don't like people who, for the sake of humanity, want to bend bananas straight."

The reaction of the public and the press to the political engagement of the intellectuals was not always one of satisfaction, and not infrequently it was characterized by bitter criticism. This was particularly true in the case of the political interventions of Heinrich Böll, a novelist internationally acclaimed, not only for the quality of his literary work (he was Nobel laureate in 1972) but for his energetic efforts, as president of the international PEN club, in behalf of the rights of persecuted and imprisoned intellectuals in the Soviet Union, Eastern Europe and Latin America.

Böll's concern over the threats to individual freedom were not solely international in focus. As a novelist, he early revealed himself to be an uncompromising social critic, and both *Billiards at Half-Past Nine* and *The Clown* were unflattering portraits of the booming economic growth of the Federal Republic that emphasized the skill with which Nazi fellow travelers had been able to insinuate themselves into the ruling class of the new democratic State. In *The Clown*, in particular, Böll's portraits of bourgeois parvenuism were as scathing as those in Theodor Fontane's novel of Wilhelmine society *Frau Jenny Treibel*, and they were hardly calculated to ingratiate the author with the new economic establishment or with the Catholic Church, of which he was a particularly bitter critic, like his fellow Catholic Carl Amery for whose book *Capitulation* he wrote an introduction. Nor was the impression of the earlier books softened by the novel *Group Portrait with Woman*, which brought Böll his Nobel Prize, for this preeminently Catholic morality was the story of the martyrdom of a woman who practiced the simple virtues of courage, responsibility, honor and love but found them unavailing in a callous and bureaucratized society that believed only in power, influence and money.

It was, however, Böll's public rather than his literary activities that aroused the liveliest indignation of his fellow citizens. The novelist was horrified when the excesses of the student left led the government to pass the so-called Radicals' Decree (*Radikalenerlass*), which forbade government employment to persons who had engaged in activity that could be described as subversive of the constitution. This he regarded as a shameful and hypocritical piece of legislation and a kind of voluntary suicide for a democratic society. In an essay entitled "Radicality and Hope," he asked, "What would have become of the Federal Republic if there had been no radicals and extremists who were intent not on their personal enrichment but upon changing existing relationships? Let us think the student movement out of our history and imagine that it never took place—how crippled would our educational system be today!"

Even to some people who admired Böll and considered themselves to be liberals, this attitude seemed perverse and blind to the havoc caused in the universities by groups that professed contempt for Böll's own values. But the novelist was unstayed, and his belief that repression nourished itself and gradually subverted the society that it was supposed to be protecting found even more forthright expression in the matter of the terrorists and the measures used against them. From the outset, Böll was convinced that public hysteria was being created by a conservative press intent on denying civil rights to anyone even vaguely associated with activities that were very loosely described as terroristic: and, when *Bild-Zeitung* in December 1971 announced in headlines BAADER-MEIN-HOF GANG MURDERS ON!, at a time when there was no firm evidence to indicate either that there was a gang or that it had committed murder, he declared angrily, "That is naked Fascism, provocation, lies and dirt!" and demanded legal injunctions to protect public opinion from this kind of calculated suggestion. The sole result of this was to bring down upon his head a chorus of strident calumniation in which he was labeled as a "sympathizer," a "spiritual father," a "helper's helper" of terrorism. In 1974, *Quick* magazine wrote, "The Bölls are worse than Baader-Mein-hof," and a speaker on Radio Free Berlin said that, "The soil of terror is fertilized with the malevolent spirit of those who sympathize with the people who commit these horrors" and did not hesitate to name Böll as one of the most dangerous of the *Sympathisanten*.

The novelist responded in numerous speeches and articles and, most effectively, in a short novel entitled *The Lost Honor of Katherina Blum* (1975), which was immediately filmed by Volker Schlöndorff and Mar-garethe von Trotta in collaboration with the author. Although it bore some general resemblance to *Group Portrait with Woman*, this was more a pamphlet than a novel, accusing the rightist press of character assassination and violation of human rights. It told the story of a woman who spent a night in her apartment with a young man who was wanted by the police, although she did not know this. Her innocent action exposed her to persecution by police and press against which she had no legal protection or recourse; and, in the end, distraught and demoral-ized, she shot the journalist who had played the leading part in hound-ing her. The book and the film created a sensation, and, although this didn't bring the personal attacks upon Böll to an end, they appear to have touched the conscience of a lot of people and to have aroused a new awareness of what was beginning to look like a well-organized conser-vative campaign against civil and intellectual freedom under the guise of concern for State security. This marked the beginning of the turning of the tide. By 1978, the nationally circulated *Stern* magazine had, in effect, joined Böll's side and was printing articles on the danger of the new security techniques to civil liberties; and, in the same year, the Filbinger case, of which more later, discredited the groups that had been the most strident in their campaign against "the sympathizers."

Böll never considered himself as a political writer, and by inclination and talent he was more akin to his contemporary the novelist Martin Walser, a master of the meticulous dissection of the frailties and foibles of the German middle class, than to the political activists Grass and Enzensberger. But, as a Christian moralist in a society that he believed was prone to evil, he felt compelled to expose that evil to the often deluded or myopic gaze of his fellow citizens and to point to its inevitable human and social consequences. Sometimes he did this with the laconic forthrightness of a police report, as he did in *Katharina Blum*; at others, he presented chilling visions of what Germany might become if those who believed in freedom were not vigilant.

Böll was at his most Cassandra-like in the novel *Precautionary Siege (Fürsorgliche Belagerung)*, a macabre picture of a society that had been captured by its fears and its shortsighted reliance upon violence to relieve them, in which the possessing class had surrendered their freedom to the policemen who protected them and led regimented, joyless lives in which every step they took, every meal they ate, every human contact and telephone call they made was monitored and recorded, in which suspicion had become a way of life and careers were destroyed by youthful enthusiasms and indiscretions, and where the relations between the generations were marked by mutual incomprehension and, fitfully, by irrational hatred. This society was epitomized by the experience of one of Böll's characters, who

> sat in the bus between Cologne and Hubreichen and read in a book called *Castro's Way*, sat there quietly and didn't notice how the people round him read newspapers with accounts of the death of Bewerlöh [a businessman killed by terrorists], and suddenly, somewhere short of Hurbelheim, the deathly silence in the bus frightened him and he looked up and noticed that everybody was staring at him, silently and with hatred, and at the book, wordlessly icy and steel-like, "as if they would strangle me at any moment," and he had become frightened, really frightened, and had almost pissed in his pants from fear and had got out in Hurbelheim and gone the rest of the way on foot. And now he wanted to get out, simply out, it didn't matter where. Anywhere where one could read books, even in the bus, without getting frightened like that.

In Böll's view, that bus was what the Bundesrepublik was in danger of becoming in the days when the antiterrorist campaign reached its height and, as long as that was so, vigilance and engagement were required of all lovers of freedom, and especially the country's independent writers.

III

In contrast to the novel, the drama had always, since Schiller's day, been regarded as having a social purpose. Indeed, Schiller had not hesitated to describe the theater as a moral institution, "the common channel through which the glow of wisdom flows from the intelligent, superior part of society and spreads itself in gentle streams throughout the whole State." It existed, not merely to entertain, but to instruct, by presenting scenes of life and the conflicts and passions of men truthfully or at least in such a way as to promote understanding. Schiller himself followed this principle in his social drama and his historical plays, most of which turned upon the theme of the seductive and destructive influence of power upon the lives of human beings, and so did such eminent successors of his as Georg Büchner and Friedrich Hebbel and Gerhart Hauptmann and Frank Wedekind and the Expressionist dramatists of the 1920s.

It was noteworthy, however, that despite the brilliance and variety of the German drama after 1945—and the British critic Ken Tynan wrote in 1964 that the contemporary German theater was the best in the world—the tradition of social responsibility was imperfectly maintained, and, instead of instruction and edification, what was provided on the stages of many theaters in West Germany was either sensationalism or an assault upon the values and sensitivities of the audience, a *Publikumsbeschimpfung*, to use the title of Peter Handke's play of 1969.

To a large extent, the organization of the theater in Western Germany accounted for this. By tradition and by postwar reorganization, theaters were freed from the commercial restraints that bound most theaters in England and the United States. Their ability to operate from one season to the next bore no direct relationship to the satisfaction that they provided their audiences, for their income came to a large extent from subsidies and subscriptions. A report in *The Times Literary Supplement* in April 1969 estimated that East and West Germany together had about 150 theaters that were visited by 60 million spectators a year. The average number of ticket subscribers per theater was close to 20,000, and each ticket sold was subsidized to the tune of about £1. This situation had the not entirely unhealthy effect of relieving theater *Intendanten* (superintendants) and directors and stage designers from the necessity of truckling to public taste; but, in all too many cases in West Germany, it heightened their belief that the way to make reputations for themselves was to be different in the most strikingly possible way from their fellows. Since most theaters had the same repertory of four or five dozen plays that were repeated at intervals, the emphasis was placed upon new productions that would impress the critics by their originality or their outrageousness.

No one has a right to object to new interpretations of old plays. Fritz Kortner's interpretation of Shakespeare's Shylock was a triumph of theatrical art when he first gave it; his persistence in repeating it without change until the end of his career was disastrous. On the other hand, one is entitled to expect of new versions a decent fidelity to the author's purpose and his text, or so one would think. In the West German theater this was not always a sound expectation. What often took place there was nothing less than an unashamed manipulation of the classics.

Schiller was so often the object of this kind of treatment that one was almost persuaded that directors were revenging themselves upon their schoolmasters for having made them memorize passages from *Maria Stuart* and *Don Carlos*. Curt Riess has written of Peter Zadek's production of *The Robbers* in 1966 that the "performers appeared in costumes and masks as if to make fun of the persons they represented. Amalie was wholly *kitschisch*, Karl came from the Wild West, Fritz from a horror film made in Hollywood. Moreover, the way in which they and the robbers comported themselves was intended to say, 'Look how stupid Schiller was! And isn't it fun to point it out!' The background . . . a real American comic strip, mixed with advertisements. Schiller, therefore, not only as comic but as predecessor of Wild West shockers!"

Hansgunther Heym's production of *Wilhelm Tell* went even further in distorting the play's characters and plot. In Schiller's play, Stauffacher and his friend Attinghausen are patriots who wish to free their country from Austrian tyranny, and Tell is a simple man who does not wish to be involved in their plans but is goaded into action by the behavior of the sadistic Austrian governor Gessler, who not only seeks to humiliate him, but does so at the risk of his son's life. In Heym's production, Gessler is a sympathetic gentleman of the old school forced to assume responsibility for policies that he does not personally approve; Tell is an asocial boor; and Stauffacher and Attinghausen are establishment figures attempting to dupe the masses, and their famous oath at the Rütli has overtones of National Socialism.

Nor was Schiller the only classical author treated in this way. Goethe's *Tasso*, a play about the difficulties that the man of letters finds in adjusting to normal society, was transformed by Peter Stein into a piece about a neurotic in which Goethe's text was rearranged to suit the director's purpose and the whole experiment seemed intended solely as an attack upon Germany's greatest poet, although for reasons that were obscure. Heinrich von Kleist's *Prince Friedrich of Homburg*, presented by the Hamburg Deutsches Schauspielhaus during the Theater Festival in Berlin in 1978, took place on a stage covered by potatoes (perhaps intended by the DDR directors Manfred Karge and Matthias Langhoff to convey the impression that the court of the Great Elector was a primitive and rural enterprise, which it was not), and the directors eliminated from the text whole passages that illuminated the relationship between the prince and his officers and abruptly changed the ending by having the hero go mad.

Even Shakespeare, who, since the days of the immortal Bowdler, has been pretty well inviolate in the English-speaking world, has enjoyed no such immunity in Germany, where, as one of "*unser Klassiker*," he has been exposed to every outrage. Zadek's *Measure for Measure*, played by a troupe of blue-jeaned and miniskirted players, two of whom practiced headstands on chairs, was an attempt, on the basis of a prose translation of the play that retained nothing of Shakespeare's language, to tell the audience what the director thought the poet should have said. The same director's production of *Othello* in Hamburg in 1976 portrayed the protagonist as a maniacal savage and Desdemona as a common prostitute, who had a lesbian scene with her maid, slouched about the stage in a variety of costumes ranging from a white evening gown to a bikini, and was finally slaughtered in a scene of Grand Guignol meticulousness that outraged the audience and caused a major *Theaterskandal*. In Alfred Kirchner's production of *The Tempest*, in Berlin's Schiller Theater in 1978, Prospero wandered about in baggy pants and galluses, less sorcerer than advance man for American imperialism, and the audience was invited to consider Caliban the true hero of the piece.

These melancholy examples are not intended to extinguish the memory of other performances of the classics that were beyond reproach—Ernst Schroeder's production of Goethe's *Faust: Second Part* in the Schiller Theater in 1970, for example, and Friedrich Beyer's production of Lessing's *Minna von Barnhelm* in the Thalia Theater in Hamburg in 1979—but it was the outrageous ones that attracted the greatest amount of attention and diverted energies that might have been put to other theatrical purposes. In this regard, it is worth noting that, in contrast to the contemporary novel, the theater has been impressive neither in its treatment of the Nazi past nor in its attention to contemporary social problems.

It is difficult to say why German dramatists seemed so reluctant to try their hand at a play about Hitler, or the actualities of life under the Third Reich, or the conspiracy of July 20, 1944. German filmmakers had some success in this direction—one thinks of Alfred Vohrer's gripping version of Hans Fallada's *Everyone Dies for Himself (Jeder stirbt für sich allein)*, in which Hildegard Knef and Carl Raddatz starred*—but theatrical experiments were less ambitious and, in a curious way, seemed for the most part to come from abroad. Both Brecht's *Fear and Misery of the Third Reich* and *Arturo Ui* were written in exile and did not wear well, since they were written with no real comprehension of the actualities of the Nazi system. Carl Zuckmayer's *The Devil's General*, written in Vermont during the war and produced for the first time in Germany in the late forties, was an exciting but contrived picture of *la dolce vita* in the Third Reich and the conflict between the SS and military officers of the old school; and his resistance drama *Song in the Fiery Furnace* was too symbolic in its technique to bring the Nazi experience to life. The most moving of the productions of the fifties that dealt with Nazism, *The Diary of Anne Frank* (1956), was written by the Americans Frances Goodrich and Albert Hackett, and the shattering drama about anti-Semitism, Max Frisch's *Andorra* (1961), which has been discussed in an earlier chapter, was by a Swiss.

The first attempt to deal with the Nazi period in a circumstantial way, that is, in a way that treated of real events and real people, was *The Deputy (Der Stellvertreter)* by the thirty-year-old Rolf Hochhuth, which had its première in the Berliner Volksbühne in 1963 under the

*This did reach the stage in 1981 as a musical revue by Peter Zadek. After seeing it, Rolf Michaelis wrote: "This revue, based on a novel of the resistance, is, not in the sexual sense but in the political, obscene."

direction of Erwin Piscator. Piscator was now at the end of his career—
he had been a pioneer in the political theater of the Weimar period and
an important influence upon Bertolt Brecht's kind of documentary and
epic drama—but he seized upon the Hochhuth play with enthusiasm,
announcing that it was one of the few real contributions to what people
now began to call "the assimilation of the past," a play that was courageous enough to name names and assign responsibility for evil to those
who committed it, and, above all, "a historical drama in Schiller's sense
of the word."

> Like Schiller's dramas, it sees the individual as the moving
> force who, in his activity, represents an idea: who is free to
> fulfill this idea, free in his insight into the necessity of "cate-
> gorical," that is, moral and human action. It is on the basis of
> this freedom, which everyone possesses, and which everyone
> possessed during the Nazi period, that we must proceed if we
> are to assimilate the past. To deny this freedom means to
> deny the guilt that everyone who didn't use his freedom to
> decide against inhumanity has taken upon himself.

This was a fair enough statement of Hochhuth's philosophy. As Hans
Mayer wrote in 1979, he was unwilling to accept the situation once
described by the dramatist Friedrich Dürrenmatt when he said, "in the
clownish spectacle of our century, in this collapse of the white race,
there are no people who are guilty or responsible any longer. Everyone
couldn't do anything about it and didn't want it to happen." Hochhuth
felt that there was no tragedy without responsible actors and moral
conflict, and he set out to write historical drama with that in mind.
Unfortunately, he was so intent on accumulating documentation to support his points that he was careless about dramatic construction, and his
plays were so long that they had to be cut drastically for production,
with consequent distortion. In the case of *The Deputy*, which was a
dramatization of the extermination of the European Jews by the Nazis,
their exploitation by German economic interests, and the failure of the
wartime Pope Pius XII to denounce the appalling crime, the cuts had
the effect of diminishing the fault of other responsible parties and placing undue emphasis upon that of the Pope.

Despite, or because of, this weakness, the play enjoyed a triumph on
the stage, and this inspired emulation, although none of the subsequent
experiments in this genre—Heinar Kipphardt's *In the Case of J. Robert
Oppenheimer* (1964) and his Eichmann drama *Joel Brand* (1965), Peter Weiss's *The Inquiry* (1965), and Hochhuth's own play about World
War II, *Soldiers* (1967)—came close to repeating its success. Indeed,
some of them seemed designed less to grapple with the Nazi past than to
place the blame for its evils on other shoulders or to prove (as was the
case with Peter Weiss's *Vietnam Discourse* in 1968) that the victors in
1945 were as capable of war crimes as the Nazis had ever been.

In the late sixties, when the agitations in the universities began, interest in the Nazi past tended to weaken, both in the general public mind and in the theater. But this changed at the end of the next decade, when many people began to be concerned about what seemed to them to be ominous signs of a growing conservative reaction with potential danger for civil liberties. A move in the Bundestag for a statute of limitations upon crimes committed during the Nazi period, the imminent prospect of the election of an archconservative as Bundespräsident, and an insistent clamor for an extension of the *Radikalenerlass* and a more uncompromising campaign against terrorism convinced some people that 1933 was not as remote as they had thought and that Bonn might still turn out to be Weimar. This mood inspired two plays about Nazism that proved that the German theater was still capable of being what Schiller had believed it should be.

The most strident of the voices on the right of the political spectrum was that of Hans Filbinger, CDU member and minister president of Baden-Württemberg, a shrewd politician who was often spoken of as the next President of the Republic. Filbinger was a bitter critic of the Social Democratic Party's Eastern policy and of its failure to deal as sternly as he would have liked with the terrorists; he was an enemy of the universities, which he regarded as springboards for terrorism and subversion; and he was a stern moral censor who, among other things, found the director of the Stuttgart Staatstheater, Claus Peymann, politically and morally objectionable and forced his dismissal. Ironically, Filbinger himself was on his way out of office before Peymann, and this was the result of a sudden announcement in the press that Hochhuth had written another play. This time, it was about lawyers in the Nazi period, particularly those who had been employed as trial judges in the armed services. It was indeed based upon the meticulously documented case of Hans Filbinger, who, while serving in such capacity during the last days of the war, had sentenced a young sailor named Walter Gröger to death for alleged desertion, a sentence that was subsequently carried out.

Hochhuth's *The Lawyers*, which exemplified his belief that "authors must articulate the bad conscience of their nation because the politicians have such a good one," finished the career of Hans Filbinger. It was not a particularly good play, requiring much reworking and cutting before it could be produced, but its effect had been felt long before it got to the stage. A much more effective dramatic commentary upon the Filbinger mentality was the 1979 play by one of Peymann's collaborators in the Stuttgart theater, Thomas Bernhard's *Before Retirement* (*Vor dem Ruhestand*). This was subtitled "A Comedy of the German Soul," a description that may have troubled some of those who saw it. Based roughly on Chekhov's *Three Sisters*, it was the story of a brother and two sisters who live alone and dream of a lost paradise, the Third Reich. Once a year, on Himmler's birthday, the brother puts on his old SS uniform, and they have a gala evening and look at faded photographs, and sometimes the brother and the older sister torment the younger sister, who is crippled and confined to a wheelchair and who reads books and newspapers and can thus, on occasion, be treated as an enemy, indeed, as an inmate of a concentration camp and have her hair cropped and be otherwise mistreated. At moments when reality breaks in upon this feast of memory, they tell themselves that their time is coming. "We now have a *Bundespräsident* [Karl Carstens] who was a National Socialist," the older sister says. "There you are!" her brother answers. "That shows how far we are again today . . . and we have a whole lot of other leading politicians who were National Socialists!"

The West German theater was not, therefore, indifferent to its duties toward the past, although its engagement in this respect was sporadic and bereft of any truly impressive work of theatrical art. On other political subjects, its record was more disappointing. One might have expected some attention to conditions in the other Germany, to the oppressive political conditions in which fellow Germans were forced to live, and to the plight of intellectuals in the DDR. The only notable attempt to deal with those problems was Günter Grass's subtle and shrewdly argued *The Plebeians Rehearse the Uprising* (1966). Grass imagined that, on June 17, 1953, when workers in East Berlin, Merseburg, Halle, Leipzig, Magdeburg and other towns rose in protest against the raising of production norms, the emasculation of their unions, and the increasing repressiveness of the Communist system, Bertolt Brecht was rehearsing his production of Shakespeare's *Coriolanus* at the Theater am Schifferdamm in East Berlin. A delegation of workers comes to him to ask him to write a manifesto for them. Instead of complying, the *Dramaturg* plays word games with them and seeks to use their agitations for his own dramatic purposes. He becomes aware of the earnestness of the situation only after the Soviet tanks have entered the city, and then it is too late.

Grass's play was a tribute to the Seventeenth of June, an event which, as he noted, had lost its real significance with the passing of the years and become a meaningless holiday marked by "empty bottles, sandwich papers, beer-corpses, and real corpses, since the traffic demands an extra dividend of sacrifices on holidays." It was also an argument for a greater degree of political engagement on the part of German artists. From the dramatists, it did not elicit much response. With the exceptions noted above, the German theater did not have much to offer in the way of political drama or social criticism in the late sixties and seventies. The outlook of dramatists like Bodo Strauss, who has been mentioned earlier, was much like that of the Theater of the Absurd that had such a vogue in the fifties: they seemed to be saying that life was so hopeless that it was not even worth defining the problems that called for solution.

IV

That sort of thing was not permitted in the German Democratic Republic, where literature was regarded not only as a social function but as an instrument of social utility, and where anyone who was privileged to be a writer was expected to use his talents to improve society and the lives of his fellow citizens. This was a challenge that appealed to many German artists after the end of World War II, and not a few writers of established reputation, who would have had no difficulty in making a lucrative career in Western Germany, chose to go instead to Socialist Germany. It was only after they had done so that they discovered that the honor of being a Socialist writer did not carry with it the freedom to determine the nature and form of their engagement or the right to insist that the aesthetic canons of their craft be observed. It was all very well for the party leadership to say, as Erich Honecker said in 1971, that "when one proceeds from the firm position of Socialism there can, in my opinion, be no taboos in the field of art and literature." The trouble was that there were always other officials, who sat on boards and commissions that had to do with literature, who were adept in discovering that this method or formulation or that stylistic device or development of plot was not good Socialism, and persistence in its use could lead to refusal of the right of publication or production, exclusion from the Writers Union and, in the last resort, expulsion from the country. From the DDR's earliest days, there was open warfare between its bureaucrats and its writers.

That this had a stifling effect upon creativity and the development of new talent goes without saying. The first years after the war saw a complete regimentation of literature, with the extension of State control over libraries, publishing houses, bookstores and theaters, and the promulgation of a stylistic canon for writers. War was declared upon Formalism—that is, any mode of expression that was symbolic or stylized or seemed to emphasize form at the expense of content; and the approved mode was declared to be Socialist Realism, which Soviet cultural boss Andrey Zdhanov had once defined as the principle that "the truthfulness and historical exactitude of the artistic image must be linked with the task of ideological transformation, of the education of the working people in the spirit of Socialism." In practice, it soon became evident, this meant an endless stream of novels about life in the factory and the fields in which the problem was always whether the norms would be met and Socialism continue to advance. Other forms of literary creation were discouraged.

These rules were binding even upon such prominent writers as Anna Seghers, the dean of East German novelists, and Bertolt Brecht, whose decision to settle in East Germany in 1948 had been publicized as proof of the superiority of Socialist over bourgeois culture. Seghers had always been suspicious of institutionalized literary dogma and, in the late 1930s, in a famous debate with Georg Lukács, had defended a liberal conception of realism that allowed artists to experiment with new forms of expression. But she lacked the vigor to take on the hard-nosed bureaucrats of the SED and, neither at the beginning nor later, fought against their ukases. Her capitulation can be seen in depressing form in her novel about the rising of June 17, 1953, *Trust (Das Vertrauen)*, which manages to overlook completely such palpable realities as the intolerable conditions that led to the agitations, which are described as manifestations of a counterrevolutionary movement similar to that led by Admiral Kolchak after the Bolshevik Revolution of 1917 and, like it, encouraged by the capitalist West.

Brecht's difficulties with the party have been described in Martin Esslin's excellent biography of the dramatist. From the very beginning, he was under pressure to abandon his famous epic style. After his production of Maxim Gorki's *The Mother* in 1951, a member of the Central Committee of the SED complained about its lack of realism, historical authenticity, and political soundness; and his opera *The Trial of Lucullus*, with music by Paul Dessau, led to a slashing attack by the party organ *Neues Deutschland* in which he was accused, not only of violating the principles of Socialist Realism, but of "a relapse into doubt and weakness," a charge serious enough to force the collaborators to appease the authorities by writing a work of propagandistic trash in the form of a choral cantata for youth groups called *Report from Herrnburg*. Until his death in 1956, Brecht was periodically belabored by the party press, which at times—after his production of Goethe's *Ur-Faust*, for example, when he was charged with pessimism, lack of respect for German culture, and mockery of the German folksong—threatened the existence of his theater. It is to his credit that he never sacrificed his artistic principles in any serious way to the pressures placed on him, but he did not escape the humiliation of public declarations of loyalty to a regime that he must have detested, like his statement of fealty after the bloody repression of the workers on June 17, 1953.

Although there were signs of growing restiveness among writers in the years after 1953, it was not until 1956, in the wake of the Twentieth Party Conference of the Communist Party of the Soviet Union that Stalinist literary criteria lost their force. What was at the time hailed as a "thaw," however, never amounted to much more than a slightly greater latitude in the choice of literary themes (production novels fell off, and there was a sudden rash of books about World War II, which included the long-time bestseller in East Germany, Bruno Apitz's novel about concentration camps, *Naked Among Wolves*). But the party was not ready to tolerate any true measure of intellectual freedom (and the revolt in Hungary and the troubles in Poland made them less so); and, when Professor Hans Mayer wrote a review on "The Current State of our Literature," in which he contrasted its meager and sickly condition with the achievements of the Weimar period, he was forbidden to broadcast it and became the object of a vitriolic personal campaign when it was published in the journal *Der Sonntag* and found it expedient, some time later, to migrate to the West.

There was some appreciation in party circles that a persistence of the differences between the party and the country's leading writers and critics would be unhealthy, and in 1959, at the so-called Bitterfeld Conference, a start was made at overcoming this. Both the outmodedness of Soviet models and the inadequacy of most of what had passed for literature in the DDR for the last ten years was admitted, and the common task was declared to be that of creating a national literature that would inspire respect at home and abroad. Under the motto, "Comrade! Seize your pen! The Socialist national culture needs you!", writers were invited to deal with contemporary problems of life in the DDR.

The response to this challenge was positive, and during the sixties literature came of age in the DDR. In a curious sense, the building of the Berlin Wall in August 1961 contributed to this by cutting the intellectuals off from the West and making literature a family enterprise, an affair "*unter uns.*" In any event, books that were real books rather than forced expressions of ideological zeal began to appear with regularity— Christa Wolf's *Moscow Stories* and *Divided Heaven*, Wolfgang Dobrowski's *The Sarmatian Time* and *Levin's Mill*, Stefan Heym's *The Papers of Andreas Lenz*, Jakov Lind's *Jacob the Liar*—and the world learned to its surprise that there were actually some good poets in the DDR—Stephen Hermlin, Peter Huchel, Christa Reinig, Günter Kunert and others.

Yet this appearance of progress toward a freer, and hence, a better literature was misleading. The culture bosses never relaxed their vigilance or their anxious search for deviation, and a writer whose works were praised one day could not be sure he would not be assailed the next. Popularity was often regarded as a suspicious sign and attracted examination and criticism. Thus, Christa Wolf, a writer who succeeded better than any other novelist of her time in describing the painful process of self-realization in Socialism, a process that, in her view, demanded honesty, freedom from wishful thinking, and what Ernst Bloch had called the "principle of hope," aroused the liveliest unease among the critical establishment; and, at the Writers Congress in May 1969, a dogmatic critique of her novel *The Quest for Christa T.* (*Nachdenken über Christa T.*) accused her of subjectivity and ambiguity and failure to emphasize that the Socialist personality's claim to happiness comes from productive involvement in the collective.

The party's treatment of Peter Hacks was even more drastic. This gifted dramatist, who emigrated from West Germany in 1955, received the Lessing Prize of the East German Academy of Arts two years later for his play *The Battle of Lobositz* and had a notable success with his *The Miller of Sans Souci* in 1958. When he turned from historical themes to contemporary ones, however, he entered a jungle filled with ideological snipers. His play *Briquettes*, which dealt with the emergence of a new Communist workers solidarity as it was reflected in a conflict between the workers of two different industries, was canceled because it supposedly emphasized negative aspects of the progress toward Socialism; and, when Hacks rewrote the play and produced it for the Berlin Festival of 1961 under the title *Problems and Power (Die Sorgen und die Macht)*, the reception was judged to be unfavorable by the party, and the play was taken off, the chief party theoretician explaining that "Hacks sees human relations in our society primarily from the viewpoint of bourgeois psychology." Four years later, when, because of the dearth of competitors, the literary establishment staged a new play by Hacks, *Moritz Tassow*, for the Berlin Festival, the Central Committee called it "obscene," and the DDR's leading theater magazine complained that Hacks had made the Communist functionary in his play a believer that "simple pragmatism . . . lifts practical utility to the status of truth," and thus a violator of Communist doctrine. Once more the play came off, and Hacks fell into such deep disfavor that he was reduced to writing plays for children.

Nor were the poets spared. East German cultural policy made the publication of any poem that did not deal with an orthodox theme in an orthodox manner a chancy business, and any evidence of modern techniques was immediately damned as bourgeois and regressive. It is not difficult to imagine the reaction of the party critics to a poem like "You haven't heard," by Christa Reinig, here translated by Christopher Middleton for *The Times Literary Supplement*.

> Of progress not another word
>   of work and pensions and percents
>   I speak (heroes, you haven't heard)
>   for the asocial elements.
>
> For letching matloes waifs and strays
>   for gipsies dreamers goofs of love
>   for working men who've had enough
>   for jailbirds oddballs refugees
>
> For the hoodlum suicide hooligan
>   for whores in houses where the lamps are low
>   and for the drunks who'll never know
>   it's a lump of star they're trampling on
>
> I speak my words as madmen may
>   for myself and others also blind
>   for all who haven't found the way
>   or got a home to find.

This was clearly too daring for publication, and it was not long before its author made her way to the West where she could receive a hearing.

A more political poet than Christa Reinig (or Peter Huchel, who was forced from his editorship of the periodical *Sinn und Form* in 1962 and effectively silenced) was the popular composer of ballads and chansons, Wolf Biermann. A dedicated Socialist but an opponent of bureaucratized totalitarianism, Biermann had the temerity to snipe at party *Bonzen* (bigwigs), State Security thugs, policies like the building of the Wall, and the glib but never realized promises of economic improvement, and his gibes had wide circulation. The party tried in various ways to discourage the poet, but after the publication of his book *The Wire Harp (Die Drahtharfe)* decided that it could no longer tolerate taunts like

> Die einst vor Maschinengewehren mutig bestanden
> fürchten sich vor meiner Gitarre. Panik

breitet sich aus, wenn ich den Rachen öffne und
Angstschweiss tritt den Büroelephanten auf den Rüssel
wenn ich mit Liedern den Saal heimsuche . . .

[Those who once stood up courageously to machine guns
are scared by my guitar. Panic
spreads when I stretch my jaws and
the sweat of fear shines on the trunks of the office elephants
when I visit the hall with my songs . . .]

In a speech at the eleventh session of the SED Central Committee,
Erich Honecker placed the poet under ban, explaining that

with his songs and poems Biermann is currently betraying
the basic tenets of Socialism. In doing so, he enjoys the be-
nevolent support and encouragement of a number of writers,
artists and other intellectuals. It is high time to take a stand
against the proliferation of alien and dangerous ideas and
inartistic junk which at the same time show strong pornographic elements.

Despite the apparent finality of this declaration, the warm support
that Biermann received from the leading members of the literary community apparently persuaded the party that it would be embarrassing
and self-defeating to declare the Bitterfeld experiment a failure and to
crack down on writers in general. For the next ten years, the cultural
policy of the DDR followed a highly erratic course, with some apparently innocuous works falling under the censor's shears while surprisingly antisystem works were allowed to see the light of day. A notable
example of the latter was Ulrich Plenzdorf's play *The New Sorrows of
Young W. (Die neuen Leiden des jungen W.)*, which caused a considerable stir at its première in Halle in 1972, by showing that young people
in the DDR did not spend all their time working for and thinking about
Socialism and that some of them at least dreamed of having real blue
jeans and preferred the music of Louis Armstrong to that of "Handel-
sohn Bacholdy" and had generational problems and unhappy love affairs.
But examples like this seemed to frighten the authorities and to
encourage the hardliners who had no use for a literature that did not toe
the party line. In the middle of the seventies an offensive against progressive writers began that took two forms. The Writers Union (*Schrift-
stellerverband*), which had been established as the social organization
and representative voice of the literary community, became the object
of a systematic policy of infiltration and exclusion, so that the more
independent of the writers were forced out or not invited to membership
on various contrived technical grounds, and their places were filled with
party bureaucrats or members of State commissions and State publishing houses. By this process, the Union lost its power to serve as a pressure group in the interest of artistic freedom and gradually became a
weapon that could be used against recalcitrant writers. In the second

place, the decision appears to have been made to use the threat of deprivation of citizenship to force the literary community into line.

This weapon saw its first use in November 1976, when Wolf Biermann was expelled from the country. Although the poet had long been deprived of publication rights in the DDR, he had continued to write, and his collections—*With Marx and Engels Tongues (Mit Marx und Engelzungen)* and *Germany: A Winter's Tale (Deutschland: Ein Wintermärchen)*—had been published in the West. His international reputation was so great (he was considered by some to be the greatest writer of satirical songs since Heine) that the government had considered it expedient to allow him to give concert tours abroad. It was an incident during one of these that the government used to make an example of him. Asked for an encore at a concert in Hamburg, Biermann said he would sing one when the announced program was finished, adding jocularly, "I'm ready for any atrocity (*Ich bin zu jeder Schandtat bereit*)." *Neues Deutschland* immediately announced that "in the media of the imperialistic German Federal Republic," Biermann had announced that he was "ready for any atrocity against the DDR." The expulsion order followed.

This time the outraged reaction of the poet's colleagues had no effect upon the party. Among those who protested directly to Party Secretary Honecker were such respected writers as Christa Wolf, Stefan Heym, Günter Kunert, Ulrich Plenzdorf, Klaus Schlesinger, Rolf Schneider, and Franz Fühmann. In May 1978, when the Writers Congress met in East Berlin, none of these writers received an invitation, and several of them were subjected to campaigns of official hectoring (Stefan Heym was accused of breach of currency laws) or backstairs denigration, the term *kaputte Typen* being applied to them by party hacks and ideological hatchetmen. In 1979, while the president of the Writers Union, Hermann Kant (the author of a tedious but scrupulously orthodox novel called *Die Aula*), and the honorary president, Anna Seghers, looked the other way, Heym, Schneider, and seven other fighters for literary freedom were eased out of the Union.

By now the situation had become a European scandal. In 1979, Günter Kunert, one of the most distinguished poets in the Democratic Republic but a dead man in a literary sense since he had protested against the expulsion of Biermann, applied for, and received, a travel visa and moved into exile in Itzehoe in Holstein. When he did so, he published a description of the campaign of falsification, obstruction, pettifoggery and calumniation that he had had to struggle against during the most creative years of his life. "Too many 'literary technicians,' " he ended his report, "have wiped their boots on me during the last decade for me to accept a single additional humiliation of that kind. These people, whom we have to thank for the indigestible brew of their unholy ideological cast of thinking, we must blame also for the oppressive losses that have afflicted DDR literature; for poets and writers whose number is still incomplete, life was made intolerable, so that, as far as they could see, no other escape remained to them except to go. I am reluctant to have to admit for myself that this is the only alternative."

11

Soldiers

If there was one thing that everybody in the West was sure about during World War II, it was that, once National Socialism was defeated, Germany would never again be allowed to have an army. This was the view of the man in the street and of the people who sat in government offices and worked on postwar planning, and it was clearly expressed in the basic occupation directive drafted in Washington in 1944–1945, the famous memorandum JCS-1067 which, in its main outlines, was accepted by the other Allied Powers at the Potsdam Conference. This document defined the principal goal of the Allies as being "to prevent Germany from ever again being a threat to the peace of the world" and stipulated that this must be accomplished by "the industrial disarmament and demilitarization of Germany" and the "continuing control over Germany's ability to conduct war." When the Allied Control Council began its work in Germany in August 1945, it issued a series of directives that forbade Germans to wear military uniforms or rank insignia or decorations or to possess weapons, munitions or explosives (with some exceptions for policemen, miners and demolition crews); it made military schools, exhibitions, and ceremonies illegal, outlawed paramilitary sports clubs and similar organizations, ordered a halt to military-related research, and ordered the destruction of monuments, placards, street signs and memorial tablets that were intended "to maintain and preserve the German military tradition . . . or to glorify military events." Zonal commanders were simultaneously ordered to pursue a vigorous policy of dismantling industries that could be used for military production.

The Cold War invalidated all of these measures. By the spring of 1948, the Soviet government had authorized the expansion, arming and garrisoning of special border forces in the Eastern zone, and in Washington and London earnest talks had begun about the necessity of building up a limited West German military force. The outbreak of the Korean War in July 1950 gave added urgency to this idea, and Western planning for the integration of a German contingent in a European defense force led, in the years that followed, to a corresponding buildup of East German forces. As a result, by 1955 each of the German states had a military establishment of its own, with the approval of its Superpower patron.

In the Western world, this development caused the gloomiest forebodings among people whose historical memory was stronger than their fear of a Communist victory in the Cold War, and in Germany too this abrupt reversal of Allied policy evoked reactions that ranged from open hostility to extreme skepticism. One West German politician said that Germans must now try to do something that they had never had any success with in the past: namely, to create an effective democracy and an effective armed force at the same time. He did not seem sanguine about the probable results. Even the soldiers, who, to their gratified surprise, were brought from retirement to plan and raise the new forces, expressed grave concern. The moral foundation of an army was as important, they pointed out, as the material one. Soldiers must have a tradition of which they could be proud. Upon what tradition, given Germany's dark past, was a new army to be built? And what support could it, after the horrors of the late war, expect from the German people?

These were difficult questions, and they were answered in different ways in the Federal Republic and in the DDR.

I

To those people who shuddered at the words German rearmament, history supplied no comfort. In the rise of Prussia to great-power status in the eighteenth century and in the imposition of its hegemony upon Germany in 1866 and Europe in the years after 1870, the army had been the crucial factor, proving the dictum of the Great Elector, Frederick William of Brandenburg, in his memorandum to his successor in 1667, "Alliances to be sure are good, but forces of one's own, upon which one can rely, are better . . . and it is these, thank God!, that have made me *considerabel* since the time when I began to have them." But the army was also the main pillar of absolutism in Prussia and in the German Empire that Prussia founded in 1871 and the chief barrier to effective parliamentary government and progress toward democracy. If it can be argued that modern German history was a prolonged constitutional struggle between conservative and liberal forces, it was clear that in the critical moments in that process, it was the army that played the decisive role, throwing its weight in every instance against the cause of popular sovereignty. In 1819, the most hopeful period of reform in Prussian history came to an end not least of all because the army got rid of the progressive elements in its own officer corps, who had been working for constitutional change, and became once more a bulwark of unredeemed absolutism. In 1848, the liberal victories of March and the efforts of the Frankfurt Parliament to unite Germany on the basis of constitutional government and individual liberty became meaningless when the Prussian army restored order in Berlin, leveled the barricades in Dresden, and put the brave but disorganized democrats of the Badenese Legion to flight. In 1866, the Prussian army's victory over the Austrians at Königgrätz was also a victory over those Prussian liberals who had, since 1860, been trying to use the budgetary rights of the parliament to establish some form of control over the military establishment. In each case, the soldiers reinforced in the minds of their supreme commanders the principle enunciated by one of their number in 1848: Against democrats, only soldiers are effective.

When the German Reich was established in 1871, after the victory over France, the soldiers seemed to believe that they alone deserved credit for that achievement. The crowning of William I in the Hall of Mirrors in Versailles resembled nothing less than a military review, for the civilian participants cut a sorry figure among the swashbuckling victors of Mars-la-Tour and Gravelotte who, with sabers jangling and decorations gleaming, crowded around the throne and shouted their jubilation as massed bands played "Heil Dir im Siegerkranz!" and the "Hohenfriedberger March" of Frederick the Great. The leader of the Catholic Party, Ludwig Windthorst, said bitterly, "Versailles is the birthplace of a military absolutism similar to that brought to flower by Louis XIV," a prophecy that the subsequent history of the Empire proved to be shrewd. Indeed, it is not too much to talk about a progressive militarization of German life after 1871. Military values permeated the world of business, producing a breed of industrialists who ran their enterprises as if they were fortress commanders, and the university community, where the student corporations adopted the ceremonials and the vices of garrison life and tried to emulate the style of the Prussian lieutenant. In the age of William II, the wealthy bourgeoisie sought to advance itself socially by seeking husbands for its daughters in the aristocratic officer corps and commissions for its sons in crack cavalry regiments, thus giving itself over to a process of feudalization that had the most profound social results. At the same time, the influence of the military in the domestic politics of the Reich was not inconsiderable. Its ever repeated demands for heightened military appropriations contributed to the financial problems that plagued every government after Bismarck's, and the advice given by its leaders concerning social policy was so catastrophic in tendency as to create a crisis atmosphere that made impossible any genuine reconciliation between the working class and the rest of society.

In foreign policy, its role was more fateful. Even so strong a leader as Bismarck had difficulty in controlling the propensity of the military chiefs to meddle in matters of foreign policy. During the wars of 1866 and 1870, Helmuth von Moltke and the "demigods" of the General Staff challenged his responsibility for the direction of State policy and tried to take the right of determining the goals and duration of the military effort into their own hands; and in 1887 Bismarck discovered that the General Staff was actually pursuing its own foreign policy and was seeking, through its agents in Vienna, to encourage the Austrians to launch a preventive war against Russia on the understanding that Germany would support them. In the years after Bismarck's fall, the tendency of the army to usurp the authority of the Foreign Office and the Diplomatic Corps became more pronounced. Operational plans for future wars were adopted that seriously limited the government's freedom of diplomatic action; and, in times of crisis, civilian leaders learned, not only that their options were severely restricted, but that military expediency was invoked to justify courses of action in which they had no confidence but which their lack of technical military knowledge made them incapable of criticizing. Germany went to war in 1914, despite the gravest misgivings on the part of the civilian leadership, because the soldiers said it was necessary; and, once the war was under way, the army arrogated to itself the right to make not only all of the military decisions, but the political ones as well. In the last analysis, the military was responsible for such critical political errors as the refusal to promise to evacuate Belgium after the war was over, which made negotiations with the Western Powers for a compromise peace impossible, and the introduction of unrestricted submarine warfare, which brought the United States into the war; and, in general, the maladroit politics of people like Hindenburg and Ludendorff led directly to the collapse of 1918, which swept away the monarchical system that the army, by its role in domestic affairs, had sought so zealously to maintain.

One might have expected the Republican regime that was established in 1918 to remember this record and to see that military influence in the new State was reduced to the barest minimum. But the Republican leaders were so dependent upon the army for support against the threat of a takeover by the extreme left that their ability to impose effective restraints upon it was negligible, and the soldiers made the most of this weakness. Under the command of Hans von Seeckt, the army recovered from the physical and psychological effects of its recent defeat and became not only an efficient force but one that was so organized that it was capable of rapid expansion when international conditions made this possible. At the same time, however, it was never fully integrated into the society that it was supposed to be protecting from internal as well as external foes. In the Reichswehr of the 1920s, dissatisfaction with the terms of the Versailles Treaty, with the forced reduction of the army and with the consequent slowing down of promotions made the officer corps contemptuous of the politicians, whom they blamed for these things, and they communicated their feelings to the troops under their command. This situation was the more dangerous because the Allies had insisted, when they wrote the military clauses of the Treaty, that Germany must not be permitted to have an army based upon conscription but would be limited to a small force (100,000 officers and men) of long-term volunteers. The effect of this was to make the Reichswehr's antirepublican stance more ominous than it might otherwise have been and to turn the army into a praetorian guard that had no real allegiance to the Republican government.

In the critical phase of the Republic's fortunes, when its democratic leaders struggled to control the horrendous social effects of the world depression, the military embarked on a political course of their own. In a series of misbegotten experiments, they sought to use the emergency powers of the Reich President to find an authoritarian answer to the Republic's problems. Heinrich Brüning, Franz von Papen, and Kurt von

Schleicher, the Chancellors of the years 1930–1932, were all chosen by the army leadership and then abandoned when they proved incapable of mastering the deteriorating political situation. In the end, the army politicians were outmaneuvered by Adolf Hitler, who had been systematically playing upon the dissatisfactions that existed in the junior officer corps and the rank and file by promising a restored and expanded military establishment once he came to power and by attacking the Republican government for lack of national spirit and failure to defend the vital interests of the State. In the first weeks of 1933, when it became clear that Hitler was at the gates, there were many people in Germany who believed that the army would not tolerate the accession to power of this dangerous political adventurer. But, after all of their frenetic and misguided political meddling, the army chiefs now adopted an elaborate pose of neutrality, and by doing so assumed a significant share of the responsibility for having delivered Germany into the hands of National Socialism.

Nor did their responsibility end there. It can be fairly said that the army was culpable for much of the horror that followed. It was in a real sense an accomplice of Hitler's in the bloody events of June 30, 1934, in which the SS, using army equipment, killed dissident elements in the SA and, at the same time, deliberately murdered some old enemies of the Führer, and its participation in this operation—and its willingness to pledge its fealty to Adolf Hitler in a public oath a few weeks later, despite the fact that two prominent officers, Generals Kurt von Schleicher and Kurt von Bredow, were victims of that Night of the Long Knives—marked the beginning of a total capitulation to the will of the dictator. This had a shameful culmination in February 1938, when the officer corps stood mutely by while Hitler contemptuously dismissed their highest commander, after bringing spurious charges of sexual misconduct against him, and assumed personal command of the Wehrmacht.

There were soldiers who regarded this lack of resistance as a disgrace and who sought to remind their fellows of an older tradition of honor and responsibility to their country. In 1938, when it became apparent that Hitler's course was bent on war, a group of officers led by General Ludwig Beck, the chief of the General Staff, sought to organize opposition to a policy that, in their view, was tantamount to national suicide. Beck believed that precisely because the German people had always had a kind of *pietas* for the army, it was the soldiers' responsibility now to protect it from destruction. "History," he wrote, "will burden these leaders with blood-guilt if they do not act in accordance with their professional and political knowledge and conscience. . . . It shows a lack of greatness and of understanding of his task when a soldier of the highest rank in times like these sees his duty and task only in the restricted area of his military assignment, without taking note of his overriding responsibility to his whole people."

But Beck knew that he could not count on the support of the majority of his fellow officers. Too many of the older ones had detached themselves from the question of political responsibility, protesting that they were only soldiers, doing their jobs; and too many of the younger ones owed their commissions and their promotions to their loyalty to the Nazi Party and their ideological zeal. Even for many of those who had become disenchanted with Hitler, moreover, the oath of allegiance that they had taken in 1934 made anything like a generals' strike unthinkable. Beck and his friends had therefore to pin their hopes on conspiratorial activity, and they proved to be neither lucky nor efficient conspirators. Their plans for a *Putsch* against Hitler at the time of the Sudeten crisis of 1938 were undercut by the capitulation of the Western Powers to Hitler's demands, a victory for the Führer that discouraged the plotters and reduced their number, and their subsequent attempts to remove him by assassination foundered either on Hitler's intuitive sense of danger and his habit of avoiding it by changing his plans at the last moment, or—as in the case of the bomb plot of July 20, 1944—on the lack of determination and the fatal hesitations of the conspirators.

A month before the attempt on Hitler's life in the Wolf's Lair at Rastenburg, one of the directors of the conspiracy, admitting that he was pessimistic about the chances of success, said, "The attempt must be made, *coûte que coûte*. . . . For it is no longer a matter of the practical goal, but of the German resistance movement's daring to make the decisive blow before the world and before history. Everything else is a matter of indifference." There was something to this, and surely Beck and Klaus von Stauffenberg and their associates proved that the army's subservience to Hitler was not total or irretrievable. But their action could not expunge the memory of the many commanding officers who continued to obey the Führer's orders long after they knew that there was no hope of victory and that their obedience was merely increasing the death toll of their own troops and prolonging the suffering of the German people. That there were high-ranking officers who cynically went on serving a man they privately believed to be a madman in the hope of winning a marshal's staff before the fighting stopped was a shameful commentary upon the moral condition to which the army had been reduced in the Third Reich, and the memory of this was not diminished by the flood of self-exculpatory literature written by former general officers in Hitler's Wehrmacht in the first postwar years.

II

No one who passed through Western Germany in the first months after the Paris Agreement of December 1954, which admitted the Bundesrepublik to membership in NATO and authorized it to raise a contingent force of 500,000 officers and men, could avoid being impressed by the scope and intensity of antimilitarism. The feeling cut across party lines. It was strongest, perhaps, in the Social Democratic Party, the bulk of whose membership held to the doctrinaire pacifism of their Weimar past, but many of the Free Democrats shared it, and it was by no means lacking in the coalition of Konrad Adenauer. The trade unions were critical of the rearmament policy that the Chancellor had made his own, and so was a large part of the leadership of the Evangelical Church. That section of German youth that was eligible for military service showed their displeasure at the prospect by howling down government defenders of the policy in Cologne and by stoning the defense minister with beer mugs in Augsburg; and the enormous success of Helmuth Kirst's antimilitarist novel *0815* and the films based upon that book and Carl Zuckmayer's drama *The Devil's General*, which portrayed the military caste and army life in the worst possible light, indicated that this negative attitude was widely shared by the general public.

It is likely that similar reactions lay under the surface in the German Democratic Republic as well, when in January 1956 the East German government promulgated a law that reorganized its existing garrisoned police units and formally established a *Nationale Volksarmee*; and it is probable that the common basis of antimilitary feeling in the DDR was, as it was in Western Germany, historical recollection, the knowledge that the possession of an army had not been a good thing for Germany in its modern history and that the military establishment had always tended to be a State within the State, inhibiting social progress and preventing the development of liberal and democratic institutions.

The government of the DDR countered this undercurrent of feeling by denying the relevance of the evil past to its announced action. In his speech before the People's Chamber on January 18, 1956, announcing the new law, the deputy chairman of the Council of Ministers, Willi Stoph, did indeed remind his auditors that "in Imperial Germany, in the Weimar Republic, and during the Nazi regime, the reactionary soldiers forged their criminal plans, oppressed the German people, including German youth, and misused them for their military goals." Those same reactionary forces, he continued, were now again at work in Western Germany, promoting their old policy "in the interest of German monopoly and finance capitalism and the Junkers under the flag of the aggressive North Atlantic Pact." But no such line of continuity could be detected in the German Democratic Republic. The revolution effected as a result of the war had broken with the past. "In the German Democratic Republic the working class, the industrious peasantry and the other active sections of society are the supporters of the army and thereby the ruling power in State and society." The very idea of opposition between the army and the rest of society, of the kind of civil-military problem that had been a constant element in German history, was now impossible. "The People's Army of the German Democratic Republic is an inseparable and constituent part of our workers' and peasants' State, which serves to protect the democratic achievements of the population and the boundaries of our Republic. The National People's Army, therefore, works in the German Democratic Republic in full agreement with the interests of the working population. In the German Democratic Republic, the foundations of militarism—monopoly capitalism and the Junkers—have been definitively destroyed. The People's Army of our

Republic is therefore the instrument that protects a people freed from imperialism; it represents, in the deepest sense, national character."

It was not possible for those charged with the task of building the new army in Western Germany to appease the forces of antimilitarism with this kind of argument. The Bundesrepublik was not a revolutionary State ruled by a single party, which claimed to govern in the interest of the working masses and exercised complete control over all of the instruments of power. On the contrary, it was a pluralistic State with a capitalistic economy, and government policy emerged by a process of conflict and compromise between various parties, pressure groups, and economic and social interests. In such a society, the argument that the new army would represent the interests of "the people" was bound to encounter a more skeptical response than in the DDR, particularly on the part of those who remembered the way in which past German armies, while claiming to represent the State, had always taken care of themselves first. Nor would such reasoning persuade those who were concerned lest the rapid buildup of the new Bundeswehr, under the pressure of a nervous American government, bring old Nazis back into public life by the military route, and who noted that already officers who had held high rank in the Wehrmacht (General Adolf Heusinger, formerly chief of the Operations Division at Hitler's Headquarters, and General Hans von Speidel, Rommel's chief of staff) occupied leading positions in the Bundesrepublik's contingent to NATO.

Army planners in the Bundesrepublik relied, therefore, not on Willi Stoph's kind of rhetoric but on concrete measures that were designed to prevent the recurrence of the perennial civil-military problem by creating a new model army for the democratic Republic. As early as the end of 1950—shortly after U.S. Secretary of State Dean Acheson had repudiated the earlier policy of demilitarization and called for the participation of West German forces in a European defensive force—the former trade union official and parliamentarian Theodor Blank was appointed commissioner of security for West Germany. With a group of former officers and the cooperation of professional men, business groups and academicians, Blank began to study the whole range of questions involved in the creation of a military establishment. Much of the work of *Dienststelle Blank*—which was later, as a result of the ratification of the Paris Treaties, absorbed by the new Defense Ministry—was technical in nature, but the most interesting and revolutionary aspect of its activity might rather be described as philosophical, for it was concerned with the formulation of the principles that should determine the inner structure and spirit of the new West German army.

It is no exaggeration to say that the officers of *Dienststelle Blank* were animated by ideals similar to those enunciated by the Prussian military reformers of the years 1807–1813. Gerhard von Scharnhorst, Hermann von Boyen, August von Gneisenau and their colleagues had also been confronted with the task of rebuilding an armed force from the bottom up after an utterly disastrous war and at a time when the army was the object of popular hatred and suspicion. They had sought to accomplish their task by the creation of a "citizen army" in which the caste system and the brutal discipline of the past would be abolished, the moral worth and personal rights of the individual soldier would be respected, and the quality of personal initiative would be valued as highly as blind obedience—a force, in short, in which Prussian subjects would be glad to serve, regarding service, indeed, as a duty of citizenship.

In the same spirit, Blank and his colleagues—notably Colonel (later General) Wolf Count Baudissin, who was the most brilliant and idealistic of the new reformers—insisted that the gulf between military and civilian society must be closed and that the army must be neither a closed body nor "a collection of robots and functionaries with weapons" but rather an organization of *Staatsbürger in Waffen*, in which citizen soldiers could acquire the technical knowledge, discipline and spirit of teamwork that were required in modern warfare, without having to undergo the dehumanizing processes that were characteristic of the older training systems. It would be an army free of *Kadavergehorsam* and *Barras*—of corpselike obedience and the kind of petty garrison-tyranny that was graphically described in Kirst's *0815*—and its soldiers would be treated like human beings, encouraged to think for themselves, and rewarded for personal initiative. In service regulations and disciplinary codes, the rights of the individual would be protected; soldiers would have the right of petition to civilian authorities and of redress of grievances; and they would enjoy freedom of opinion, assembly and discussion.

Finally, service in the new army would be based on a broad conception of military education that would include, for both officers and men, not only technical training but political instruction and impartial discussion of historical questions and contemporary events in Germany and other countries. Its guiding principle would be what came to be called *Innere Führung* or moral leadership. It was intended to overcome the political apathy of the younger generation and to give it motivation and a sense of the importance of serving, and in this sense it was reminiscent of von Boyen's ambitious plan to make the Prussian army of 1814 "the school of the nation." It was influenced also by the reflection that "unpolitical soldiers" had served Germany badly, and that the political naiveté of the German officer corps in the interwar period had helped bring Hitler to power.

While these measures were being formulated in *Dienststelle Blank*, it became apparent that parliament was also determined to assert its authority in military affairs, not only to prevent an infiltration of the new military establishment by old Nazis but also to remove the possibility that control over the future army would be lodged in any single pair of hands, a Seeckt *redivivus* or a second Hindenburg. Its determination on the first count became manifest in July 1955, when the government submitted a bill to the Bundestag calling for the raising of 6000 volunteers as the first step towards recruiting an army. To the exasperation of the American military, who wanted to see Germans in uniform as quickly as possible, the Bundestag refused to approve the request until a thirty-eight-member Personnel Advisory Committee had been established by law to screen all appointments to the rank of colonel and above. This body included such well-known opponents of National Socialism as Fabian von Schlabrendorff, who once tried to kill Hitler, Annedore Leber, the widow of the Lübeck Socialist leader, Julius Leber, who died for his resistance activities, General Fridolin von Senger und Etterlin, who had refused to allow the Gestapo to infiltrate his command in Italy, and Dr. Otto Rombach, former mayor of Aachen, who had been dismissed from his post by the Nazis in 1933. Through the Committee's work, which lasted from 1955 to 1957, the Bundestag exercised, as the New York *Times* noted, "absolute control over the officer personnel" of the army in its formative period. It examined six hundred cases, unfavorably in one hundred of them, and it showed its independence by rejecting four officers for permanent rank who had performed important services in the Blank organization. Thanks to their services, there was little danger that the new officer corps would become a refuge for antidemocratic elements or even that its members would model their style upon that of soldierly paragons like Seeckt and Schlieffen. When the first seven German officers reported for duty at SHAPE headquarters, there was, a reporter for *Der Spiegel* noted, "no heel-clicking, no piercing looks, no clipped nods, no spirited strides, no harsh voices." The officers were in civilian clothes and looked like "diplomats who had forgotten their umbrellas."

That parliament had no intention of relinquishing its control over Bundeswehr policy was shown in July 1956, when formal legislation on the organization of the armed forces and provisions for conscription were enacted. As part of the military laws, the Bundestag created the office of parliamentary defense commissioner, a kind of ombudsman who was empowered to receive complaints from officers and private soldiers but was also given unrestricted powers of investigation into any aspect of life in the armed forces and was required to report his findings on special problems to the Bundestag and to make periodic reports in writing on the general internal condition of the armed forces.

It would have been too much to expect that the raising of the Bundeswehr, a process that lasted until 1965, when the twelve divisions authorized by the Paris Agreement of 1954 were ready for service, would be accomplished without incident. As one commanding general said in 1964, "In all matters that affect the armed forces, people in the Bundesrepublik react neuralgically. The reasons lie in our history. Established democracies act more generously. And the public here too will have gradually to learn to stop regarding normal consequences of rapid growth with a lack of goodwill." He was referring to the tendency of press and public to feel that any complaint by an army officer about the inhibiting effect of the new political criteria upon normal training schedules was a sign of military insubordination and to view every reported case of mistreatment of recruits by NCOs as a sign of a return to the brutal training methods of the old army, without pausing to consider whether the fault might not lie with the lack of sufficiently experienced NCOs and junior officers. But there were enough of these incidents in the ten years of expansion to feed popular suspicion, and in 1964 this received new nourishment when the parliamentary defense commissioner, the former Admiral Hellmuth Heye, published an alarmist report on conditions in the army in the popular weekly illustrated magazine *Quick*. In this series of articles, Heye said things that had not been included in his written report to the Bundestag: namely, that unless prompt remedial action were taken, the Bundeswehr would develop, in an undesirable fashion, into a force with tomorrow's weapons but trained in the spirit of yesterday. He said that there was strong opposition in the officer corps to the *Innere Führung* and the idea of the citizen-soldier, and that there were dangerous signs of regression—indeed, of the military establishment again becoming a State within the State.

In the hullabaloo that followed, a few reasonable voices were raised to point out that there doubtless were, among the older troop commanders, some who viewed the democratic reforms skeptically, but that if their complaints became too egregious, the government possessed all of the powers needed to discipline them. Meanwhile, the possibility of the armed forces becoming a State within the State was not nearly as great as that of their being forced into isolation in German society, a tendency that was already so pronounced that officers preferred not to wear their uniforms in public lest they attract attention and, in certain quarters, abuse.

Members of the Bundeswehr suffered, indeed, from a complex of problems that were in a true sense unique. The armed forces that they served had neither the independence enjoyed by other national forces, since they were subordinated to an international command, SHAPE, and dependent upon its directives, nor the popular and party support enjoyed by the military in Britain and France, for the political parties that had created the Bundeswehr in 1956, because it was necessary, had maintained a critical distance from it ever since, and their attitude was reflected in public opinion. They were expected to inculcate in their troops the qualities that would sustain them in the field if war should come, while at the same time refraining from violating their civilian rights and values, a difficult task when one was forced to deal wth recruits from an affluent and permissive society that had small respect for the military virtues. The nature of the structure of command was hardly calculated to supply them with guidance or inspiration, for the Bundestag, remembering the way in which military chiefs like Seeckt had defied civilian control in the Weimar period, had carefully avoided appointing a chief of army command, placing the power of supreme command in the hands of the minister of defense and his civilian state secretaries. In 1966, when General H. Trettner, the inspector general of the armed services, sought to have this corrected by making the inspector general a deputy of the defense minister with a share in the power of command, this was repudiated as an example of military politics, and

Trettner was forced to resign, which he did with some bitterness, saying, "We are obedient, and we want to remain obedient. But, if we are treated as we have been up to now, the combat forces will get out of hand when things are serious, or—what would be worse—they won't do anything at all."

This was perhaps less a threat than an expression of frustration, a frustration felt by many officers who lacked the social prestige that the military had once possessed in Germany and still enjoyed in other countries, whose professional ethic of duty and discipline found little response in society as a whole, and who were at the same time deprived, because of the sharp caesura that the year 1945 had made in German history, of any real connection with the past and, hence, of any continuity of tradition. This was a painful deprivation. The German encyclopedia, the Grosse Brockhaus, defines tradition as "one of the decisive characteristics that make a person a person. He lives from the experiences, the knowledge, the insights of his forebears." Without this gift, a person lacks perspective and orientation and, if he is a soldier, suffers a diminution of professional stature. As a writer in the newspaper *Die Welt* said, "An army without a sense of tradition would be degraded to a technical facility whose purpose was killing, in which self-sacrifice would likewise be devalued into a technical waste product."

The Defense Department had not been unmindful of this problem, and in July 1965 defense minister Kai-Uwe von Hassel issued a memorandum, the result of six years of study and discussion, entitled "Bundeswehr and Tradition." In thirty theses, this directive sought to relieve the identity problem felt by many members of the Bundeswehr by urging them to take a critical but sympathetic view of the past and to find in it their own models for inspiration and emulation.

For the guidance of the Bundeswehr, the *Traditionserlass* pointed out that, throughout their history, the German armed forces have always honored such qualities as love of country, as distinct from vulgar nationalism, conscientious fulfillment of duty without expectation of praise or reward, obedience and loyalty to the supreme authority representing the people and the State, and "freedom in obedience," or the willingness to take upon oneself the responsibility for acting for the common good, even at the risk of one's life. This last principle was to be seen in the latitude that German troop leaders had always possessed, until Hitler's time, so that their personal initiative was never stultified by the strategical or tactical plan of the overall commander; on a different level, it was exemplified by the bravery of those officers who risked their lives for the sake of conscience in resisting the crimes and injustices of the Nazi regime, even though they had to break their oath of allegiance to their supreme commander.

Addressing itself to the delicate question of the army's role in politics, the directive stressed the individual rather than the corporate aspect of the problem. "Political participation and shared responsibility," it stated, "have belonged, since the time of the Prussian reforms, to the good traditions of German soldierly life." And then, with a perhaps unconscious echo of General Ludwig Beck's memorandum of 1938, it added, "He who follows a false tradition of the unpolitical soldier and restricts himself to his military craft neglects an essential part of his sworn duty as a soldier in a democracy."

The memorandum went on to note some specifically soldierly values that had manifested themselves and been honored in German military history—such as the ability to make decisions under the pressure of time and circumstance and to live with the consequences (again perhaps an unconscious echo, this time of Clausewitz's famous chapter "On Military Genius")—and mentioned, among the spiritual qualities that had been characteristic of outstanding German soldiers such things as generosity and chivalry, comradeship and compassion, valor and sacrifice, composure and dignity in failure and success, modesty in comportment and style of life, and discipline of spirit, speech and body. It concluded by stating that the connection with the past found its visible expression in the black-red-gold flag, which was the symbol of civic responsibility and of the German aspiration toward the "unity and law and freedom" mentioned in the national anthem, in the eagle of the federal coat of arms, which was the oldest German symbol of sovereignty and the idea of law, and in the Iron Cross as symbolic of morally constrained soldierly valor; and it listed the occasions on which word and symbol should combine to awaken in the soldier a consciousness of tradition (parades, oath-taking, memorial services, and grand tattoos).

It will be noted that the directive of July 1965 held firmly to the principles of the *Innere Führung* and the idea of the citizen-soldier, while at the same time demonstrating the connection between these ideas and the values of the Prussian reformers of 1807–1813 and the members of the officers' resistance against Hitler. In doing this, and in stressing the military and spiritual values that soldiers in the Bundeswehr could share with the most admirable of their predecessors, it sought to give the armed forces a past in which they could take pride while at the same time emphasizing their responsibility to the democratic society of which they were a part. And, on the whole, the directive did help to relieve the feeling of rootlessness that had affected members of the Bundeswehr and to reduce their impatience with the strains caused by the necessity of reconciling military discipline with the rights of the individual soldier. In the fifteen years that followed the promulgation of the *Traditionserlass*, the feeling of being isolated became much less pronounced in the Bundeswehr than it had been in the early 1960s, although, as we shall see, it was capable of revival.

In the DDR also, while the government continued to dissociate itself, for ideological purposes, from much of the German past, it did not underestimate the importance of tradition and the effect that a sense of continuity could have upon the morale of the armed forces. The development of the uniform illustrated this. The first East German military units, the so-called Garrisoned Police of 1948, wore police blue, but in 1952, when the attempt to conceal the buildup of an East German army was finally abandoned, they received Soviet-style military uniforms.

These proved to be unpopular with both the troops and the general public and, after the National People's Army was formally established, a uniform was adopted that was virtually the same as the field gray of the Wehrmacht of the Hitler period. In a speech justifying this, Willi Stoph declared:

> There are important progressive traditions in the military history of our people which found their expression in the uniform. German imperialism and Fascism . . . degraded it as a symbol of military and national honor. In the National People's Army, the German uniform will have a true patriotic meaning as an expression of resolute readiness for the defense of our democratic achievements. In these uniforms, but with red armbands, the armed workers of 1918 chased out the Kaiser; the Hamburg workers, the miners of the Ruhr, workers and peasants from Saxony and Thuringia fought against the nationalist Free Corps and the reactionary Reichswehr. In these uniforms in World War II, many officers and soldiers came forward in the National "Free Germany" Committee against the Hitler Fascist Army.

Stoph scoffed at the uniform of the West German Bundeswehr as having no roots in the German past and, indeed, as being an international capitalistic costume foisted on the Bundeswehr by NATO.

Not content with these historical connections, the party authorities also proceeded to appropriate the Prussian tradition in the persons of the leaders of the Reform Party—Scharnhorst, Gneisenau, Yorck von Wartenburg, and Blücher—whose statues in the Opera Square in the Forum Fredericianum in Berlin were now illuminated by night and whose military exploits were celebrated in the Museum of German History housed in the *Zeughaus* (Armory) at the head of Unter den Linden. This association commended itself, not only because some of these soldiers had progressive political views (Gneisenau, indeed, having been regarded by the Prussian court as a Jacobin), but because they had all urged the necessity of an alliance with Russia to defeat Napoleon. But the old Prussian style was submerged in that of the Wehrmacht in the traditional exercises that were now celebrated in front of the *Neue Wache,* the former military headquarters of Berlin, which now housed a memorial to the victims of Fascism and militarism. Here there were daily changings of the guard, effected with all the ceremonial of the Wilhelmine and Hitler armies, and, periodically, more elaborate reviews in which, *mit klingendem Spiel,* jackbooted and helmeted troopers moved, grim-faced and implacable, down Unter den Linden and, as they reached the *Neue Wache,* changed their pace to the old *Gänseschritt* (goosestep), their legs rising in stiff precision and smashing back to the pavement, while their fellow citizens looked on, if not with satisfaction, at least with respect.

Such traditional shows were much less frequent in West Germany and not always accepted so passively. Indeed, on May 6, 1980, the holding of a Grand Tattoo to celebrate simultaneously the swearing-in of new recruits and the twenty-fifth anniversary of membership in NATO led to a bloody clash between antiwar demonstrators and police that caused injuries to 257 policemen, 27 of whom were seriously hurt, and to at least 50 of those protesting the ceremony.

The Grand Tattoo (*Grosses Zapfenstreich*) is the most elaborate of military spectacles and is reserved for moments of solemnity and commemoration. Its origins lie in the days of the Prussian-Russian alliance against Napoleon, and much of the choreography that determines the way in which troops are marched on and ordered, to the music of massed bands and the shrilling of fifes, is modeled upon Russian practice, as is the dramatic climax of the review, the command "Helmets off! To prayer!", which is followed by the playing of the hymn "*Ich bete an die Macht der Liebe* (I pray to the power of love)" to the music of Christian Gregor. There is nothing provocative or bellicose about this ceremony, which is indeed a moving evocation of the tradition of comradeship and, as such, particularly appropriate to the swearing-in of new recruits. Why, then, the *Krawall* in Bremen?

Partly, one gathers, because of the coupling of the initiation ceremony with the celebration of membership in NATO, whose recent decision to proceed with atomic rearmament had aroused violent public controversy and concern over the damage it would do to relations with the Soviet Union. Partly also because the *Zapfenstreich* was held in Bremen, at the insistence of a *Bürgermeister* who had lost contact with the left wing of his own party, the SPD, and had underestimated the depth of their antimilitarism, and who had, in addition, not sufficiently taken into account the fact that his city was the seat of the most radical university in Germany. And partly, finally, because it was announced that the chief speaker on the occasion of the Tattoo would be the newly elected President of the Federal Republic, Karl Carstens, a man for whom the Young Socialists, academic youth, and the left in general had no respect, and whose extreme conservatism and checkered political past (he was described by some as an "old Nazi") made his participation seem a challenge. This combination of circumstances invited demonstrations on the day of the Tattoo, and groups of pacifists, opponents of nuclear weapons, Young Socialists, members of the Evangelical youth movement, advocates of citizens' initiative (Greens), and opponents of NATO gathered to protest against the "military spectacle" as contrary to democratic values and dangerous to peace. These peaceful demonstrations gave an opportunity for well-organized criminal elements, Communist students and *Chaoten,* armed with Molotov cocktails, chains, stones and clubs, to launch a murderous attack upon the police reserves.

The events in Bremen caused a sensation throughout the country and touched off a confused debate in which some people questioned the wisdom of such ceremonies and, indeed, of all efforts to build tradition in an organization like the Bundeswehr, since this could only run counter to democracy by creating elite-thinking. Defense Minister Hans Apel responded in an essay in *Der Spiegel* by pointing out that many groups and associations in the Federal Republic (churches, trade unions, parties) cherished their own traditions, and that it would be manifestly unfair to deny this right to the military. In the twenty-five years its existence, the Bundeswehr had demonstrated its absolute loyalty to the democratic order; it had remained true to the principles of *Innere Führung* and the conception of the soldier as "*Staatsbürger in Uniform*"; and the fact that it desired to celebrate the traditions that it had inherited from the past and from a quarter of a century's service in the cause of European peace, not in the privacy of the garrison, but in public, sharing its pride with its fellow citizens, deserved praise rather than reprobation.

This was persuasive, but it could not disguise the fact that the damage had been done and that the Bundeswehr had been rudely reminded that its acceptance in the society it served was not yet complete.

III

It is necessary to inquire now into the strength, efficiency and reliability of the two German armies, bearing in mind that anything said with respect to the last of these questions must be highly conjectural.

According to the 1979 edition of John Keegan's *World Armies*, the Bundeswehr comprised the following forces:

Field Army	340,000
Territorial Army	441,000
Navy (154 vessels, mostly small craft)	38,000
Air Force (509 combat aircraft)	110,000
Paramilitary Forces:	
Federal Border Police	20,000
Länder Alert Police	15,000
Reserves:	
Army	615,000
Navy	27,000
Air Force	85,000

The Field Army, which consists of the major fighting forces, is under overall NATO operational command, the highest independent national command being at corps level. It is organized in three corps of three to four divisions each, each division having three brigades, and one independent division based in Schleswig-Holstein, which works with the Danish army. There are twelve divisions in all (four armored, four armored infantry, two infantry, one mountain and one airborne). Each division has a sizable complement of combat and support units (armored reconnaissance battalions, heavy artillery and rocket battalions, antiaircraft, signals and engineer battalions, and helicopter squadrons). Appropriately for a contingent force in an international army, the Bundeswehr draws its equipment from various national sources and has the advantage of choosing weapons that have proved their efficiency in competitive tests. Most of its small arms are German-made, including the assault rifle and the machine guns; the mortars are Israeli; the heavy artillery and rockets are mostly American; the tanks are American M-48s and German Leopards, the latter gradually superseding the former.

The Territorial Army's main task is to defend the rear areas in time of war. It comprises Home Defense Groups, Light Infantry Battalions, and Security Companies, each with its distinct mission and largely manned, in peace time, by reservists. Of the paramilitary forces, the Border Police is equipped with light armored vehicles, mortars, antitank weapons, 20 mm cannon, and infantry small arms. It operates entirely within a 30 km zone along the Federal Republic's borders but could, in the case of a threat to "the existence of free democratic order" of the Republic, be used as the government directed. The Police Alert Units are garrisoned police intended to counter threats to civil order.

Since the Bundeswehr's mission in time of war would be to stop a thrust from the east and since this would almost certainly take the form of a land offensive, it is logical that the lion's share of the military budget should go to the army, and that the navy should play a modest role. On the assumption that the major responsibility for protecting the northern flank will fall to the air and naval forces of Britain and the United States, the German government has generally resisted the enlargement of its naval contingent to NATO. In 1964, it comprised only 120 vessels (7 destroyers, 6 frigates, 53 minesweepers, 49 torpedo boats, and 5 submarines). Fifteen years later this number had increased only to 154, although the Naval Air Arm has been built up to a force with 134 combat aircraft, including three fighter-bomber squadrons. The Air Force itself, which in time of war would have the mission of supporting the ground forces, has overcome the difficulties caused by the unreliability of its first-line combat plane, the accident-prone Starfighter, and now has 35 squadrons, 16 of which are fighter-ground-attack squadrons. It is equipped also with Sidewinder antiaircraft missiles, Pershing 1A SSM missiles, and SAM batteries with Nike Hercules rockets.

Measured by European, rather than Superpower, standards, this is a formidable enough fighting force, the more so because the quality of its training is high, both at the basic level and in the specialist schools for NCOs and the relatively new Bundeswehr universities for career and long-service officers. Because the Bundeswehr has not been engaged in actual combat, no very realistic estimate can be made of its efficiency. But professional judges give it high marks on the basis of its equipment, now the best in NATO, and its performance in maneuvers. Its twelve divisions are considered to be the backbone of the NATO order of battle, and in NATO's autumn maneuvers in 1980 they showed a clear superiority, in articulated movement, use of armor, and command at the middle level, over the United States 7th Army.

A graver problem—and here we come to the question of the reliability of the Bundeswehr in time of war—is that posed by the high incidence, since the late 1960s, of conscientious objection to any form of service that involves the possibility of having to kill or be killed. This affects not only people being called up for service but conscripts who are already serving. In each of the years from 1971 to 1973, 25,000 of the former appealed for exemption on the grounds of conscience, and 2000 serving conscripts asked for discharge; and these figures have not sensibly diminished since then. Indeed, the example of General Gert Bastian, commander of the 2nd Panzer Division, who in January 1980 asked for retirement because he believed that NATO's rearmament plans were inviting war with the Soviet Union, and the events of May in Bremen may encourage an increase in the numbers seeking to avoid military service.

This is not an immediately vital threat to a peacetime army in which long-term volunteers form 55% of total strength. But the number of active soldiers applying for release from duty has raised some doubts about the effectiveness of the *Innere Führung*. In 1978, Defense Minister Apel, in a frank moment, said, "The greatest danger in my eyes would be if our political education produced only hypocrites who knew how to adjust to circumstances and no republicans in uniform who knew why they defend this Republic." And this in turn poses the question about the reliability of the nonregular components of the Bundeswehr if war came, particularly in view of the fact that the forward units of the enemy would probably be East Germans.

In 1761, during the Seven Years War, Thomas Abbt wrote an essay called "Dying for the Fatherland," in which he argued that, when a person was born in, or decided to live in, a country whose laws protected him and which interfered with his freedom only in matters that affected the best interests of the whole, then that was his fatherland, and it had the right to demand of its subjects love and affection and, if need be, the supreme sacrifice of life, which should be made willingly and, indeed, joyfully. Cowards and cynics might laugh at this, but that was only because they were incapable of understanding the "pleasure of death"—not of the kind of death that came to the voluptuary or the animal but "which calls our soul like a Queen from its prison rather than strangling it as a slave in its cell and which finally gives the blood that flows from our veins to the suffering fatherland, that it may drink and live again." The rewards of such willingness to die were a heightened life and a new honor and wider horizons for the soul.

The argument was not original—one finds it in Plato's *Crito*—and it was often repeated after Abbt's time, in Hölderlin's "Death for the Fatherland," for example,

> O nehmt mich, nehmt mich mit in die Reihen auf,
> Damit ich einst nicht sterbe gemeinen Tods!

Umsonst zu sterben, lieb ich nicht, doch
Lieb ich, zu fallen am Opferhügel

Fürs Vaterland, zu bluten des Herzens Blut
Fürs Vaterland—

[O take me, take me with you into the ranks,
So that I do not die a common death!
I desire not to die in vain, yet
I would love to fall on the hill of sacrifice

For the Fatherland, to bleed my heart's blood
For the Fatherland—]

in the verses of Theodor Körner and Ernst Moritz Arndt during the
Wars of Liberation against Napoleon and of others like them during the
wars of 1866 and 1870, and finally in the patriotic outpourings of 1914,
like Bruno Frank's rapturous cry when the war came

Frohlockt, ihre Freunde, dass wir leben
Und dass wir jung sind und gelenk!
Nie hat es solch ein Jahr gegeben,
Und nie war Jugend solch Geschenk!

[Rejoice, friends, that we are alive
And that we are young and nimble!
Never has there been a year like this,
And never was youth such a gift!]

and Karl Bröger's proud lines

Dass kein fremder Fuss betrete den heimischen Grund,
Stirbt ein Bruder in Polen, liegt einer in Flandern wund.
Alle hüten wir deiner Grenzen heiligen Saum.
Unser blühendstes Leben für deinen dürrsten Baum,
    Deutschland!

[That no foreign foot should violate our native soil,
One brother dies in Poland, one lies wounded in Flanders.
We all guard the sacred hem of thy boundaries.
Our most blooming life for thy most withered tree,
    Germany!]

And yet, as early as the eighteenth century, questioning voices were
heard. In Nicolai's novel *Sebaldus Nothanker,* the protagonist is asked
by his wife to preach a sermon on Abbt's "Dying for the Fatherland,"
which has just been published. He is reluctant and complains, in a passage that is not irrelevant to twentieth-century conditions, "Where in

this Germany, torn by war and devastation, can one today find the fatherland? Germans fight against Germans. The contingent of our prince is in one army, and in our own land people are recruiting for another. Which party should we join? Whom should we attack? Whom should we defend? For whom should we die?"

Almost two hundred years later, in 1955, Hermann Heimpel, professor of history in Göttingen, came back to Abbt's theme and, at a memorial service in Hannover, delivered an address called "On Death for the Fatherland," in which he declared that, as a result of two world wars, the concept had lost its meaning. "The *Technisierung* of war," he said, "will always lead to the totalization of war and thus deprive dying for the fatherland of its old nobility, because it fastens upon the nonsoldier as much as upon the soldier." It was high time, he added, that people realized "there is no problem in Europe, no interest of the fatherland that is still so holy that it should be allowed to serve as a motive for allowing the incalculable beast of modern war to be given its freedom again—no Saar territory, no eastern territory, and not even German unity. . . . The salient characteristic of modern war is not the dying for the fatherland but the terrible destruction of masses of people."

How pervasive this feeling is among persons old enough to be eligible for military service in Western Germany and how it would affect the reliability of the Bundeswehr in a war that would pit the two Germanies against each other it is impossible to say, but surely the question is not an irrelevant one.

According to the International Institute for Strategic Studies in London, the armed forces of the German Democratic Republic had the following components in 1979:

Army	107,000 active, 305,000 reserve
Air Force	36,000 (335 combat planes)
Navy	16,000 (200 ships, mostly small craft)
Paramilitary Forces	571,500

That fear of the army recovering its autonomy is not a purely Western phenomenon, despite Willi Stoph's proud words in 1956, is shown clearly enough both in the command structure of the armed forces and by their relationship with the Soviet Union. As in the Federal Republic, the armed forces are immediately subordinate to the minister of national defense, who commands them in accordance with the laws and decrees of the People's Chamber; but the true controlling body is the Socialist Unity Party (SED), through its Commission for National Security, its National Defense Council, and the Security Department of its Central Committee. These bodies watch over the actual working of the armed forces as an instrument of State; political representatives and party branches in the various military units see to it that the political views of personnel do not vary from orthodoxy, and the party's youth organization has branches for soldiers that also serve to promote conformity. Compulsory political education is much more thorough than in the Federal Republic, officers being subjected to eight hours of political indoctrination a month and other ranks much more than that, and all officer personnel are under constant surveillance by the Ministry of State Security. In addition, the party maintains large security forces—over 70,000 border guards and alert police forces, as well as paramilitary combat groups in all major populated areas—with which to discourage any independent activity by the armed forces of which the party disapproves.

As for the Soviet Union, its basic suspicion of any new German army, even one enrolled in its own alliance system, is shown by the fact that the National People's Army has been restricted in size and is currently the smallest of the Warsaw Pact armies in proportion to population and the second smallest in absolute terms. The Commander of the Group of Soviet Forces in Germany exercises complete operational control over the armed forces, which are almost entirely dependent upon the Soviet Union for small arms and field weapons, since the German Democratic Republic, unlike the Bundesrepublik, has not been allowed to develop an arms industry of its own.

Despite these controls, the National People's Army (NVA), which is the most important of the services, has developed into an efficient force, well trained and well armed—indeed, if one could judge from the equipment displayed in the parade in East Berlin marking the thirtieth anniversary of the DDR in October 1979, armed with up-to-date armored combat vehicles and some of the newer Soviet rocket launchers and helicopters, in addition to new Soviet T-72 tanks. It has performed with superior competence in Warsaw Pact maneuvers since 1963; it took part in the operation against Czechoslovakia in 1968, although its participation lasted only five days and was under close Soviet supervision; and, starting in the late sixties, it fulfilled more independent missions in Africa and the Middle East where, apparently with the assent of its Warsaw Pact allies, it began to supply advisers and experts to a number of governments and revolutionary movements, including Angola, Mozambique, Libya, Algeria and Ethiopia. It was reported in 1978 that as many as 1200 East German soldiers were acting as advisers and instructors for artillery, communications, logistics and security questions in Algeria and 450 in Libya; and military schools in the DDR were helping to train officers from South Yemen, Ethiopia, Angola and Syria. NVA units were also reported to have taken part in fighting in Ogaden and Eritrea. All in all, the East Germans were as active and as numerous in Africa as the Cubans, and their influence in the Middle East was greater and was growing.

But the NVA's principal mission is in Europe, as part of the battle line of the Warsaw Pact, in which it belongs to the First Strategic Echelon, which presumably means that it would be immediately involved in any clash between East and West. How would it be likely to comport itself in such circumstances?

The incidence of antimilitarism has not been negligible in the DDR, and since 1962, when universal military service was introduced, conscientious objection to service has bulked sufficiently large as to cause periodic debates about appropriate treatment of objectors, in which, as we have seen, the Evangelical Church has played an important part. How strong latent opposition to war is among serving conscripts, who comprise about 55% of the NVA rank and file, and how much stronger it might become if the NVA found itself confronted with the Bundeswehr, it is impossible to guess, beyond noting that the answer would depend on how well ideological indoctrination stood up to that test.

The educational program of the NVA has endeavored, on the one hand, to teach devotion to the Socialist Fatherland and unquestioned loyalty to both the Soviet Union and the other "brother armies" of the Warsaw Pact. It has also, as the American military analyst Donald Hancock has pointed out, stressed negative values as a means of building a militant patriotism, and the most important of these has been "hatred against enemies of the people." Since these include fellow Germans who happen to live in the Federal Republic, it is possible that this part of the educational mission is even more difficult than that of inculcating brothership with the Czechs and the Poles. It is possibly for this reason that the party leadership decided, as early as the 1950s, that military-political education could not be delayed until young people were recruited into the armed services, and as a result lectures about the army and its mission became part of school curricula. In 1968, the Ministry of Education announced: "The Socialist military education of scholars is a firm part of class-oriented education. It must . . . be differentiated according to the different age groups of young people and children. It is a matter of awakening in the students a readiness to defend the DDR and Socialism at any time."

A pamphlet on Socialist military education that appeared in 1974 was less delicate in stating its objectives. "Education in hate," it said, "does not stand in conflict with the noble goals of Socialism. Hate is the necessary consequence of the working class's fight for liberation and of the fact that the achievements of the Socialist State community are today actively threatened by imperialism." Four years later, against the protests of the Evangelical Church, the party decreed that, even though military indoctrination was already pervasive in the instruction of every subject from geography to music from kindergarten onward, a special subject, *Wehrkunde* or Military Science, would now be compulsory in the ninth and tenth grades of the elementary schools.

It is clear that this heightened emphasis upon military-political education was a defensive measure to counter Western influence in a period of political détente in which the DDR was receiving many visitors from the Federal Republic. But it may also have been a sign of lurking fear in party headquarters concerning the willingness of their fellow citizens, and indeed their soldiers, to take up arms against their brothers across the border. In March 1978, the Berlin Rundfunk broadcast an extraor-

dinary verse in a program called "New Soldier Songs in Discussion."
Entitled "My Brother, My Enemy," this read:

> Der dort drüben steht mit der Waffe,
> könnte mein Bruder sein.
> Doch was ist ein Bruder?
> Kain erschlug Abel.
> Märchen erzählen von feindlichen Brüdern,
> doch auch das beweist nichts.

> Der da mein Bruder sein könnte,
> mag sanft sein und friedfertig.
> Aber er hat eine Waffe,
> gehorcht seinen Oberen,
> die sind meine Feinde.

> Der dort drüben steht mit der Waffe,
> könnte mein Bruder sein.
> Aber er ist auch der
>   Heim-ins-Reich Holer,
> billiges Werkzeug der Eroberer,
> gefühllose Waffe der Raubmörder.
> Mensch, vielleicht Bruder,
> jedoch benutzbar zum Tod
> und also mein Feind!

> [That one, standing over there with the gun,
> could be my brother.
> But what is a brother?
> Cain killed Abel.
> Fairy stories tell of hostile brothers,
> but even that proves nothing.

> That one, who might be my brother,
> may be gentle and peaceable.
> But he has a gun,
> obeys his superiors,
> who are my enemies.

> That one, standing over there with the gun,
> could be my brother.
> But he is also the Home-to-the-Reich promoter,
> cheap tool of conquerors,
> heartless weapon of greedy murderers.
> Human being, perhaps brother,
> yet useful for killing
> and therefore my enemy!]

A government that must resort to such blatant forms of indoctrination can hardly be fully confident of the reliability of the instruments on which it must rely in time of war. In both of the pacts that divide Europe, each of which has raised the cry "The Germans to the front!", the unanswerable question is posed: What would German soldiers do if commanded to fire upon each other?

12

Berlin: Athens on the Spree and City of Crisis

In September 1935, with a college friend, I traveled from Munich to Berlin with the intention of having an interview with the United States ambassador there, William E. Dodd. In private life, Mr. Dodd was a distinguished historian of the American South, the biographer of Jefferson Davis, and the editor of Woodrow Wilson's papers, and it was about historical rather than current diplomatic questions that we wished in the main to consult him. In truth, he was a better scholar than he was ambassador, although his deficiencies in the latter respect did him no discredit. He so detested the Nazis that, although it proved in the long run to be self-defeating, he found it almost impossible to have any dealings with them. This he made violently clear even in our short talk, which was otherwise unremarkable.

During our stay in the city, we lived in a *Christliche Hospiz* (a kind of YMCA) on the Mittelstrasse, a block away from Unter den Linden and only a little further from Bahnhof Friedrichstrasse. It was an excellent location from which to visit the galleries on the Museum Island and to explore the charms of Berlin Middle—the Gendarmenmarkt and the little streets between the Spree arm and the river proper, which were the locale of Wilhelm Raabe's novel *The Chronicle of Sperlingsgasse*—and we made the most of the opportunity. In the evenings, we went further afield. In those days it was almost compulsory for outlanders to visit Haus Vaterland on the Potsdamer Platz, a garish establishment run by Kempinski that sought, under one roof, to provide, in their proper setting and accompanied by appropriate music, the local food and drink of every part of Germany. Thus, as we discovered when we went there, the house included a Hamburg sailors' pub, a Grinzing wine restaurant filled with Viennese waltzes, a Berlin *Weissbierstube*, a Rhenish restaurant with a view of the river and the town of Bacharach and—perhaps a tribute to German *Wanderlust*—a *Wild West Stube*, which featured a band in sombreros and chaps, a stuffed cinnamon bear, two faded university pennants (Princeton and Notre Dame), and, periodically, a violent storm in what appeared to be the Rocky Mountains.

On another evening, we walked from our lodging, through the Brandenburger Tor and the Tiergarten to the Budapester Strasse and on, past the Zoo and the Kaiser Wilhelm Church, to the Kurfürstendamm, a broad and brightly lighted boulevard flanked with cafés and beer halls and motion picture theaters, where we went to the UFA Palast and listened to Jan Kiepura sing in one of those innocuous musicals that were the staple of the German film in the Nazi years.

When one visits Berlin today, all that seems incredibly remote. The Potsdamer Platz, once so full of traffic that Paul Boldt, from his seat on the terrace of the Café Josty, wrote

> Der Potsdamer Platz in ewigem Gebrüll
> Vergletschert alle hallenden Lawinen
> Der Strassentrakte: Trams auf Eisenschienen,
> Automobile und den Menschenmüll

> [The Postdamer Platz in never-ending roaring
> Turns to a glacier all the resounding avalanches
> In the streets: the trams on iron rails,
> The automobiles, and the human throngs]

is today a waste in which nothing moves, a field of fire for East German soldiers. Haus Vaterland is long gone, and so is Café Josty, and the same is true, or almost so, of the Kaiser Wilhelm Church, for nothing but the ruins of the tower remain, preserved to remind Berliners of the consequences of war. No one who lives in the Mittelstrasse today is permitted to walk past the Brandenburger Tor. The Tiergarten is forbidden territory and, although the glare of the lights from the Kurfürstendamm can be seen on dark nights, its pleasures are as remote to those who live in Berlin Middle as Khatmandu. The Wall sees to that. It is possible to go in the other direction, but only under strict control, and the transit fee demanded by the East German authorities gets higher all the time and is already prohibitive for ordinary West Berliners.

The physical separation of the city has been the most radical change in Berlin's social life in its long history. Berlin has had walls before—in the middle ages and during the reign of King Frederick William I, who in 1735 built a new wall around the then much enlarged town to facilitate the collection of customs duties—but those barriers had held the Berliners together. This one divided them, and its effects were deep and traumatic.

Whether Berlin can survive indefinitely in its present riven state is a question that no one can answer with any assurance. Here we can only consider some of the factors that will affect its future, not neglecting those forces of continuity that have sustained Berlin throughout its history.

I

The city's origins are relatively recent compared with those of Roman foundations like Vienna, Augsburg and Cologne. This is because the

Romans never succeeded in establishing themselves to the north or to the east of the Elbe River, and that area remained for centuries the preserve of nomadic tribes—Germans, like the Suevians and the Semnonians of whom Tacitus spoke with respect, and Slavs, who crossed the Vistula and the Oder in the seventh and eighth centuries and pressed toward the west. It was not until the end of the twelfth century that conditions became favorable for anything like town development and that came as a result of a German *Drang nach Osten* that was designed to claim the area, which came to be known as the Mark, for the Holy Roman Empire. This was led by a series of bellicose and able imperial margraves, beginning with Albert the Bear of the House of Askanier, who subjugated or expelled the Slavs. It was while this was going on that Berlin had its beginnings, and it was not by accident that the bear became its symbol, since the Askanians were its first protectors.

The settlement started at a transit point for merchants at a ford or causeway on the river Spree, where traders coming from the east or the west had to unload their goods before either continuing their journey by land or shipping their bales downstream by boat to the chain of lakes called the Havel and thence to the Elbe and the sea. Around this crossing, which was called the Mühlendamm, there grew a double town, on the east side of the stream a community of merchants and victuallers called Berlin, with its marketplace, the Molkenmarkt, and church, named after St. Nicholas, the patron saint of merchants, and, on the west side, a community of fishermen called Cölln, with its own church, named after St. Peter, who had, of course, been a fisherman himself. Thanks to the peaceful conditions established by the Askanian margraves, the town prospered, thanks to a lively trade in grain, timber, fish and hides from Russia that flowed through its entrepôts on their way to Hamburg, and it was so important a commercial center that in the fourteenth century it became a member of the Hanseatic League. It developed as a typical medieval town, with a patriciate of great merchants and nobles, a *Bürgertum* of masters of trades and handicrafts, organized in guilds, a Jewish community, and a sizable transient population; and, like other medieval towns, its subjects were proud of their privileges, which included the right to tax foreign traders, to mint money, and to exercise self-government without interference by the margraves.

The days of peaceful progress came to an end at the beginning of the fourteenth century when the Askanian line died out. In the period that followed, the town was drawn into the struggle between Emperor Ludwig of Bavaria and the Papacy, a dispute that caused outbursts of anticlericalism that sometimes took violent forms, as in the case of the murder and burning of Provost Nicholas of Bernau by a mob in 1324, which led to the town's being placed under papal ban. The lack of strong imperial authority in the Mark encouraged local strongmen to prey upon itinerant traders, unprotected villages, and, eventually, the townsmen themselves. In 1380, one of these, Ritter Erik Falke auf Schloss Saarmund made a raid upon Berlin and, after extensive pillage, burned it to the ground; and this led to emulation, and the period of the robber barons set in. The most successful of these were Dietrich and Johann von Quitzow, members of the Pomeranian nobility, who terrorized the whole of the Mark, virtually putting a complete stop to Berlin's trade and making it hazardous to venture beyond the town walls. In later years, a veil of romance fell over the exploits of the *Raubritter*, and in 1888 Ernst von Wildenbruch wrote a play called *The Quitzows* that was a great favorite of the country gentry when they visited Berlin, but the town *Bürger* at the beginning of the fifteenth century could hardly have been expected to take the same view, and they must have longed for a strong hand to restore law and order in the Mark.

Relief was, in fact, on the way, for in 1411 the Emperor appointed Burggraf Frederick of Nuremberg, of the House of Hohenzollern, as Statthalter of the Mark, and this vigorous prince made short work of the freebooting nobles. Provided with auxiliary troops, supplies and ammunition by the *Bürger* of Berlin (the bells of the town's churches were melted down for cannonballs), Frederick in 1414 broke the power of the Quitzows in the open field and then hammered their forty fortresses and strong points to pieces with his guns. For his efficiency, he was made hereditary margrave and Kurfürst, or Imperial Elector, the first in a long line that stretched to the first years of the eighteenth century when the Hohenzollern received the title King of Prussia.

Unfortunately, Frederick saw no reason to permit the Berliners to return to the happy independence of the *status quo ante bellum*. His keen eye had noted that the Mühlendamm was the strategic key to the whole of the Mark, and he desired to bring it under his personal control by building a residence in Berlin. The alarmed citizenry were able to fob him off with material compensation, but his successor, Kurfürst Frederick II (Iron Tooth) proved to be a more stubborn suitor. When the Berliners refused his request for privileges in the town, he fomented strife between local factions and then intervened to put it down, simultaneously seizing and holding farms at Tempelhof and other outlying town possessions as a pledge until he received the right to build a strong point, his *Zwing-Cölln*, on the island between the two arms of the Spree.

Once this was completed in 1451, the Hohenzollern were the masters of Berlin. The medieval liberties of the *Bürger* were systematically eroded, and the town became the residence of the Kurfürsten and the capital of the Mark, governed by a bureaucracy of trained administrators who were educated at the Cöllnische Ratschule and, after 1574, in the famous Berlinische Gymnasium zum Grauen Kloster (where Otto von Bismarck was later to go to school), and who superseded the old local government in all important functions. These changes were made more palatable to the citizenry by the improvement of economic conditions that accompanied them. During the days of brigandage, the center of commercial activity in eastern Germany had shifted from Berlin to the Leipzig Fair. But the coming of the Kurfürsten attracted bankers and court purveyors, as well as new trades—clothiers, embroiderers, hatters, goldsmiths, swordmakers and manufacturers of luxury goods—and prosperity returned.

The first Kurfürsten were proud of their new capital and lavished attention on it, encouraging their courtiers and officials, by tax privileges and land grants, to build fine houses, introducing a water system, and beginning the plastering of the streets. But much of this progress was negated by pestilence (in 1546, 1576, 1588 and 1611) and war. The religious strife of the sixteenth century did not leave Berlin untouched, and, during the Thirty Years War, it was pillaged by both Gustavus Adolphus and Wallenstein, and its population sank from 12,000 to less than half of that figure. It was only after Frederick William, the Great Elector, came to the throne in 1640 that recovery began. A man of vision and determination, Frederick William built up a standing army that was strong enough to prevent the depredations that had ruined his predecessors, and his victory over the Swedes at Fehrbellin in 1675 was hailed by the Berliners as a promise of security and new hope.

> Berlin, jetzt freue dich,
> Der Feind ist überwunden!
> Mark, jauchze und sey froh,
> Dein Schrecken ist gebunden!
>
> Du bist durch diesen Sieg
> Von solcher Furcht befreit,
> Gott wird dir helfen noch
> Und ferner stehen bey.
>
> [Berlin, now rejoice,
> The foe is overcome!
> Mark, exult and be happy.
> Thy terror is contained!
> Thou art by this victory
> Freed from such terror,
> God will help thee still
> And stand by thee.]

Nor were they disappointed. In the last years of the Great Elector, commercial activity expanded, partly as a result of the completion of a canal between the Oder and the Spree, new industry began to come to Berlin, particularly textiles to supply the needs of the army, the population recovered, reaching 10,000 in 1680 and then sextupling in the next thirty years, and new residential areas were established outside the old Berlin-Cölln borders, in districts called Friedrichswerder and Dorotheenstadt. These were largely populated by Huguenot refugees from France, to whom the Great Elector opened the town by his Potsdam Edict of November 8, 1685; and this French element, which numbered 5000 before the end of the century and which continued to grow, not only contributed to Berlin's economic development, establishing linen and silk manufactures and specializing in jewelry and other fine crafts, but had an important and permanent effect upon the town's culture and its language, which is still filled with French expressions that lend piquancy to Berlin conversation.

It was at the end of the seventeenth century that Berlin witnessed the beginning of that flowering of the arts and the sciences that led local patriots to call it the Athens on the Spree (*Spreeathen*), and it is important to note that the leading role in this was taken by a woman, Sophie Charlotte, the wife of the Great Elector's successor Frederick. The great-granddaughter of James I of England, and the granddaughter of the unfortunate Elizabeth who married the Winter King, Sophie Charlotte possessed the spirit and gaiety of the Stuarts without their propensity to recklessness and obtuseness. Carefully educated at the court of her father, Ernst August, who was Prince Bishop of Osnabrück and, after 1679, Duke of Hannover, she grew up speaking French, Italian and English as well as her mother tongue, had an excellent knowledge of Latin, was a good musician, and was interested in both the natural sciences and philosophy. Philosophy was, indeed, almost a family specialty, for Sophie Charlotte's aunt, the Princess Elizabeth, was an enthusiastic follower and personal friend of Descartes, and both Sophie Charlotte and her mother delighted in debates with Leibniz, who was a kind of family friend.

When Sophie Charlotte was married to the Kurprinz of Prussia in 1682, she went to a court that had for two generations been almost exclusively preoccupied with questions of power and survival and had had neither the time nor the energy to consider that the prestige of a great State must always depend to some extent upon the attention that it pays to arts and letters. Her husband, who became Kurfürst in 1688 and the first King in Prussia in 1701, had some sense of this lack and tried to repair it by means of opulence and show, commissioning Johann Arnold Nering to beautify his city and Andreas Schlüter to remodel the castle in monumental baroque style and to build an armory, the handsome Zeughaus that still stands at the head of Unter den Linden. Schlüter was the author also of the majestic equestrian statue of the Great Elector that stood originally on Neher's Long Bridge over the Spree but now graces the forecourt of Schloss Charlottenburg.

That castle, which was originally called Schloss Lietzenburg and stood in the old village of Lietzow some distance west of Berlin proper, Sophie Charlotte made a center of the arts, for she was less interested than her husband in buildings and monuments. Here select audiences were able to hear programs of chamber music and, despite the disapproval of the Lutheran Church, the first operas ever played in Berlin, and here the Queen brought together poets and foreign scholars, like Samuel Pufendorf, and divines, like the eloquent Pietist preacher Jakob Spener and his distinguished opposite number, the leader of the Reformed congregation, Daniel Jablonski, to discuss books like Pierre Bayle's *Dictionary* and to debate problems like ecumenism and the possibility of the union of the confessions. She took a lively interest in the activities of the Academy of Arts, which had been founded under Schlüter's direction in 1696, and persuaded her husband to balance it with an Academy of Sciences, of which her friend Leibniz became the first president and which soon included in its membership Germany's leading scientists, like the astronomer Gottfried Kirch. A woman of beauty and wit, Sophie Charlotte could write on her deathbed: "I go now to satisfy my curiosity about the basic causes of things, which Leibniz was never able to explain to me, about space, and the infinite, about being and nothingness; and for the King my husband I prepare the drama of a funeral, which will give him a new opportunity to demonstrate his magnificence."

During the reign of King Frederick William I, nothing more was done to enhance the beauty of the growing city, for the King was interested mainly in laying down exercise grounds for his troops, like Tempelhof Field (the scene of the airlift of 1948), to which he provided access by extending Friedrichstrasse to the Hallesches Tor and building a highway through the district of Kreuzberg. Economically, however, Berlin continued to flourish, and its population was nearing 100,000 when Frederick II took the throne in 1740. This monarch, whose military exploits made Prussia a European power of the first rank, insisted that its capital have public buildings worthy of this new position. He was the designer of the so-called Forum Fredericianum, between the royal palace and the Zeughaus, and it was during his reign that the Opera, the Royal Library, the palace of Prince Henry that housed the University after it was founded in 1809, and the pantheonlike building that became St. Hedwig's Church were built, a collection of architectural triumphs to which the broad avenue Unter den Linden was a fitting approach, particularly after it had been embellished by the Brandenburger Gate, built by Karl Gotthard Langhans during the reign of Frederick's successor and crowned by the famous quadriga of Gottfried Schadow.

Considering the disruptions caused by war in the years from 1740 to 1745 and 1756 to 1763 and the fact that the city suffered two occupations by foreign troops (the Austrians in 1742, for one day, and the Russians for a longer period in 1760), the intellectual vitality of Berlin during Frederick's reign was remarkable. It was in those years, as we have seen, that Nicolai and Moses Mendelssohn made the city an important center of the European Enlightenment; and it was at that time that Berlin's distinguished theatrical and musical tradition was established with the première of Lessing's *Minna von Barnhelm* in 1767 and the performance of Goethe's *Götz von Berlichingen* in 1774, and with the founding of a successful opera and ballet theater under the direction of the composer Karl Heinrich Graun. It is worth noting also, since Berlin became known in the nineteenth century as the "newspaper city," that its first newspapers were founded in Frederick's reign, including the *Vossische Zeitung*, which was to continue publication until Adolf Hitler put an end to the free press in 1933. At the same time, although with no great encouragement from the King, who preferred French men of letters to German *Naturwissenschaftler*, Berlin became the gathering place of a remarkable group of pioneers in scientific research and its practical applications, like the mathematician Leon-

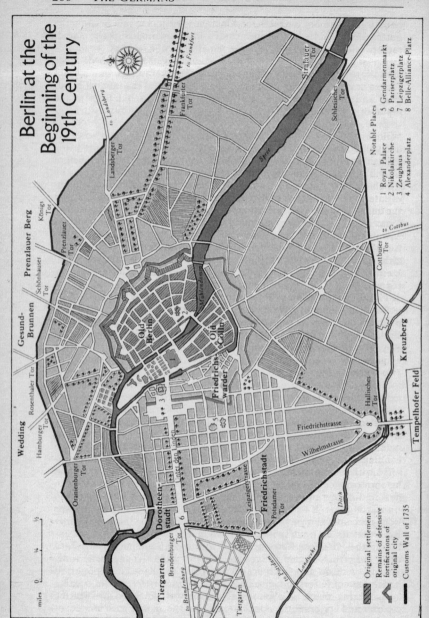

Berlin at the
Beginning of the
19th Century

Notable Places

1 Royal Palace   5 Gendarmenmarkt
2 Nikolaikirche   6 Pariserplatz
3 Zeughaus   7 Leipzigerplatz
4 Alexanderplatz   8 Belle-Alliance-Platz

◻ Original settlement

◣ Remains of defensive
   fortifications of
   original city

▬ Customs Wall of 1735

miles 0 ¼ ½

hard Euler, the botanist Johann Gleditsch, who laid out Berlin's first botanical garden, and the chemists Pott and Hermstedt, who experimented with dyes for industrial use. Finally, another sign of vitality, the city grew rapidly, reaching 150,000 inhabitants in the year of Frederick's death, a modest enough figure by modern standards, but one that caused a severe housing shortage that made it necessary to build additions to many of the existing two- and three-story buildings and to replace others with buildings with four stories.

Even so, during the reigns of Frederick William II and Frederick William III, there was no significant expansion of the city outward. The lively intellectual activity of the years before the Prussian defeat by the French in 1806—the days of Rahel Varnhagan's salon and August Iffland's theater—took place within the confines of the Frederician city, which was not much larger than that of the Great Elector. Indeed, even as late as the 1830s, when Berlin had more than 250,000 inhabitants, the bulk of the population lived along the two arms of the Spree or in the areas flanking Unter den Linden. Some of the rich nobility had built new villas in the area that came to be known as the Tiergarten, but the wealthy bourgeoisie maintained their residences in the Friedrichsstadt, although they might, like Jettchen Gebert's uncles and aunts in Georg Hermann's novel, spend their summers in rented lodgings in the outlying villages of Charlottenburg and Schöneberg.

The forces that brought the remorseless growth of Berlin, until it reached its gigantic twentieth century proportions, were economic and political; and it was the coming of industrialism that started the process. Berlin's first steam engine was bought by State funds in 1800 for the Royal Porcelain Manufactory, much to the alarm of people living in the neighboring streets, and the first iron foundry and machine works were also within the confines of the old city. But it was soon discovered that more space was needed for industrial operations, and entrepreneurs turned northward, where open land stood at their disposal in the suburb of Wedding and the adjoining area called (ironically, one might think, considering the uses to which it was put) Gesundbrunnen (Health Springs). On the Chausseestrasse in Wedding, Egells's foundry and machine works was established in 1821 and became the prototype and training ground for Berlin industry, all of the leading manufacturers serving their apprenticeship there. In 1837, August Borsig established his iron works in Wedding and, four years later, produced his first locomotive, for the railroad age had now begun, and Berlin's first stretch of track, to Potsdam, had been built in 1838. Other entrepreneurs followed Borsig's lead—Werner Siemens and Georg Halske, founding another Berlin tradition, built their first plant in Kreuzberg in 1847 but soon moved to their present location in Wedding—and, as the tendency toward large-scale organization accelerated and was encouraged by the establishment of new technical schools, the whole area north of the Frederician city was industrialized.

As this happened, all of the social ills attendant upon industrialization were visited upon the city. One of the first to recognize this, as we have seen, was Bettina von Arnim, who, when she volunteered to organize medical assistance for the poor during the cholera epidemic of 1831, became aware of the dreadful misery in the already well developed slums in the northern districts and who subsequently spent much of her abundant energies on attempts to inspire the government to alleviate it. Bettina's *This Book Belong to the King* (1843) was Berlin's first sociological report on the results of economic expansion.

Another observer who made the same point was Ernst Dronke, later an associate of Marx and Engels, who visited Berlin in 1846 and wrote a book about what he saw that led to his arrest and imprisonment for two years for lèse majesté and subversion. Like Bettina, Dronke described the "stinking hovels" in which the poor were huddled, but he noted that private enterprise was seeking to improve these conditions by the erection of large buildings with many rooms, in which hundreds of tenants could be accommodated. This development marked the beginning of the spread of the so-called *Mietskaserne*, or rental barracks, gigantic erections of many floors and rooms that received light from a series of backcourts (*Hinterhöfe*), which also served as areas for hanging out the wash, exchanging gossip, and entertainment. As the city grew, this was the characteristic lodging for millions of people in working-class areas in Wedding, Prenzlauer Berg, Kreuzberg and Neu-Kölln, and in the last years of the nineteenth and the first of the twentieth century Heinrich Zille won the affection of Berliners by the skill with which he captured the spirit of the *Hinterhof* culture with his crayon and brush.

The ally of industry in promoting the expansion of the city was politics, for in 1870 Berlin ceased to be merely the principal city in Prussia and became the capital of the new German Reich, and what followed was an unparalleled building boom, not only in the inner city but in the suburbs as well. Henry Vizetelly, an Englishman who visited Berlin in the seventies, wrote in his amusing, and often prejudiced, *Berlin Under the New Empire* (1879), "In the Prussian capital, scaffoldings and buildings in course of construction constantly arrest the eye. In the outskirts of Berlin new quarters are still being laid out, new streets planned, new houses rising up everywhere. Until quite recently, so many new structures were in course of erection that one was led to imagine the capital of the new Empire had been handed over to some Prussian Haussmann to expend a handsome share of the French [war indemnity] in its extension and improvement." In the old Friedrichsstadt, the Wilhelmstrasse, once a quiet residential street for aristocratic families, was transformed by the erection of new mansions for rich industrialists and bankers like August Borsig and Paul von Schwabach and official buildings to house the Prussian and Reich ministries, the Chancellor's staff, and the Foreign Office. New hotels to serve the needs of official visitors and tourists sprang up like mushrooms—the Adlon on the Wilhelmstrasse, the Central, the Kaiserhof, the Bristol and the Esplanade close by—and, where Unter den Linden crossed the Friedrichstrasse, Café Bauer and Kranzler appealed to the fashionable and the idle. South of Unter den Linden, on the Jägerstrasse, the new Reichsbank rose in

1875, and the nearby Behrenstrasse was soon the center of the Deutsche and Bleichröder banks and other commercial houses. At the south end of the Friedrichsstadt, between the Spittelmarkt and Belle Alliance Platz, the Mosse and Ullstein publishing houses began to build their newspaper empire, and Wolff's Telegraph Bureau became the center of an extensive *Zeitungsviertel*.

Meanwhile, the wealthy bourgeoisie were moving west and south, building luxury apartments along the Landwehr Canal on the edge of the Tiergarten and substantial homes in Schöneberg and Charlottenburg. In the early seventies, the heroine of Fontane's *Irrungen, Wirrungen* lived in a gardeners' colony on the west side of the Tiergarten, about where Bahnhof Zoo now stands, and could walk through open fields to the village of Wilmersdorf to the southwest. But after Bismarck had the idea of constructing his own Champs-Elysées to Berlin's equivalent of the Bois de Boulogne in the wooded Grunewald in Zehlendorf, this was soon no longer possible. His creation, the Kurfürstendamm, and the new streets that radiated out from it, soon brought Wilmersdorf and Steglitz closer to the old city center, while creating new living space for the growing middle and professional classes and the small tradespeople and white-collar workers. The manual workers, who paved the new streets and built the new buildings and serviced the machines of Borsig and Siemens, continued to live in the meaner streets of Wedding and Friedrichshain and Kreuzberg and Neu-Kölln.

By the 1880s, the living area occupied by people who considered themselves to be Berliners was already so enormous that the problem of improving the internal communications net demanded constant attention. In the inner city, the favored method of transportation was for a long time the droschke or single-horse carriage, and from the 1840s onward there were also horse-drawn omnibuses. For longer trips, however, what was needed was a system that could carry large numbers of passengers with regularity and speed, and this was first provided in the seventies by the establishment of a horse-drawn train on rails, first between Charlottenburg and the city center, and then on a rapidly expanding network of lines that, in 1896, carried 154 million passengers. By that time, the days of the horse were numbered. As early as the seventies, a circular steam railway system had been established on tracks that followed the course of the old customs wall of 1735, which had been leveled in 1867–1868; and in 1882 this was supplemented by the new city railroad (*Stadtbahn*), which served other points outside the circle, making it possible, for instance, for Berliners who wanted to picnic by the water to do so by taking the train from the Friedrichstrasse Station to Wannsee, the largest of the Havel lakes.

Meanwhile, Siemens and Halske had begun to experiment with electrification, and the world's first electrical streetcar had appeared in Lichterfelde in 1881; and within twenty-five years the whole street railway system had been transformed by the introduction of electrified trams and autobuses. Finally, in 1897, the construction of an electrified surface and underground railway—the present-day *U-Bahn*—was under way, and before the First World War its main line ran all the way from Warschauer Bridge in Friedrichshain via the Schlesisches Tor, the Hallesches Tor and the Zoo Station to the new Olympic Stadium (1913) in the West End, with branch lines running north to the Schönhauser Allee in Gesundbrunnen, south to the Innsbrucker Platz in Schöneberg, and south and west through Wilmersdorf to Dahlem Dorf and Zehlendorf. Since population kept growing and followed the expansion of the transportation net, it was only logical that these outlying towns and districts should, for administrative efficiency, be amalgamated with the original Berlin center, and this was done by a law of April 27, 1920, which created a Greater Berlin with a total area of 88,000 hectares—large enough to accommodate the cities of Frankfurt, Munich and Stuttgart together—and almost 4 million inhabitants.

During this rapid process of growth, Berlin had become an industrial center of world importance, known particularly for the production of heavy machinery and machine tools, electrical and chemical products, fine textiles and porcelains, and articles of *haute couture*. It had also more than lived up to its reputation as the Athens on the Spree. The first half of the nineteenth century had seen the founding of the University by Humboldt, Fichte, and Schleiermacher and its recognition as the dominant German center of philosophical and historical studies as a result of the work of Hegel, Niebuhr and Ranke, and this was matched by a literary revival and a new flowering of musical activity that opened with the premiére of Weber's *Der Freischütz* in 1821 and Felix Mendelssohn-Bartholdy's performance of the long forgotten Matthew Passion of Johann Sebastian Bach in 1829. As early as 1824, the novelist Jean Paul wrote to a Berlin friend, describing the city as a "mountain state of German culture, social, aesthetic and philosophical."

But even this renaissance, remarkable because it followed so swiftly upon the defeat of 1806 and seven years of subjugation to Napoleon, was nothing to the cultural explosion of the period from 1870 to 1914. Under the Empire, the University acquired a world reputation, with natural scientists like Hermann Helmholtz, Rudolf Virchow and Robert Koch, historians like Theodor Mommsen and Heinrich von Treitschke, sociologists like Ferdinand Tönnies and Georg Simmel, and philosophers like Wilhelm Dilthey and Ernst Cassirer. In the field of literature, Berlin was the city where the major work of the Social Realists Friedrich Spielhagen, Fontane and Sudermann was accomplished and a new era in the theater was inaugurated with the foundation in 1889 of *Die Freie Bühne*, dedicated to the cause of modernity and presenting the works of Ibsen and Strindberg as well as new German dramatists like Hauptmann and Wedekind. In the pictorial arts, the "Berlin Secession"—a group that included Max Liebermann, Lovis Corinth, Käthe Kollwitz, Max Slevogt, Ernst Barlach and Max Beckmann—broke through the conventions of tradition and showed the possibilities of an artistic style that was both boldly innovative and socially aware; and in music Berlin was a showplace of conductors of international renown, with as many as three hundred concerts a year. The very atmosphere of

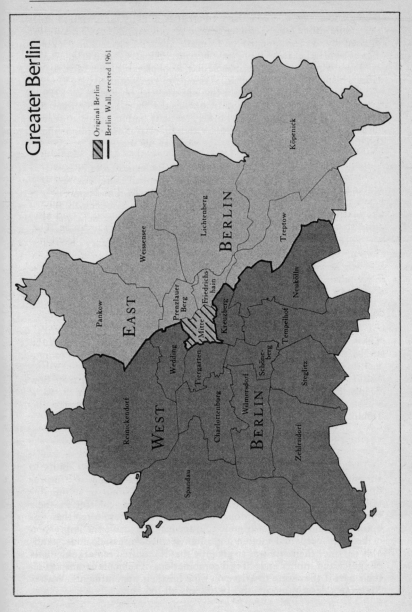

Greater Berlin

Original Berlin
Berlin Wall, erected 1961

Köpenick

Weissensee

Lichtenberg

BERLIN

Treptow

Pankow

EAST

Prenzlauer
Berg

Friedrichs-
hain

Mitte

Neukölln

Kreuzberg

Wedding

Tiergarten

Tempelhof

Schöne-
berg

Reinickendorf

WEST

Charlottenburg

Wilmersdorf

Steglitz

BERLIN

Spandau

Zehlendorf

the city seemed to be conducive to creative activity, and something of the exhilaration felt by young people in this vibrant capital was expressed by the protagonist of Conrad Alberti's novel *The Old and Young* when he talked of "the nervous, endlessly quivering Berlin air . . . which works upon people like alcohol, morphine, cocaine, exciting, inspiring, relaxing, deadly: the air of the world city."

This artistic vitality survived the war and the revolution of 1918 to inspire new triumphs of the spirit during the short-lived Weimar Republic. Indeed, the inner force of this great city and its ability to survive disaster astonished some observers with a reflective turn of mind, and in January 1919 Count Harry Kessler wrote in his diary:

> In the evening in a cabaret in the Bellevuestrasse. Racy Spanish dancer. In the middle of her number a shot cracked in from outside. Nobody paid any attention. Minimal impression of the revolution on big city life. This life is so elemental that even a world-historical revolution like the present one does not cause any essential disturbance in it. The babylonian, the immeasurably deep, the chaotic, the mighty characteristics of Berlin have become clear to me only through the revolution, in showing that this awful movement can cause in the much more awful pendular rhythm of Berlin only small local irritations, as when an elephant receives a stab with a pocket knife. He shakes himself but strides on as if nothing had happened.

The same point was made by Alfred Döblin in his great novel of the 1920s, *Berlin Alexanderplatz*, in which the city itself was the protagonist, majestic, sentient, invulnerable, enduring.

But Adolf Hitler and Walter Ulbricht were soon to demonstrate how deeply the city could be wounded, and its durability, after their work was accomplished, was less certain than it seemed to Kessler and Döblin.

II

Throughout its history, the dynamic vitality of the city, its ability to surmount natural catastrophe and political crisis, and its future-orientedness affected the temperament and the humor of its inhabitants. Berliners tended to be energetic, ebullient, colorful in their speech, quick at repartee, prone to sentimentality, more often than not optimistic, and in time of trouble courageous. They gave the impression of being in perpetual motion and often seemed harassed, understandably so, since their city was so gigantic that it required remarkable feats of agility and timing and shrewd combinations of vehicular transport on their part if they were to arrive on time for their appointments. Walter Mehring's description of the 1920s was all too apt:

Die Linden lang! Galopp! Galopp!
Zu Fuss, zu Pferd, zu zweit.
Mit der Uhr in der Hand, mit'm Hut auf 'm Kopp,
Keine Zeit! Keine Zeit! Keine Zeit!

[Along the Linden! Gallop! Gallop!
On foot, in a cab, in twos.
With the watch in the hand and the hat on the head,
No time! No time! No time!]

They were generally and unabashedly loquacious, for so much happened around them every day that they were anxious to describe it and to give their reflections on it to anyone they met. One rarely met a taciturn Berliner, and there was much to Kurt Tucholsky's judgment that "the Berliner cannot converse. Often one sees two people talking to each other, but they are not conversing; they are reciting their monologues to each other. Berliners can't listen either. They merely wait, completely intent, until their opposite number stops talking, and then jump in."

This flow of speech was relieved in most cases by a lively turn of phrase and great richness of language. Berliners were good *causeurs* who brought to their task the gift of telling description and a good store of illustrative anecdotes; and students of Berlin humor have been fascinated by the high incidence, in their conversational rhetoric, of sometimes subtle and sometimes elaborate antithetical constructions. Walther Kiaulehn has argued that this had historical roots. About twenty years after Martin Luther's revolt against the Church of Rome, the city councils of Berlin and Cölln begged Kurfürst Joachim II to introduce the communion in the Evangelical Lutheran form, and he did so in a ceremony in the St. Nicholas Church in Spandau on November 1, 1539. Subsequently, constant reading of the New Testament accustomed Berliners to think in terms of opposites—"The first will be the last!", "Only he who is humbled shall be raised!", and the like—and this invariably influenced their style in lighter moments.

As an example, Kiaulehn gives the Berliner's description of the poet Stefan George as someone "who looks like an old woman who looks like an old man," but many other illustrations of antithesis and inversion can be found. There is, for instance, the story of the intoxicated man staggering hopelessly around and around a *Litfasssäule*, one of the circular pillars used for advertising that have been common in Berlin since 1854, and lamenting loudly, "*Entsetzlich! Lebendig einjemauert!*" ("Dreadful! Walled in!"); and there is a more contrived story from East Berlin about Brezhnev's dying and being condemned to walk through all eternity arm in arm with Golda Meir, a powerful conversationalist. One day he sees another couple and recognizes Walter Ulbricht, paired with Gina Lollabrigida. "Comrade Ulbricht!" he says sharply. "What kind of punishment do you call this?" Ulbricht answers sheepishly, "It's not my punishment, Comrade Brezhnev! It's her punishment!"

Of somewhat different order was what was usually meant when one talked of Berlin wit: the qualities of *Schnoddrigkeit* and *Schlagfertigkeit*. The first, a kind of juvenile insolence, was a natural product of the peculiar democracy of the big city, in which everyone was fair game for a witticism. It was the humor of the *Schusterjunge* (shoemaker's apprentice) in Kiaulehn's story of Biedermeier Berlin, who was whistling his way down Unter den Linden when he became aware of the imposing figure of General Field Marshal Friedrich von Wrangel and fell silent. Flattered by this mark of respect, Wrangel said, "*Na*, why don't you go on whistling?", to which the urchin replied, "When I look at you, I have to laugh, and when I laugh, I can't whistle." It was the cheekiness of the fourteen-year-old youth stopping by an obviously pregnant woman waiting for a bus, and saying pleasantly, "*Na, Frollein, ooch schon verlobt?*" ("Ah, Fräulein, engaged already too?").

The much vaunted *Schlagfertigkeit*, or quickness of repartee, was attributed by local patriots to the city's air (*Berliner Luft*), which was supposed to put all the senses on the *qui vive*. It was more likely due to the competitive spirit induced by urban life. Whatever its cause, it was much respected, and its finest products became part of the lore of the city. Frederick William IV, who had the misfortune to be on the throne when the revolution of 1848 erupted and who was an otherwise unfortunate ruler, was nevertheless admired in Berlin for the brilliance of his verbal sallies, like his response to the citizens of Gumbinnen who petitioned for the right to change the name of the stream on which their town was situated, the Pissa. The King wrote: "Granted. Recommend Urinoco." The banker Carl Fürstenberg's *Schlagfertigkeit* has been noted already, but he had many competitors in his time, notable among whom was the Reichstag deputy Adolf Hoffmann, whose wit was enhanced by the fact that he spoke in a broad Berlin dialect with its customary disregard of the difference between the dative and accusative forms of the personal pronoun. As a member of an investigative commission, Hoffmann was once interrogating a merchant of dubious reputation, who suddenly said, "I refuse to talk with you. You always confuse *mir* and *mich*." Hoffmann replied, "That is so, but not punishable. But you are always confusing *mein* and *dein*, and that's why you're here and why you've got to answer me."

In argument, Berliners were apt to demonstrate an exaggeration of threat and epithet, as well as gifts of fantasy and hyperbole, that were not found in other parts of Germany. Herbert Schöffler has suggested that this too is rooted in the nature of the milieu, and that the very fact that Berlin was for so long unique among German cities for its unlimited possibilities freed the imagination of its citizens from the restrictions imposed by nature and probability, inspiring grotesque admonitions like "I'll paste you one that will leave you peeping out of your ribs like a monkey in its cage!" and unexpected but richly satisfying descriptive insults like "You haven't got all your cups in the cupboard!" The art of insult was much cultivated in Berlin and sometimes assumed philosophical dimensions, as in the sympathetic and almost envious remark, "*Du hasts gut, du bist doof!*" ("You're lucky. You're dumb!")

The strong strain of irony in Berlin humor was attributed variously to the nature of the environment, the sand of the Mark and the infertility of the soil, the Voltaireianism of Frederick II, and the mixture of the original population with French and Jewish elements. While not rejecting these explanations out of hand, Theodor Fontane believed that they were less important than the fact that, since the coming of the Kurfürsten, Berlin had never enjoyed the freedoms that other towns possessed, since its police force and judicial system were in the hands of the royal power and that, since the censorship deprived them of free speech, Berliners used satire and irony to defeat it. However this may be, it was certainly true that Berlin wit always seemed to flourish in repressive conditions: during the operation of the Socialist Law in the nineteenth century, during the censorship of the First World War, and especially during the Third Reich, when the policies and mannerisms of Germany's new rulers were the subject of a national body of underground humor (*Flüsterwitz*) to which Berlin made its characteristic contribution. At the time of the Concordat with the Papacy in February 1933, the story circulated in Berlin that Goering had gone to Rome to facilitate an agreement and had sent a telegram to Hitler reading, "Plenary powers exceeded. Rome burning. Pope imprisoned. Tiara suits me fine. Your Holy Father"; and after the burning of the Reichstag there were dozens of jokes about Goering's dangerous habits with matches. The Berliner's love of riddles found almost unlimited expression during the Nazi years ("Why is the Third Reich like a streetcar?" "Because a *Führer* stands in front of both, while inside people are constantly paying and no one can jump off!"), as did their habit of stating their true longings in ironical verse.

> "Heil Hitler!" ist der Deutsche Gruss
> Den jeder Deutscher sagen muss.
> Doch eines Tages gibt es Krach.
> Dann sagt man wieder "Juten Tach!"

> ["Heil Hitler!" is the German Greeting
> That everybody has to say.
> But one day the crash will come,
> And then we'll all say "Good day!" again.]

This kind of humor flourishes today on the other side of the Wall. Thus, one hears: "What is the difference between Erich Honecker and a bad telephone connection?" "Nothing. Hang up and try again!" ("*Nix. Aufhängen und wiederwählen!*")

Under all the bustle and the wordiness (*die grosse Schnauze*) and the cockiness lay unmistakable qualities of devotion and firmness. The Berliner loved his city with a deep affection that could elicit, even from a

man like the theater critic Alfred Kerr, who was feared for the savagery
of his reviews, a remarkable degree of sentimentality.

> Vor mir steht ein Strauss von Flieder
>   Und ein grüner Weinpokal;
> Und der Kellner bringt in müder
>   Gangart mein bestelltes Mahl.
>   Draussen unter schwülem Himmel
>   Seh ich Droschkengäule ziehn.
>   Fernes Strassenbahngebimmel.
>   Juniabend in Berlin.

> [Before me stands a bouquet of lilac
>   And a green wine glass;
> And the waiter, moving wearily,
>   Brings my ordered meal.
>   Outside, under the sultry sky,
>   I see cab horses passing.
>   The distant clanging of trams.
>   June evening in Berlin.]

Away from his city, the Berliner was only half himself and, like the two
tourists in the Harz in Fontane's novel *Cécile*, compared everything he
saw with something at home, and found his new life without savor.
Before the First World War, Alfred Lichtenstein expressed this feeling
of emptiness in a fine poem with a Goethean fall:

> In fremden Städten treib ich ohne Ruder
> hohl sind die fremden Tage und wie Kreide.
> Du mein Berlin, Du Opiumrausch, Du Luder.
> Nur wer die Sehnsucht kennt weiss was ich leide.

> [In strange cities I move without a rudder
> hollow are the strange days and like chalk.
> O my Berlin, you opium ecstasy, you hussy!
> None but the yearning heart knows what I suffer!]

and in our own time Wolf Biermann has sounded the same note:

> Ich kann nicht weg mehr von dir gehn
> Im Westen steht die Mauer
> Im Osten meine Freunde stehn,
> Der Nordwind ist ein rauher.

> Berlin, du blonde blonde Frau
> Ich bin dein kühler Freier
> dein Himmel ist so hunde-blau
> darin hängt meine Leier.

[I can't go away from thee any more
In the West stands the Wall
In the East stand my friends
The north wind is raw.

Berlin, thou blonde, blonde woman
I am thy cool suitor*
thine heaven is so wretchedly blue
my lyre hangs on it.]

It was this love for their city that sustained Berliners when the hard times came, the days of Hitler's war, and the occupation, and what seemed to be the perpetual Berlin crisis of the postwar years. During the last stages of the Second World War, the English, who knew from their own experience what aerial bombardment was like, expressed reluctant admiration for the people of Berlin who, under a weight of bombs that was greater and more unremitting than that of the Blitz of 1940, dug themselves out every morning and, as well as they could, went about their daily chores. They received no moral encouragement from their Führer, who had washed his hands of them when he perceived that the war was lost: and they expected and wanted none, for Berlin had not been a city that responded with much sympathy to the Hitler style or shared his grandiose expectations. They comforted themselves with small jokes, saying that the war would be over when one could travel by *S-Bahn* from the Eastern to the Western Front, and with a sense of local pride, defining cowardice as volunteering for front-line duty in order to escape the nightly peril in Berlin. They watched the destruction of their city with dismay, but they did what they could every day to control the damage as they did what they could later to remove it and start rebuilding.

When the war ended, they soon discovered that, however they might rebuild, they could not hope that their city would resume its central position in German life. The division that the Cold War brought to Germany as a whole was soon replicated in Berlin. The interallied agreements of 1944–1945 stipulated that the city, while situated within the Soviet occupation zone, should have a special status and be under the authority of the Allied Kommandatura, an agency of the four Powers. For convenience it was divided into four sectors, one for each of the Allied military commands, but there was to be a native municipal government, with an Oberbürgermeister and a Magistracy, to run the city under Allied supervision. From the beginning, unhappily, it was clear that the Soviet authorities were intent upon bringing the whole of the city under their ideological control. The first city commandant, the Soviet General Nikolai Bersarin, saw to it that the city government was staffed almost exclusively with Germans who had received their train-

---

*The drink known as *eine Berliner Weisse* (a kind of wheat beer sometimes flavored with a raspberry or juniper syrup) is also known as "a cool blonde."

ing during the war in Moscow, and the first postwar years saw earnest attempts by the restored German Communist Party (soon transformed into the Socialist Unity Party or SED) and the Soviet-sponsored Cultural Union for Democratic Renewal to communize the political and cultural life of the city.

These maneuvers failed to impress a population that was already alienated by the misconduct of the Soviet garrison, and the failure of their policy was doubtless a factor in the Soviet resort to stronger measures, the blockade of the city in 1948–1949. This *coup de main* was, as we have seen, defeated by the resistance of the Berlin people under the leadership of Ernst Reuter, which was so unequivocal and determined that the Western Powers were encouraged to take the gamble with the air lift that eventually defeated the Soviet purpose. The blockade did, however, put an end to united city government. Soviet reprisals against Reuter and his associates Louise Schroeder, Walther Schreiber, Otto Suhr and Willy Brandt led them to move their headquarters from the Rathaus of Berlin Middle to that of the district of Schöneberg, which henceforth became the government center of West Berlin. At the same time, on October 7, 1949, the SED declared that the Soviet sector of Berlin was the capital of the newly established German Democratic Republic.

It was during the blockade that Günter Neumann had written the confident song "*Der Insulaner verliert die Ruhe nicht*" ("The Islander doesn't lose his cool"), and the old Berlin saying "*Uns kann keener*" ("No one can touch us") became an expression of self-congratulation. But the threat to the freedom of West Berlin did not go away. It came back in more menacing form in November 1958, when Premier Khrushchev announced that, unless Allied troops garrisoned in West Berlin were withdrawn within six months, the Soviet Union would conclude a separate treaty with the DDR, relinquishing its occupation rights and powers, after which time the Western Powers would have to negotiate with the DDR over rights of access to Berlin, and the latter, as a sovereign State, would have the right to deny such access. Against this ultimatum, the West stood firm, and it was never carried out; but the building of the Wall on August 13, 1961, which deprived West Berliners of access to the eight eastern districts of their city, underlined their isolation and shook the easy confidence of the postblockade years. The unasked questions were now unavoidable. Did the Islanders have the physical and psychological resources necessary to assure their independence? Were tradition and love of their city and the courage demonstrated so often in Berlin's history enough for survival?

III

A casual visitor to West Berlin in the seventies might find these questions puzzling, for the external appearance of the city was one of blooming health and vitality. The Kurfürstendamm was ablaze with neon and lined with smart restaurants and cafés like the Bristol and Mehring's, and the windows of the KaDeWe on the Wittenberg Platz and Wertheim's in the Walther Schreiber Platz were filled with articles that vied in elegance with anything to be found on Regent Street and Fifth Avenue. More impressive perhaps than these evidences of material prosperity were the abundant signs that West Berlin was still very much Sophie Charlotte's city, with a symphony orchestra that was probably the best in Europe, an excellent opera company, and theaters like the Schiller Theater and the Volksbühne and the Theater am Halleschen Ufer with a proved reputation for innovation and bold experiment, with the rich treasures of the Dahlem Museum and the National Gallery, the great new Memorial Library, without its peer in Germany, and a cluster of academies and research centers, and with a lively literary life on the local level in Schöneberg and Steglitz and Kreuzberg.

Yet all this was belied by depressing demographic evidence that West Berlin was losing its vital energies. Its population, which stood at about 2,105,000 in 1949 and rose to 2,229,000 in 1957, turned downward in the following year and in 1964 began a steady decline that brought it down to 1,926,000 in 1977, of whom only 1,737,000 were natives. More significant than the total figure was the structure of the population, which showed the worst age profile in Germany. At the end of 1976, 22.8% of West Berlin's inhabitants were over sixty-five years of age, as opposed to 13.2% in Western Germany, and only 15.8% were under fifteen years, as opposed to about 25% in the Bundesrepublik. Moreover, about 20,000 more West Berliners died every year than were born, and this loss was not replenished by the natural inflow of new inhabitants from the surrounding area, because the DDR allowed only those over sixty-five to move to the West. Of the years that followed the building of the Wall, only 1969 and 1970 showed a positive inflow and that was composed largely of Turkish and Yugoslav *Gastarbeiter* (guest workers). After 1970, more people left the city every year than entered it. In 1976, for instance, 41,566 native West Berliners emigrated, while 30,015 people came to the city from the West. But a large number of the latter were students or young people in apprenticeship who would not stay permanently in the city.

Particularly disturbing were the effects of these population tendencies upon the city's working force, which declined steadily in relation to the total population. In 1970, 3000 more German workers left the city than came to it, and between 1971 and 1975 the excess of departures over arrivals increased from 5.6% to 27%. The West Berlin Senate sought to counter this trend by an attractive schedule of inducements for West German workers—travel and resettlement costs, tax-free assistance for home construction, family allowances and the like—that was not entirely without effect. Even so, it was estimated in 1971 that every third person who was drawn to the city by these advantages changed his mind sooner or later and left it, either because he was dissatisfied with his working or living conditions or because he was affected by the Berlin form of claustrophobia, the fear of being caught without hope of escape if the city fell to the forces of the East, a feeling that did not entirely disappear even after the conclusion of the Four Power Treaty of 1971 and the Basic Treaty of 1972, since those agreements did not put a complete stop to threats from the DDR and interference with traffic to West Berlin. Indeed, the constantly reiterated SED argument that East Berlin was an integral part of the DDR, while West Berlin was not part of the Bundesrepublik—a theory that contradicted the basic intent of the treaties—indicated that the DDR leaders did not regard the Berlin question as having been regulated definitively.

Another reason for concern about the future of the city, which was not unconnected with the shrinking of the labor force, was the decline of the number of its commercial and industrial enterprises. Between 1961 and 1970, the number of industrial firms decreased from 3500 to 2370, with a minimal number of new establishments. Particularly significant was the fall in the number of locally bound and financed enterprises, and the tendency toward concentration of industry in the hands of large firms like Siemens, AEG Telefunken, Schering, BMW/Daimler Benz, some of which had their headquarters in Western Germany and had no fixed commitment to the city.

West Berlin's economic viability, which had a direct bearing upon its political independence, depended in the last analysis upon the Federal Republic, which subsidized it to the extent of $2 billion a year, which came out of the pockets of West German taxpayers. This financial relationship was uncomfortable for both parties. In their proud independence, the Berliners had no very warm affection for their brothers to the west. When they used the word *drüben* ("over there"), it was not always clear whether they meant Leipzig or Düsseldorf. They were flattered when foreign observers emphasized the difference between them and the citizens of the Bundesrepublik, as the Swedish writer Lars Gustafsson did at the beginning of the seventies:

> Two countries could not be more different than the scarred, clever Berlin with its lively sharp intellect, with its revolutionary groups, its Marxist day care centers, its blue, red, white pamphlets, its street cafés and bookstores, Berlin, this mysterious smithy of the forces of the future, imprisoned behind high walls and minefields in the middle of a hostile, clay-grey military dictatorship with endless fields of potatoes, this Berlin, that knows everything, has experienced everything, and has long accepted its condition, and the stupid, money-distended Bundesrepublik with its supermarkets, its portable TV sets, and its creaking pompous furniture, thick rugs, glass table covers, and settees of black leather and steel tubes.

For their part, the West Germans had mixed feelings about Berliners, and it was probably safe to say that the admiration and sympathy that they felt for them in moments of crisis like 1948 and 1961 gave way, in quiet times, to older feelings of dislike and distrust. Berlin was never greatly loved in the rest of Germany. To many Germans in the nineteenth century, it was an alien place, and Konstantin Frantz, a political writer admired by Wagner, wrote in 1879 that it was better suited to be the capital of a Jewish Reich than a Germanic one. Romantics like Adolf Bartels and Wilhelm Schäfer and Julius Langbehn were convinced that its influence upon German culture was unwholesome, and Friedrich Lienhard called for a union of *Volk* and *Land* against literary Berlin and modernism, raising the battle cries "*Bestürmt wird nun die schwarze Stadt!*" ("Now we shall storm the black city!") and "*Los von Berlin!*" ("Away from Berlin!"). In the 1920s, visitors from the provinces were apt to be shocked and disoriented by the tempo of the city, and Erich Kästner once described this feeling in verse:

> Sie stehen verstört am Potsdamer Platz
> Und finden Berlin zu laut.
> Die Nacht glüht auf in Kilowatts.
> Ein Fräulein sagt heiser: 'Komm mit, mein Schatz!'
> Und zeigt entsetzlich viel Haut.
>
> Sie wissen vor Staunen nicht aus und nicht ein.
> Sie stehen und wundern sich bloss.
> Die Bahnen rasseln. Die Autos schrein.
> Sie möchten am liebsten zu Hause sein
> Und finden Berlin zu gross.
>
> Es klingt, als ob die Grossstadt stöhnt,
> weil irgendwer sie schilt.
> Die Häuser funkeln. Die U-Bahn dröhnt.
> Sie sind das alles so gar nicht gewöhnt
> Und finden Berlin zu wild.
>
> Sie machen vor Angst die Beine krumm
> Und machen alles verkehrt.
> Sie lachen bestürzt. Und sie warten dumm
> Und stehen auf dem Potsdamer Platz herum,
> bis man sie überfährt.
>
> [They stand confused on the Potsdamer Platz
> and find Berlin too noisy.
> The night is ablaze with kilowatts.
> A girl says hoarsely, "Come with me, my treasure!"
> And shows an awful lot of skin.
>
> In their amazement they don't know which way to turn.
> They just stand and wonder.
> The trains rattle. The autos shriek.
> They would rather be at home
> and find Berlin too big.

It sounds as if the big city were groaning
because someone was scolding it.
The houses sparkle. The U-Bahn drones.
They're just not used to all that
and find Berlin too uncivilized.

From fear they get their legs tangled
and do everything wrong.
They smile in dismay. And they wait stupidly,
and stand around on the Potsdamer Platz,
until someone runs over them.]

After 1945, when Berlin ceased to be the national capital and the
center of Germany's political life, hostility toward it was modified but
did not entirely disappear. The things about the city that the Swede
Gustafsson found attractive were regarded with suspicion by many
West Germans, who were easily persuaded that the intellectual freedom
of the city simply played into the hands of Communism and who blamed
the West Berlin university movement for having spread subversion all
over the country. It would be impossible to estimate how many West
Germans felt on occasion resentful about having to pay taxes to support
a city that permitted such things to go on, but there was no doubt that
such resentment existed and was potentially dangerous.

The behavior of the transient population (students, *Ausgeflippte*, city
district Indians, communards and anarchists) also threatened the stability and the economic future of West Berlin, since these elements were
apt to visit their indignation over issues that angered them upon the city
itself, in irrational attacks upon property. On May 9, 1970, in protest
against the American incursions into Cambodia, 8000 demonstrators
gathered on the Hardenbergstrasse between Ernst Reuter Platz and the
Zoo Station, a large number of whom surrounded the America House
with the obvious intention of storming and destroying it. Failing to dis-
perse this mob with fire hoses, the police launched what may well have
been the last cavalry attack in German history, an assault by forty-eight
mounted policemen. Like many similar attacks by horse in wartime, this
one failed because of a lack of reserves; after driving the demonstrators
as far as the Steinplatz, the cavalry was met with a hail of missiles,
which killed two horses and wounded thirty others, and they were forced
to retire. For the next three quarters of an hour, until the police reformed and drove them into the Technical University, one group of
demonstrators built a barricade in front of the Renaissance Theater,
while others overturned automobiles and smashed the windows of banks
and companies like the IBM corporation, using flagpoles from the Ernst
Reuter Platz to demolish those in the upper stories of the buildings. All
in all, about a million DM in damages was caused in this fracas, and
250 policemen were injured.

A similar manifestation of irrational violence came in Christmas
week in 1980 as a result of the perennial housing shortage in Berlin,

which was aggravated by real-estate speculators and contractors who systematically bought up buildings, evicted the tenants, and then left the houses vacant until they could be either modernized or torn down to make way for new ones. In 1980, at a time when 80,000 people were looking for living quarters, 7000 apartments were standing empty. This situation was particularly acute in Kreuzberg, a district which in recent years had attracted so many Turkish *Gastarbeiter* that they constituted 40% of the population, as well as large numbers of students, young unemployed people, and the so-called *"Freaks und Alternativler"* who found it a congenial place in which to practice their unconventional way of life. The Senate's program of large-scale renovation and reconstruction in Kreuzberg (which had had some positive results in the neighborhood of the Mehring Platz) slowed down in 1979 and 1980 and, by leaving many buildings vacant that were targeted for later replacement, exacerbated the problem caused by the manipulations of private speculators. In exasperation, groups of young people began in 1979 to occupy empty buildings, and, by the end of 1980, twenty-one buildings were filled with squatters.

The possibility of resolving this situation by negotiation with the Senate, which was the objective of some of the squatters, was lost because of injudicious reaction on the part of the police, whose attempt on December 12, 1980, to prevent the occupation of another house on the Fraenkelufer aroused a general fear that an attempt would be made to clear all of the occupied houses of squatters. This led to demonstrations on the Fraenkelufer and at the Kottbuser Tor, in which violent elements took over, and groups of young people smashed the windows of banks and supermarkets. Sixty-three people were arrested by the police, and twenty-three more in renewed incidents in the days that followed. The militants now announced that, if all those detained were not released, it would not be only Christmas trees that burned at Christmas, and they made good their threat by transferring their destructive activities to the Kurfürstendamm, where banks and businesses chosen at random were their targets. All told, there were sixteen cases of serious damage besides the window-smashing spree on the Kurfürstendamm during Christmas week, including a branch bank in Neu-Kölln, a post office in Wilmersdorf and a church; and on December 27 the main hall of the U-Bahn station in Dahlem Village, a thatch-roofed building that dated from 1912 and was much admired as an architectural curiosity, was gutted by fire.

The Senate subsequently made a generous arrangement with the squatters, granting them leases on the apartments they had seized and reasonable compensation for improvements they may have made and promising alternative quarters for people evicted as a result of the Senate's renovation program. But this did not obviate the damage done by the militant forays along the Kurfürstendamm, the violence of which, one observer wrote, made the student riots of the sixties look like civilized protests. The *Berliner Morgenpost* fulminated against "these vagabond people . . . , dropouts of every kind, *Fixer* [drug dealers] and ordinary criminals." This was language that was not unusual in an Axel Springer newspaper, but it was not unlikely that it reflected the opinion of many Berlin inhabitants, who had long been concerned about the presence in their midst of people who were not "real Berliners," were deeply offended by their style of life and willing to attribute to them responsibility for the enormous increase in the illegal use of drugs (10,000 heroin addicts by the middle of 1978, according to a Senate estimate) and of youthful criminality, and were frightened and enraged by their explosive and destructive violence.

Even if one disregarded the negative effect of the kind of incidents described here upon West German and foreign firms that were considering investment or establishment of branches in West Berlin—and it was probably not inconsiderable—their divisive consequences within the city itself were potentially too serious to be overlooked. The *Frontstadt* had met the crises of 1948–1949 and 1961 with a united will, its people standing together against the external enemy. In 1980, Berliners no longer seemed to have that common bond, and that was a serious loss, given the other problems—political, economic and demographic—that confronted them.

PART THREE

Present
and
Future

13

Democracy and Nationalism

During the winter of 1795–1796, in order to answer hostile and unintelligent criticism of a recent undertaking, Friedrich Schiller collaborated with his friend Goethe in writing over five hundred satirical epigrams, which were eventually called *Xenien* (gifts to departing guests) and published in *The Muses Almanach for the Year 1797*. Most of them had specific targets, but one of the most frequently cited was addressed to the German people and read:

> Zur Nation euch zu bilden, ihr hofft es,
> Deutsche, vergebens,
> Bildet, ihr könnt es, dafür freier zu
> Menschen euch aus.
>
> [You hope in vain, Germans, to make
> yourselves a nation.
> Train yourself rather—you can do it—
> to be freer human beings.]

It is impossible to say with any hope of assurance what was in the minds of the two poets when they wrote this distich, but we do know that, in the same year that it was composed, Schiller, in his *Letters on the Aesthetic Education of Mankind*, had expressed concern about the effects that the new spirit of nationalism awakened by the French Revolution was having upon individual freedom. It seems likely, therefore, that the epigram to the Germans was intended as a warning. Schiller and Goethe had little faith in the political capacity of their countrymen. They were aware that, for reasons rooted in history (Schiller was not the historian of the Thirty Years War for nothing), they had an excessive, almost self-emasculating, respect for authority. What they were saying, in effect, was that the Germans should not aspire to national power until they had acquired, and learned to use, the moral and civil freedom that was required to control it.

The course of German history in the 150 years that followed this literary exercise demonstrated how little influence even the greatest of poets are likely to have upon events. It is true that, in the first part of the nineteenth century, the leaders of the movement that aspired to make a united German nation out of the fragmented members of the Germanic Confederation were as inimical to absolutism as they were to particularism and that their objectives were the ones defined in Hoffmann von Fallersleben's *Song of the Germans* (1840),

> Unity and Law and Freedom
> For the German Fatherland.

But after their hopes of attaining these goals by popular revolution collapsed in 1848, the intensity of their desire for nationhood led them to subordinate everything else to it. "No one may be criticized," said one of their leaders, Karl Twesten, "for giving precedence to the issue of power at this time and maintaining that the issues of freedom can wait." Because of this capitulation, the national State that came into existence in 1871, the Bismarckian Reich, was an authoritarian structure that was based on a constitutional theory that specifically repudiated the idea of popular sovereignty, and, in its brief and power-obsessed career, it denied to its citizens any opportunity to grow in self-reliance and political responsibility. Not the least important of the causes of the destruction of the German Empire of 1871–1918 was the absence of constitutional restraints upon, or effective democratic opposition to, its heedless course; and not the least tragic aspect of the failure of the hapless Republic that succeeded it was the lack of enough energetic and dedicated people who combined the willingness to assume responsibility for building a new realm of freedom with the practical arts necessary to solve the problems that stood in the way of its realization.

The beneficiary of that failure was Adolf Hitler, whose claim that he alone was capable of restoring the lost honor and glory of the German nation appealed to the credulous, and who used the power that they gave him to destroy that nation beyond the hope of any recovery.

Or so it might seem. Certainly, as we consider the state of Germany and Europe almost forty years after Hitler's defeat and death, it is worth asking ourselves whether the first part of the Goethe-Schiller epigram is not as true today as it was at the end of the eighteenth century, although perhaps for different reasons. But before we consider that problem, it would be appropriate to address ourselves to the second part of the distich and to ask the extent to which the civic failures of the past have been remedied in the last four decades. What is the state of German freedom? How healthy is German democracy?

I

Two years before Hitler came to power, the philosopher Karl Jaspers wrote a book called *The Intellectual Situation of Our Time*, which appeared as the 1000th volume of a highly regarded series called *Sammlung Göschen*. In 1978, recalling this circumstance, the sociologist Jürgen Habermas asked fifty intellectuals to write essays for a book with a similar title (*Stichworte zur "Geistigen Situation der Zeit"*), which appeared a year later as the 1000th volume of the series *Edition Suhrkamp*. The result was a fascinating volume, although—not surprisingly, given the leftist orientation of the contributors and the implied invitation to compare 1979 with 1931—one that was touched with a not inconsiderable amount of cultural pessimism. Two ideas in particular tended to recur in the various essays: that the Federal Republic was confronted with a "crisis of legitimacy" and that the development of a truly democratic consciousness had been impeded by the "weight of history."

When one considered the progress and achievements of the Federal Republic since 1949, both of these propositions were a bit surprising. At the very time that Mr. Habermas's colleagues were writing their essays, public opinion polls were indicating a remarkable level of support for the democratic form of government. In November 1978, the Allensbach Institute of Demoskopie, West Germany's most respected center for the study of public opinion, posed the question, "Do you believe that the democracy that we have in the Federal Republic is the best State form, or are there others that are better?" Seventy-one percent of those polled felt that it was the best form; only 11% felt that there were better ones, and 18% were undecided. Asked in another poll, held at about the same time, whether "all in all, we really have a good political order or not," 2% of the respondents answered "very good"; 37%, "good"; 42%, "good enough" ("*es geht*"); 12%, "nothing special"; and 4% made no judgment. Finally, again in November 1978, the Allensbach Institute asked a more elaborate question, but one that was certainly evocative of Weimar memories: "When one thinks of all the difficulties that come upon us . . . do you believe that we can . . . master them with our democratic form of State, with several parties in the Bundestag, or will these difficulties require a one-party system with a strong government at its head?" Seventy-seven percent voted for the former alternative, as opposed to 70% of those asked the same question in December 1976–January 1977 and 66% of those interrogated in April 1975. Only 9% thought a one-party system would be required, as opposed to 13% in December 1976–January 1977 and 18% in April 1975. Taken at their face value, these polls hardly support fears about declining faith in democracy.

On the other hand, as we have had occasion to observe, there were generational differences of attitude, and these are not reflected in the polls cited. People who had reached maturity in the late sixties and seventies did not always feel the same commitment to the Republic as their elders, who remembered the war and the occupation, and who were likely to be proud of Germany's swift recovery and establishment of democratic institutions and to believe that theirs was the freest society in the world. The younger generation was more inclined to question this satisfaction, to find inadequacies in the existing system, and to challenge the accepted orthodoxies by various kinds of extraparliamentary opposition. The student movement of the sixties and seventies, the environmental protection and antinuclear movements, and even the still small neo-Nazi groups of the late seventies were all evidence of this, and, to the extent that they resorted to antidemocratic behavior, they represented a discordant and disturbing political force. To this extent, one could talk of a crisis of legitimacy.

The degree to which the burden of history hampered the development of democracy in Germany was more difficult to assess. Certainly there was little obvious piety for the past, and schoolteachers were constantly bemoaning the lack of historical interest shown by their students. Civic celebrations of earlier epochs, when they occurred, were free of emotional intensity. Visitors to the Hohenstaufen Exhibition in Stuttgart in 1976 and the Nuremberg exposition of 1978 celebrating the 600th anniversary of the reign of Charles IV of Luxemburg were not invited to take pride in the glories of the old Reich and would not have responded if they had been, for what did Frederick Barbarossa mean to the average citizen of the Federal Republic? When plans were made to hold a Prussian Exposition in West Berlin in 1981, the committee charged with the arrangements agonized over the problem of how they were going to present a reasonably accurate impression of Prussian history to a people who had apparently forgotten the Hohenzollern and had repudiated militarism so completely that they sometimes appeared to regard their own Bundeswehr with irritation and lack of sympathy.

Another indication of apparent indifference to history was the fact that the names of the great men of the past were rarely invoked in political discussion. Frederick II was no longer a symbol of national will, and, as for Bismarck, the waning evocative power of his name was indicated by polls held during the years 1950–1971 by the Allensbach Institute, which asked the question: "In your opinion which great Germans accomplished the most for Germany?", offering a choice between Konrad Adenauer, Bismarck, Ludwig Erhard, Frederick the Great, Theodor Heuss, Adolf Hitler, "other monarchs and generals," "democratic politicians," "writers, artists and philosophers," "scientists and inventors," and "others." Bismarck's share of the vote was 35% in 1950 but declined steadily thereafter, reaching a low point of 13% in December 1966, the year after his 150th birthday. By the late seventies, he appeared to have become so remote and indistinct a figure that the dramatist Rolf Hochhuth, not usually an admirer of great men, wrote an essay in *Der Spiegel* entitled "Bismarck the Classic," in which he roundly criticized German historians for their inadequate appreciation of their country's greatest statesman and said that the three volumes of the Iron Chancellor's *Table Talk* should be required reading for his countrymen, since they were "the only books in the German language whose human *and* political stature (the rarest combination there is) places them on the level of Shakespeare's historical plays." The lack that Hochhuth complained of was corrected by Lothar Gall's excellent biography of Bismarck in 1979, which was on the best-seller list for many weeks, but neither it nor Hochhuth's rather excessive praise of the old man's humanity seemed likely to start a "Bismarck wave" or to reverse the generally ahistorical tendency in Western Germany.

But one does not escape the influence of history simply by forgetting the names and the dates. One's behavior may be profoundly affected by inherited attitudes, and it is important to inquire concerning the degree to which this is true in contemporary Germany, particularly since contemporary critics, like Hans Mommsen in his essay in the Habermas volume, have claimed that "emancipation in the intellectual realm has not kept pace with the remarkable economic, technological and social upswing of the Federal Republic," and have attributed this to the continued influence of authoritarian forms of behavior and traditional mental patterns.

One can find evidence to support this if one takes the trouble to get beneath the surface of the political process in Western Germany and, as the indefatigable pollsters have been doing for the last thirty years, to investigate the motives and assumptions of the participants. Consider, for example, the question of voter turnout at elections. Americans, whose own record of participation in the electoral process is scandalously bad, are generally impressed when they hear that 85% or more of the West German electorate goes customarily to the ballot boxes. But this seems somewhat less impressive when one learns, from questionnaires concerning motivation, that almost half of the voters interrogated admit that their behavior is rooted, not in any feeling that they are participating in the democratic decision-making process, but rather in the belief that their duty as a citizen requires it. Indeed, the connection between their expression of opinion by means of the ballot and the decisions that the government eventually takes is by no means clear to most of them, if one can believe the results of an Allensbach poll that asked the question: "Do you have the feeling that one has, as a citizen, influence upon the decisions of the federal government, or is one powerless?" Between 1975 and 1978, the percentage of respondents giving the latter answer varied between 55% and 48%. At the same time, the number of those who, in response to supplementary questions, felt that the influence that they had was not great enough never exceeded 25% and was generally much lower. The reason for this apparent satisfaction with a system that half of them believed gave them no effective influence on affairs emerged from yet another poll made in 1971, which indicated that a very high percentage of respondents, 48%, when asked to define the State, regarded it as synonymous with the government, while 12% said that the word made them think of laws. This, one interpreter has pointed out, looks uncomfortably like a confirmation of that deference to authority that was a fixed characteristic of German political attitudes in the eighteenth and nineteenth centuries.

In a fascinating article on tradition and change in the German political culture, in which he has availed himself of the results of political polling over the last three decades, the Augsburg political scientist Theo Stammen cites two other pieces of evidence that seem to reflect traditional modes of thought. The first is the low percentage of party membership in contrast to the very high percentage of participation in elections. Asked if they would be prepared to enter a party, 7% of the respondents in 1952 said "Yes" and 85% "No." In 1960, the relative figures were 14% and 78%; in 1975, 15% and 78%. The heavy negative vote in 1952 may have been influenced to some extent by memory of the pressures exerted in order to compel party membership during the Nazi years, but the fact that it did not change significantly in the next twenty-three years would appear to indicate that the traditional German tendency to value private virtues over public ones was a more effective cause. It was once said that the average German had a three-point credo: (1) The State equals the officials; (2) Politics destroys character; and (3) The best government is a good administration. The reluctance of a large majority to commit themselves by party membership to active participation in politics suggests that that kind of prejudice against politics is still very much alive. In this connection, Stammen's other datum is also relevant: in a 1976 poll that posed the question: "If you had a son or daughter, would you be happy, or not happy, to see him or her become a politician?", 43% of those respondents with sons said that they would be unhappy and only 19% that they would be the reverse; 40% of those with daughters said that they would be unhappy and 20% the opposite. Fifty-one percent were also in agreement that politics was a "more unfair and ruthless" business than other occupations.

It would perhaps be a mistake to take these echoes of the past too seriously, particularly since there is evidence that the attitudes mentioned are currently showing signs of modification in local and regional politics, in the activities of citizens' initiative groups and of the various components of the Green (environmentalists, opponents of nuclear energy and the like) voting lists. But since the end of the Adenauer era, a period in which the democratic culture of the Federal Republic seemed to have established and consolidated itself on stable foundations, other tendencies, also reminiscent of the past, have emerged that cannot be dismissed so lightly.

The first is an almost neurotic sensitivity to signs of economic trouble, accompanied by a tendency, alluded to earlier in our discussion of money, to react with pessimism and undemocratic behavior. When the triumphant economic miracle of the fifties faltered for the first time at the beginning of the next decade, and when the Erhard government proved incapable of mastering the recession, the unease in the country was reflected, not only in significant changes in the federal government (the coming of the Great Coalition), but in the sudden emergence of the National Democratic Party (NPD) and of the Extra-Parliamentary Opposition (APO). The not insignificant influence of these groups in German politics came to an end when the recession was brought under control by the vigorous policies of Karl Schiller, but the fact that they existed at all revealed that there were antidemocratic forces in German society that could be mobilized quickly, and that the democratic culture was more than normally vulnerable to signs of economic instability.

The worsening of economic conditions in 1974–1975, which was the result of stagnation accompanied by inflation and was complicated by the effects of the Arab oil embargo of 1973, did not have the same kind of political results but was nevertheless marked by a significant loosening of the social consensus upon which the political culture rested and the beginning of disputes between the social partners. Chancellor Schmidt's vigor in attacking the malaise, and increases in the amounts spent on social services, including support for the close to one million unemployed in 1976, helped to alleviate the situation; but by 1977 there were serious labor-management disputes, and people began to talk anxiously about polarization. ("A ghost goes around in Bonn," Ralf Dahrendorf wrote in 1978. "The ghost of polarization.") By the end of the decade, when it began to appear that the economic slowdown was not a mere cyclical phenomenon but a long-term process caused by what one economist called "the middle-aging of the West German economy," and when other alarming symptoms were noted (an increasing budget deficit, some slippage of the mark, and new disputes between labor and management over the question of co-determination in the steel industry and the use of lockouts against striking workers), the reaction in the country was not merely one of concern and indignation, as in other democracies confronting the same problems, but—at least in some quarters—one that questioned the democratic system itself. It was the economic malaise that produced all the talk about a "crisis of legitimacy" and led, in neoconservative circles, to the invention of the word *Unregierbarkeit* ("ungovernability") as a new criticism of the democratic system. Neither of these terms had much popular resonance, but their appearance, like the re-emergence at the beginning of the eighties of a small but vocal right-radical minority, was not reassuring to anyone with a historical memory.

In the second place, the political culture of the Federal Republic showed a relatively low tolerance for nonconformity and dissent and a distressing tendency, particularly on the right of the political spectrum, to attempt to counter it by means of legal disabilities and prohibitions. Much of the reaction to the student movement of the sixties was disturbingly reminiscent of the anti-Burschenschaft campaign of the 1820s and of Bismarck's attacks upon the Catholics and the Socialists in the 1870s. However one might justify the Radicals' Law of January 1972 (and there was certainly something to be said for regulations that denied government employment to known enemies of the constitution), there was little doubt that it was administered in many cases with an excessive zeal and a latitude of interpretation (there were cases of people being denied jobs, not because they had openly opposed the democratic order, but because they seemed "indifferent" to it) that seemed to assume that any form of dissent was reprehensible. In a provocative article called "The Difficulties of Protecting a Constitution," Ulrich Greiner pointed to

the thousands of "recognizances" and the growing number of people under surveillance. A permanent feeling of being controlled is created in them. When, in an otherwise relatively free country, pressure suddenly materializes from above, there are only two possible kinds of reaction: the one that is

publicly desirable with gradations from . . . loyalty to the
State to accommodation and hypocrisy, and one that is certainly not desired, which begins with doubts concerning the
justice and fairness of our social order and ends with radical-
ism. The author Peter Schneider has formulated it this way:
"Anyone who is declared to be an enemy of the constitution
becomes one."

When terrorism reached its height in the seventies, it elicited not only
demands for firm measures against the terrorists themselves but much
talk about the necessity of acting against people who were loosely called
"sympathizers" with terrorism. This was often justified with the slogan
"No freedom for the enemies of freedom!", which, as Theo Stammen
pointed out, had a persuasive ring until one remembered that it came
from the mouth of Louis de Saint-Just, the French Jacobin who was the
most extreme advocate of the use of terror against political opponents
and hardly a model of good democratic practice. All in all, the tendency
of many Germans, in time of controversy over issues that touched them
nearly, to view the political process as a conflict between Friend and
Foe—a theory that the political scientist and Nazi sympathizer Carl
Schmitt had once recommended as a healthy corrective to the pluralism
of Weimar—was another indication of the ambivalence of their democratic conviction.

Finally, it was not reassuring to note the increasing use of violence in
domestic controversy, which had its origins in the student movement
and the APO in the sixties but became characteristic in the seventies of
other opponents of the social-liberal consensus, particularly groups inimical to consumerism, nuclear energy, and the kind of environmental
damage that they associated with capitalism. Inspired by utopian aspirations that could not be satisfied by the electoral process, they used the
only weapons that promised to advance their goals—obstruction, disruption and force—often justifying their use of them in the way that
earlier Romantics in German history had done, as a defiant high treason against reason.

It was significant of the vulnerability of the democratic system to this
reversion to the kind of political irrationality that played such a fatal
role in the Weimar period that the left-wing youth organizations of both
the Social Democratic and Free Democratic parties, the JUSOs and the
JUDOs, were touched by it and, indeed, allowed their electoral tactics
to be influenced by it. In the parliamentary campaign in the autumn of
1980, they formed part of the crowds that disrupted speeches by the
CDU-CSU candidate Franz-Josef Strauss in Cologne, Essen and Hamburg, pelting the podium in Cologne's Sport Hall with eggs and toma-
toes, drowning out the speaker's voice with choruses of "Heil Hitler!
Stop Strauss!", scuffling with the police, cutting television and light
cables, and doing everything in their power to deny Strauss his constitutional right of free speech. It was understandable that the frustrated
candidate should have shouted, after similar scenes in the Burgplatz in

Essen, "You would have been the best students of Dr. Joseph Goebbels, the best supporters of Heinrich Himmler! You are the best Nazis that ever existed!"

The violence of these confrontations paled before that shown in the struggle over nuclear energy, particularly in the village of Brokdorf in the vicinity of Hamburg. Plans to build an atomic reactor here aroused the opposition of anti-nuclear-power groups as early as 1976, and there was a series of peaceful protests over the next four years. By the beginning of 1981, however, the course was set toward violence. On February 2, groups of militants broke windows, plundered shops and shot at the police with catapults during a demonstration in Hamburg; and on February 28, 50,000 demonstrators advanced on Brokdorf, including action groups bent upon disruption by all possible means. One hundred twenty-eight police were wounded in battles in which their opponents threw gasoline bombs and other missiles, and in related actions the Brokdorf construction chief had his home fire-bombed, and Molotov cocktails were thrown into courthouses in Glückstadt and Itzehoe.

It was true, of course, that other democracies had not been entirely free of the tendencies and weaknesses noted here, but those countries had not had the history of political incapacity and democratic failure that Germany had had either. That fact added weight to Wolfgang J. Mommsen's rueful admission that, "despite all the perfection of our social institutions and the manifest stability of our political system we have not yet developed that measure of calm composure in the face of extreme political opinions that is characteristic of older mature democracies, in spite of their often incomparably more difficult social problems." It also underlined the concern of those who wondered how many Brokdorfs the democratic system could stand before there was a renewed cry for a more authoritarian stance by the government.

By the beginning of the 1980s, it was clear that the Federal Republic had problems more serious than any experienced during the Adenauer period and that the democratic culture was not as firmly consolidated as had been imagined earlier. But this did not prevent the system from operating more successfully than most of its sister democracies, both in coping with the problems that were unique to it and those that it shared with other advanced capitalistic states; and the bulk of the Republic's citizens seemed to realize this when they went to the polls in October 1980. Indeed, in those elections, the voters acted as if they did not feel as powerless as some of the pollsters said they did, for they cast their ballots with marked discrimination. In an election that pitted the two strongest, most experienced, and most intelligent politicians of their generation against each other, the voters chose Helmut Schmidt over Franz-Josef Strauss as much because of their memory of Strauss's violation of democratic principles in the *Spiegel* case of 1962, his too militant record as defense minister, the irrationality of his attacks upon *Ostpolitik*, and his attempt to label the Social Democrats as a party of traitors as because of Schmidt's solid record of achievement in foreign policy, his social reforms and his success in keeping inflation and unemployment down to levels that aroused the envious attention of the British and the Americans.

At the same time, they voted more enthusiastically for Schmidt than they did for his party, which alienated many of its supporters by the tactics of its left wing and by evidence of mismanagement and corruption in some local organizations. The immoderate attacks upon Strauss in the northern cities and the role of the JUSOs in the anti-Bundeswehr demonstration in Bremen caused defections from the SPD in both Hamburg and Bremen, where the Green List attracted 2.3% and 2.7% of the vote respectively, and in Essen and Cologne, which they lost to the CDU. Much of the strength that the SPD had hoped to pick up from voters put off by Strauss went instead to their coalition partner, the FDP, perhaps an indication that the demands of their left wing for a more aggressive reform program offended the basic conservatism of the independent voters.

In general, aside from the increase in liberal strength, the election results contained no surprises and indicated no erosion of support for the system. There was some falling off in total participation (88.7% as opposed to 90.7% in 1976 and 91% in 1972), but not enough to corroborate fears that the electorate was losing interest in the parties or the electoral process. The CDU-CSU remained the strongest political grouping, with 16,900,370 votes, or 44.5% of the total, which represented a loss of 4.1% since 1976. The SPD, with 16,262,096 votes, 42.9%, did only marginally better than in 1976, and showed a falling off of 3% (a million votes) since 1972. The big winner, in relative terms, was the FDP, with 4,030,608 votes (10.6% of the total) as opposed to 2,995,085 (7.9%) in 1976 and 3,129,982 (8.4%) in 1972. The significant voting shifts all took place between the major parties. Of the eight other groups listed on the ballot, only one received an appreciable vote, the Green List with 1.5%, far less than the 5% needed for representation in the Bundestag.

Indeed, the election of October 1980 and the two parliamentary elections that preceded it underlined the failure of extremist parties of the left or the right to demonstrate any significant appeal to the voters, a fact that would appear to support the American political scientist Nicholas Katzenstein's judgment that, while realignments and perhaps transformations of Western Germany's system of elite collaboration were possible in the period ahead (a gradual erosion, for example, of the relations between the SPD and the trade unions), "the institutional form of mass political participation . . . [was] unlikely to be challenged in the 1980s." Barring an economic disaster or a drastic change of power relationships in Europe, West German democracy, despite its internal problems, seemed as stable as anything could be in a problematical world.

II

In February 1981, the retiring chief of the West German mission in East Berlin, Günter Gaus, gave an interview to representatives of the newspaper *Die Zeit*, during which he gave his personal impressions of the country he was leaving. He regarded it, he said in his opening remarks, as a German country, indeed, "more German than the Federal Republic."

This intrigued the reporters, who urged the minister to dilate upon the theme, which he did by making four points. In his view, he said, "the diminished tempo of industrialization [had] preserved certain positive values and—in the form of resentments occasionally expressed with respect to other people—some negative values from the last hundred years of German history longer" in the DDR than in the Federal Republic. The DDR had become "less watered down (*eingeschmolzen*), less reduced to conformity (*nivelliert.*)"

In the second place, there was in the DDR "a conscious inclination toward history." It was, to be sure, selective, as it was in the West. "Insofar as we do it at all, we too look for our heritage in what suits us. But [in the DDR] the much more conscious historical inclination leads to the fact that specific figures and specific epochs . . . become impressed upon the consciousness much more strongly" than in the West.

"The third point I want to make," Gaus continued, "also has to do with the adaptation of the cultural legacy, in which we are very negligent and the DDR very conscious of its goal, and that is the lack of embarrassment with which folklore and folk songs are cultivated, on the level of high art as well as in quite simple, even banal, local club activities, whereas in our case the generation of the fifties usually had to take a detour through American folklore in order to overcome the shyness with respect to German folk songs that the Nazis had left them with."

Finally, "people [in the DDR], who had to adapt themselves, and who also understood how to adapt themselves, are—for reasons that are in part obvious and regrettable—confined to their country. And that also marks them."

The interesting thing about these remarks was the extent to which they appeared to be informed by a conviction that West Germans had paid a high price for overcoming the historical gulf that had existed between Germany and the West and for becoming, politically, economically and culturally, part of the Western World. They had, the minister suggested, lost something of their essential substance in the years that had passed since the end of the Third Reich; the cosmopolitanism and materialism of the West had eroded their individuality as a people; and they had sacrificed native cultural values, inwardness and a sense of community and the folkways inherited from the past, to the seductions of the consumer society. The similarity of Gaus's views and those people in Western Germany, particularly on the left, who were alienated by what they considered to be the excesses of capitalism and who called for a return to older and simpler ways, was apparent. It was doubtful, however, whether very many of those critics of the consumer society would have concluded that, because the DDR had not experienced the cultural changes that dynamic capitalism caused, it represented an appropriate model for their utopian longings. If the DDR was not affected by the uglier aspects of modern life, it was also deprived of its conveniences. If inwardness and a sense of community survived in the DDR, it was to a large extent because—as Minister Gaus admitted—its citizens were confined to their country, and because, in a land where dissent was forbidden, one either capitulated to the demands of the community or withdrew into oneself. Being more German than the West Germans also meant being less free than the West Germans.

Parenthetically, it is worth noting that the inclination to history that appeared to impress Gaus—the invocation of the names of Goethe and Schiller, Heine and Lessing, Scharnhorst and Gneisenau—was less a genuine historical consciousness than an attempt to give people who were subjected to a system imported from the Soviet Union something with which they could identify. For this purpose, and doubtless to emphasize the importance of loyalty and obedience and dedication to the State, the Prussian past had been revived and Christian Rauch's statue of Frederick the Great had been put back in its old place on Unter den Linden after thirty years of absence. But Prussianism meant more than obedience; it stood for liberalism and toleration and enlightenment, qualities that were not viewed with any favor by the functionaries of the SED. The correspondent for *Die Zeit* Joachim Nawrocki has written:

> The DDR is rather Wilhelmine than Prussian with all its *Brimborium* [fussiness] and its *Zackigkeit* [spit and polish], its tightly structured, fossilized hierarchies and chains of command. Strictly speaking, it is true that the organization of State and society has been changed much more radically since the end of the war than in the Federal Republic. But a lot has changed astonishingly little: the appearance of little towns and villages, the landscape, above all, the relationship between the citizen and authority, the lack of a full voice (*Unmündigkeit*) and the absence of any political alternative. . . . It's only that many things have received different names. What used to be called *lèse majesté* is now called "public denigration" and "State-hostile provocation."
>
> It is perhaps more than a superficial impression if one looks at the physiognomies of the party and State functionaries, let's say in the photo of the signing of the Basic Treaty, and notes unmistakable differences from the West German officials. The DDR people could almost all fit, with Kaiser William moustaches, into Heinrich Mann's *Der Untertan* or [Carl] Zuckmayer's *Hauptmann von Köpenick*.

When Erich Honecker became Party Secretary in 1971, there was some expectation that an era of progressive change might be beginning, for the new leader seemed to recognize that, in a country where few people believed any longer in the promises of Marxism, tangible improvements were the only means of increasing loyalty to the State. But his attempts to implement this idea soon encountered difficulties. The relaxation of controls over literary activity inspired such an outburst of creative energy and new ideas that it soon frightened the SED establishment, while the decision to allow West-marks to circulate as a second currency, in order to enable DDR citizens to buy Western products in State-run Inter-Shops, also backfired. Not everyone had the opportunity to acquire West-marks, and the experiment merely raised unfulfillable expectations. The importation of 10,000 Volkswagen automobiles from the West had the same boomerang effect. The cars cost too much (30,000 East-marks), and there were too few of them to meet the needs of people who had, in some cases, been waiting for seven years for an automobile. The net result of these experiments, then, was to increase both the regime's economic instability, already suffering from an unfavorable trade balance of 3 to 4 billion mark a year, and popular dissatisfaction with the inferiority of local products to Western ones and the inaccessibility of the latter to all but a select few in the upper ranks of the State service.

As long as the grumbling remained subterranean and unorganized, it was tolerated, but whenever it found expression in systematic criticism, the government felt compelled to resort, as it did in the case of the too-unbuttoned writers, to its only remaining weapon, punitive action. The era of limited free expression came to an end, as we have seen, with the expulsion of Wolf Biermann from the country in November 1976. In the next twelve months, the same fate befell the writers Thomas Brasch, Reiner Kunze, Sarah Kirsch, Jürgen Fuchs and Hans Joachim Schädlich, the songwriters Gerulf Pannach and Christian Kunert, and the actors Manfred Krug and Eva-Maria Hagen. The *Germanist* Hellmuth Nitsche was exiled because he had dared to write President Carter about violations of the human rights provisions of the Helsinki Agreement of 1975, and the medical doctor Karl-Heinz Nitschke because he had circulated a petition on the same subject. In all of these cases, the crimes committed were irritating but trivial in the eyes of the SED leadership, who did not regard the views of humanists and scientists with any seriousness and believed that deprivation of citizenship was the most expeditious way of dealing with them.

Much more threatening to those in the seats of power was criticism from people within the party itself, whose Marxist credentials were unimpeachable and who dared to use their orthodoxy against the policy and practice of the SED. To the party ideologues, such dissent was a contradiction in terms, for it was their view that, in a classless society, which they claimed the DDR to be, no objective political or social basis existed for an opposition. When, therefore, the natural scientist Robert Havemann undertook to write theses challenging the assumptions of the current leadership, they reacted by placing him, not for the first time, under house arrest; and, when the East Berlin economist Rudolf Bahro wrote an analytical study called *The Alternative: A Critique of the System of "Real Socialism,"* in which he attacked the regime's denial of theoretical discussion and argued that the existing system had not liberated the working class but merely subordinated it to a party bureaucracy, the State Security forces arrested him on trumped up charges of espionage.

If the arrest and subsequent imprisonment of Bahro was intended to stop criticism within party ranks, it did not succeed in its purpose. On the contrary, it aroused deep unease among midlevel functionaries and dedicated younger officials who had long chafed under the yoke of the SED *Bonzen* and led some of them to begin the formation of an oppositional movement. In January 1978, *Der Spiegel* printed a manifesto, comprising thirty typescript pages, that had been composed by a group of self-styled "democratic and humanist-thinking Communists in the DDR" who had "illegally formed [themselves] into a Union of Democratic Communists of Germany (BDKD) because the circumstances still permit no possibility of legal organization."

The authors of this paper, who asked for the support of like-minded people in the Federal Republic, declared their goal to be that of "working for a democratic-Communistic order in all of Germany, in which all human rights are fully realized for every citizen, according to Marx's saying that all of the circumstances under which human beings are oppressed, scorned, and enslaved creatures must be abolished." In specific terms, they declared themselves to be

> against the one-party dictatorship, which is a dictatorship of the Secretary and the Politbüro clique;

> against the dictatorship of the proletariat, which is a dictatorship of the bureaucracy over the proletariat and against the whole people;

> for party pluralism, for freedom, according to [Rosa] Luxemburg, is always the freedom of those who think differently;

> for an independent parliament that emerges from the free decision of the voters;

> for an independent supreme court, where every citizen can bring his complaints against the misuse of power. Even in Prussia, a miller could win his case against the King. In "real Socialism" the powerless spirit has to humble itself before unspiritual power without being able to call for legal protection;

> for a government that is free from Central Committee *Apparatschiks* who are blind to reality (*lebensfremd*);

> for the abolition of "democratic centralism" in party, State, and society, since it is a centralism that is opposed to democracy.

The manifesto was a curious compound of utopianism, naiveté (particularly when it ventured to make economic proposals), and polemical sharpness, being especially vituperative when dealing with "the red popes in the Kremlin," who were accused of atomizing the working class movement, and their helots in the DDR, of whom the authors wrote:

> No ruling class in Germany has ever been so parasitic and has sealed itself off so completely as the two dozen families who use our country as a self-service shop. None has ever allowed itself to build such excessively golden ghettoes in the woods, which are guarded like fortresses. None has so shamefully corrupted and enriched itself with special stores and private imports from the West, with decorations and premiums and special clinics, and pensions and gifts, as this caste.

Although its genuineness was questioned in some quarters, experts on Communism in the West concluded, on the basis of language and other internal evidence, that it was what it claimed to be, and this conclusion found support in the unusual violence with which the SED attacked the document as a fabrication of the Western intelligence community. There was no way, of course, of judging how large the underground movement was for which the manifesto spoke; but that dissidence existed within the party seemed beyond doubt.

The possibility that Erich Honecker might attempt to appease it by making even partial concessions to the manifesto's democratic demands was entirely out of the question. The Party Secretary was well aware that the Soviet government, already unhappy about his experiment with the Inter-Shops, would probably react to any structural reform of the system with a demand for his ouster, and he was, in any case, too much of a realist to believe that an unpopular regime could long survive once it began to show weakness. As the DDR entered the fourth decade of its existence, therefore, there was every indication that it would continue to fit Wolf Biermann's description of it as "an unattractive, fear-inspiring police State, which screws foreign currency out of its unhappy children and locks its Communist critics either in or out, a State in whose coat of arms it is not the hammer and compass that are appropriate but the bludgeon and the muzzle."

III

In 1960, in his inaugural address as the Federal Republic's second President, Heinrich Lübke, after touching on several of the controverted problems of the day, came to that of national reunification. This, he declared, "remains *the* question of our national life . . . on which we are all united, irrespective of party and religious affiliation. In the long run, Germany will not remain separated, either by absurd boundaries or by brutal disruption of personal ties; for it would be an insoluble contradiction if those who today concede to the people of Asia and Africa their right to freedom and self-determination should deny us Germans this natural right."

As in many of the President's later public utterances, there was more pathos than logic in this statement, and one was left wondering what particular miscreants he believed to be showing favoritism toward which particular Asians and Africans. But Mr. Lübke could not be faulted for stressing the importance of the issue. Since the beginning of the Cold War, when the border between the Western occupation zones and the Soviet zone changed from a temporary to an apparently permanent frontier, the question of reunification was one on which millions of West Germans held strong views, either for personal or moral-humanitarian or patriotic or ideological reasons, either because they had relatives or friends from whom the arbitrary division of Germany separated them or because they felt a sense of obligation to fellow Germans who they knew were suffering from the harsh political and economic conditions in the DDR or because their national pride was offended by the fragmentation of a Germany that had once stretched

> From the Meuse unto the Memel,
> The Tyrol to the Baltic Sea

or because they believed that reunification would represent a turning of the tide against the menace of Communism. Similarly, the issue was important on the other side of the iron curtain that divided Germany, on the one hand to people who hoped that reunification might liberate them from a regime that they detested and, on the other, to the DDR leadership who manipulated it, as we shall see, in their propaganda and their relations with the government of the Federal Republic.

In the West, the fervor of reunification sentiment diminished with the passage of the years, although even in the eighties it was not a concept that could be lightly flouted. In the first years, it appeared to be an entirely practical goal. In 1949, when the Parliamentary Council met to draft a Basic Law for the new West German government, its members were, as we have seen, reluctant to be seen as committing themselves to a rump Germany, and consequently wrote a preamble that described the Basic Law as a means of providing a government "for a transitional period," until the reunification of the country was effected. It was possible, in the days of the close collaboration between Konrad Adenauer and John Foster Dulles, when the Americans were talking about "rolling back" Communism, to believe that that transition would be short. But the failure of the Western Allies to move when the East German workers rose on June 17, 1953, shook the credibility of the "policy of strength," and after the failure of the Geneva Summit of 1955 and Adenauer's trip to Moscow, it became clear that there was no hope of an imminent solution of the national question. Even so, both the Adenauer and the Erhard governments persisted stubbornly in their refusal to recognize the legal existence of another German State and their policy of breaking relations with other governments that were of a different opinion in this regard. Unfortunately, this Hallstein Doctrine, as it was called, which had been conceived as a weapon in the "policy of strength" strategy and was designed to isolate and weaken the DDR and persuade it to seek union with the West, was more and more regularly flouted by the Third World nations it was intended to intimidate.

The *Ostpolitik* of the Great Coalition and the Brandt government was inaugurated in full recognition of the stalemate of the older policy. Indeed, Brandt and his colleagues had reached the conclusion that fixation upon the reunification issue was both unrealistic and shortsighted. It maintained the tension between the two Germanies at a dangerously high level, thus contributing to the fragility of European peace, and it was indifferent to opportunities for *ad hoc* arrangements that might contribute to the well-being of fellow Germans in the DDR. Yet, as he pursued his policy of détente, Brandt discovered how great the symbolic importance of the reunification issue was to many German politicians. He wrote in his diary about how amazed he was, during his term as foreign minister in the Great Coalition, over how "fearfully and aggressively groups in the CDU, among them members of the cabinet, behaved when the sacrosanct Hallstein Doctrine was touched. The illusion that one could still accumulate credit in the world with the obstinate claim that the Federal government alone represented Germany, that one could simply stop developments, or get anywhere with fossilized positions, was hardly to be overcome."

Later, when he was his own man, his task was no easier, for the German right wing was opposed to the *de facto* recognition of the DDR that was implicit in Brandt's formulation "two States within one nation." During the second round of talks in Kassel, demonstrators in the streets carried placards reading

> *Volksverräter Hand in Hand—*
> *Willi Stoph und Willy Brandt!*

> [Traitors to the people in collusion—
> Willi Stoph and Willy Brandt!]

and, as the treaties moved toward conclusion, the CDU-CSU fought them every step of the way, claiming that Brandt's policy was in violation of the preamble of the Basic Law and thus unconstitutional. Since, in both the eastern treaties and the Basic Treaty of 1972 between the Federal Republic and the DDR, the former reserved the right to work for reunification by peaceful means, the Supreme Constitutional Court could find no merit in these charges against the Federal Chancellor, although it went on record with an interpretation of the preamble of the Basic Law that declared that it was the legal duty of all political agencies to encourage a "permanent striving after reunification."

This judgment touched off a heated discussion of how, in view of the new relations with East Germany, the subject should be treated in school curricula, which were currently under fire because of new revelations that students had little knowledge of, or interest in, the reunification question. At the end of 1978, the education ministers and Senators of the West German *Länder* further confused an already muddled question by trying to prove that the treaties had not destroyed the essential unity of the nation. This they did by a brace of definitions that they recommended for school use: first, that "the German nation continues to exist as a linguistic and cultural unit"; and, second, that "the German nation continues to exist as a State people that has no common State, but whose subjects, unaffected by separate regulations in the DDR, possess the united German State affiliation." As the Socialist minister Horst Ehmke has written, it is doubtful whether these definitions were either politically realistic or pedagogically communicable.

After a long period of quiescence, during which the diplomats worked hard to give substance to the normalization process that Brandt had set in train in the early seventies, the reunification debate flared into life again in the first weeks of 1981. The occasion was the interview, alluded to earlier in this chapter, between Günter Gaus and reporters of *Die Zeit*. In the course of this, Gaus complained that many people in the West had not yet accepted the fact that for the foreseeable future there were going to be two independent sovereign German States living side by side, and that the more they knew about each other the more tolerable the relationship would be. Unfortunately, there were too many West German patriots who made speeches about the German nation on Sundays, always equating that term with the Bismarck Reich of 1871 and always implying that Reich must be restored by bringing "the part" that had broken away back into union with the West. It was high time, Gaus said, that his fellow citizens in the Federal Republic took a longer historical view. The German nation was not synonymous with the Bismarck Empire, which, in any case, had lasted only seventy-five years. Over the centuries, the nation had assumed many different forms, and might again. "For a relationship with the DDR that has perspective," the minister continued, "we need to think seriously and profoundly about Little Germany (*Kleindeutschland*) and Great Germany (*Grossdeutschland*) and about the real meaning of federalism, and about what the middle of Europe has become, for good or evil. . . . The two German States exist and, to all intents and purposes, will exist longer than the present generation. There is no sense in going on talking about the DDR from the political and psychological perspective of 1949."

Then, answering one of his interrogators, who pointed out that concepts like "national unity" had wide currency and asked how they could be given substance, Gaus answered:

> We must as far as possible give up using the concept of the nation any longer, because when we do we fall into the danger of indulging in shadow-boxing again. Specifically, we again give people in the DDR an opportunity to say: "Here comes the old *revanchiste* around the corner, who won't recognize that there are two German States here that exist independently of each other and are each sovereign in their own right."

These blunt observations put the cat among the pigeons for fair, and there was a predictable cry of protest, members of the CDU-CSU in particular expressing outrage over Gaus's requiem for the Bismarck Reich and accusing him of constitutional impropriety and political naiveté. The resultant debate, however, had little of the duration and bitterness of the earlier fight against the eastern treaties; and, indeed, the most interesting thing about it was that it seemed to inspire an intriguing tactical shift of position with respect to the national question by the leadership of the SED.

In *The Communist Manifesto*, Karl Marx had written that the workers have no fatherland until they seize political power and constitute a nation of their own, on principles that are fundamentally different from those of the bourgeois society that they have overcome. In accordance with this, the leaders of the SED, when they addressed themselves to the question of divided Germany, took the line that, since 1949, there had been two German nations: a nation of workers and farmers and "real Socialism," and a capitalist nation that was doomed to disappear in time. The gulf between them was absolute and unbridgeable. Walter Ulbricht once said that the nation of the Krauses had nothing in common with the nation of the Krupps, even though they spoke the same language.

This did not mean, however, that the SED policymakers could be indifferent to the question of reunification. Even the most convinced Socialist had ties with the West that had to be acknowledged, and there were ideological reasons for reassuring him that the separation would not be permanent. At the SED party conference in 1954, when Walter Ulbricht touched on this theme, he used language that could, with the change of a single word, have been put in the mouth of Heinrich Lübke.

> We are for the unity of Germany, because the Germans in the west of our homeland are our brothers, because we love our fatherland, because we believe that the restoration of the unity of Germany has an irrefragable legal validity and that anyone who dares to contest this law will be destroyed.

The SED program of 1963 defined the goal of the party to be "the restoration of German unity," while at the same time attributing the present division of Germany to the actions of the "imperialistic Western Powers in conspiracy with West German monopoly capitalism," thus intimating that the precondition of reunification was the destruction of capitalism in the West.

The way in which SED propagandists used the reunification issue was always influenced by tactical considerations. In the days when the Federal Republic was seeking to isolate the DDR and was claiming the sole right to speak for Germany in world affairs, it was important to attempt to neutralize this by playing the national card, if only to remind other countries that Germany did not stop on the west bank of the Elbe. When *Ostpolitik* was inaugurated, however, and the West Germans began to make earnest attempts to establish a working relationship with the DDR, the SED became uncomfortable with the intrusiveness of the Westerners and the increased influence of Western ideas and products upon their subjects. The unity of Germans was consequently downplayed, and the official policy became one of delimitation, or *Abgrenzung*. In 1974, the paragraph in the constitution of 1968 that defined the DDR as "a Socialist State of the German Nation," which strove to overcome "the division of Germany forced upon the German Nation by imperialism" and to effect "the step by step closing of the gap between the two German States until they join on the basis of democracy and Socialism," was deleted, and the new paragraph read simply, "The German Democratic Republic is a Socialist State of workers and farmers." *Abgrenzung* remained the party line for the next six years, finding its most determined expression in October 1980, when, in a speech at Gera, Erich Honecker made a violent attack upon the Federal Republic and demanded that normalization of relations would require the recognition by the Federal Republic of a separate East German State citizenship (something the West has always refused to acknowledge), and when this was followed by a fivefold increase in the transit fees required of West German visitors to the DDR, a move that seemed calculated to reduce the number of Western visitors radically.

Barely four months later, however, while West Germans were debating Günter Gaus's suggestion that the time had perhaps come to delete the word "Nation" from the dialogue between the two Germanies, the SED Secretary abruptly changed his course, or at least his language. At a meeting of district delegates in East Berlin, Honecker referred to politicians in the West who tried to convey the impression that reunification meant more to them than their pocketbooks.

> We should like to say to them: Be careful! One day Socialism will knock at your door, and, when the day comes on which the workers of the Federal Republic go about the Socialist transformation of the Federal Republic of Germany, then the question of the unification of the two German States will be posed in completely new form. As to how we would decide then, there should be no question of doubt.

It would be difficult to say whether Honecker was chiefly influenced by the desire to appear more German than the representatives of the West German government, or by the hope of appealing to West German workers who were now feeling the economic pinch, or by the desire to win the approval of his own citizens, who had responded with less than enthusiasm to the party's attempt to inspire them with a separate "Socialist State consciousness." If the last, the Secretary may have been a bit annoyed by the enthusiasm of his audience's applause, which indicated that even State functionaries could be moved by the emotional appeal of the reunification issue.

Yet, of course, Günter Gaus was correct when he said that people who kept using the word "Nation" were shadow-boxing; and this applied to politicians on both sides of the Wall. Just as the division of Germany had been the result of external factors, specifically, the deterioration of relations among the Great Powers, so would any fundamental change in the relationship between the two parts of the country depend upon the state of world politics. Indeed, even minor adjustments were apt to be determined by changes in the international climate. There was little doubt, for example, that the Soviet invasion of Afghanistan, the subsequent cooling of East-West relations, and concern over the situation in Poland had a direct influence upon Honecker's speech at Gera and the attempt to diminish the flow of Western visitors to the DDR. As for the larger question of whether and when Germany would be reunified, there was no likelihood of its being decided by Germans alone. In his state of the nation address in 1979, Helmut Schmidt showed that he at least was under no illusions on this score, when he said:

> The idea that one day a State of 75 million Germans could arise in the middle of Europe arouses concern in many of our neighbors and partners in Europe. . . . We ought not overlook the fact that, in the eyes of others, the German division is today part of the European balance of power that secures peace in Europe. . . . In our geopolitical position, and with our recent history, we Germans cannot allow ourselves a political schizophrenia, which on the one hand pursues a realistic policy of peace and at the same time carries on an illusionary debate about reunification. . . . Readiness for reality is needed, if our will to peace is to prevail.

This did not mean that German reunification was an impossibility; only that, as the Chancellor added, it would come, in all probability, only after a long period of peace. Given the state of the world, in short, there seemed to be no good reason to doubt the continued relevance of Schiller's epigram.

Appendix

"The Awful German Language"

In the days when Bismarck was the greatest man in Europe, an American visitor to Berlin, anxious to hear the Chancellor speak, procured two tickets to the visitors' gallery of the Reichstag and hired an interpreter to accompany her there. They were fortunate enough to arrive just before Bismarck intervened in a debate on a matter of social legislation, and the American pressed close to her interpreter's side so as to miss nothing of the translation. But although Bismarck spoke with considerable force and at some length, the interpreter's lips remained closed, and he was unresponsive to his employer's nudges. Unable to contain herself, she finally blurted, "What is he *saying*?" "Patience, madam," the interpreter answered, "I am waiting for the verb!"

There is no doubt that the structure of the German language, which was based upon the Latin, with its rigid rules for indirect discourse and its search for elegance in encapsulation, has been a source of exasperation and helplessness for foreign visitors. In her famous treatise on Germany, Mme. de Stael complained that there was no good conversation to be had in the country because the grammatical construction of the language always put the meaning at the end of the sentence and thus made impossible "the pleasure of interrupting, which makes discussion so animated in France." Mark Twain, in a famous essay called "The Awful German Language," was more vigorous in his complaints. "An average sentence in a German newspaper is a sublime and impressive curiosity," he wrote. "It occupies a quarter of a column; it contains all ten parts of speech—not in regular order but mixed; it is built mainly of compound words constructed by the writer on the spot and not to be found in any dictionary . . . ; it treats of fourteen or fifteen different subjects, each enclosed in a parenthesis of its own, with here or there extra parentheses which re-enclose three or four of the minor parentheses, making pens within pens; finally, all the parentheses and re-parentheses are massed together between a couple of king-parentheses, one of which is placed in the first line of the majestic sentence and the other in the middle of the last line of it—after which comes the VERB, and you find out for the first time what the man has been talking about; and after the verb—merely by way of ornament, as far as I can make out—the writer shovels in 'haben sind gewesen gehabt geworden sein' or

310

words to that effect, and the monument is finished. . . . To learn to read and understand a German newspaper is a thing which must always remain an impossibility to a foreigner."

Yet the grammatical structure of a language is something that can be learned, and, in the German case, this is not as difficult as Mark Twain said it was. One has the feeling that his criticism is misdirected, and that the most frequent cause of foreign misunderstanding is not the sometimes clumsy form assumed by written and spoken German but rather the difficulty of determining what is actually being said. The non-German reader often has the impression of trying to cut his way through the jungles of words, many of which have no precise meaning, a good percentage of which are clearly redundant, and some of which appear to be superfluous. Nor is this an entirely mistaken impression. At various times in its recent history, the German language has proved to be alarmingly vulnerable to abstractness and density, overornamentation and linguistic xenophobia, and ideological manipulation. In inflicting these wounds upon a language which, at the end of the eighteenth century was a model of *claritas et elegantia*, philosophers, professors, Romantic intellectuals, soldiers and bureaucrats, editors of journals, guardians of morality, and agents of totalitarianism have all played their part, and the cumulative effect of their influence is still apparent and still represents a formidable barrier to effective communication with the outside world.

I

The creator of the German language, Heine wrote in his *History of Religion and Philosophy in Germany*, was Martin Luther; and this is no exaggeration, for whatever might be said of the literary products of Germany's various regional dialects, the foundations of a common German literary experience did not exist until the Monk of Wittenberg provided it. This he did with his translation of the Bible and his political and theological pamphlets, which were couched in a new language of incomparable lucidity and richness, vigorous and flexible in its expression and suited equally to the requirements of exposition and argumentation, of satire and humor. Luther made meaningless the gibe of his antagonist Emperor Charles V, who once said that the German language was fit only for speaking to horses; and when the new printing press made possible the dissemination of his writings to every part of the German states, his German rapidly became universal literary language. Because Luther's Bible is still widely read, its stylistic influence is not negligible even today.

The effect of the Lutheran model was, however, sharply diminished by the devastating results of the religious wars. During the Thirty Years War, Germany was overrun by mercenary armies of every nationality, and this caused the degeneration of language that one sees reflected in the songs of the *Landsknechte*, which are often polyglot mixtures like

Wir kamen vor Friaul
Wir kamen vor Friaul
Da hatt'n wir allesamt gross' Maul
Strampedemi
Alami presente al vostra signori

Moreover, the ascendancy of France in the years after the Peace of Westphalia threatened to compound the effects of the war and to destroy the cultural independence of the German states. With an insidious rapidity, French became the language of culture and elegance in Germany, and it was perhaps only natural that writers who desired a large audience should either abandon their own tongue or seek to make it conform to the requirements of French style. Among patriotic German writers, this aroused the liveliest apprehension, and one of them, the novelist Johann Michael Moscherosch, condemned "à la mode" literature and wrote scornfully of "our little Germans who trot to the French and have no heart of their own, no speech of their own, but French opinion is their opinion, French speech, food, drink, morals, and deportment their speech, food, drink, morals and deportment, whether they are good or bad."

This concern found more positive expression at the end of the seventeenth century in the writings of the philosopher Gottfried Wilhelm von Leibniz and the jurist Christian Thomasius. As president of the newly established Academy of Sciences in Berlin, Leibniz felt some responsibility to act as a spokesman in matters of German culture and, in two important essays on language, he argued that the best way for his countrymen to free themselves from foreign models would be to make their own language as effective an instrument for serious discourse as the French language was. To promote this end, he called for a serious program of improvement, embellishment and analysis, as well as the preparation of scientific lexica and dictionaries for current and archaic usages and technical terms.

Thomasius not only echoed these recommendations, but, in his university teaching at Leipzig and Halle, sought to give practical encouragement to the study of an effective native style by breaking the monopoly that Latin had had up to this time in university instruction and giving his lectures on language in German. He also wrote a series of philosophical works in the vernacular and, more important, founded the first German literary journal to make a serious attempt to reach a general audience. This experiment was not particularly successful, for Thomasius seems to have been incapable of divesting himself of his professorial manner; but others profited from his mistakes, and the early eighteenth century saw an explosion of journalistic activity that sought to emulate the current success of *The Tatler* and *The Spectator* of Joseph Addison and Richard Steele in England. Indeed, a good part of the contents of the so-called "moral journals" in Germany was made up of imitations or translations of their English models. This was not without positive benefit to the development of a German literary language, for something of the urbanity of English style crept in, and imitation of English models tended to discourage the too heavy German reliance upon the encapsulated style.

By this time the war against French influence had been won and much of the scientific and analytical work that Leibniz had called for had been accomplished. This progress was consolidated and the German language given a new stability in 1748 with the publication of Johann Christian Gottsched's *Establishment of a German Art of Speech, according to the Models of the Best Writers of the Past and Present Centuries*. Gottsched had the temerity to lay down firm rules and standards for modern usage, seeking to combine the best features of dialect German with that of the language of model writers since the time of Opitz; and, although he was attacked on the grounds of pedantry and conservatism, his standard German found general acceptance. In the fifty years that followed, German prose style found a new maturity in the epistolary style of Christian Fürchtegott Gellert, the novels of Christian Martin Wieland, and the critical writings of Gotthold Ephraim Lessing, who, despite his successful campaign to found a truly national theater, did not scruple to emulate Voltaire's prose style, which he translated into a clear muscular German of great intensity and bite.

It was, however, reserved for Johann Wolfgang Goethe to combine and harmonize all of the linguistic developments of the previous century. Born and raised in a city whose culture was impregnated with Imperial memories and Lutheranism, he understood, even before the meeting with Johann Gottfried Herder in 1770, which he called the turning point in his poetic life, that language, if it is to remain alive, must return frequently to its own past for replenishment. During his university years and his apprenticeship as a writer, he was strongly influenced by Gellert's emphasis on the natural style and by the theoretical writings of Friedrich Gottlieb Klopstock, who insisted on the importance of imagination, emotion and freedom from artificiality. All of these influences came together in those early works that so dazzled the German world—the drama *Götz von Berlichingen* and the novel *The Sorrows of Young Werther*—and found superb expression in *Wilhelm Meister's Apprenticeship*, where they were enhanced by Goethe's fertility in verbal experimentation and invention and his unique gifts of penetration and intensity. After *Wilhelm Meister*, no one had any reason to feel that the German language was in any sense inferior, in expressiveness or beauty, to that of any of its neighbors.

There were those, however, who were not satisfied with this achievement. Nietzsche, a notably clear writer, was fond of remarking that the German mind found no particular merit in clarity—that on the contrary it "loves clouds and all that is obscure . . . the uncertain, unformed, shifting, growing of every kind [it] feels to be 'profound.'" At the very moment when Gellert and Wieland were counseling Germans to write graceful, lucid and unadorned prose, this advice was being scornfully rejected by J. G. Hamann as alien to German culture. The model of style should, he argued, be found in the divine disorder of nature and in the reveries of biblical prophets seeking God, and to show what he meant he couched his own writings—as Eric Blackall, the British authority on the development of the German language, has written—in tangled, highly symbolic language, full of sibylline references and interruptions and intercalated quotations, which were powerful and striking but more often unintelligible, aphoristic and obscure. The difficulty of understanding Hamann's writings did not hurt—indeed, perhaps for the reasons advanced by Nietzsche, it seemed to enhance—his reputation; he came indeed to be known as the "mighty magus of the north." His style infected German prose writers like Jean Paul, with the result that the novels and stories of that brilliant and original writer are virtually inaccessible to the Western World, and they fascinated Herder and the young Hegel.

It is Hegel, much more than Hamann, who must bear responsibility for making stylistic obscurity respectable in academic and scientific writing. Philosophers before him had relatively little difficulty in expressing their views in reasonably straightforward language. Leibniz, for example, had believed that German might well become the ideal language for philosophy precisely because of its concreteness, which would facilitate lay understanding. Hegel himself was capable, at least in his youth, of writing a good plain style, as his essay "The Constitution of Germany" of 1788 demonstrates. But by the time he had begun work on *The Phenomenology of the Spirit*, which was to appear in 1807, he had abandoned his relative lucidity for a prose that has been the despair of legions of earnest students. Why he should have done this is by no means clear. One of his English editors, J. N. Findlay, has confessed that there is "much in the *Phenomenology* which is enigmatic, and one cannot always see why the route to Absolute Knowledge should wind through just these peculiar thickets." It is his guess, he continues, that Hegel was "swayed in his choice of words by a burgeoning unconscious," that "an afflatus seized him in the Jena lecture-rooms, an afflatus perhaps unique in philosophical history, which affected not only his ideas but his style, and which makes one at times only sure that he is saying something immeasurably profound and important, but not exactly what it is."

From the time when he went to the University of Berlin in 1817 until his death in 1831, Hegel occupied an almost monarchical position in German intellectual life. The profound influence that he exerted on other important figures—Ferdinand Lassalle, for example, and Karl Marx, and Leopold von Ranke and the whole of the Prussian historical school—need not concern us here. What has to be noted is that, as far as the style of academic discourse was concerned, his ascendancy can only be described as deplorable in its results. It persuaded minds less fertile and productive than his own that the hallmark of the intellect was abstraction and impenetrability, and it was responsible, at least in university circles, for the still prevalent notion that a work that can be read without difficulty need not be taken seriously. It is doubtless true that the elitism characteristic of the university system reinforced this conclusion, the dense and involuted style taking the place once occupied by Latin as the barrier separating the world of learning from the plebs. However that may be, in a society in which the professor was taken perhaps more seriously than he deserved, the emergence of a professorial style could not help but have deleterious effects upon the general state of the language.

A different kind of obscurity was introduced by the Romantic movement of the early nineteenth century, which was led in its revolt against the rationalism of the Enlightenment to the discovery that the language of Gottsched and Goethe was not adequate to its needs and which sought to supply what was lacking by nonliterary means. This was, given the nature of the movement, natural enough. In his study of language, *After Babel*, George Steiner has noted that conflicts between the artist and the middle class tend to make the former scornful of the prevailing idiom and that preoccupation with the unconscious and subconscious strata of the individual personality has the effect of eroding the generalized authority of syntax; and these observations fit the case of the Romantics admirably. In sharp contrast to such a socially well-adjusted person as Goethe, who was as proud of his service as minister of mines in the Grand Duchy of Weimar as he was of his poetry, the Romantics, with some exceptions, thought of themselves as artists who were doomed by their special gifts to be misunderstood by the rest of society. At the same time—and here again they differed from writers like Goethe and Schiller and Lessing—they were less interested in the real world than they were in a world that was created by people like themselves, in which the normal rules did not apply—a realm of fantasy, wonder and terror.

It was obvious to them that such a world could not be described and its secrets disclosed in the language of the moral weeklies or of Schiller's political dramas. It was difficult, indeed, to see how words alone could give an adequate impression of the depth of feeling, the intensity of experience, and the nobility of soul of the lonely outsiders about whom the Romantics delighted to write. They were convinced that the artist had feelings that lay beyond the emotional range of ordinary people and that he was capable of thoughts that lay too deep for tears. How then were these to be communicated? The Romantics' answer was by the creation of mood through symbol, incantation and music.

In a Romantic story there was rarely any systematic development of character or situation. The characters were one-dimensional and had no independent existence, serving for the most part as reflections of the protagonist's own thinking, as embodiments of his private hopes and fears. The action had no logical pattern or continuity but was for the most part a sequence of moods, evoked sometimes by stereotypical descriptions of nature (which, in the stories of Joseph von Eichendorff, seldom vary in any important detail), by the use of recurring symbols (the moon breaking through the clouds, or posthorns in the night), and by charged words that were intended to mean much more than they said. In the Romantic vocabulary, *Sehnsucht*, a much used term, does not mean a focused kind of desire but is really a portmanteau word that may mean anything from a melancholic feeling of affinity with nature to a hopeless recognition that the world is out of joint. In Ludwig Tieck's story "Der blonde Eckbert," the literal meaning of the word *Waldeinsamkeit* (forest solitude) is less important than its sound, which is intended to evoke a mood of regret for lost innocence and a desire to flee from the delusions of the real world into the security of a simpler past. The Romantic style depended upon a language that was both illogical and inexact, in which words had no precise meanings and were, in fact, intended to be imprecise, to arouse desires or doubts or apprehension or that vague sentimental feeling that a later irreverent generation was to call "soul-tickling" (*Seelenschmus*). The result was a cloudy dreamlike prose which was intended to be felt rather than comprehended and which tended to dissolve if subjected to the process of translation into English or French—a prose, in fact, that resembled music more than speech.

Nor was this an accident. If fantasy was the Romantics' stock in trade, music was the ally of fantasy. It fascinated the writers of this generation, and the nineteenth-century German cultural philosopher Wilhelm Dilthey once pointed out that the form of many Romantic stories was often designedly musical, a contrived exercise in tone and modulation. Similarly, when purely literary expedients failed them, the Romantics were apt to fall back upon musical substitutes. In Tieck's stories and in Eichendorff's, the narrative is frequently interrupted by songs which are intended either to give emotional coloration to an incident or to tell readers what the characters are feeling. Here again one senses a Romantic conviction that language is inadequate to express the depth and complexity of the individual soul and the innermost meaning of life, and that music is the proper vehicle for this, and is, indeed, the true German language.

This feeling found encouragement in the writings of that most Romantic of philosophers, Arthur Schopenhauer, whose vogue was so great in mid-century Germany. In a remarkable passage in the third book of *The World as Will and Idea*, Schopenhauer talks about music as "a universal language in the highest sense, which has roughly the same relationship to the universality of concepts as these have to individual things. . . . This intimate relationship which music has to the true essence of all things explains why, when appropriate music sounds in any scene or action or event or environment, it seems to open up to us its most secret meaning and supplies the most accurate and intelligible commentary upon it. For music is different from all the other arts in the sense that it is not a copy of the appearance or, more accurately, the adequate objectivity of the Will but the unconditional copy of the Will itself and, therefore, to everything that is physical in the world it is the metaphysical, to every appearance it represents the essence (*das Ding an sich*). One could in consequence just as well call the world embodied music as embodied Will: hence it is understandable why music throws every painting—indeed every scene of actual life and the world—into bold relief in heightened significance."

What this means in any practical sense, it is not easy to say, but it clearly assigns a magic power to music. Indeed, Schopenhauer rejected Leibniz's commonsense definition of music as an unconscious exercise in arithmetic by the mind that doesn't know it's counting (*exercitium arithmeticae occultum nescientis se numerare animi*) and changed it to read an unconscious exercise in metaphysics by the mind which doesn't know it's philosophizing (*exercitium metaphysices occultum nescientis se philosophari animi*), a subtle enhancement that was gratifying to the Romantic temperament.

This elevation of music at the expense of language was resisted by nineteenth century enemies of Romanticism. Leaders of the Young Germany movement like Karl Gutzkow and Ludwig Börne and Naturalists like Heinrich Hart regarded music as a suspicious art which, by its appeal to the emotions, was an enemy of reason, the cause of which, they believed, was best advanced by their own kind of hard and uncompromising prose. But the claims of prose were rejected by the Romantics with contumely. In his essay "Richard Wagner at Bayreuth" in 1872, Friedrich Nietzsche declared that language was "a terrible sickness" that was oppressing all human development, that it was a malevolent power that thwarted human aspiration so that "when people seek through mutual understanding to work together, the madness of general concepts—yes, of mere word-sounds—seizes them and . . . the creations of their common meaning are stamped with the sign of misunderstanding . . . [with] the emptiness of those imperious words and concepts. . . . And so one is the slave of words; under this compulsion no one can reveal himself any longer . . . and few can save their individuality." Only music could correct this situation, Nietzsche wrote, for music was "the enemy of all conventions, all artistic alienation, and all lack of comprehension between individual and individual. Music is the return to nature and simultaneously the purification and transformation of nature. . . . In its art rings the sound of nature transformed into love."

It was not difficult for people who had this kind of reverence of music to become convinced that to become attuned to its more profound language gave one a moral superiority over the glibber peoples of the word. The thesis of Thomas Mann's *Reflections of an Unpolitical Man*, which appeared during the First World War, was that the use of language for analytical reasons was antithetical to the musically contemplative German mind, and the book contained extraordinary attacks upon Mann's brother Heinrich for having failed to appreciate the superiority of German *Kultur* and for having become a *Zivilisationsliterat*, a scribbler in behalf of Western ideas of civilization and a defender of France, a country in which politics and "its twin sister literature" had supplanted music and "usurped the highest rank in the social-artistic interest of the nation."

Nietzsche, after his break with Wagner, altered his view and wrote that music was "a drug of the worst sort, especially dangerous to a nation given to hard drinking and one that vaunts intellectual ferment for its power both to intoxicate the mind and to befog it"; and Mann too, when the course of history convinced him that Germany's musicality was a weakness rather than a sign of cultural superiority, reversed his position. In *The Magic Mountain* (1924), the German protagonist's mentor Settembrini warns him that music is an opiate that militates against clarity of expression and thought ("Beer, tobacco, and music! Behold your fatherland!"), whereas "the word [is] the glory of mankind, it alone imparts dignity to life. Not only [is] humanism bound up with the word . . . but so [is] humanity itself." He deplores the fact that Germans have come to have an uneasy relationship with language and describes this as a danger to the world. "You do not love the word," Settembrini says, "or you have it not, or you are chary with it to unfriendliness. The articulate world does not know where it is with you. My friend, that is perilous. The word, even the most contradictory word, preserves contact."

Later still, at the end of the Second World War, Mann came back to the problem, which, indeed never ceased to trouble him and which was to be the principal theme of his last great novel, *Doktor Faustus*. In a speech entitled "Germany and the Germans," he referred to a passage in *Cousin Pons*, in which Balzac describes a German musician who was a master of harmony but always left the voice parts to his French collaborator. His country, Mann said, had suffered deeply from this tendency to prefer the music to the words. "Such musicality of the soul must be paid for dearly in other spheres—in the political, the sphere of the common life of human beings."

II

The deleterious effects of professorial profundity (sometimes called *Hegelei*) and of the fantasy and musicality of the Romantics were well developed long before Germany became a unified nation. When the campaign that was to achieve that goal got under way, another threat to the economy and clarity of the language appeared, this time in the patriotic rhetoric of the middle class that was the main support of the national movement. The literary style of the bourgeoisie resembled their taste in furniture; it tended to be both ostentatious and overstuffed. A typical example is a speech delivered by Gabriel Riesser in 1859, the so-called "Schiller Year" which celebrated the hundredth anniversary of the poet's birth and in the course of which, by means of a selective reading of his works, he was metamorphosed into a champion of German unity.

Introduced by a flourish of trumpets, Riesser began his speech with the words, "May the echo of the thousand-voiced jubilation that has pierced your ears in those tones that have now died away, riot forth in your souls! The noble creation of music, dedicated to the glorification of the memory of a great man, has never found a worthier subject, has never proclaimed a loftier, more universal festival mood than in this movement," continuing in this vein of insistent idealism, false pathos, and verbal bombast for well over an hour. In his interesting book *The Philistines' Ideology*, Hermann Glaser has analyzed the diction and style of Riesser's speech and found that every thirty-third word is a term of enhancement—that is, a comparative or a superlative—and that, in addition, there are many adjectival enhancements, like "mighty roaring," "lofty tones," "powerful genius," and the like. To emphasize that Schiller was noble, sublime, mighty, lordly, and incomparable, the appropriate words were generally embellished, the adjectives "*hoh*" and "*hoch*" (high, lofty) appearing sixty times. The dead poet was characterized as the embodiment of "the loftiest and noblest development," as "the pure flowering of the natural, the most beautiful bloom, the sweetest fruit," and as possessing "the tenderest and deepest sensitivities, the purest spirituality, the highest powers, and the most elemental and childlike emotions," all in the same sentence.

This relentless parade of superlatives, this piling up of synonyms, this smothering of nouns under the weight of adjectives, this constant straining for noble effect by mere verbosity represented a grave threat to the language as a means of communication. But this was not appreciated by Riesser's auditors, who regarded his stylistic tumescence as the height of eloquence. Nor was it only in this kind of public oratory, an activity that by its very nature appears to invite verbal extravagance, that the bourgeoisie approved and appeared to desire this swollen style. In the family magazines that supplied much of their literary entertainment, the same excesses appear, often heightened by that combination of moralizing and sentimentality that has earned the name *Kitsch*. This was the stock-in-trade of *Die Gartenlaube*, the most widely read of such journals in the years form 1850 to 1900 and a mirror both of the enlightened humanitarianism of the liberal bourgeoisie and of its literary and stylistic preferences.

In a preface directed "to all friends and readers" in the first issue of *Die Gartenlaube*, the stylistic tone was clearly set. "Greetings in the name of God, dear people in the German Land!" the editors wrote. "When you sit in the long winter evenings in the circle of your loved ones in the cosy chimney corner, or in the spring, when the white and red blossoms fall from the apple trees, with a few friends in the shadowed arbor, then read our magazine. May it be a paper for the House and the Family; a book for the big and the small, for anyone who has a warm heart beating behind his ribs and still takes joy in the Good and the Noble. . . . And, over all of it, may the breath of Poesy float like the fragrance from the blossoming flower, and may you be reminded of Home in our *Gartenlaube*, in which you find that good German tenderness of feeling (*Gemütlichkeit*), which speaks to the Heart. So try it with us, and, therewith, may God be with you!" If this suffered less from flatulence than the style of Riesser's speech, it was nevertheless indicative of an all too prevalent tendency to use language in a way that hid the sharp edges and angles of reality under sentimental stereotypes and subordinated the explicit meaning of words to their evocative power. It was a language that could be used to exalt the ordinary events of domestic life to a degree that might have baffled Mark Twain as much as the German newspaper did but was apparently highly congenial to the majority of *Die Gartenlaube*'s readers. Certainly, this kind of prose was widely imitated. The journals of Cosima Wagner are largely composed in it. Cosima and her husband do not simply arise in the morning; instead, they "gloriously salute this day." They do not go quietly to bed as ordinary people do; rather "in exalted tiredness [they] give [themselves] to rest." Even after the more cultivated sections of the bourgeoisie grew ashamed of it, this style persisted in the sentimental novels of E. J. Marlitt and Hedwig Courths-Mahler, which were the staple reading of the lower middle class.

The establishment of the German Empire in 1871 subjected the language to new strains that arose from the changed political conditions. The role played by the Prussian army in unifying Germany had profound social effects, among which was a widespread veneration of the Prussian General Staff, which was credited with the victories over Austria and France, and a tendency on the part of the wealthy middle class to regard the acquisition of reserve commissions in the officer corps as socially necessary for their sons; and it was inevitable that the language could not remain unaffected by these developments.

The metaphors of power began to affect newspaper editorials, parliamentary speeches, university lectures, and historical writing; and a new unconditionality of language marked both Heinrich von Treitschke's lectures on politics at the University of Berlin and the speeches of the industrialist Stumm Hallberg, and other *Geheimratsübermenschen* (supermen of the business world) who seemed to regard their factories as military commands.

At the same time, as the feudalization of the middle class proceeded, private discourse was affected by what came to be called the Prussian style. This apparently originated during the Napoleonic period in the diffidence and inarticulateness of King Frederick William III, who spoke in fragments, allowing verb forms or single phrases to stand for whole sentences. In time, this lapidary form of communication hardened into a peremptory, somewhat insolent ("*schnoddrig*") garrison and casino language (*Kommisston*), which was admired and used outside the army because it seemed to be the style of a superior caste and, in some cases, because its employment, in imperious formulations like "*Bisschen dalli!*" or "*Weitermachen!*" or "*Schnauze!*", seemed to connote qualities of decisiveness and moral force.

It should be noted parenthetically that, within the army itself, and particularly in the staff and the professional schools, the literary standard was high. Staff officers were trained to write an uncluttered and economical prose, and a remarkable number of them developed into writers of some distinction. At the beginning of the nineteenth century, Clausewitz demonstrated the ability to discuss the most complicated of strategical questions in graceful and readily intelligible prose; Helmuth von Moltke's letters from Turkey in the 1830s had literary qualities of the highest order; and the memoirs of the wars of 1866 and 1870 by the artillery commander Prinz Kraft zu Hohenlohe-Ingelfingen were written in a prose as energetic and vibrant as the war accounts of the distinguished journalist (and later novelist) Theodor Fontane. As the century progressed, however, and warfare was mechanized, so was the style of its practitioners; and the writing of the Schlieffen generation of staff officers was marked by a growing incursion of technical jargon.

Two other developments of the nineteenth century deserve at least cursory attention. The first was the result of the progressive bureaucratization of society, which brought with it the proliferation of the lifeless, redundant, legalistic prose that is characteristic of statute books and instructions for the completion of income tax forms. Christian Morgenstern made fun of this in his poem "The Magistracy," in which his hero Korf, who has received a citation from the police to appear in court for purposes of identification and registration, replies in a bureaucratese designed to discourage further requests.

Korf erwidert darauf kurz und rund: ¦
"Einer hohen Direktion
stellt sich, laut persönlichem Befund,

untig angefertigte Person
als nichtexistent im Eigen-Sinn
bürgerlicher Konvention

vor und aus und zeichnet, wennschonhin
mitbedauernd nebigen Betreff,
Korf. (An die Bezirksbehörde in——.)"

Staunend liest der anbetroffene Chef.

[Korf writes:—"To the Worshipful Direction
May the undermanufactured mention
That, whereas, per personal inspection,

He is found and filed with due attention
as—say—nonexistent as within
Civil juridicular convention,

Now he, albethough he is not seen,
Condeplores above regard. (Undated!)
Yours . . . *Korf.* (To the Magistrate's Court in——.)"

Which upsets the Old Chief concernated.]

Bureaucracies are singularly humorless, and Morgenstern's spoof did not prevent their spread or alter the fact that bureaucratic language has a seductive power and leads some people to believe that it invests prose with weight and authority. There were lots of such people in Germany.

Finally, the grace and effectiveness of the language were endangered by regressive and xenophobic tendencies in Imperial Germany that survived the First World War and became even stronger during the Weimar Republic. These were largely the result of that fear of modernity which, as we have seen elsewhere in this volume, affected part of German society and found expression in hostility toward the city, idealization of rural life, and—as a result of the agitations of certain patriotic groups in the decades before the First World War and after the defeat of 1918—a fear of contamination by foreign ideas. With respect to language, the result was an enthusiasm for archaic formulations and prose that was rich in reference to blood and soil, as in Hermann Löns's stories about the Lüneburg Heath and the work of the Rhinelander Wilhelm Schäfer, who wished to destroy the dominance of Berlin over German cultural life and to return German literature to the *Volk*, and tried to do this by means of his *The Thirteen Books of the German Soul* (1922), which was written in a contrived and contorted prose best described as bogus-Allemanic.

The activities of these *Heimatdichter*, as they were sometimes called, found expression also in a new effort to cleanse the language of foreign words, which was the aim of Eduard Engel in his popular work *Entwelschung: Verdeutschungswörterbuch*, which first appeared in 1917. In the late seventeenth century, when the possibility of an irreversible corruption of the German language by foreign terms was very real, Leibniz had called for an energetic effort to prevent this. But Leibniz had favored the elimination only of those foreign terms for which there were effective German equivalents, and he had recognized that there were many non-German words that were not only useful but enriched the language. Engel would admit of no such exceptions. Like a new Hermann the Cherusker in front of the Roman legions, he laid about him, exterminating the Latin tags beloved by German parliamentarians (*panem et circenses, rebus sic stantibus*), the term long used to designate the graduate of a Gymnasium (*Abiturient*), the description of the profession that Bismarck had practiced (*Diplomatie*). For these, he insisted, with what can only be regarded as insensitivity, *Brot und Vergnügen, wie die Dinge stehen, Abgangsschüler*, and *Staatenverkehr* would do as well. *Die Toilette* he insisted must be replaced according to the sense implied, by either the clumsy *Ankleidezimmer* or the faintly ridiculous *Abort* ("off-place"). As for the succulent *Bouletten*, beloved by Berliners who were proud of the Huguenot contribution to their city and its language, Engel suggested, rather offensively, that they should be renamed *Klösse*, like Bavarian dumplings, which they did not resemble.

III

It was during the Third Reich that all of the tendencies remarked upon here reached their most extreme expression. The rush of new converts to the National Socialist movement in the first days after Hitler's accession to power—the so-called *Märzgefallene*—included the great majority of the holders of university chairs and of the intellectual community, and these people brought the professorial style to new heights of complexity in their efforts to justify the new regime and establish its roots in Germany's history and cultural tradition. In these exercises, the philosopher Martin Heidegger played a stellar role, proclaiming that Hitler and the German people were bound by fate and "guided by the inexorability of that spiritual mission that the destiny of the German people forcibly impresses upon its history." At the same time, the militarization of the language, which had begun after 1871, received new impetus, for the combative stance of the NSDAP seemed to require a language that would fit it, and the air rang with words like *Kampf, Schlacht, Einsatz, Einheit, Front* and *Durchbruch*, borrowed from the vocabulary of the army, and awkward compounds of these that gave a military tone to literally anything the new government interested itself in, a word like *Arbeitsschlacht* referring to the campaign to reduce unemployment, *Erzeugungsschlacht* to the Nazi program for increasing the birthrate, *Ernährungsschlacht* to its agricultural policy, and so on. Thus, if the harvest was good, this would be announced jubilantly in the *Völkischer Beobachter*, the official party newspaper, as "a breakthrough (*Durchbruch*) in East Prussia."

The style of the new regime was an eclectic one. It availed itself freely of the inflated and sentimental mode to which the lower middle class, which formed the bulk of party membership, had become accustomed. Its use of superlatives and adjectival prefixes of enhancement, like *einmalig* (unique), *historisch* (historical), *Welt* (world) and *gross* (great), was unrestrained, the Führer's actions rarely being described as of less than "world historical importance"; and its penchant for pathetic effect and *Kitsch* can be seen in any analysis of the language of speeches made on the occasion of the Führer's birthday.

It was colored also by the hatred of foreign terms that was characteristic of the *Heimatdichter* (the Reich Chamber of Culture was perpetually engaged in cleansing operations) as well as by their blood-and-soil terminology (BLUBO) and their penchant for archaicisms. The working force of a factory was often called *die Gefolgschaft* (the body of followers), a word that had an old German ring and connotations of vassalage and fealty and unquestioned service under natural leaders. But despite these affectations and an antiurban tone that one finds, for example, in Joseph Goebbels's contemptuous use of the noun "asphalt" and the invented verb *asphaltieren* ("The Jew *asphaltiert* with crooked phrases and slippery promises"), the language of the Third Reich was replete with technical terms borrowed from the selfsame modern industry that the agrarian Romantics hated, and Hitler himself was fond of using foreign terms for effect, not always, it should be added, correctly or appropriately.

In the years before the party assumed power (later known officially as the *Kampfzeit* or time of struggle), the American economist and publicist Peter Drucker once heard a Nazi speaker telling a crowd of farmers, "We don't want higher bread prices! We don't want lower bread prices! And we don't want bread prices to remain the same! We want *National Socialist* bread prices!" The language of National Socialism mirrored this kind of contempt for rationality. Hitler's speeches were designed to break down the emotional resistance of his hearers rather than to appeal to their intellectual faculties, and his greatest oratorical efforts, at the annual party conferences in Nuremberg, depended, like the Romantic prose of the early nineteenth century, upon symbol and ritual and music for their magical power. His language, which was often incomparably clumsy and vulgar, drew its strength from the *Stimmung* (mood) created by nonliterary means. In Nazi usage words like "intelligence" and "objectivity" were bad words; "feeling" and "will" were good ones. Alfred Rosenberg, the philosopher of the movement, railed against people who moved on purely logical paths, "advancing from one conclusion to another . . . on the basis of the axioms of reason." It was necessary to get rid of "the whole bloodless intellectualistic garbage heap of purely schematic systems." Hitler certainly agreed. It was not, in his view, the duty of good Germans to analyze situations and take considered action. They were supposed to "feel," to "hear the voice of blood," to "sense the ecstasy of destiny" (a term invented by Heidegger), and then to act with "hardness" and "fanaticism" as their leader commanded.

Fanatisch and *hart* were much-used Nazi words, and, as Viktor Klemperer has pointed out in his absorbing analysis of the language of the Third Reich, they were always used in a sense that was opposite to their pre-1933 meaning, which had negative associations with madness in the one case and brutality in the other. Under the new dispensation, to be hard was to be strong, unyielding and heroic, and to be fanatical was to be dedicated to the cause and ready to make any sacrifice for it. *Fanatisch* was a word to which Hitler became increasingly addicted during the Second World War, and, to the despair of his staff officers, he used it as the key to all problems. His speeches to them were all variants of one made late in the conflict, in which the Führer said:

> Originality is something like a will-o'-the-wisp if it isn't based on steadfastness and fanatical tenacity. That's the most important thing in all human existence. People who only get fancies and ideas and that sort of thing . . . won't accomplish anything . . . One can make world history only when, in addition to a good head, an active conscience, and an eternal watchfulness, one has a fanatical steadfastness, a power of belief that makes a person a warrior to the very marrow.

"Fanatic" and "hard" were not the only words to which the Nazis assigned new meaning. The once respectable words "system" and "systematic" now became suspect, for the noun *das System* was used as a term of reprobation for the Weimar Republic and the moral obliquity and cultural degeneration that the Nazis insisted had been its principal characteristics. The modest word "organic" was exalted to mean something like "true to, and arising from, the blood and soil of the fatherland." Thus, "organic," when used with "philosophy" deprived the noun of its meaning and referred to a kind of feeling that rejected the tyranny of reason. "*Rücksichtslos*," which once meant "without consideration" and was vaguely pejorative, now—at least when it was applied to patriotic Germans—acquired the positive sense of "energetic" and "intent on achieving one's goal." Similarly, to do something blindly (*blindlings*) no longer signified thoughtless action; on the contrary, "blind obedience" was almost as admirable as "fanatical steadfastness."

This subversion of the language was intended to change the way the German people thought about politics and life, and it was promoted by all of the resources of the government. The Nazi Party exercised complete control over the educational system and the instruments of mass communication, and the minister of culture and propaganda, Joseph Goebbels, used that power shrewdly, with the intention, he once said, of propagating a "terminology compatible with our philosophy of State." Goebbels issued explicit directives to the press, listing the subjects that should receive attention and the manner in which they should be treated and providing lists of formulations that were approved and words that were henceforth forbidden. (Thus, on December 13, 1937, an "urgent instruction" stipulated that "from today the word *Völkerbund* [League of Nations] will no longer be used by the German press. This word no longer exists.") Similar directives applied to schoolbooks, and the result was an imposed uniformity of language that constricted expression and influenced thinking. How, for instance, could the constant association of certain adjectives with certain nouns help but form stereotypes that allowed for no exceptions? If the Versailles Treaty was called "shameful" and "criminal" every time it was mentioned in print or in public discourse, it became difficult to consider the possibility that it might have redeeming features.

During the Nazi period, such stereotypes systematically poisoned the German mind. Granted that anti-Semitism had existed in Germany long before Hitler was a political force, it is hard to believe that the German people would have tolerated the enormities of his treatment of the Jews if it had not been for the relentless use of adjectives like "cunning," "sneaky," "deceitful," "corrupt," "lecherous," "treasonable," "cowardly," "parasitic" and "rootless" in every context in which the word "Jew" appeared, if it had not been for the constant association of the Jews with the defeat of 1918, the Treaty of Versailles, and the threat of Communism, and had the Nazis not invented frightening words that were designed not only to discourage contact with the Jews but to make them appear subhuman and bent upon defiling the purity of the German race—words like *Judenknecht* (Jewboy), *Judenhure*, (Jewish whore) and *Volksverratёr* (traitor to the people) for Germans who had Jewish friends, and *Blutschande* (defilement of the blood) and *Rassenschande* (racial defilement) for erotic relations with them.

Hitler's declaration of war on Poland in September 1939 spurred the managers of the language of the Third Reich on to new forms of manipulation. It is significant that the first communiqué was phrased in such a way as to disguise Germany's responsibility for the coming of the war: "Since yesterday morning we have been answering the enemy's fire." Subsequently, in contrast to the generally sober and reasonably exact army bulletins of the First World War, Nazi communiqués were either wildly exaggerated, which was true of the years of victory, when superlatives seemed likely to discourage the enemy and to still the apprehensions of a population that had not greeted war with enthusiasm, or, once the tide of battle had turned, evasive and mendacious. After 1942–1943, the use of words like "retreat," "withdrawal" or "defeat" did not appear in the war bulletins and were forbidden to the press. Alternative formulations like "setback" were permissible in contexts that implied a temporary situation. Lines were not supposed to be "broken" by the enemy but "straightened" by the Germans, a euphemism that discreetly veiled the losses involved. German troops, who were always "brave" or "heroic" (adjectives that were not allowed to be used for the enemy), were never "thrown back" by the enemy; they "detached themselves" or, when it was impossible to deny the fact that an encirclement by the enemy was in progress, they "fought themselves free." The trouble with this sort of thing was that it was belied by what was said by soldiers returning from the eastern front and by the mounting casualty lists; and people began to read the bulletins with a critical eye. Klemperer tells of a friend who, in December 1941, told him that the war was going miserably in Africa and, when asked how he knew, pointed to the words "our heroically fighting troops" in the latest bulletin. "*Heldenhaft* sounds like an obituary," he said. "You can count upon it."

The practice of euphemism was used also to hide the realities of National Socialist domestic policy from the German people. From the very beginning of the regime, the Nazis had been ingenious in inventing impersonal terms for dreadful things, borrowing them sometimes from the world of mechanics. The term *Gleichschaltung*, which encompassed the abolition of political parties and the trade unions in 1933–1934 and the subsequent elimination from public and professional life of persons whom the Nazis regarded as dangerous or undesirable, is an engineering term meaning "putting into the same gear"; it was sufficiently abstract and technical to divert the mind from the thought of what it might mean in human terms. For what happened during the Night of the Long Knives in June 1934 and inside camps like Dachau, the words *töten* and *niedermachen* (kill) were too explicit to be employed freely; *liquidieren* and *entledigen*, words from the world of business meaning to finish the job, had the advantage of turning the victims into objects. Similarly, the program for the killing off of the mentally ill and retarded was discreetly masked by the word "euthanasia," which was sufficiently unknown and imprecise in meaning to hide the brutal facts.

In the procedures that were followed in the course of murdering 6 million European Jews, the same verbal delicacy was observed. The policy received the designation "the Final Solution"; and the fate of the victims—according to H. J. Adler, who was an inmate of Theresienstadt and other extermination camps and had occasion to study the jargon of the executioners—was variously described as "wandering off" (*abwandern*), "evacuation," "sending away" (*abschieben*), "ghettoizing," "rubbing out" (*ausmerzen*) and—in his view—one of the most ghastly of the Nazi formulations—"special handling" (*Sonderbehandlung* or SB). The death squads went about their grisly business under the name *Sonderkommandos*.

The language of bureaucracy was also a boon to those who wished to impersonalize the operations of the death camps. Much of the correspondence of Rudolf Hoess, the commandant of Auschwitz, was concerned with quotas and rates of disposal and sounded as if he were the manager of a synthetics firm or a factory for the conversion of waste materials. In July 1941, when Hermann Goering, the plenipotentiary for the Four Year Plan, wanted to let Reinhard Heydrich know that the the official machinery of the government would be at his disposal for the killing off of the Jewish population, he wrote:

> As supplement to the task that was entrusted to you in the decree dated January 24, 1939, to solve the Jewish question by emigration and evacuation in the most favorable way possible, I herewith commission you to carry out all necessary preparations with regard to organizational, substantive and financial viewpoints for a total solution of the Jewish question in the German sphere of influence in Europe.
>
> Insofar as the competencies of other central organizations are hereby affected, these are to be involved.

It is doubtful whether one could find a more shameful example of the language of the Third Reich, unless it were the mawkishly sentimental and morally illiterate speech of Heinrich Himmler to the SS Group Leaders in Posen in October 1943 in which he said:

> I want to speak here before you in all openness about a very delicate subject. Among us it should be talked about quite openly, but despite this we shall never talk about it in public. . . . I mean the evacuation of the Jews, the extermination of the Jewish people. This is one of those things that one says easily enough. "The Jewish people will be exterminated," says many a party comrade. "OK—stands in the program—elimination of Jews—extermination—we'll do it." And then they come, the 80 million worthy Germans, and every one has his good Jew. It's clear; the rest are all swine; but this one is a first-class Jew. Of all the people who talk that way, none has seen it happen, none has been through it. The most of you know what it means when a hundred corpses are lying together, when five hundred are lying there, or

when a thousand are lying there. To have seen that through and while doing so—leaving aside exceptions owing to human weakness—to have maintained our integrity, that has made us hard. This is an unwritten and never-to-be-written page of glory in our history.

IV

One of the principal themes of Günter Grass's novel *Dog Years* is the role played by language in creating National Socialism, propagating its doctrines, and hiding its crimes, and the book is filled with devastating attacks upon the manipulators and corrupters of the German tongue. In the section devoted to the climax of the war, Grass shows the Third Reich expiring to the accompaniment of an endless and mindless stream of military communications couched in Heideggerian prose. "The Nothing is coming-to-be between enemy armor and our own spearheads," one of these reads. "The Nothing will be after-accomplished on the double. Each and every activity of the Nothing attuned to distantiality will be substantivized in view of final victory, so that later, sculptured in marble or shell-lime, it may be at-hand in a state of to-be-viewedness."

This passage may have been in Peter Dimitriu's mind when, in October 1977, he wrote an article in *Le Monde*, warning that the malevolent combination of the language of power and that of philosophy was still at work in the German Federal Republic. It would be difficult, he wrote, to find in England and France anything comparable to the constant citing, in any context, of philosophers like Hegel, Marx, Ernst Bloch, Nietzsche, Oswald Spengler, Max Stirner and Herbert Marcuse to justify violence, and the language itself reflected this situation. Words like *bezwingen, bewältigen, überwinden* had connotations of force that were absent in their French equivalents "vaincre," "surmonter," "dépasser"; *richterliche Gewalt* was clearly more threatening than "pouvoir judiciare"; and so was *Gewaltakt* compared to "acte de violence." Such metaphors, M. Dimitriu continued, appeared in discussions of ideas, in political and administrative jargon, in advertising, and in sports reporting. It was perhaps possible to make too much of this, but surely it was not insignificant that, when the English talked about the power to constrain, they used the word "control," whereas the Germans said *Verfügungsgewalt*.

Dimitriu's concern is a reflection of the entirely understandable French fear of a German relapse into Nazism, but there have been no significant signs of this in the years that have passed since Hitler's Reich came tumbling down, and a balanced view would indicate that the language, like the country, has freed itself from the imprint of National Socialism.

That it was able to do so—to cleanse itself of the perversions and corruptions of the Nazi experience and to demonstrate its ability to speak in a new key and to meet the needs of a pluralistic society—was the result of a combination of forces. In the first years after 1945, the Occupying Powers played their part by their policies of re-education and denazification and by the discretion they employed in granting licenses for the operation of newspapers and radio stations. After sovereignty was restored to Western Germany, the various regional ministries of education made a major contribution by their hard work in purging school curricula of materials that were tainted by association with National Socialism or written in the style of the Third Reich. A new generation of writers, led by Hans Werner Richter, began in 1947 to try, by periodic meetings and the force of their own example, to build a new literature on the basis of a liberated language, an effort that Günter Grass, who was a member of the group, commemorated in 1979 in his novel about the state of the German language at the end of the Thirty Years War, *The Meeting at Telgte.* And, not least important, the sharp impetus to modernization that was provided by the "economic miracle" of the 1950s, the revolution in communications that brought the outside world closer to Germany than it had ever been before, and the accelerated rate of change that characterized all industrial society in the second half of the twentieth century had the effect of making the Nazi experience recede into an indistinct past.

As the Nazi stamp upon language disappeared, so did the rhetorical excesses that had been the products of nineteenth century nationalism and the military images and the inflated *Schwulst* that had been characteristic of both the Wilhelmine and the Nazi political style. It would be difficult to compile a book called "Parliamentary Eloquence in the German Federal Republic" because, with a few exceptions, Bonn politicians have avoided the high-flown phrase and opted for plain speaking, even at the cost of dullness, and newspapers, even in their *Feuilleton* pages, have tended to do the same. In an age of prosiness, there was, moreover, no place for the excesses of the Romantic style, with its emphasis on symbolism and its inarticulate search for deeper meanings. The vogue that Hermann Hesse enjoyed among the university generation in the United States in the 1960s was nonexistent in Germany, and the prose of Ernst Jünger no longer had the power to inspire imitation.

In the place of these influences came new ones: first of all, the flood of English and American expressions that entered the language during the occupation period and later, more persistently, when television became well established and American features became a regular and popular part of its programs. Language purists deplored the excessive eagerness with which their countrymen sought to anglicize or Americanize their speech, and they had some reason to do so, since many of the adopted words and expressions had no clear meaning in their new context. These, however, having no merit but modishness, soon disappeared. The borrowings that have established themselves have done so, either because they say something without the clumsiness of the older word— *Wochenende* for *Ende der Woche, Filterzigaretten* for *Zigaretten mit Mundstück, Importe* for *Einführen, frustriert* for the inexact *un-*

erfüllt—or because they are part of an international language that defies translation—computer, stress, hobby, hot jazz, jeans. It seems clear that these and such direct translations of new American expressions as *Umweltverschmutzung* (environmental pollution) have enriched the language.

Whether the influence of the advertising profession has been equally positive is more doubtful. There are those who hold that the greatest contribution to forthrightness of speech since the days of Martin Luther has been the advertising jingle, and certainly there is a charming directness to

> Ganz furchtbar schimpft der Opa.
> Die Oma hat kein PAECH-BROT da
>
> [Grandpa's cursing wakes the dead;
> Grandma gave him no Paech's bread!]

or

> Was Sauerstoff für Deine Lunge,
> ein guter Wein für Deine Zunge,
> und für dein Herz 'ne Schmusekatze,
> Das ist TOPHEAD für Deine Glatze.
>
> [Oxygen is for the lungs;
> Good red wine delights the tongue;
> A cuddly girl will get you hot;
> TOPHEAD's for that mean bald spot!]

But when one leaves the verse for the prose, the charm disappears, and one encounters, as Hans Weigel has written, "a new language . . . , a language that was never spoken, that doesn't exist, that can't exist, that ought not exist, in which we are preached at, whispered to, hinted at . . . by hucksters of the representative sample, cross-section analysts of powdered soups, bards of body-odor and bad breath, psalmists of under-arm moistness." The inventions of such people are less a sign of linguistic vitality than a cheapening of language for purely material ends.

It is possible, of course, that non-Germans, particularly those from Western countries, will experience relatively little difficulty in comprehending what is being said in advertising-German, for the style transcends national boundaries and the message is the same in all languages. But what of the accessibility of the language in general? To what extent does it facilitate foreign understanding of Germany?

At the outset, it may be remarked that a Mark Twain *redivivus* would find German newspapers less impenetrable than they were in the nineteenth century. It is true that the interminable sentences that he complained of can still be found in leading journals like the *Frankfurter Allgemeine Zeitung* or the *Süddeutsche Zeitung*, although far less frequently than was once the case. But papers like Axel Springer's chief organ *Die Welt* cultivate a more succinct style, and the popular press, of which *Bild-Zeitung* is the most widely read example, go in for short sentences, one-paragraph stories, and a lively but simple idiom.

But this is misleading. The greatest barrier confronting the foreigner who seeks an understanding of contemporary Germany by reading its journals and books is that there seems to be no universally accepted standard High German anymore. A mastery of the dignified and somewhat stuffy style of the *Frankfurter Allgemeine Zeitung* does not prepare one to unravel the complexities of *Der Spiegel*, a weekly journal that is written in radical-chic German that is designed to be outrageous and abounds in unusual combinations and linguistic inventions; and the problems awaiting the foreigner in the world of scholarship are even more formidable. The professorial style was always, as we have seen, an obstacle to easy comprehension, but at least it was true, in the days before Hitler, that there was a rough uniformity of view in the attitudes that university faculty members held regarding social and political problems. This can no longer be counted on, and the result has been a perceptible increase in the amount of general theorizing that has crept into contemporary scholarship. It is not easy to find a recent book in history in which the author applies himself to his subject without writing a fifty-page theoretical preface first. Moreover, the theorists always seem to belong to schools, and the schools have private languages that have to be understood if the works of their members are to be properly appreciated. This is not easy for the foreigner who may not have learned to recognize, from the employment of terms like *systemimmanent* and *umfunktionieren*, what wavelength he is supposed to tune into. He is apt to feel the same inadequacy as earlier foreigners did when confronted with the symbols and the charged words and the flights into music of the Romantics.

To gain an understanding of the variability of political view and position in the German Federal Republic is no easier, particularly if one intends to try to learn something about the attitudes of the extreme critics of the existing political and social system. Here again a special language is encountered, that of the *Chaoten* and the *Spontis*, of the anarchists and the *Flipperlebensgemeinschaften*, an idiom called *Rotwelsch*, made up of liberal borrowings from the jargon of the underworld and from the Marxist theoreticians, in which the police are always *Bullen* or a *Faschistenpack* and political awareness requires participation in *Befreiungsaktionen*, at the risk of being *geklaut* and forced to sit in the *Knast*, in order to undermine the *verlumpte Staat* and to achieve a *höhere Lebensqualität*. Here again the nuances and shadings implicit in the terms used are not easily perceived by the outsider.

Finally, there is the problem of the German Democratic Republic, which has a totalitarian regime and a totalitarian theory of language, which means that 18 million Germans in the East, who use the same language as their brothers in the Federal Republic, are being taught systematically to use it in a different way and for a different purpose. Georg Klaus, one of the DDR's leading philosophers of speech, makes no bones of the fact that, in the eyes of the East German regime, the purpose of language is to change "the attitudes of people in production and public life and their moral behavior, so that the goals of Socialism may be maximally achieved."

To promote this end, language is controlled and manipulated—in much the same way as it was during the Third Reich—by regulations formulated by the government and imposed upon the school system, the news agency ADN, and the central organ of the Socialist Unity Party, *Neues Deutschland*. The emotional charging of words, the excessive use of superlatives, the preference for terms taken from the military vocabulary, the sharp schematization that eliminates neutral valuations in favor of black-white dichotomies, the insistent use of invective, and the constant repetition of stereotyped epithets that were the stock-in-trade of Goebbels are in use once more. So, moreover, are words that are also used in the West but have, in the DDR, a profoundly different meaning—words beginning with the prefix "peace" or the adjectives "people's" and "popular," words like "coexistence" and "relaxation of tension" and "human rights" and "democracy." It is for this reason that, when agreements have been made with the German Democratic Republic, Western diplomats have sometimes been unpleasantly surprised by the meaning later assigned by the government of the DDR to wording that they had accepted and had thought they understood.

When Willy Brandt met Willi Stoph in Erfurt in 1970, they had two private talks, with no one else present. There was no need for an intermediary or interpreter, they decided, Stoph remarking, "We both know German." This was accurate, as the sequel showed, only in the most formal sense. The fact is that German—the same German—is not the language of all Germans. This does not make things easy for the foreign student of the contemporary German scene.

Bibliography

This bibliography does not pretend to be comprehensive. It merely lists, chapter by chapter, the books and articles that I have found helpful and that readers in search of amplification may find it useful to consult.

Chapter 1: Historical Perspectives

Barraclough, G. *The Origins of Modern Germany*. Rev. ed. Oxford: 1947.

Berlin, Isaiah. *Against the Current: Essays in the History of Ideas*. New York: 1980.

Brunschwig, H. *Société et romantisme en Prusse au XVIIIe siècle*. Paris: 1973.

Gay, Peter. *The Bridge of Criticism*. New York: 1970.

————.*The Enlightenment: An Interpretation*. 2 vols. New York: 1966, 1969.

Gershoy, Leo. *From Despotism to Revolution, 1763–1789*. New York: 1944.

Möller, Horst. *Aufklärung in Preussen: Der Verleger Friedrich Nicolai*. Berlin: 1974.

Ohff, Heinz. "Die liberalen Preussen," *Der Tagesspiegel*. Berlin: Sonntagsserie, Sept. 17, 1978–Oct. 29, 1978.

Riehl, W. H. *Die bürgerliche Gesellschaft*. 9th ed. Stuttgart: 1897.

————.*Land und Leute*. 9th ed. Stuttgart: 1899.

Sagarra, Eda. *A Social History of Germany, 1648–1914*. New York: 1977.

Schnabel, Franz. *Deutsche Geschichte im neunzehnten Jahrhundert*. Herder ed. Freiburg: 1964, vol. 1. Book 1.

Schöffler, Herbert. *Kleine Geographie des deutschen Witzes*. Göttingen: 1955.

Troeltsch, Ernst. "The Ideas of Natural Law and Humanity." In Otto Friedrich von Gierke, *Natural Law and the Theory of Society*. Trans. and ed. by Ernest Barker. 2 vols. Cambridge, England: 1934.

Walker, Mack. *German Home Towns, 1648–1871*. Ithaca: 1971.

Wedgewood, C. V. *The Thirty Years War*. London: 1938.

Chapter 2: Politics in a New Key

Binder, David. "Brandt's Mark." *New York Times*, May 12, 1974.

Bracher, Karl Dietrich. *Theodor Heuss und die Wiederbegründung der Demokratie in Deutschland*. Tübingen: 1965.

Brandt, Willy. *Begegnungen und Einsichten: Die Jahre 1960–1975*. Hamburg: 1976.

———.*My Road to Berlin*. New York: 1960.

Craig, Gordon A. *From Bismarck to Adenauer: Aspects of German Statecraft*. Rev. ed. New York: 1965.

Davison, W. Phillips. *The Berlin Blockade*. Princeton: 1958.

———.Dönhoff, Marion Gräfin. *Die Bundesrepublik in der Ära Adenauer: Kritik und Perspektiven*. Reinbek bei Hamburg: 1963.

Dornberg, John. *The Other Germany*. New York: 1968.

Edinger, Lewis J. *Kurt Schumacher*. Stanford: 1965.

———.*Politics in West Germany*. 2nd ed. Boston: 1977.

Gatzke, Hans W. *Germany and the United States: "A Special Relationship?"* Cambridge, Mass.: 1980.

Golay, John Ford. *The Founding of the Federal Republic of Germany*. Chicago: 1958.

Grosser, Alfred. *Germany in Our Time: A Political History of the Postwar Years*. New York: 1971.

Hartrich, Edwin. *The Fourth and Richest Reich*. New York: 1980.

Hiscocks, Richard. *The Adenauer Era*. New York: 1966.

Katzenstein, Peter J. "Problem or Model? West Germany in the 1980's." *World Politics*, XXIII (1980), Number 4.

Ludz, Peter Christian. "Von der Zone zum Ostdeutschen Staat." *Die Zeit*, October 1974.

Mann, Golo. "Konrad Adenauer: Staatsmann der Sorge," *Frankfurter Allgemeine Zeitung*, February 14, 1976.

Richter, Hans Werner. ed. *Die Mauer, oder Der 13. August*. Reinbek bei Hamburg: 1961.

Stern, Carola. *Ulbricht: Eine politische Biographie*. Cologne: 1964.

Weyrauch, Wolfgang, ed. *Ich lebe in der Bundesrepublik: Fünfzehn Deutsche über Deutschland*. Munich: n.d.

Chapter 3: Hitler and the New Generation

Améry, Jean. "Adolf Hitler: Verbrecher—Ja; Verräter—Nein." *Die Zeit*, June 16, 1978.

———"Die Zeit der Rehabilitation: Das Dritte Reich und die geschichtliche Objektivität." *Frankfurter Rundschau*, April 10, 1976.

Bracher, Karl Dietrich. *Die Auflösung der Weimarer Republik*. 2nd ed. Stuttgart: 1957.

Craig, Gordon A. "What the Germans are Reading about Hitler." *The Reporter*, July 16, 1964.

Fest, J. C. *Hitler*. Trans. from the German. New York: 1974.

Haffner, Sebastian. *Anmerkungen zu Hitler*. Munich: 1978.
"Hitler kam von ganz alleine an die Macht." *Der Spiegel*, Number 34/1977.
Janssen, Karl-Heinz. "Wir—zwischen Jesus und Hitler." *Die Zeit*, July 7, 1978.
Klose, Werner. "Hitler in der Schule." *Die Zeit*, December 16, 1977.
Meinecke, Friedrich. *The German Catastrophe*. Cambridge, Mass.: 1950.
Schoenbaum, David. "What German Boys Say about Hitler." *New York Times Magazine*. January 9, 1966.
Syberberg, H. J. *Hitler, un film d'Allemagne*. Paris: 1978.
————.*Syberbergs Filmbuch*. Munich: 1976.
Vogt, Hanna. *The Burden of Guilt*. Trans. from the German. New York: 1964.

Chapter 4: Religion
Brunschwig, *Société et romantisme*.
Craig, Gordon A. *Germany, 1866–1945*. Oxford: 1978.
Dickens, A. G. *The German Nation and Martin Luther*. London: 1974.
Dilthey, Wilhelm. *Das Leben Schleiermachers*. 2 vols. Göttingen: 1966–1972.
Durnbagh, Donald R. *The Believers Church: The History and Character of Radical Protestantism*. New York: 1968.
Forster, Karl. "Kirche in einer säkularisierten Gesellschaft." In *Dreissig Jahre Bundesrepublik: Tradition und Wandel*, Josef Becker, ed. Munich: 1979.
Friedenthal, Richard. *Luther: Sein Leben und seine Zeit*. New ed. Munich: 1979.
Gritsch, Eric W. *Reformer Without a Church: The Life and Thought of Thomas Müntzer*. Philadelphia: 1967.
Heer, Friedrich. *Europäische Geistesgeschichte*. Stuttgart: 1957.
Heine, Heinrich. *Religion and Philosophy in Germany: A Fragment*. Trans. from the German. Boston: 1959.
Minder, Robert. "Das Bild des Pfarrhauses in der deutschen Literatur." In *Kultur und Literatur in Deutschland und Frankreich*. Frankfurt am Main: 1962.
Rosenberg, Hans. "Theologische Rationalismus und vormärzlicher Vulgärliberalismus," in *Politische Denkströmungen im deutschen Vormärz*. Göttingen: 1972.
Sagarra, *Social History*.
Thadden, Rudolf von. *Die brandenburgisch-preussischen Hofprediger im 17. und 18. Jahrhundert*. Berlin: 1959.
Vigener, Fritz. *Drei Gestalten aus der modernen Katholizismus: Moeller, Diepenbrock, Döllinger.* Munich: 1926.

Chapter 5: Money

Amery, Carl. *Capitulation: The Lesson of German Catholicism.* Trans. from the German. New York: 1967.

Fischer-Fabian, S. *Berlin-Evergreen.* Frankfurt am Main: 1975. ("Spiel mit Millionen-Carl Fürstenberg")

Goethe, Johann Wolfgang. *Faust. Parts 1 and 2.* Trans. by George Madison Priest. New York: 1941.

Hartrich, *Fourth and Richest Reich.*

Klass, Gert von. *Stinnes.* Tübingen: 1958.

The Marx-Engels Reader, Robert C. Tucker, ed. 2nd ed. New York: 1978. "On the Jewish Question" and "Economic and Philosophic Manuscripts of 1844."

Mayer, Hans. *Anmerkungen zu Richard Wagner.* Frankfurt am Main: 1966.

Muhlen, Norbert. *The House of Krupp.* New York: 1959.

Schopenhauer, Arthur. *Werke in zwei Bände.* Werner Breda, ed. Munich: 1977. "Aphorismen zur Lebensweisheit," chapter 3.

Sombart, Werner. *Der Bourgeois: Zur Geistesgeschichte des modernen Wirtschaftsmenschen.* Munich: 1913.

Stern, Fritz. *Gold and Iron: Bismarck, Bleichröder and the Building of the German Empire.* New York: 1977.

Stern, Selma. *Jud Süss: Ein Beitrag zur deutschen und zur jüdischen Geschichte.* Munich: 1973.

Strieder, Jacob. *Jacob Fugger the Rich, Merchant and Banker of Augsburg.* Trans. from the German. New York: 1931.

Wagner, Richard. *Die Musikdramen*, Joachim Kaiser, ed. Munich: 1978.

Wallich, Henry C. *Mainsprings of the German Revival.* New York: 1955.

Chapter 6: Germans and Jews

Arendt, Hannah. *Rahel Varnhagen: The Life of a Jewish Woman.* Rev. ed. New York: 1974.

Börne, Ludwig. *Werke in zwei Bände.* Helmut Bock and Walter Dietze, eds. Berlin: 1964.

Dönhoff, Marion Gräfin. "Eine deutsche Geschichtsstunde." *Die Zeit.* February 9, 1979.

Goldmann, Nahum. "Juden und andere Deutschen." *Die Zeit,* February 2, 9, 1979.

Grunfeld, Frederic V. *Prophets Without Honor.* New York: 1979.

Habe, Hans. "Fassbinder und das hässliche Gesicht des Antisemitismus." *Die Welt am Sonntag.* April 4, 1976.

Heine, Heinrich. *Werke.* Martin Greiner, ed. 4 vols. Frankfurt am Main: 1968.

Hellendall, F. "Heinrich Heine and Düsseldorf—A City Afraid of Its Great Son." *Monatshefte für deutsche Unterricht*, LXIII, No. 1 (1971).

Hermand, Jost. "Heines frühe Kritiker." In *Der Dichter und seine Zeit.* Wolfgang Paulsen, ed. Heidelberg: 1970.

" 'Holocaust': Die Vergangenheit kommt zurück." *Der Spiegel,* Number 5/1979.

Joll, James. *Three Intellectuals in Politics.* New York: 1960.

Kessler, Count Harry. *Walther Rathenau: His Life and Work.* Trans. from the German. New York: 1930.

Luther, Martin. *Works.* Trans. and ed. by Jaroslav Pelikan and Helmut T. Lehman. St. Louis and Philadelphia: 1955–1975. See especially Vol. 47 ("On the Jews and Their Lies.")

Mayer, Hans. *Aussenseiter.* Frankfurt am Main: 1975.

"Nur Nix." *Der Spiegel,* Number 9/1969.

Pulzer, Peter. *The Rise of Political Anti-Semitism in Germany and Austria.* New York: 1964.

Rathenau, Walther. *Tagebuch, 1907–1922.* Hartmann Pogge von Strandmann, ed. Düsseldorf: 1967.

Reich-Ranecki, Marcel. *Über Ruhestörer: Juden in der Deutschen Literatur.* Munich: 1973.

Sammons, Jeffrey L. *Heinrich Heine: The Elusive Poet.* New Haven: 1969.

Treitschke, Heinrich von. *History of Germany in the Nineteenth Century.* Ed. and with an introduction by Gordon A. Craig. Chicago: 1975.

Uedey, Gert. ed. *Materialien zur Hans Mayer "Aussenseiter."* Frankfurt am Main: 1978.

Uthmann, Jörg von. *Doppelgänger, Du mein bleicher Geselle.* Stuttgart: 1976.

Varnhagen, Rahel. *Briefwechsel.* Friedhelm Kemp, ed. 4 vols. Munich: 1966–1968.

Wagner, Cosima. *Diaries, 1869–1877.* New York: 1978.

———.*Diaries, 1878–1883.* New York: 1980.

Chapter 7: Women

Bebel, August. *Die Frau und Sozialismus.* Leipzig: 1887.

Brandt, Willy. ed. *Frauen Heute: Jahrhundert Thema Gleichberechtigung.* Cologne: 1978.

Braun, Lily. *Memoiren einer Sozialistin.* 2 vols. Munich: 1909.

Bridenthal, Renate and Claudia Koonz. "Beyond *Kinder, Küche und Kirche:* Weimar Women in Politics and Work." In *Liberating Women's History: Theoretical and Critical Essays,* Berenice A. Carroll, ed. Urbana, Ill.: 1976.

Brunschwig, *Société et romantisme.*

Die Frau in der DDR: Fakten und Zahlen. Staatsverlag der DDR. Berlin: 1975.

Frauen im Aufbruch: Frauenbriefe aus dem Vormärz und der Revolution von 1848. Fritz Böttger, ed. Darmstadt: 1979.

Das Gewissen steht auf. Lebensbilder aus dem deutschen Widerstand. Annedore Leber, ed. Berlin: 1954.

Hackett, Amy. "Feminism and Liberalism in Wilhelmine Germany." In *Liberating Women's History.*

——.*The Politics of Feminism in Wilhelmine Germany.* Dissertation, Columbia University, 1976.

Huch, Ricarda, ed. *Carolinens Leben in ihren Briefen.* Leipzig: 1914. *Keiner schiebt uns weg: Zwischenbilanz der Frauenbewegung in der Bundesrepublik.* Lottemi Doormann, ed. Weinheim: 1979.

Martens, W. *Die Botschaft der Tugend.* Stuttgart: 1968.

Martiny, Anke. "Berufsbild: Parlamentarierin." *Frankfurter Allgemeine Zeitung,* March 31, 1979.

Mayer, *Aussenseiter* ("Judith und Dalila").

Müller-Seidel, W. *Theodor Fontane: Soziale Romankunst in Deutschland.* Stuttgart: 1975.

Nettl, J. P. *Rosa Luxemburg.* 2 vols. London: 1966.

"Nur die Krumen vom Tisch der Männer: *Spiegel*-Report über Frauenarbeitslosigkeit in der Bundesrepublik." *Der Spiegel,* Number 2/1978.

Quataert, J. H. *Reluctant Feminists in German Social Democracy, 1885–1917.* Princeton: 1979.

Rühmkorf, Eva, and Eva, Marie von Münch. "Wer kämpft für die Frauen:" *Die Zeit,* July 11, 1980.

Sagarra, *Social History.*

Sanford, Jutta S. *The Origins of German Feminism.* Dissertation, University of Michigan, 1978.

Wie emanzipiert sind die Frauen in der DDR? Beruf, Bildung, Familie. Hertig Kuhrig and Wulfram Speigner, eds. Cologne: 1979.

Chapter 8: Professors and Students

Bleuel, Hans Peter, and Ernst Kunnert. *Deutsche Studenten auf dem Weg ins Dritte Reich.* Gütersloh: 1967.

Brunschwig, *Société et romantisme.*

Craig, *German History, 1866–1945,* chapters 6, 11, 18.

"Deutschlands Professoren: Götter oder Fachidioten?" *Der Spiegel,* Number 8/1968.

Eichendorff, Josef von. "Halle und Heidelberg." In *Erzählungen,* Werner Bergengruen, ed. Manesse Verlag, n. d.

Fallon, Daniel. *The German University: A Heroic Ideal in Conflict with the Modern World.* Boulder, Colorado: 1980.

Jarausch, Konrad. "Sources of German Student Unrest, 1815–1848." In *The University in Society,* Lawrence Stone, ed. 2 vols. Princeton: 1974.

Kuhn, Helmut et al. *Die deutsche Universität im Dritten Reich.* Munich: 1966.

McClelland, Charles E. *State, Society and University in Germany, 1700–1914.* Cambridge, England: 1980.

Mason, Henry L. "Reflections on the Politicized University: The

Academic Crisis in the Federal Republic." *Bulletin of the American Academy of University Professors.* Autumn 1974.

Paulsen, Friedrich. *The German Universities.* Trans. from the German. New York: 1906.

Pross, Harry. *Vor und nach Hitler: Zur deutschen Sozialpathologie.* Freiburg im Breisgau: 1962.

Treitschke, *History of Germany* (on the Burschenschaft).

Chapter 9: Romantics

Becker, Jillian. *Hitler's Children: The Story of the Baader-Meinhof Terrorist Gang.* Philadelphia: 1977.

Bergmann, Klaus. *Agrarromantik und Grossstadtfeindschaft.* Mersenheim am Glau: 1970.

Bloch, Ernst. *Zur Philosophie der Musik.* Frankfurt am Main: 1974.

Brunschwig, *Société et romantisme.*

Craig, *Germany, 1866–1945*, chapters 9, 13.

Dilthey, *Das Leben Schleiermachers.*

Glaser, Hermann. "Die Diskussion über den Terrorismus: Ein Dossier." *Aus Politik und Zeitgeschichte: Beilage zur Wochenzeitung Das Parlament*, June 24, 1978.

Goltz, Bogumil. *Die Deutschen.* Insel Bücherei, No. 357. Leipzig, n.d.

Lowenthal, Leo. *Erzählkunst und Gesellschaft.* Neuwied and Berlin: 1971.

Mann, Thomas. "Deutschland und die Deutschen" and "Deutsche Ansprache—Ein Appell an die Vernunft." In *Reden und Aufsätze*, II. Oldenburg: 1965.

Mayer, *Anmerkungen zu Richard Wagner.*

Mosse, George L. *Masses and Man: Nationalist and Fascist Perceptions of Reality.* New York: 1980.

Nietzsche, Friedrich. *Jenseits von Gut und Böse.* Kröner, ed. Stuttgart: 1976.

Riehl, *Die bürgerliche Gesellschaft*, Part 1, chapter 4.

Schmiedt, Helmut. *Karl May: Studien zu Leben, Werk und Wirkung eines Erfolgsschriftsteller.* Hain: 1979.

Sontheimer, Kurt. *Anti-Demokratisches Denken in der Weimarer Republik.* Munich: 1962.

Stern, Fritz. *The Politics of Cultural Despair: A Study in the Rise of the German Ideology.* Berkeley: 1961.

Sternberger, Dolf. *Panorama, oder Ansichten vom 19. Jahrhundert.* Düsseldorf: 1938.

Chapter 10: Literature and Society

Daiber, Hans. *Deutsches Theater seit 1945.* Stuttgart: 1976.

Dönhoff, Marion Gräfin. "Radikalität? Ja—und warum." *Die Zeit*, October 28, 1977.

Esslin, Martin. *Brecht: The Man and his Work.* New York: 1959.

Franke, Konrad, ed. *Erzähler aus der DDR*. Tübingen, Basel: 1973.
"The German Theater in the 1960's." *The Times Literary Supplement*, April 3, 1969.
Kunert, Günter. "Jetzt ist es endgültig genug!" *Die Zeit*, November 9, 1979.
Leonhardt, Rudolf Walter. "German Literary Letter." *New York Times Book Review*, January 10, 1965.
Mayer, Hans. "Die Toten bleiben jung." *Die Zeit*, May 26, 1978.
"Poems from East Germany." *The Times Literary Supplement*, February 20, 1964.
Riess, Curt. *Theaterdämmerung, oder das Klo auf der Bühne*. Hamburg: 1970.
Seyppel, Joachim. "Ist Literatur Hochverrat?" *Die Zeit*, June 8, 1979.
Steffen, Jochen. "Gleiche Brüder auf verschiedenen Wege: Günter Grass und Hans Magnus Enzensberger." *Die Zeit*, February 7, 1975.
Vaterland, Muttersprache: Deutsche Schriftsteller und ihr Staat von 1945 bis heute. Klaus Wagenbach, Winfried Stephan and Michael Krüger, eds., with a foreword by Peter Rühmkorf. Berlin: 1979.
"Verstörung bis zur Resignation: Schrifsteller Kongress in Ostberlin." *Die Zeit*, May 12, 1978.

Chapter 11: Soldiers

"Bundeswehr und Tradition" (Traditionserlass, 1.7.65), *Wehrkunde*, 10/1965.
Craig, Gordon A. "Germany and NATO: The Rearmament Debate, 1950–1958." In *NATO and American Security*, Klaus Knorr, ed. Princeton: 1959.
——. "NATO and the New German Army." In *Military Policy and National Security*, W. W. Kaufmann, ed. Princeton: 1956.
——.*The Politics of the Prussian Army, 1640–1945*. Oxford: 1955.
Hancock, M. Donald. *The Bundeswehr and the National People's Army: A Comparative Study of German Civil-Military Polity*. Denver: 1973.
Heimpel, Hermann. "Über den Tod für das Vaterland." In *Kapitulation vor der Geschichte? Gedanken zur Zeit*. 3rd ed. Göttingen: 1956.
"Heye's Meinung über die Bundeswehr." *Süddeutsche Zeitung*, June 20–21, 1964.
International Institute for Strategic Studies. *The Military Balance, 1978–79*. London: 1979.
——.*Strategic Survey 1979*. London: 1980.
Keegan, John. *World Armies 1979*. London: 1979.
Mosen, Wido. *Bundeswehr—Elite der Nation? Determinanten und Funktionen elitärer Selbsteinschätzungen von Bundeswehr Soldaten*. Neuwied, Berlin: 1970.
Die nationale Volksarmee der Deutschen Demokratischen Republik: Eine Dokumentation. Gerhard Schmenke, ed. Berlin: 1961.

Nawrocki, Joachim. "Hoffmanns Afrikakorps: DDR Militärhilfe." *Die Zeit*, May 26, 1978.

———. "Honecker ruft die DDR-Jugend ans Gewehr." *Die Zeit*, June 30, 1978.

Schmidt, Helmut. *Beiträge*. Stuttgart: 1967.

"Wir haben euch Waffen und Brot geschickt." *Der Spiegel*, Number 10/1980.

Chapter 12: Berlin: Athens on the Spree and City of Crisis

Baedecker, Karl. *Berlin: Reisehandbuch*. Freiburg im Breisgau: 1964.

———. *Berlin und Umgebung*. Leipzig: 1906.

Berlin: Stimmen einer Stadt. 2nd ed. Berlin: 1973.

Berliner U-Bahn. Hans D. Reichardt, ed. Düsseldorf: 1974.

Dronke, Ernst. *Berlin*. Rainer Nitsche, ed. Darmstadt: 1974.

Entwicklung und Probleme Westberlins in den 70er Jahren. Institut für Internationale Politik und Wirtschaft der DDR. Berlin: 1978.

Frauen im Aufbruch (on Bettina von Arnim).

Hier schreibt Berlin: Ein Dokument der 20er Jahre. Herbert Günther, ed. Munich: 1963.

Hildebrandt, Dieter. *Deutschland deine Berliner*. Hamburg: 1973.

Ingwerson, Erhard. *Berlinische Anekdoten*. 2nd ed. Berlin: 1965.

Kerr, Alfred. *Caprichos: Strophen des Nebenstroms*. Berlin: 1926.

Kessler, Graf Harry. *Tagebücher, 1918–1937*. Frankfurt am Main: 1961.

Kiaulehn, Walter. *Berlin: Schicksal einer Weltstadt*. 3rd ed. Berlin: 1958.

Klotz, Volker. *Die erzählte Stadt*. Munich: 1969.

Krüger, Wolfgang. "Berlin wartet auf Menschen." *Die Zeit*, December 1, 1961.

Lange, Annemarie. *Berlin zur Zeit Bebels und Bismarcks*. Berlin: 1972.

———. *Das wilhelminische Berlin*. Berlin: 1967.

Laufenberg, Walter. Berlin (West): *Nachkriegsentwicklung und Entwicklungschancen unter besonderer Berücksichtigung des Reiseverkehrs*. Frankfurt am Main: 1978.

Masur, Gerhard. *Imperial Berlin*. New York: 1970.

Meyer, Hans. *Der richtige Berliner*. Walter Kiaulehn, ed. Munich: 1966.

Mehring, Walter. *Der Zeitpuls fliegt! Chansons, Gedichte, Prosa*. Hamburg: n.d.

Schöffler, *Kleine Geographie des deutschen Witzes*.

Seyppel, Joachim. *Nun O Unsterblichkeit: Wanderungen zu den Friedhöfen Berlins*. Berlin: 1964.

Sichelschmidt, Gustav, ed. *Die gespiegelte Stadt: 200 Jahre Gedichte über Berlin*. Berlin: 1971.

Springer, Robert. *Berlin, die deutsche Kaiserstadt*. Darmstadt: 1878.

Vandrey, Max. *Der politische Witz im Dritten Reich*. Munich: 1967.

Varnhagen von Ense, K. A. "Königin Sophie Charlotte von Preussen."

In *Biographische Denkmale*. 3rd ed., 3rd Part. Leipzig: 1872.

Vizetelly, Henry. *Berlin Under the New Empire*. 2 vols. London: 1879.

Vogel, Werner. *Führer durch die Geschichte Berlins*. Berlin: 1966.

Chapter 13: Democracy and Nationalism

Brandt, Willy. *Begegnungen und Einsichten*.

Dahrendorf, Ralf. "Polarisierung überm Teppich und drunter: Das eigentliche deutsche Problem." *Die Zeit*, February 10, 1978.

"Die Elbe—ein deutscher Strom, nicht Deutschlands Grenze: Ein *Zeit*-Interview mit Günter Gaus." *Die Zeit*, February 6, 1981.

Habermas, Jürgen, ed. *Stichworte zur "Geistigen Situation der Zeit."* 2 vols. Frankfurt am Main: 1979.

Hochhuth, Rolf. "Bismarck, der Klassiker." *Der Spiegel*, Number 31/ 1978.

Janssen, Karl-Heinz. "Deutsche Einheit—ein langer Seufzer?" *Die Zeit*, February 13, 1980.

Ludz, Peter Christian. *Deutschlands doppelte Zukunft*. Munich: 1974.

"Das Manifest der ersten organisierten Opposition in der DDR." *Der Spiegel*, Numbers 1, 2/1978.

Mommsen, Hans. "Aus Eins mach Zwei: Die Bi-Nationalisierung Rest-Deutschlands." *Die Zeit*, February 13, 1981.

Nawrocki, Joachim. "Einheit à la SED." *Die Zeit*, March 6, 1981.

"Sprengsatz Brokdorf." *Der Spiegel*, Number 8/1981.

Stammen, Theo. "Politische Kultur—Tradition und Wandel." In *Dreissig Jahre Bundesrepublik*, Becker, ed.

"Wir müssen an der Nation festhalten: *Zeit*-Gespräch mit Friedrich Zimmermann." *Die Zeit*, February 27, 1981.

Chapter 14 (Appendix): "The Awful German Language"

Bergsdorf, Wolfgang. *Politik und Sprache*. Munich: 1978.

Berlin. *Against the Current*.

Blackall, Eric A. *The Emergence of German as a Literary Language*. Ithaca: 1978.

Dilthey. *Das Leben Schleiermachers*.

Engel, Eduard. *Entwelschung: Verdeutschungswörterbuch*. Rev. ed. Leipzig: 1918.

Glaser, Hermann. *Spiesserideologie*. Rev. ed. Cologne: 1974.

Klemperer, Viktor. *Die unbewältigte Sprache*. 3rd ed. Darmstadt: n.d.

Stael, Mme. de. *De l'Allemagne*, Comtesse Jean de Punge, ed. 4 vols. Paris: 1958–1959.

Steiner, George. *After Babel*. New York: 1975.

——. *Language and Silence*. New York: 1967.

Twain, Mark. "The Awful German Language." In *A Tramp Abroad*, II. New York: 1879.

Weigel, Hans. *Die Leiden der jungen Wörter: Ein Antiwörterbuch*. Zürich, Munich: 1974.

Index

Abbt, Thomas, 254, 255, 256
Abs, Hermann J., 115 f
Adenauer, Konrad, 36, 41, 43, 44–48, 49, 50, 52, 55, 78, 116, 218, 242 f, 292, 294, 304
Ahlwardt, Hermann, 140
Alberti, Conrad, 274
Allensbach Institut für Demoskopie, 291, 293
Amery, Carl, 98, 123, 222
Améry, Jean, 70, 78
Andersch, Alfred, 214
Anti-militarism, 47, 49, 243, 251 f, 254–6, 258–60, 298
Apel, Hans, 252, 254
Architecture, baroque, 91, 92
Army, Prussian and German, 15, 66, 72, 109, 110, 238–42; and language, 320 f. See also Bundeswehr, National People's Army
Arndt, Ernst Moritz, 255
Arnim, Achim von, 157
Arnim, Bettina von, 157, 270
Ascher, Saul, 131, 132
Asmussen, Hans, 97
Augsburg, 22, 91, 106, 107, 262
Austria, 92, 110, 129, 140

Baader, Andreas, 187, 210, 212, 223
Baader, Franz von, 94
Bach, Johann Sebastian, 92, 272
Bahr, Egon, 57
Bahro, Rudolf, 301, 302
Bamberg, 92, 128
Banking, 106, 107 f, 113 ff, 129, 137
Barth, Karl, 97
Basedow, Johann Bernhard, 150
Baudissin, Wolf Count, 245
Baum, Vicki, 162, 214

Bäumer, Gertrud, 160
Bavaria, 43, 71, 72, 91, 92, 96
Bebel, August, 37, 155, 157; 160
Beck, General Ludwig, 241–2, 249
Beethoven, Ludwig van, 25
Belgium, 112, 240
Benjamin, Walter, 176
Berlin: after 1945, 38–39, 279–86; arts and sciences, 266–9, 272–4, 281; demographic problems, 281; Four Power Agreement, 1971, 58, 282, 287; history and growth, 262–74; housing problem, 1980, 285 f; Khrushchev ultimatum (1958), 47, 280; rising of June 17, 1953, 51, 52, 230, 304; Wall, 1961, 48, 52–3, 55, 56, 80, 233, 262, 280; wit and humor, 113, 275–7
Berlin, Sir Isaiah, 31
Bernhard, Thomas, 229
Bethmann Hollweg, Theobald von, 207
Biermann, Wolf, 234–6, 278 f
Bild-Zeitung, 219 f, 223, 330
Bismarck-Schönhausen, Otto von, 10, 15, 45, 63, 74, 77, 89, 93, 94, 109, 113, 115, 119, 139, 239, 271, 292, 295, 310
Blank, Theodor, 244, 245, 246
Blankenhorn, Herbert, 47
Bleichröder, Gerson von, 115, 116, 119, 137, 139
Bloch, Ernst, 52, 176, 200, 210, 233, 328
Böll, Heinrich, 98, 216, 219, 222–4
Bonhöffer, Dietrich, 97
Börne, Ludwig, 132, 135, 317
Bossmann, Dieter, 77–79
Boyen, Hermann von, 244, 245
Bracher, Karl Dietrich, 65, 69

343

Brandt, Willy, 35, 37, 38, 55, 56, 58 f, 185, 187, 280, 306, 332; *Ostpolitik*, 187, 229, 305
Braun, Lily, 161
Brecht, Bertolt, 214, 230, 231, 232
Bremen, 87, 251, 254, 298
Brentano, Clemens von, 130, 157, 195
Brentano, Lujo, 175
Bruck, Arthur Moeller van den, 208, 209
Brüning, Heinrich, 111, 115, 183, 240
Büchner, Georg, 225
Bullock, Alan, 66
Bülow, Bernhard von, 175
Bundeswehr, 47, 49, 80, 242 f, 292; Personnel Advisory Committee, 246; strength and reliability, 252-6; tradition, 248-9, 251-2. *See also* Anti-Militarism
Burckhardt, Jakob, 70
Bureaucracy, 22, 26, 88, 321 f

Capitalism, 26, 107, 108 f, 116-8, 219, 299 f; crash of 1873, 118 f, 137; inflation of 1923, 23, 120 f
Carstens, Karl, 230, 251
Celan, Paul, 215
Center Party, 92, 93, 95, 96, 183
Chamberlain, Houston Stewart, 67
Chamisso, Adalbert von, 130, 195
Charlemagne, 16
Charles V, Emperor, 18, 106, 311
Christian Democratic Union (CDU-CSU), 36, 41, 43, 49, 55, 78, 99, 298, 305
Chrysostom, St. John, 127
Cinema, 70, 71, 78, 79, 115, 145, 223, 227
Clausewitz, Karl von, 158, 249
Clay, General Lucius D., 38
Cologne, 24, 44, 262
Commerce, 16, 22, 107, 129, 263
Communism, 66, 77, 79, 85, 108, 123, 124, 185, 279 f, 284, 304
Communist Party (KPD), 37, 48, 50, 51, 183
Conant, Grace Richards, 76
Courths-Mahler, Hedwig, 320
Czechoslovakia, 52, 56 f, 61, 257

Dahlmann, F. C., 172
Dahn, Felix, 139
Dahrendorf, Ralf, 295

Dante Alighieri, 33, 105
Dawidowicz, Lucy, 73
De Gaulle, Charles, 48
Democracy, 34, 41, 238, 290 ff
Denmark, 21, 252
Dernburg, Bernhard, 142
Dilthey, Wilhelm, 316
Döblin, Alfred, 214, 274
Dohm, Christian Wilhelm von, 130, 132
Dohm, Hedwig, 160
Döllinger, Bishop Josef Ignaz, 93, 100
Dönhoff, Countess Marion, 10, 146
Dresden, 105, 238
Dronke, Emil, 270
Duckwitz, Georg, 57
Dühring, Eugen, 138
Dürer, Albrecht, 7
Dürrenmatt, Friedrich, 145

Edinger, Lewis J., 41, 49
Education, 30, 61, 206 f; in Democratic Republic, 103, 136; schools, 74-9, 86, 88, 146, 264; women's, 149 f, 153, 162. *See also* Universities
Ehmke, Horst, 37, 306
Eichendorff, Josef Freiherr von, 179, 191, 192, 193, 194, 196 f, 315
Einstein, Albert, 29, 141, 176, 203
Engel, Eduard, 322
Engels, Friedrich, 85, 136
Ensslin, Gudrun, 168, 187, 212
Enzensberger, Hans Magnus, 186, 214, 215 f, 219-21, 222, 224
Erasmus, Desiderius, 107
Erhard, Ludwig, 41, 43-4, 45, 55, 56, 292
Erler, Fritz, 37
Europe: Coal and Steel Community, 46; Common Market, 46, 48; Defense Community (EDC), 46, 47. *See also* North Atlantic Treaty Organization

Fairy tales, 193, 200
Falk, Viktor von, 23
Falkenberg, Dietrich von, 19
Fascism, 69, 79, 144, 187
Fassbinder, Rainer Werner, 144
Faulhaber, Cardinal, 96
Ferdinand II, Emperor, 19, 91
Fest, Joachim C., 66-8, 70, 78, 144
Feuerbach, Anselm, 158

Fichte, J. G., 32, 131, 272
Filbinger, Hans, 188, 229, 233
Flick, Friedrich, 111 f
Fontane, Theodor, 89, 157, 213, 222, 271, 272, 277, 278, 321
Forster, Georg, 29, 151
Forster, Thérèse, 151
Forte, Dieter, 106
France, 15, 17, 23, 26, 31, 33, 48, 86, 88, 109, 112, 119, 120, 135, 161, 191, 239, 247, 269; attitudes toward Germany, 10, 21; French Revolution, 29, 89; Huguenots, 129, 165. *See also* Napoleon Bonaparte
Franck, Sebastian, 107
Francke, August Wilhelm, 87 f, 150, 172
Frankfurt am Main, 87, 272
Frankfurter Allgemeine Zeitung, 144, 330, 331
Frankfurter Rundschau, 124
Frederick I, King of Prussia, 266 f
Frederick II, King of Prussia, 27, 29, 130, 239, 267, 277, 292, 300
Frederick William, the Great Elector of Prussia, 129, 238, 265, 269
Frederick William I, King of Prussia, 22, 87, 88, 262, 267
Frederick William III, King of Prussia, 89, 269
Frederick William IV, King of Prussia, 158, 276
Free Democratic Party (FDP), 36, 49, 55, 187, 296, 298
Freytag, Gustav, 107, 139
Frisch, Max, 227
Fugger, Jakob, 106, 107, 114
Fürstenberg, Carl, 113 f, 276

Gartenlaube, Die, 319 f
Gaus, Günter, 298–300, 306, 307, 308
Gellert, Christian Fürchtegott, 313
Genscher, Hans-Dietrich, 59
Gentz, Friedrich von, 153
George, Stefan, 70
German characteristics and traits, supposed and attributed: anti-modern, 66, 119, 204, 205–7, 299, 300; antipolitical, 67, 174, 293–4; dedication to work ethic, 112 f; deference to authority, 10, 22, 23, 32, 34; diversity, 24; formlessness, 199; individualism, 31, 33, 34, 192; parochialism, 17,

24 f; preoccupation with Germanness, 25, 31, 32; sociability, 24; xenophobia, 9, 26, 29, 31, 322
German Democratic Republic (DDR), 49, 50–4, 55, 57, 58, 69, 280, 298 ff; anti-modernity, 300; cultural policy, 54, 230–6, 301; economic policy, 50, 301; opposition, 51, 52, 230, 301–3, 304. *See also* National People's Army
German Federal Republic, 34, 35 ff, 290 ff; Basic Law, 39–41, 49, 59 f, 78, 187, 304 f; Bundestag, 40, 46, 47, 58, 245, 246; Constitutional Court, 40, 188; economic policy and development, 11, 35, 43 f, 55, 56, 58, 59, 112, 123–4, 213, 222, 294 f, 329; elections, 46, 55, 56, 297 f; Extra-Parliamentary Opposition (APO), 294, 296; Federal Council, 40, 49, 188; foreign policy, 47 f, 57 f, 59, 99, 187, 229, 304 f, 307 f; Radicals Decree (*Radikalenerlass*), 187 f, 222, 229, 295 f. *See also* Bundeswehr
German language, 30, 310–32; in Democratic Republic, 331 f
Germany: medieval period, 16–18; Reformation, 18, 83–5, 129; Thirty Years War, 18–21; Enlightenment, 26–30, 31, 33, 88 f, 127, 130 f, 149–53, 191, 192, 267; Napoleonic period, 32; revolutions of 1848, 33, 90, 116, 159, 160, 173, 181, 197 f, 238; unification, 1871, 16, 21, 33, 63, 239, 290; Empire, 33, 118 f, 137; Weimar Republic, 7, 34, 35, 39, 40, 44, 48, 49, 110, 115, 120 f, 207 f, 240 f; Third Reich, 9, 10, 75, 76, 77, 241, 242, 277; occupation after 1945, 35 ff, 43, 45 f, 112, 121–3, 237, 279, 329; reunification question, 45, 47, 48, 304–9
Gervinus, Georg Gottfried, 172
Gisevius, Hans Bernd, 66, 69
Glaser, Hermann, 319
Glotz, Peter, 189
Gneisenau, August Count Neidhart von, 32, 300
Goebbels, Joseph, 39, 74, 323, 325
Goering, Hermann, 77, 277, 327
Goethe, Johann Wolfgang, 15, 27, 63, 133, 172, 196, 226, 232, 278, 289, 300, 315; *Faust: Part One*, 7, 149;

Faust: Part Two, 104, 120, 227; *Götz von Berlichingen*, 7, 149, 267, 313; *Hermann und Dorothea*, 26; *Wilhelm Meisters Lehrjahre*, 28, 149, 192, 313
Goldmann, Nahum, 144, 145
Goldschmidt, Jakob, 115, 116
Gollwitzer, Helmuth, 54, 55, 99, 123
Gottsched, Johann Christian, 313, 315
Grass, Günter, 55, 145, 186, 214, 216 f, 219, 221 f, 224, 230, 328, 329
Great Britain, 15, 17, 23, 26, 31, 33, 47, 48, 62, 72, 88, 109, 110, 161, 247, 253; influence on language, 312; views of Germany, 15
Green List, 251, 298
Gregory VII, Pope, 16
Grillparzer, Franz, 63
Grimm, Jakob and Wilhelm, 172
Grimmelshausen, Hans-Jakob, 20
Grotewohl, Otto, 37, 51
Gryphius, Andreas, 19 f, 22
Gustavus Adolphus, King of Sweden, 18, 19, 265

Habermas, Jürgen, 290, 291, 293
Hacks, Peter, 233 f
Haffner, Sebastian, 68, 69, 70
Hamann, J. G., 30, 314
Hamburg, 20, 23, 24, 263; Brokdorf demonstrations, 296 f
Hanseatic League, 21, 106
Hanslick, Eduard, 199
Hardenberg, Karl August von, 32
Harich, Wolfgang, 52
Hartrich, Edwin, 122
Hauff, Wilhelm, 195
Hauptmann, Gerhart, 208, 225
Havemann, Robert, 301
Hebbel, Friedrich, 153, 156, 225
Hegel, Georg Friedrich, 8, 32, 40, 62, 126, 158, 272, 314, 328; Young Hegelians, 90
Heiber, Helmut, 66
Heidegger, Martin, 208, 323, 328
Heimpel, Hermann, 256
Heine, Heinrich, 29, 84, 127, 132–6, 141, 158, 191, 236, 300, 311
Heinemann, Gustav, 60
Heinse, Johann Jakob, Wilhelm, 196
Henry IV, Emperor, 16
Herder, Johann Gottfried von, 30–32, 313, 318

Hermand, Jost, 133 f
Herwegh, Emma, 159, 168
Herwegh, Georg, 158, 165
Herz, Henriette, 130
Hess, Rudolf, 80
Hesse, Hermann, 329
Heuss, Theodor, 36, 39–41, 45, 60
Heye, Admiral Hellmuth, 247
Heym, Stefan, 233, 236
Himmler, Heinrich, 73, 229, 327
Hindenburg, Field Marshal Paul von Beneckendorff und, 77, 240, 245
Hintze, Otto, 63
Hippel, Theodor Gottlieb, 150, 153
History and historians, 63–74, 299, 314
Hitler, Adolf, 8, 9, 10, 34, 35, 36, 37, 38, 49, 51, 61–3, 96, 97, 113, 115, 121, 140, 143, 164 f, 177, 182 f, 191, 203, 208, 209, 210, 218, 227, 241, 242, 245, 249, 267, 274, 277, 279, 290, 292, 323–28; historians on, 63–74; in schools, 74–80. *See also* Resistance Movement
Hochhuth, Rolf, 98, 227, 228, 229, 292
Hoess, Rudolf, 77
Hoffmann, E. T. A., 195, 198
Hohenzollern dynasty, 86, 175, 264, 292
Hölderlin, Friedrich, 16, 254
Honecker, Erich, 53 f, 102, 103, 124, 231, 235, 236, 300, 303, 308, 309
Humboldt, Alexander von, 130
Humboldt, Karoline von, 152 f
Humboldt, Wilhelm von, 21, 32, 130, 152 f, 173, 272
Humperdinck, Engelbert, 201
Hungary, 47, 106, 232
Hutten, Ulrich von, 71, 72, 83, 107

Iden, Peter, 124
Industrialization, 26, 66, 127, 137, 158, 269 f
Industry, 109–13, 119, 129, 141 f, 204, 239, 269
Irving, David, 72, 73, 74

Janssen, Karl-Heinz, 74
Jaspers, Karl, 145, 290
Jens, Walter, 219
Jesus, Society of, 91, 94, 95
Jews in Germany, 69, 97, 112, 126,

165, 179, 263; anti-Semitism before 1945, 8 f, 67, 75, 116, 127 ff, 131 ff, 137 ff, 140, 143, 182, 206, 326; anti-Semitism after 1945, 136, 143 ff; in economic life, 114, 119, 137; emancipation, 130 f, 140; Holocaust (Final Solution), 62, 73, 75, 76, 77, 79–80, 143, 145 f, 215, 228, 326–8; Holocaust television film, 79, 145 f

John Paul II, Pope, 101 f

Joll, James, 142

Joseph II, Emperor, 131

Jünger, Ernst, 208, 329

Kaas, Monsignor Ludwig, 96

Kant, Immanuel, 29, 30, 126

Kantorowicz, Alfred, 52

Kästner, Erich, 218, 283

Katzenstein, Peter, 49, 298

Kempowski, Walter, 216

Kepler, Johannes, 25

Kerr, Alfred, 278

Kessler, Count Harry, 274

Ketteler, Bishop Wilhelm Emmanuel von, 94 f

Khrushchev, Nikita, 47, 53, 280

Kiaulehn, Walter, 275, 276

Kiesinger, Kurt-Georg, 55, 185

Kirst, Helmuth, 243, 245

Kleist, Heinrich von, 7, 226

Klemperer, Viktor, 324, 326

Klepper, Jochen, 77

Klinger, Friedrich Maximilian, 196

Klopstock, Friedrich Gottlieb, 313

Klose, Werner, 75, 76, 79

Kolping, Adolf, 94

Körner, Theodor, 255

Kortner, Fritz, 225

Kotzebue, August von, 181

Kraus, Karl, 29

Krüger, Heinz, 61

Krupp, Alfred, 109 f, 112, 113

Kuhnen, Michael, 80

Kunert, Günter, 233, 236

Küng, Hans, 100 f

Kunze, Reiner, 301

Lagarde, Paul de, 138, 204, 205 f, 207, 208

Langbehn, Julius, 206 f, 209, 283

Lange, Helene, 159, 160

Lasker, Eduard, 137

Lassalle, Ferdinand, 314

Lavater, Johann, 29

Leber, Julius, 56

Leibniz, Gottfried Wilhelm von, 88, 226, 267, 312, 317

Leider, Frida, 7, 162

Leiser, Erwin, 70

Lenz, Siegfried, 214, 216

Leo XIII, Pope, 94

Lessing, Gottfried Ephraim, 28 f, 30, 130, 131, 139, 227, 267, 313

Liberalism, 32 f, 36, 40, 55, 119, 238 f, 290

Lichtenberg, Bernhard, 97

Lichtenberg, Georg Christoph, 29

Lichtenstein, Alfred, 278

Liebermann, Max, 141, 272

Liebknecht, Karl, 78

Liszt, Franz, 154, 158

Literature, 30, 31, 132–6, 155–7, 162, 205, 207, 212; Romanticism, 190–7; Young Germany, 157, 197, 317; in Federal Republic, 214–24; in Democratic Republic, 145, 214, 218, 230–6

Löns, Hermann, 205, 322

Lortzing, Albert, 26

Louis Ferdinand, Prince of Prussia, 130

Lübke, Heinrich, 303, 307

Ludendorff, General Erich, 136, 137, 176, 240

Lukács, Georg, 176, 231

Luther, Martin, 10, 25, 26, 63, 84–6, 95, 102, 106 f, 113, 134, 128 f, 275, 311, 330

Luxemburg, Rosa, 77, 168

Magdeburg, 20, 51; destruction of, 1631, 18–19

Mann, Golo, 45, 62, 65, 141

Mann, Heinrich, 113, 207, 208, 213, 300, 317

Mann, Thomas, 11, 67, 117, 194, 196, 209, 213, 216, 317 f

Maria Theresia, Empress, 129

Marlitt, E. J., 320

Marr, Wilhelm, 138, 139

Marx, Karl, 108 f, 116, 121, 124, 136, 141, 155, 158, 198, 201, 219, 307, 314, 328

Maser, Werner, 64, 74

Maximilian I, Emperor, 18, 106

May, Karl, 71, 198, 201–3

Mayer, Hans, 104, 116, 143, 144, 145, 146, 214, 228, 232
Mecklenburg, 20, 22, 86
Mehring, Walter, 274
Meinecke, Friedrich, 63, 176
Meinhof, Ulrike, 168, 169, 210, 212, 223
Mendelssohn, Moses, 129 f, 151, 267
Mendelssohn-Bartholdy, Felix, 272
Menzel, Wolfgang, 135
Metternich, Clemens von, 153, 181, 192
Michaelis, Caroline, 151, 152, 153
Middle class, and attitudes of, 22, 31, 33, 66, 106, 116f, 119, 120, 157, 179 f, 197, 203 ff, 224, 239, 263, 318 f, 320
Mill, John Stuart, 154, 155
Minder, Robert, 89
Moltke, General Field Marshal Helmuth Count von, 239
Mommsen, Hans, 293
Mommsen, Theodor, 140, 173, 174, 175, 272
Mommsen, Wolfgang J., 297
Monde, Le, (Paris), 78, 328
Morgenstern, Christian, 321
Moscherosch, Johann Michael, 312
Moser, Karl Friedrich, 23
Mozart, Wolfgang Amadeus, 7
Munich, 7–8, 9, 19, 23, 91, 92, 272
Münzer, Thomas, 85, 86, 106
Music, 7, 26, 116–8, 141, 193, 195, 196, 199–201, 299, 316 f

Napoleon Bonaparte, 23, 24, 30, 89, 92, 131, 250, 251, 255
National Democratic Party (NPD), 49, 55, 294
National People's Army (NVA), 243; strength and reliability, 256–60; tradition, 249. See also Anti-Militarism
National Socialism, 79, 177 f; and language, 322 ff; in literature, 216–18; neo-Nazism, 80, 292
National Socialist German Workers Party (NSDAP), 55, 65, 80, 97, 164
Nationalism, 31, 32, 34, 45, 46, 49, 63, 94, 131, 289 f, 304 ff
Naumann, Friedrich, 95
Netherlands, 17, 20, 23, 110, 121
Ney, Elly, 7

Nicolai, Friedrich, 27 f, 29 f, 130, 255 f, 267
Niemöller, Martin, 96, 97, 98,
Nietzsche, Friedrich, 138, 154, 191, 199, 313, 317 f
North Atlantic Treaty Organization (NATO), 242, 247, 251, 252, 253 f
Novalis (Friedrich von Hardenberg), 192 f, 196, 203
Nuremberg, 22, 77, 87, 116, 199, 324; trials, 112, 122

Ohnesorg, Benno, 186
Otto I, Emperor, 16
Otto-Peters, Luise, 159

Papen, Franz von, 96, 115, 240
Paulsen, Friedrich, 175, 180
Peasantry, 204–5
Pieck, Wilhelm, 54
Piscator, Erwin, 228
Pius IX, 93
Pius XII, 228
Plenzdorf, Ulrich, 235, 236
Poe, Edgar Allan, 126, 127
Poland, 21, 31, 52, 56, 57, 61, 72, 99, 106, 232, 309, 326
Pomerania, 20, 22
Press, newspaper, 185, 220, 221, 223, 246 f, 267, 271, 285 f, 330, 332
Prussia, 15, 17, 20, 22, 86 f, 88, 90, 94, 129, 155, 158, 248, 249; reform period, 1807–13, 32, 244 f, 250; rising against Napoleon, 32; constitutional struggle, 1860–66, 33, 238 f

Quitzow, Dietrich and Johann von, 106, 264

Raabe, Wilhelm, 89, 139, 261
Raddatz, Fritz J., 65
Ranke, Leopold von, 71, 72, 173, 272, 314
Rathenau, Walther, 141–3
Reinig, Christa, 233, 234
Religion, 11, 18, 19, 22 f, 29, 49, 83 ff, 106, 164; Catholicism, 90–4, 95, 96 f, 99–102, 188; Christianity and the Jews, 127 ff, 131; in Democratic Republic, 83, 102–3, 258; in Federal Republic, 83, 98–102; and National Socialism, 96–8; Pietism, 86–90, 148 f, 266; Protestant churches, 84–90, 94, 95, 97, 98, 99 f

Resistance movement, 66, 76, 89, 165, 241–2, 249

Reuter, Ernst, 36, 38–9, 50, 56, 280

Richter, Hans Werner, 54, 55, 186, 214, 216, 329

Richter, Jean Paul, 272, 314

Riehl, W. H., 24, 137, 204

Riesser, Gabriel, 318 f

Rilke, Rainer Maria, 118, 205

Rode, Wilhelm, 7

Romanticism, 11, 190–212, 283, 296; cultural pessimism, 204–7; in Federal Republic, 210–2; and language, 315–7; political, 39, 70, 207–10

Ropp, Ivan, 70

Rothschilds, banking dynasty, 114, 115

Rühmkorf, Eva, 168

Sachs, Hans, 116, 199

Sagarra, Eda, 129, 149

Sailer, Bishop J. M., 93, 94

Sand, Karl Ludwig, 181

Sauckel, Fritz, 165

Sauer, Wolfgang, 65

Saxony, 20, 25, 87, 88, 90, 116

Scharnhorst, Gerhard Johann David von, 32, 244, 250, 300

Scheidemann, Philipp, 37

Schelling, Friedrich Wilhelm Joseph von, 126

Schiller, Friedrich, 30, 63, 107, 149, 151 f, 154, 196, 224 f, 225 f, 228, 229, 289, 300, 315, 318 f

Schiller, Karl, 56, 294

Schlegel, August Wilhelm, 151

Schlegel, Friedrich, 130, 151, 192

Schleicher, General Kurt von, 115, 241

Schleiermacher, Friedrich Daniel Ernst, 90, 130, 151, 272

Schlieker, Willy H., 11

Schlözer, A. L., 150

Schlözer, Dorothea, 150, 153, 158

Schmidt, Auguste, 159

Schmidt, Helmut, 38, 59, 295, 296, 297, 309

Schmitt, Carl, 208, 209

Schneider, Paul, 97

Schneider, Rolf, 236

Schoeffler, Herbert, 24, 276

Schoenbaum, David, 77

Scholl, Hans and Sophie, 8, 165

Schopenhauer, Arthur, 108, 153, 154, 156, 200, 316 f

Schöpflin, Johann Daniel, 172

Schramm, Percy, 64 f

Schröder, Gerhard, 56

Schubert, Franz, 7, 195

Schumacher, Kurt, 36–38, 39, 40, 41, 50, 56

Schwind, Moritz von, 26

Seeckt, General Hans von, 240, 245, 246, 247

Seghers, Anna, 231, 236

Smith, Logan Pearsall, 15

Social Democratic Party (SPD), 36, 37, 41, 50, 58, 59, 95, 96, 155, 160, 161, 163, 183, 185, 187, 188, 221, 222, 251, 296, 298; Godesberg program, 1959, 38, 49, 166; Great Coalition (1966), 55 f, 305

Socialist Unity Party (SED), 36, 37, 50, 51, 102, 231, 232, 257, 280, 282, 301, 302

Sombart, Werner, 105, 108

Sophie Charlotte, Queen of Prussia, 266, 281

Soviet Union, 36, 37, 38, 45, 50, 51, 52, 57, 62, 122, 124 f, 222, 230, 231, 232, 237, 251, 254, 257, 258, 279 f, 300, 309

Spa Conference (1920), 110, 112, 142

Speer, Albert, 77, 165, 166

Spener, Philipp Jakob, 86 f, 266

Spengler, Otto, 328

Spiegel, Der, 64, 78, 171, 246, 252, 302, 331; *Spiegel* case, 48, 218, 297

Springer, Axel, 220, 223, 230, 286

Stael, Germaine de, 191, 310

Stammen, Theo, 293 f, 296

State: authority and power of, 40, 49; cult of, 32, 33, 63

Steffen, Jochen, 221

Stein, Friedrich Karl vom und zum, 32

Steiner, George, 315

Stern, 223

Stern, Fritz, 115, 207

Sternberger, Dolf, 198

Sternheim, Carl, 207

Stinnes, Hugo, 110 f, 112, 113, 121

Stoecker, Adolf, 95, 139

Stoph, Willi, 57, 243, 244, 250, 256, 305, 332

Strauss, Bodo, 124, 230

Strauss, David Friedrich, 90

Strauss, Franz-Josef, 56, 296 f, 298
Streicher, Julius, 8, 178
Strousberg, Bethel, 119, 137
Stuttgart, 229, 272
Süddeutsche Zeitung, 331
Süss-Oppenheimer, Joseph, 114 f
Syberberg, Hans Jürgen, 71

Tacitus, 11, 147 f, 262
Tagesspiegel, Der (Berlin), 72
Taylor, A. J. P., 71
Terrorism, 168, 187, 211–2, 224, 296
Thadden, Elisabeth von, 165
Theater, 145, 153, 162; in Democratic
    Republic, 214, 232–4, 235; in Feder-
    al Republic, 224–30
Thiers, Adolphe, 21
Thomasius, Christian, 172, 312
Tieck, Ludwig, 130, 190, 196, 316
Tilly, Johann von, 18–19
Times, The (London), 15
Tirpitz, Grand Admiral Alfred von,
    175
Treitschke, Heinrich von, 135 f, 138,
    139, 140, 180, 272, 320
Trevor Roper, H. R., 66
Troeltsch, Ernst, 33, 34, 176
Tucholsky, Kurt, 23, 136, 174, 275
Twain, Mark, 310 f, 330

Uhlich, Leberecht, 90
Ulbricht, Walter, 50–53, 102, 103, 274,
    275, 307
United States of America, 31, 33, 38,
    43, 47, 48, 100, 185, 237, 240, 253
Universities, 62, 162, 170 ff, 312; *Bur-
    schenschaft,* 181 ff, 185, 295; and
    National Socialism, 177 f, 183; after
    1945, 69 f, 184–9, 210, 229, 284,
    296; professors, 170–8; students, 11,
    55, 166, 177, 179–84, 210, 211
Uthmann, Jörg von, 126, 127

Varnhagen von Ense, Rahel (Levin),
    130, 132, 269
Vatican, 91, 93, 96, 100 ff, 106
Veit, Dorothea, 130, 151
Versailles Treaty, 1919, 120, 143, 240,
    325
Vienna, 139, 262; Congress of, 1814–
    15, 21, 153
Vogt, Hanna, 76
Voltaire, François Arouet de, 26, 27

Vossische Zeitung, 155, 267

Wagner, Cosima, 138, 139, 198, 320
Wagner, Richard, 8, 25, 61, 71, 116–8,
    138–9, 156, 196, 198–200, 317
Walker, Mack, 26
Wallenstein, Albrecht von, Duke of
    Friedland, 18, 265
Wallich, Henry C., 123
Walser, Martin, 224
Wars: Thirty Years, 1618–48, 18–21,
    23, 77, 91, 107, 205, 265, 289, 311,
    329; Seven Years, 1756–63, 129,
    254; Napoleonic, 23, 32; Austro-
    Prussian, 1866, 21, 110, 238; World
    War I, 22, 63, 66, 141, 142, 240, 255;
    World War II, 71, 72, 326; Korean,
    44, 46, 237; Vietnamese, 185, 187
Warsaw Pact, 257, 258
Weber, Carl Maria von, 7, 193, 272
Weber, Max, 173, 176
Wedekind, Frank, 225
Weisenborn, Günther, 219
Welt, Die, 330
Westphalia, Peace of (1648), 20, 21,
    24, 91, 312
Wichern, J. H., 95
Wieland, Christian Martin, 313
William II, Emperor, 10, 95, 113, 175,
    239
Winckelmann, Johann Joachim, 28
Windthorst, Ludwig, 239
Wirth, Josef, 142
Wolf, Christa, 233, 236
Wolff, Christian, 88, 172
Women, 11, 90, 147 ff; and the En-
    lightenment, 149 ff; during the Wei-
    mar Republic, 161–164; and Nation-
    al Socialism, 163–5; in Democratic
    Republic, 169; in Federal Republic,
    147, 166–9; Federation of Women's
    Associations, 159, 160, 161; *Mutter-
    schutz* League, 160, 168; Socialist
    women's movement, 160 f
Württemberg, 20, 23, 86, 90, 96, 114
Würzburg, 22, 91, 92

Zadek, Peter, 226, 227 n
Zeit, Die, 10, 74, 300, 306
Zetkin, Klara, 161
Zille, Heinrich, 270
Zinsendorf, Count Nicholas Ludwig
    von, 88